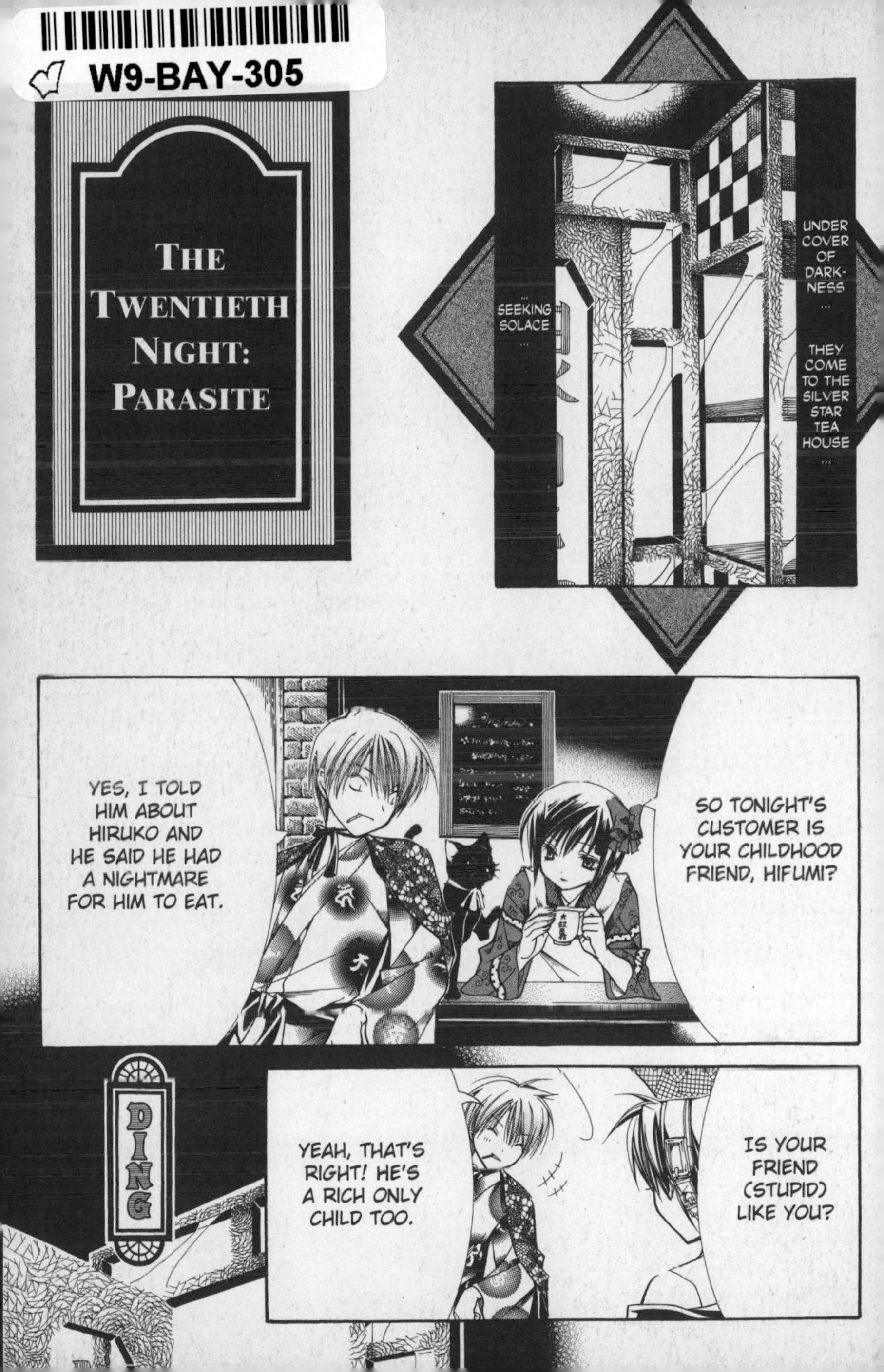
UNDER COVER OF DARKNESS...
THEY COME TO THE SILVER STAR TEA HOUSE...
...SEEKING SOLACE...
THE TWENTIETH NIGHT: PARASITE
SO TONIGHT'S CUSTOMER IS YOUR CHILDHOOD FRIEND, HIFUMI?
YES, I TOLD HIM ABOUT HIRUKO AND HE SAID HE HAD A NIGHTMARE FOR HIM TO EAT.
IS YOUR FRIEND (STUPID) LIKE YOU?
YEAH, THAT'S RIGHT! HE'S A RICH ONLY CHILD TOO.
DING

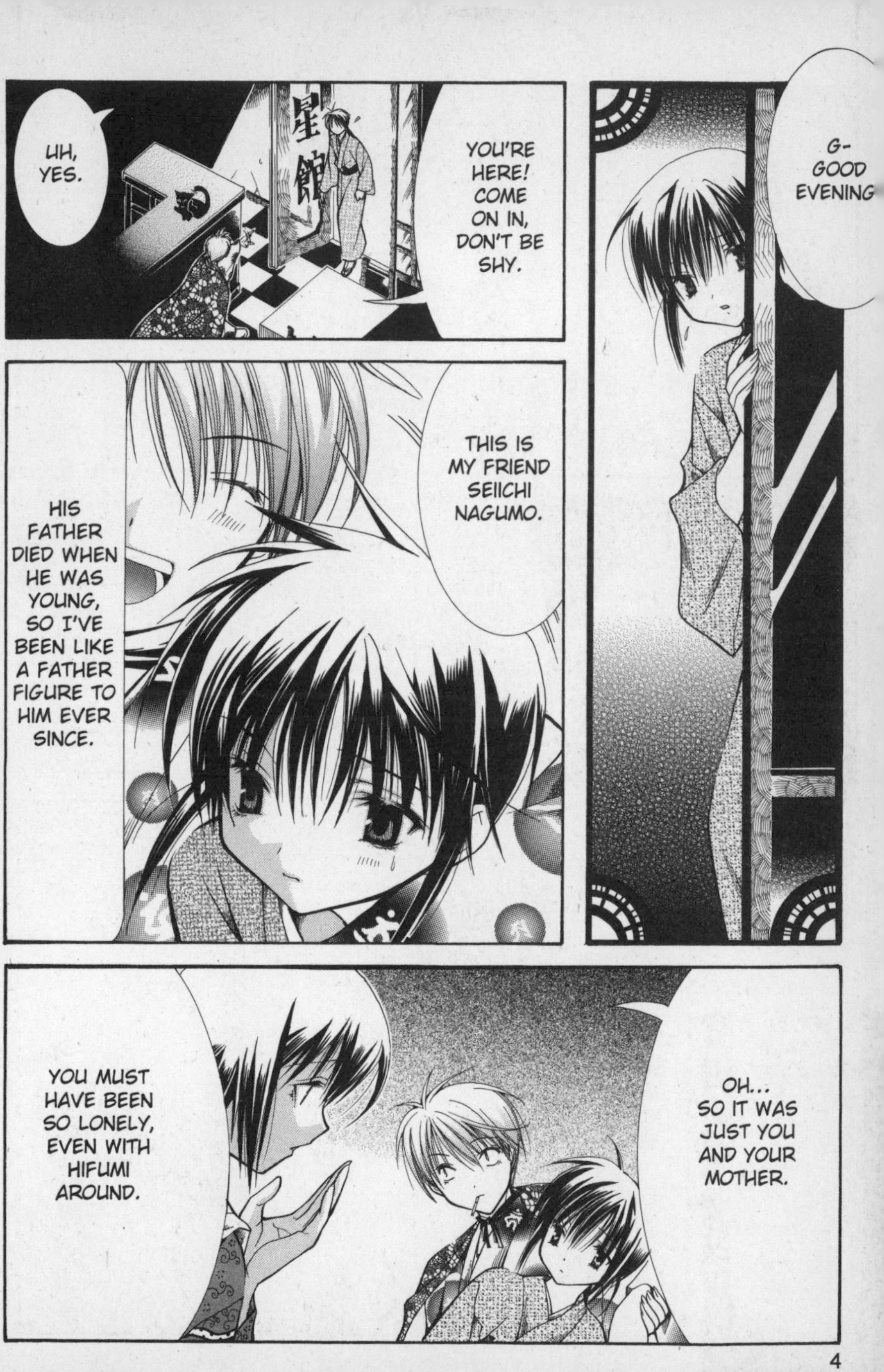
G-GOOD EVENING
YOU'RE HERE! COME ON IN, DON'T BE SHY.
星館
UH, YES.
THIS IS MY FRIEND SEIICHI NAGUMO.
HIS FATHER DIED WHEN HE WAS YOUNG, SO I'VE BEEN LIKE A FATHER FIGURE TO HIM EVER SINCE.
OH... SO IT WAS JUST YOU AND YOUR MOTHER.
YOU MUST HAVE BEEN SO LONELY, EVEN WITH HIFUMI AROUND.

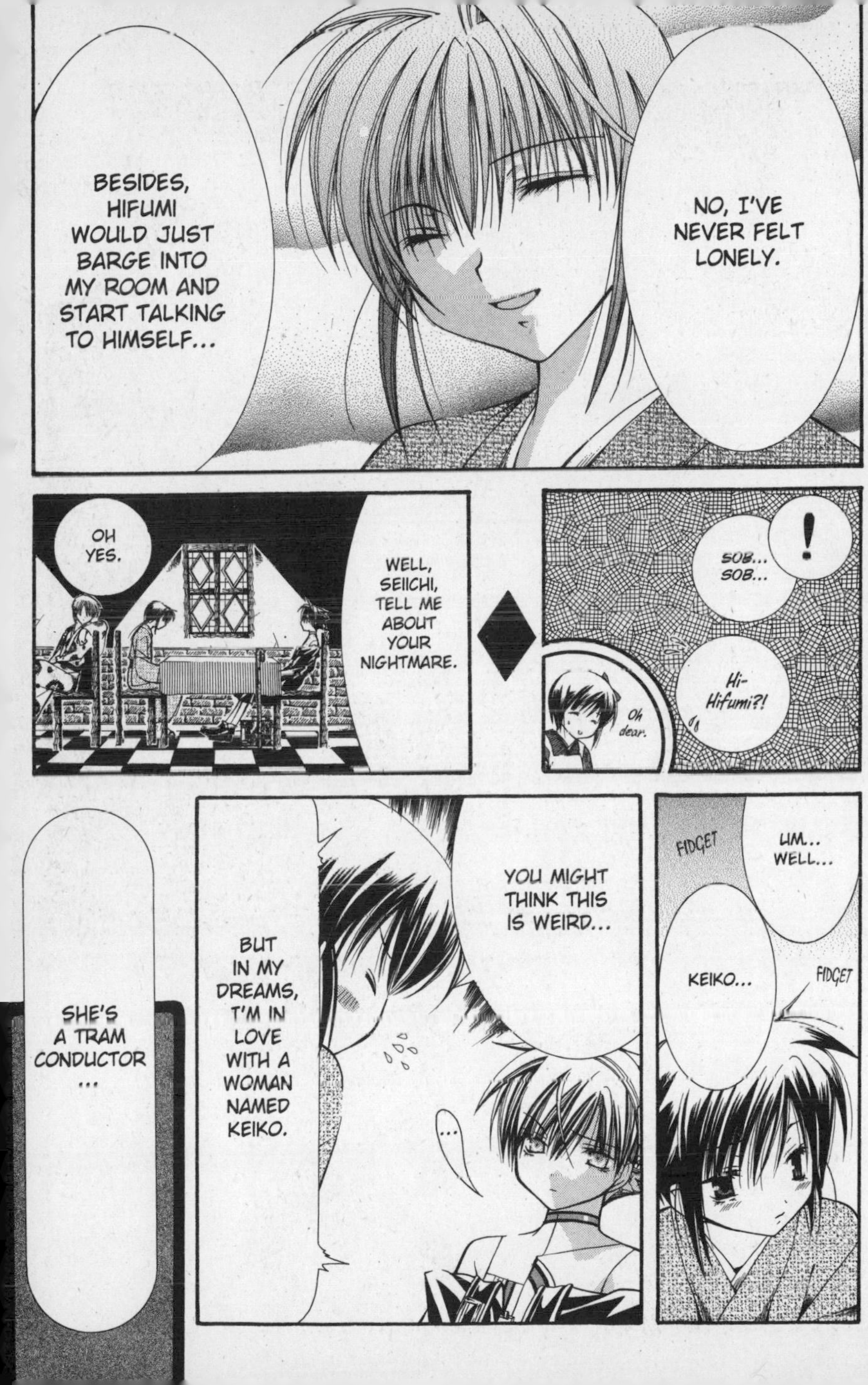
NO, I'VE NEVER FELT LONELY.
BESIDES, HIFUMI WOULD JUST BARGE INTO MY ROOM AND START TALKING TO HIMSELF...
!
SOB... SOB...
Hi-Hifumi?!
Oh dear.
WELL, SEIICHI, TELL ME ABOUT YOUR NIGHTMARE.
OH YES.
FIDGET
UM... WELL...
KEIKO...
FIDGET
YOU MIGHT THINK THIS IS WEIRD...
BUT IN MY DREAMS, I'M IN LOVE WITH A WOMAN NAMED KEIKO.
...
SHE'S A TRAM CONDUCTOR ...

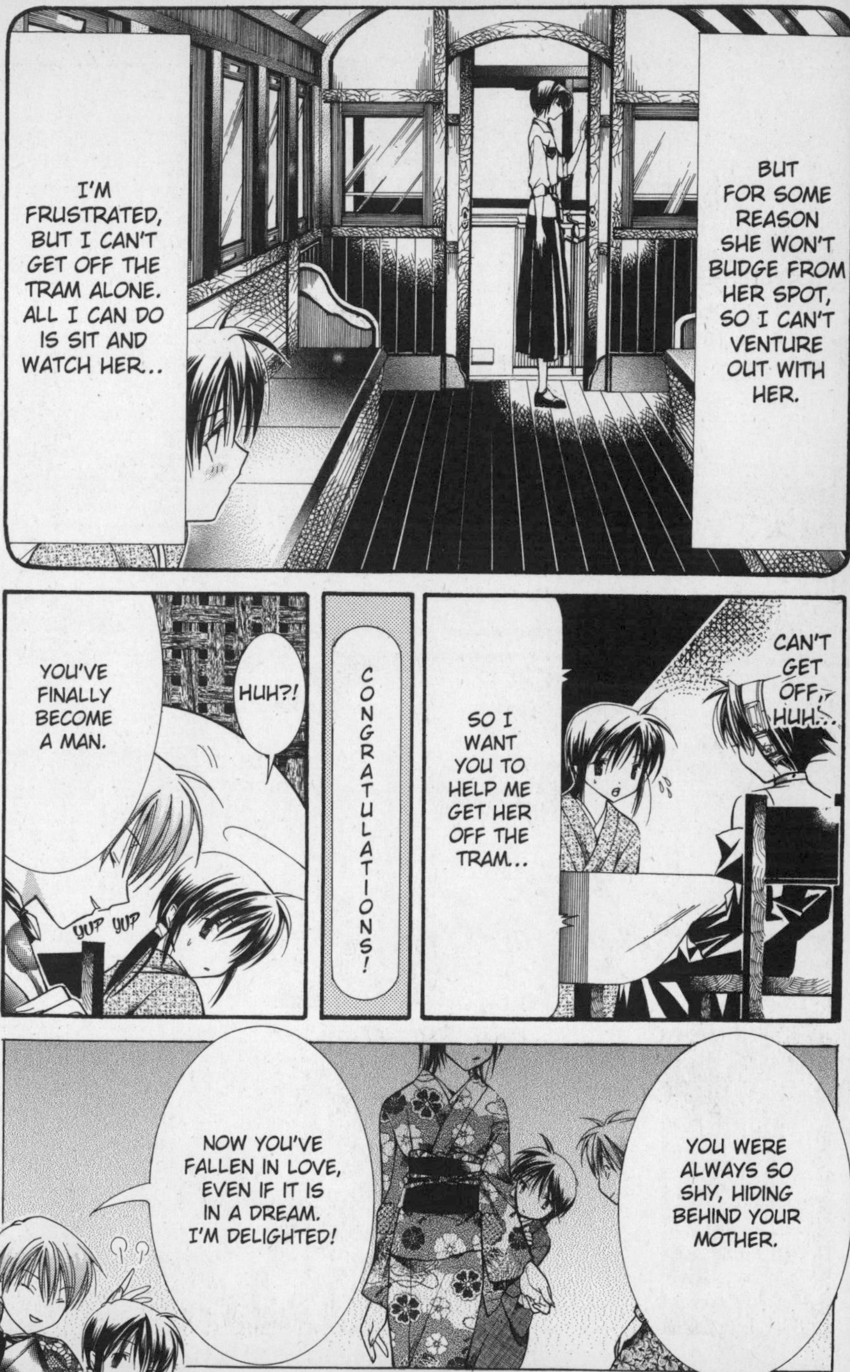
BUT FOR SOME REASON SHE WON'T BUDGE FROM HER SPOT, SO I CAN'T VENTURE OUT WITH HER.
I'M FRUSTRATED, BUT I CAN'T GET OFF THE TRAM ALONE. ALL I CAN DO IS SIT AND WATCH HER...
CAN'T GET OFF, HUH...
SO I WANT YOU TO HELP ME GET HER OFF THE TRAM...
CONGRATULATIONS!
HUH?!
YOU'VE FINALLY BECOME A MAN.
YUP YUP
YOU WERE ALWAYS SO SHY, HIDING BEHIND YOUR MOTHER.
NOW YOU'VE FALLEN IN LOVE, EVEN IF IT IS IN A DREAM. I'M DELIGHTED!

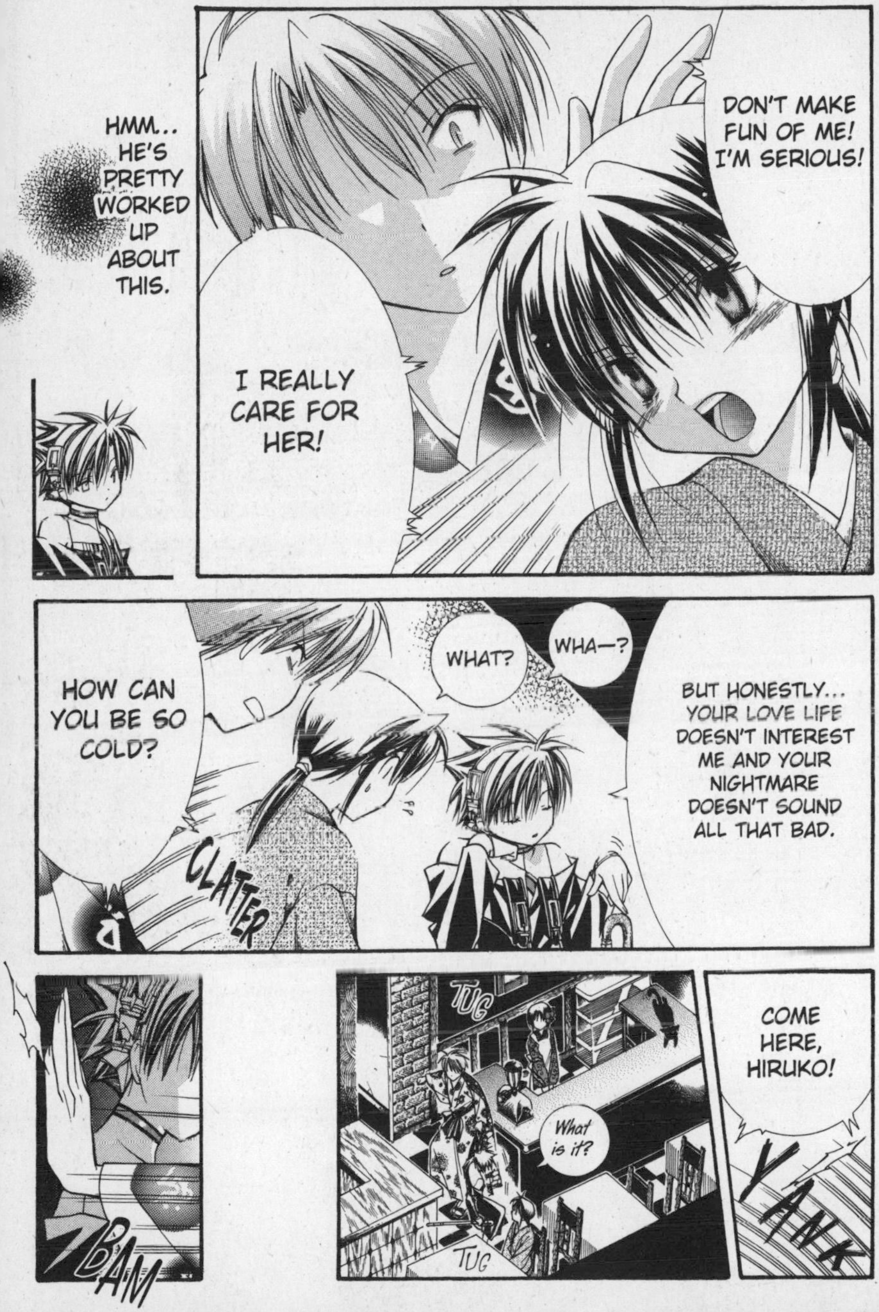
DON'T MAKE FUN OF ME! I'M SERIOUS!
I REALLY CARE FOR HER!
HMM... HE'S PRETTY WORKED UP ABOUT THIS.
BUT HONESTLY... YOUR LOVE LIFE DOESN'T INTEREST ME AND YOUR NIGHTMARE DOESN'T SOUND ALL THAT BAD.
WHA—?
WHAT?
HOW CAN YOU BE SO COLD?
CLATTER
COME HERE, HIRUKO!
YANK
TUG
What is it?
TUG
BAM

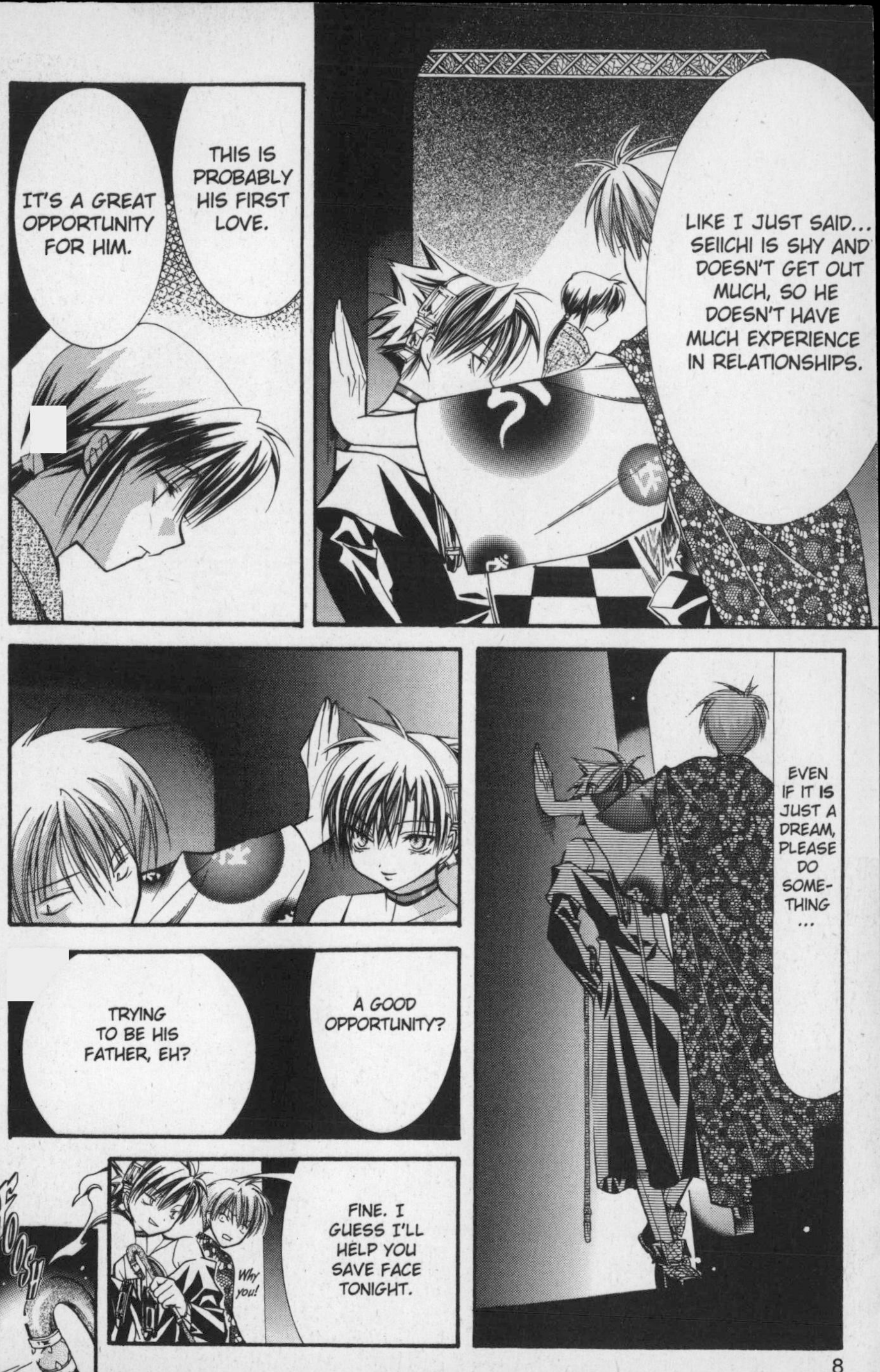
LIKE I JUST SAID... SEIICHI IS SHY AND DOESN'T GET OUT MUCH, SO HE DOESN'T HAVE MUCH EXPERIENCE IN RELATIONSHIPS.
THIS IS PROBABLY HIS FIRST LOVE.
IT'S A GREAT OPPORTUNITY FOR HIM.
EVEN IF IT IS JUST A DREAM, PLEASE DO SOME-THING ...
A GOOD OPPORTUNITY?
TRYING TO BE HIS FATHER, EH?
FINE. I GUESS I'LL HELP YOU SAVE FACE TONIGHT.
Why you!
FOOSH

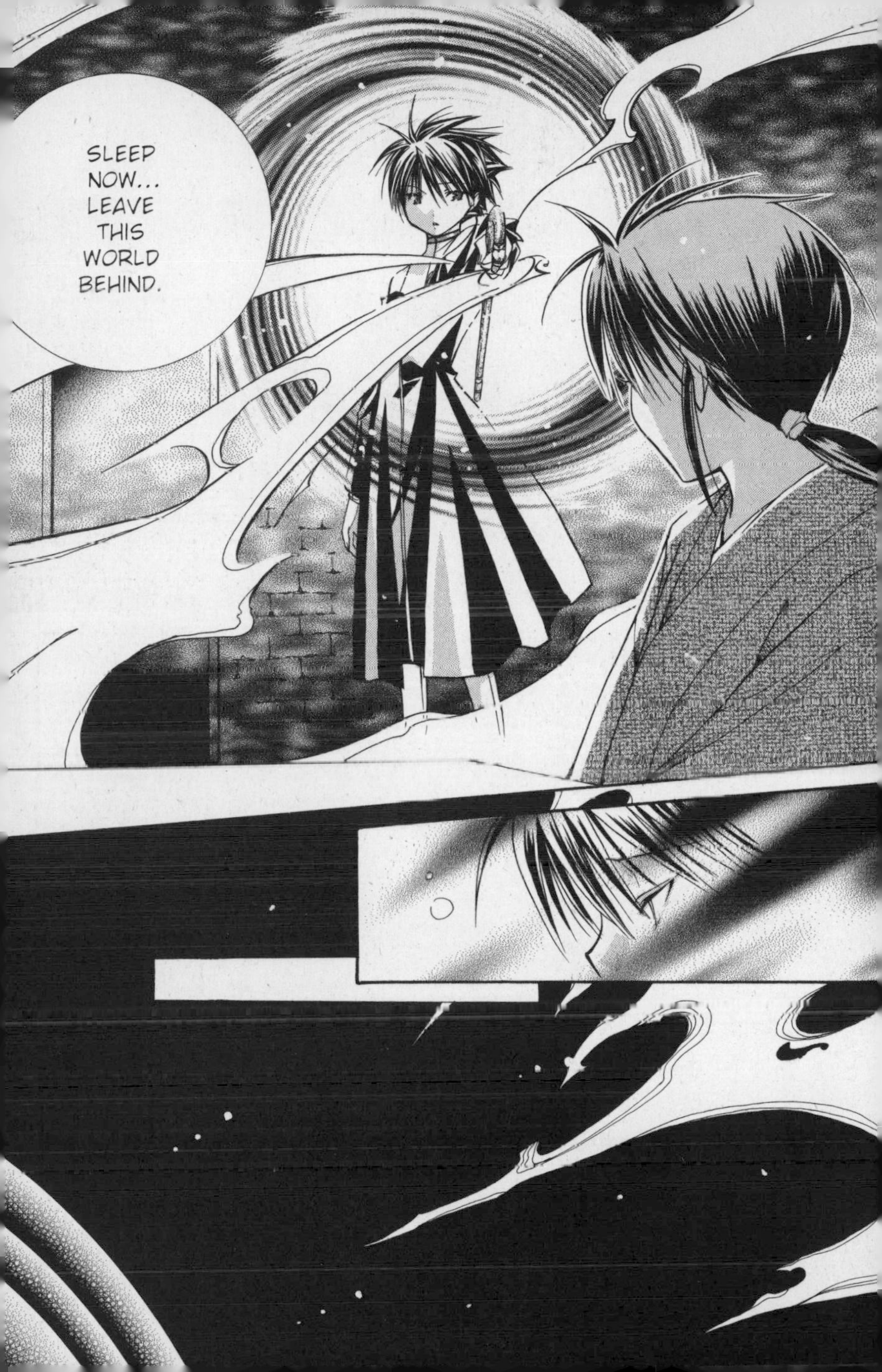
SLEEP NOW... LEAVE THIS WORLD BEHIND.

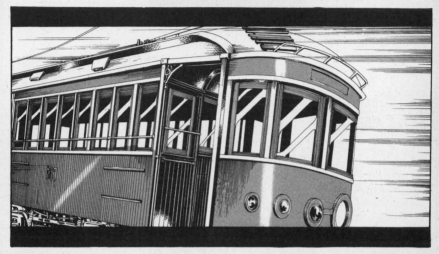

IT'S PRETTY SHAKY.

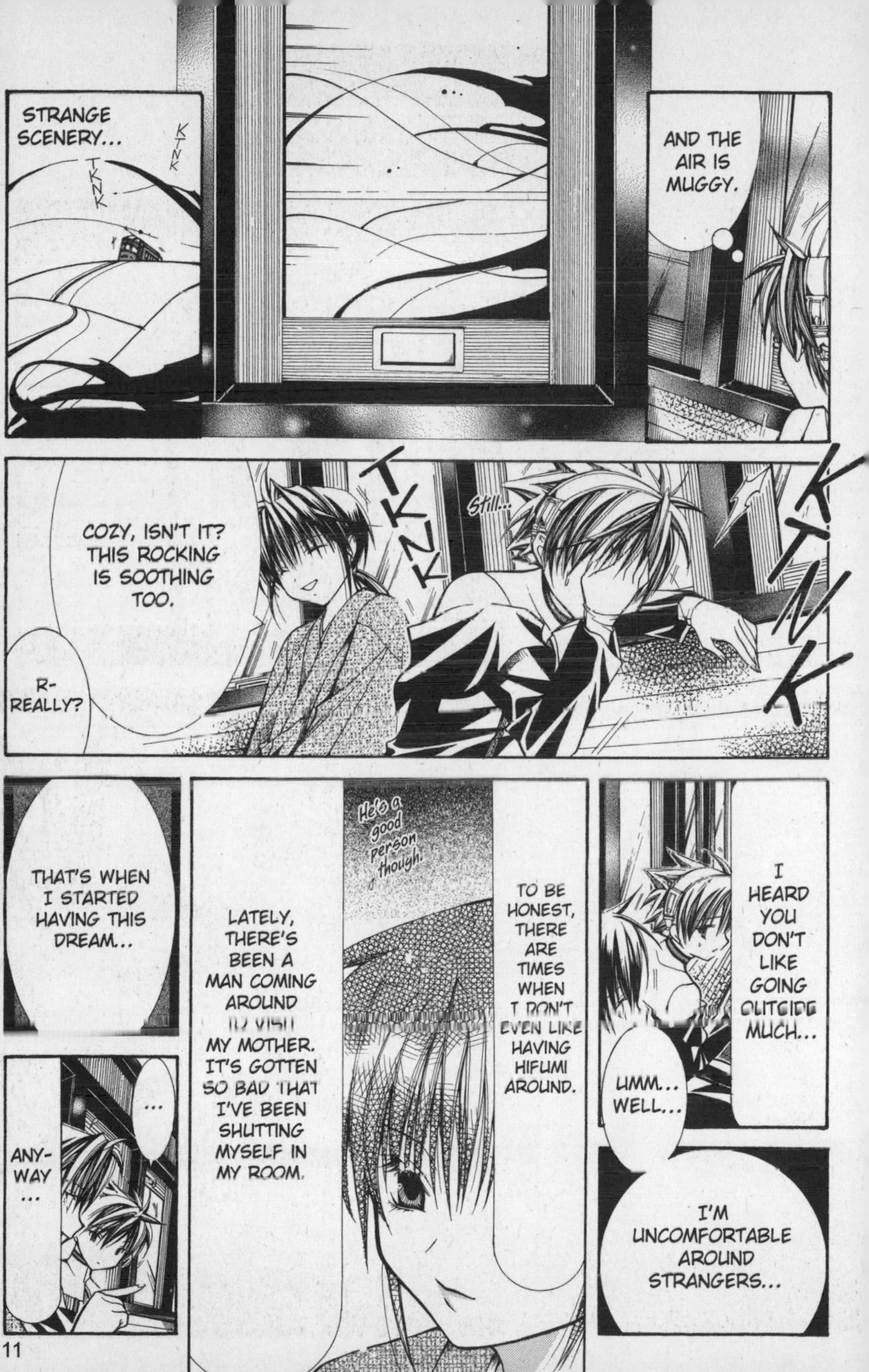
AND THE AIR IS MUGGY.
...
STRANGE SCENERY...
KTNK
TKNK
KTNK
Still...
TKNK
COZY, ISN'T IT? THIS ROCKING IS SOOTHING TOO.
R-REALLY?
I HEARD YOU DON'T LIKE GOING OUTSIDE MUCH...
UMM... WELL...
I'M UNCOMFORTABLE AROUND STRANGERS...
TO BE HONEST, THERE ARE TIMES WHEN I DON'T EVEN LIKE HAVING HIFUMI AROUND.
He's a good person though.
LATELY, THERE'S BEEN A MAN COMING AROUND TO VISIT MY MOTHER. IT'S GOTTEN SO BAD THAT I'VE BEEN SHUTTING MYSELF IN MY ROOM.
THAT'S WHEN I STARTED HAVING THIS DREAM...
...
ANYWAY...

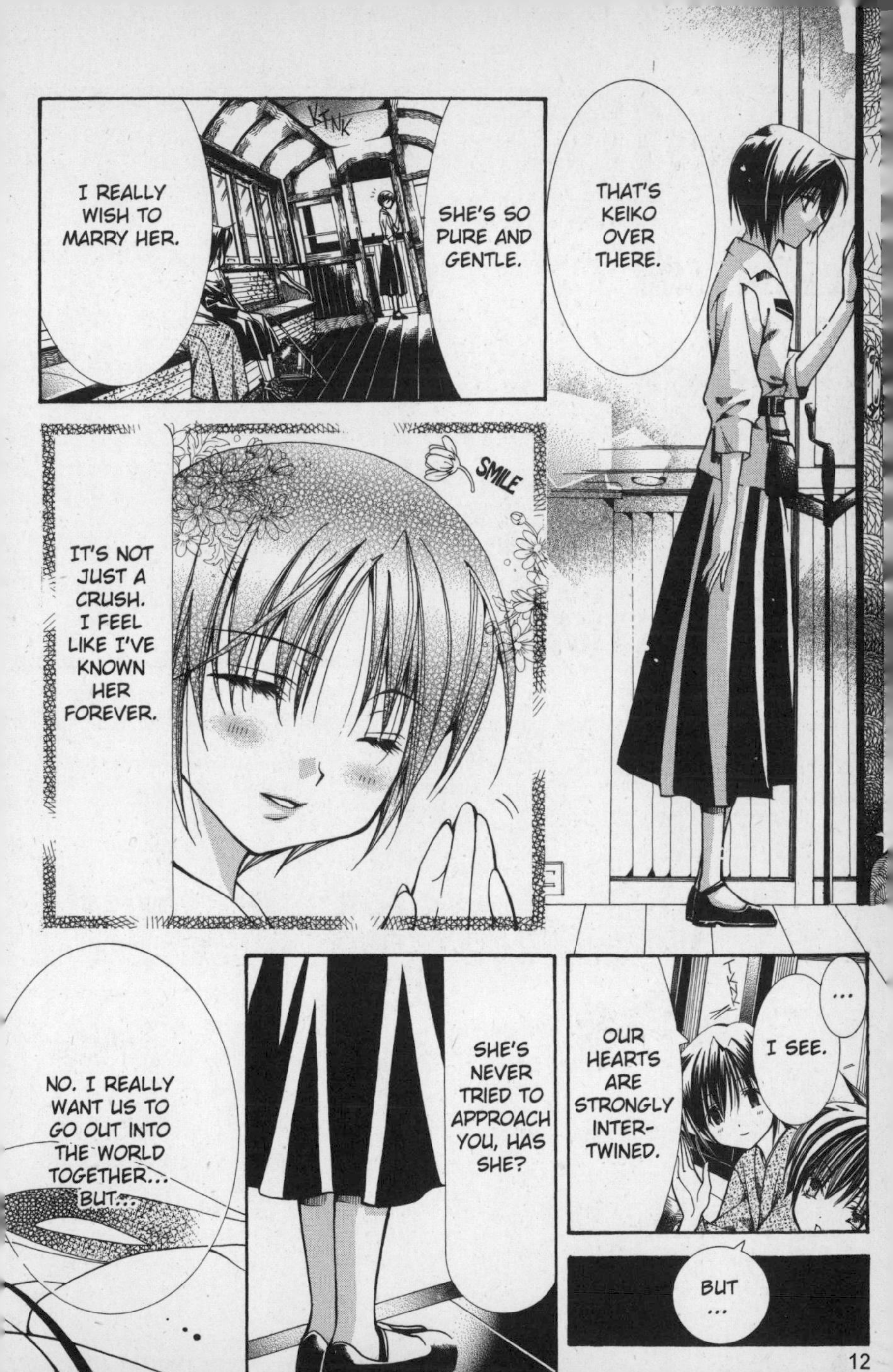
THAT'S KEIKO OVER THERE.
KTNK
SHE'S SO PURE AND GENTLE.
I REALLY WISH TO MARRY HER.
SMILE
IT'S NOT JUST A CRUSH. I FEEL LIKE I'VE KNOWN HER FOREVER.
...
I SEE.
TKNK
OUR HEARTS ARE STRONGLY INTER-TWINED.
BUT ...
SHE'S NEVER TRIED TO APPROACH YOU, HAS SHE?
NO. I REALLY WANT US TO GO OUT INTO THE WORLD TOGETHER... BUT...
...

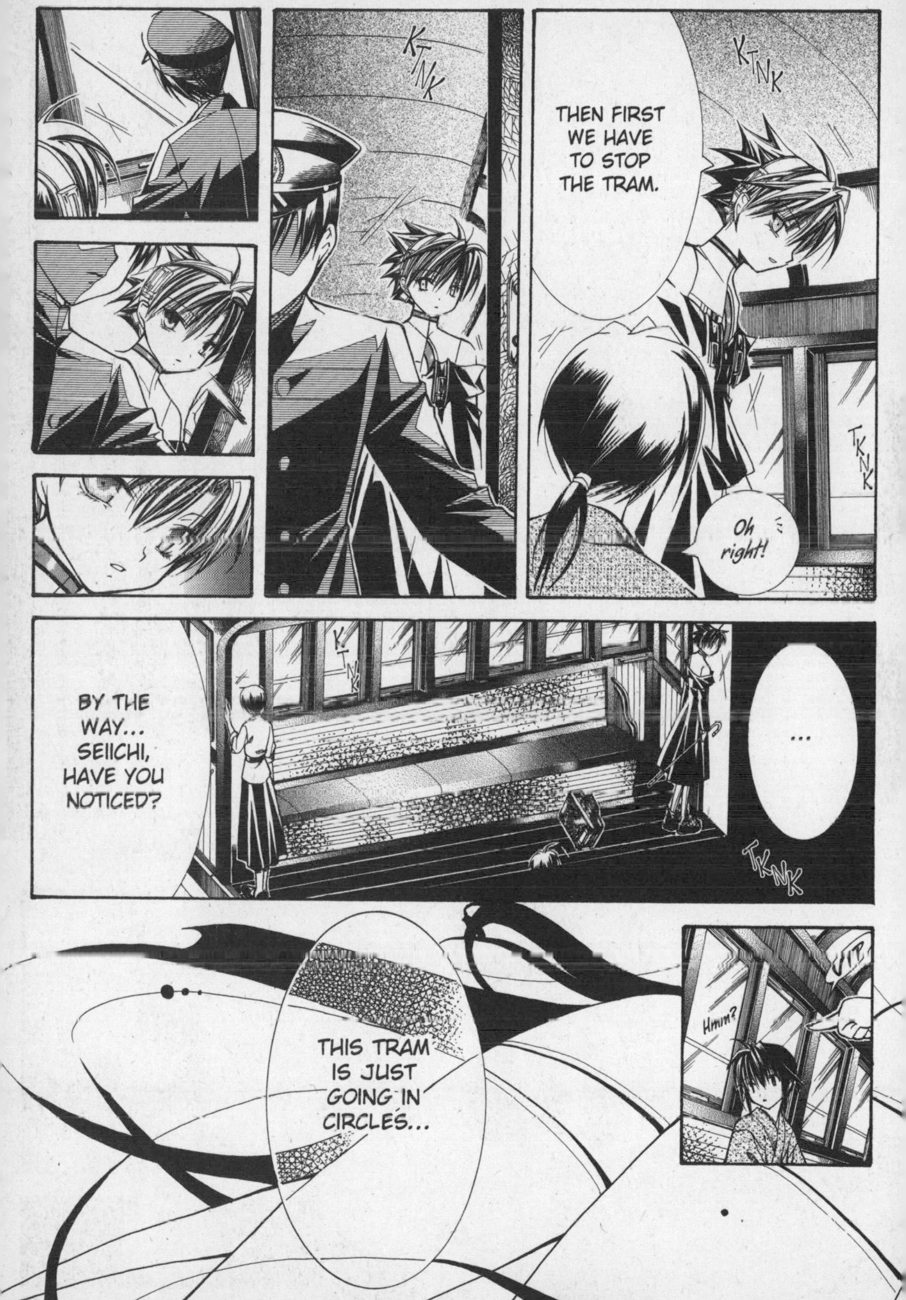
KTNK
THEN FIRST WE HAVE TO STOP THE TRAM.
TKNK
Oh right!
KTNK
...
TKNK
KTNK
BY THE WAY... SEIICHI, HAVE YOU NOTICED?
VIP
Hmm?
THIS TRAM IS JUST GOING IN CIRCLES...

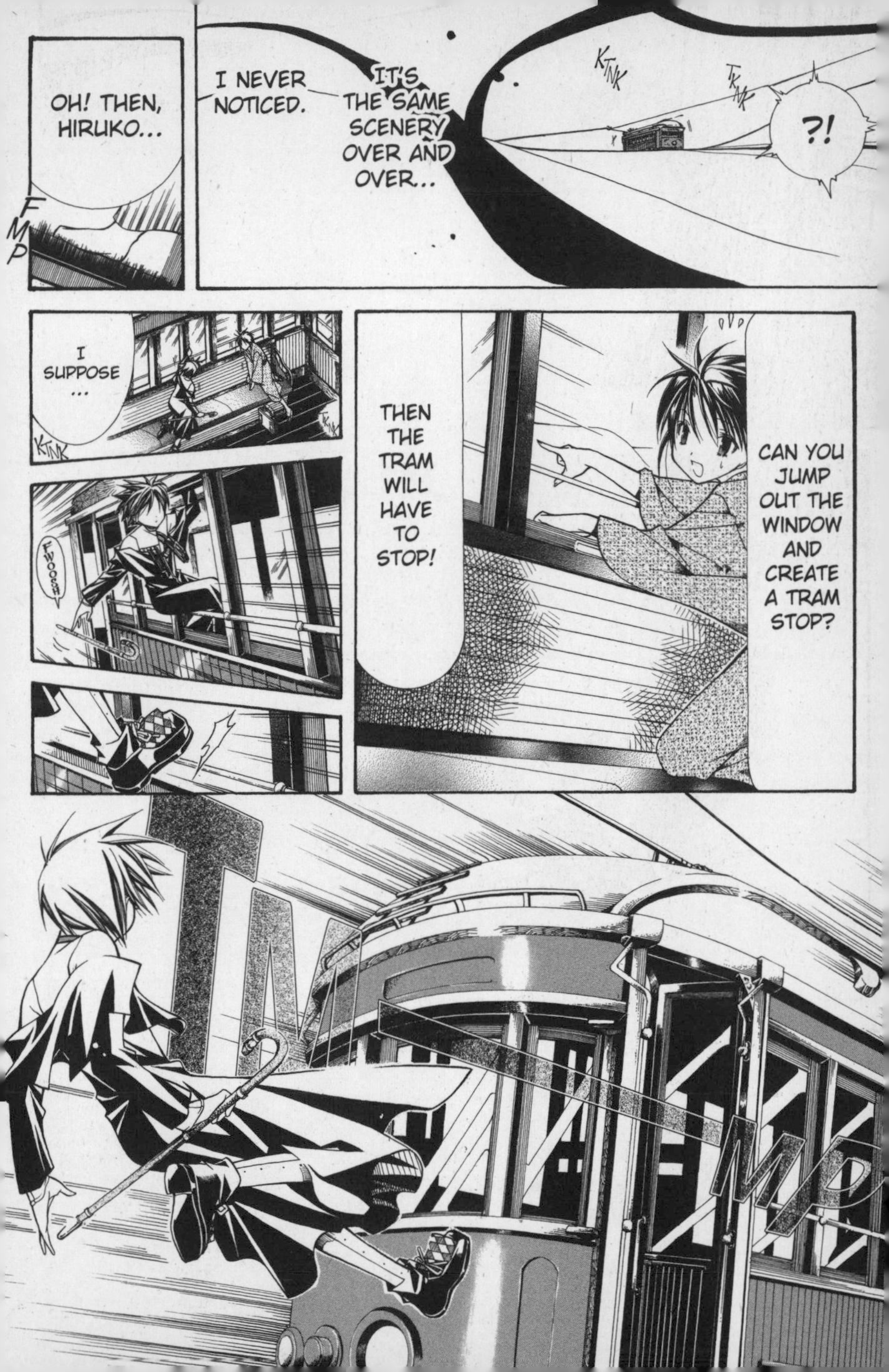

?!
KTNK
TKNK
IT'S THE SAME SCENERY OVER AND OVER...
I NEVER NOTICED.
OH! THEN, HIRUKO...
FMP
CAN YOU JUMP OUT THE WINDOW AND CREATE A TRAM STOP?
THEN THE TRAM WILL HAVE TO STOP!
I SUPPOSE ...
TKNK
KTNK
FWOOSH
TMP

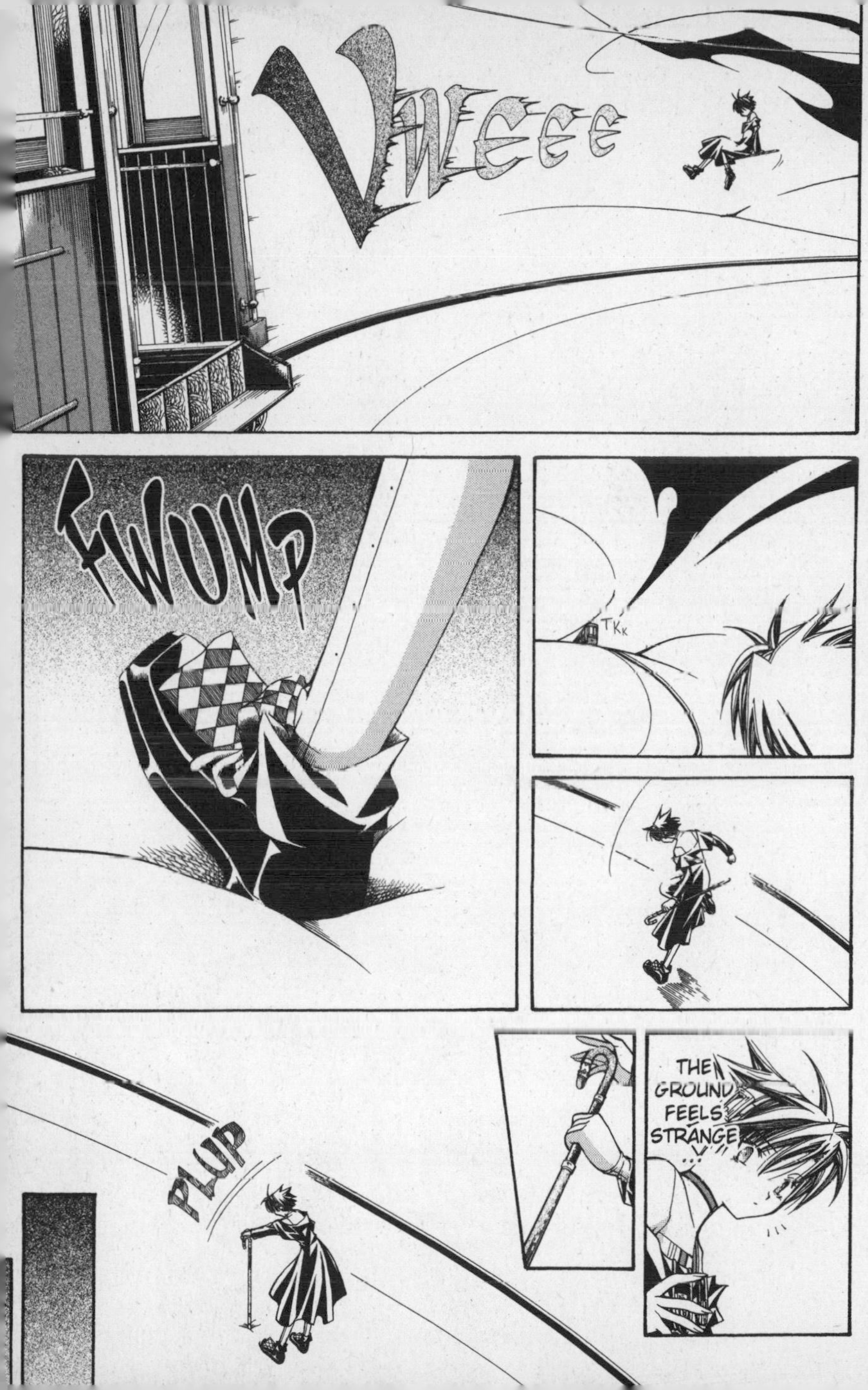
VWEEE
TKK
FWUMP
THE GROUND FEELS STRANGE...
PLUP

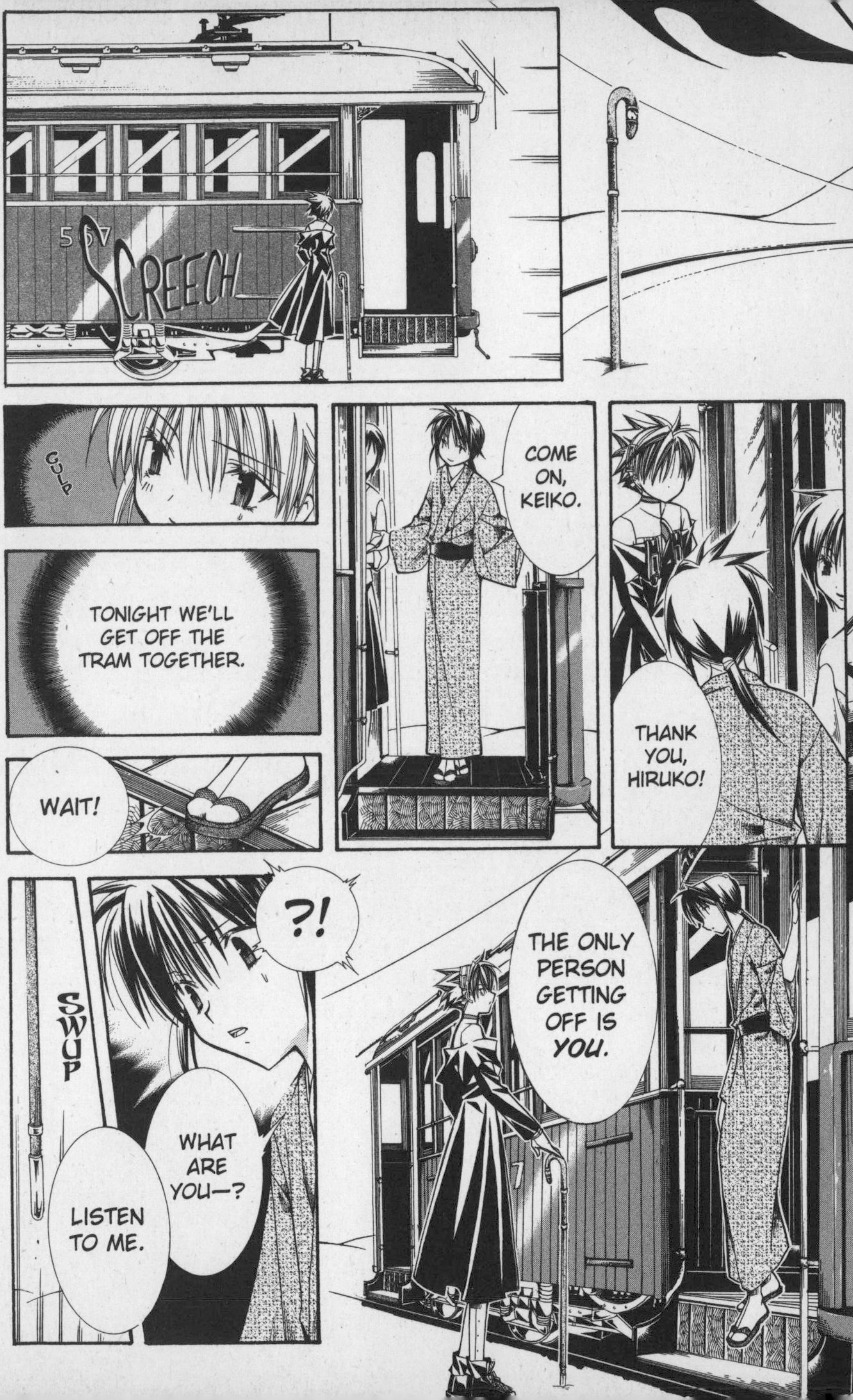
SCREECH
THANK YOU, HIRUKO!
COME ON, KEIKO.
GULP
TONIGHT WE'LL GET OFF THE TRAM TOGETHER.
WAIT!
THE ONLY PERSON GETTING OFF IS *YOU*.
?!
SWUP
WHAT ARE YOU—?
LISTEN TO ME.

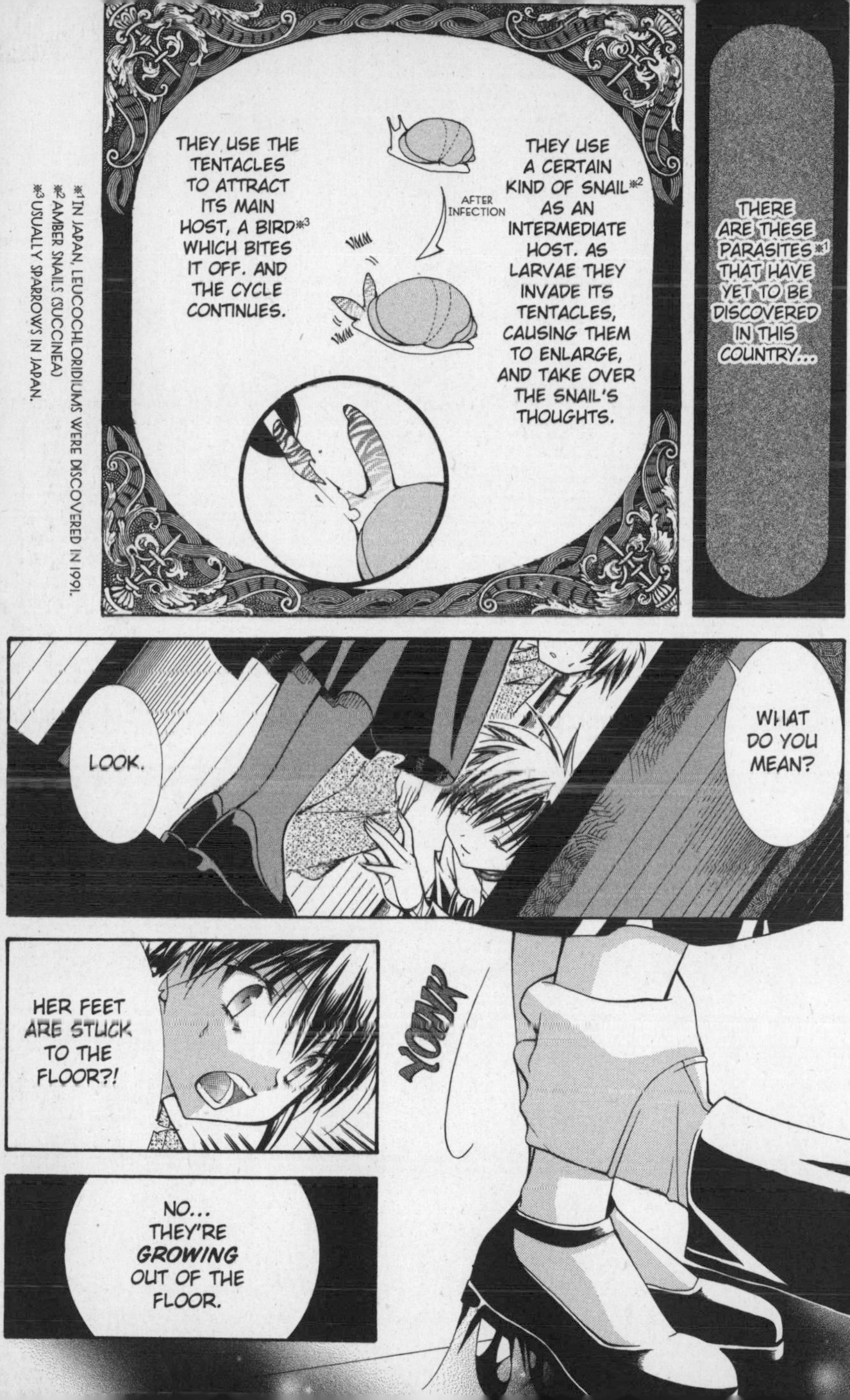
THERE ARE THESE PARASITES※1 THAT HAVE YET TO BE DISCOVERED IN THIS COUNTRY...
THEY USE A CERTAIN KIND OF SNAIL※2 AS AN INTERMEDIATE HOST. AS LARVAE THEY INVADE ITS TENTACLES, CAUSING THEM TO ENLARGE, AND TAKE OVER THE SNAIL'S THOUGHTS.
AFTER INFECTION
VMM
VMM
THEY USE THE TENTACLES TO ATTRACT ITS MAIN HOST, A BIRD※3 WHICH BITES IT OFF. AND THE CYCLE CONTINUES.
WHAT DO YOU MEAN?
LOOK.
YOINK
HER FEET ARE STUCK TO THE FLOOR?!
NO... THEY'RE ***GROWING*** OUT OF THE FLOOR.

※1 IN JAPAN, LEUCOCHLORIDIUMS WERE DISCOVERED IN 1991.
※2 AMBER SNAILS (SUCCINEA)
※3 USUALLY SPARROWS IN JAPAN.

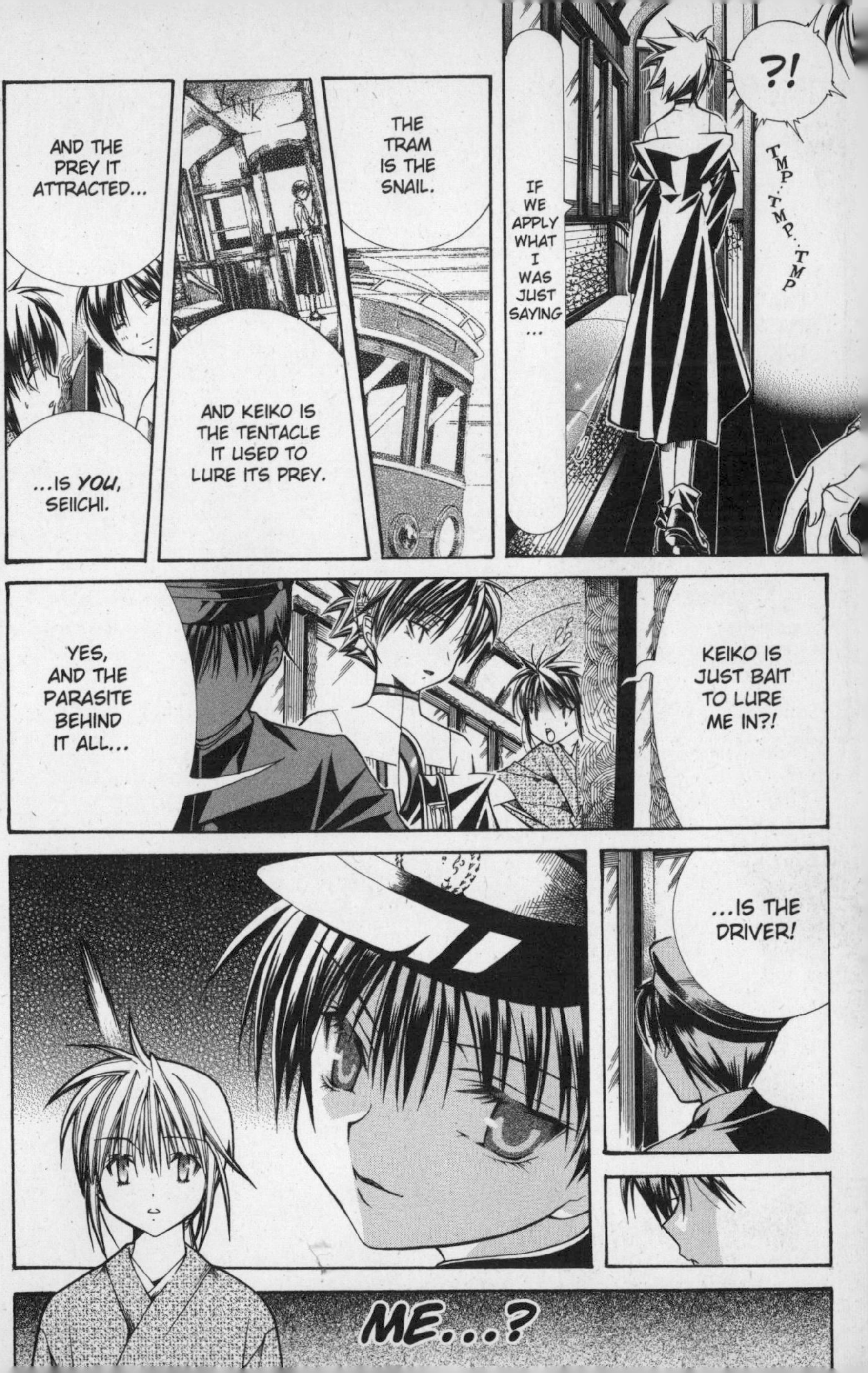
?!
TMP.. TMP.. TMP
IF WE APPLY WHAT I WAS JUST SAYING...
THE TRAM IS THE SNAIL.
AND KEIKO IS THE TENTACLE IT USED TO LURE ITS PREY.
AND THE PREY IT ATTRACTED...
...IS *YOU*, SEIICHI.
KEIKO IS JUST BAIT TO LURE ME IN?!
YES, AND THE PARASITE BEHIND IT ALL...
...IS THE DRIVER!
ME...?

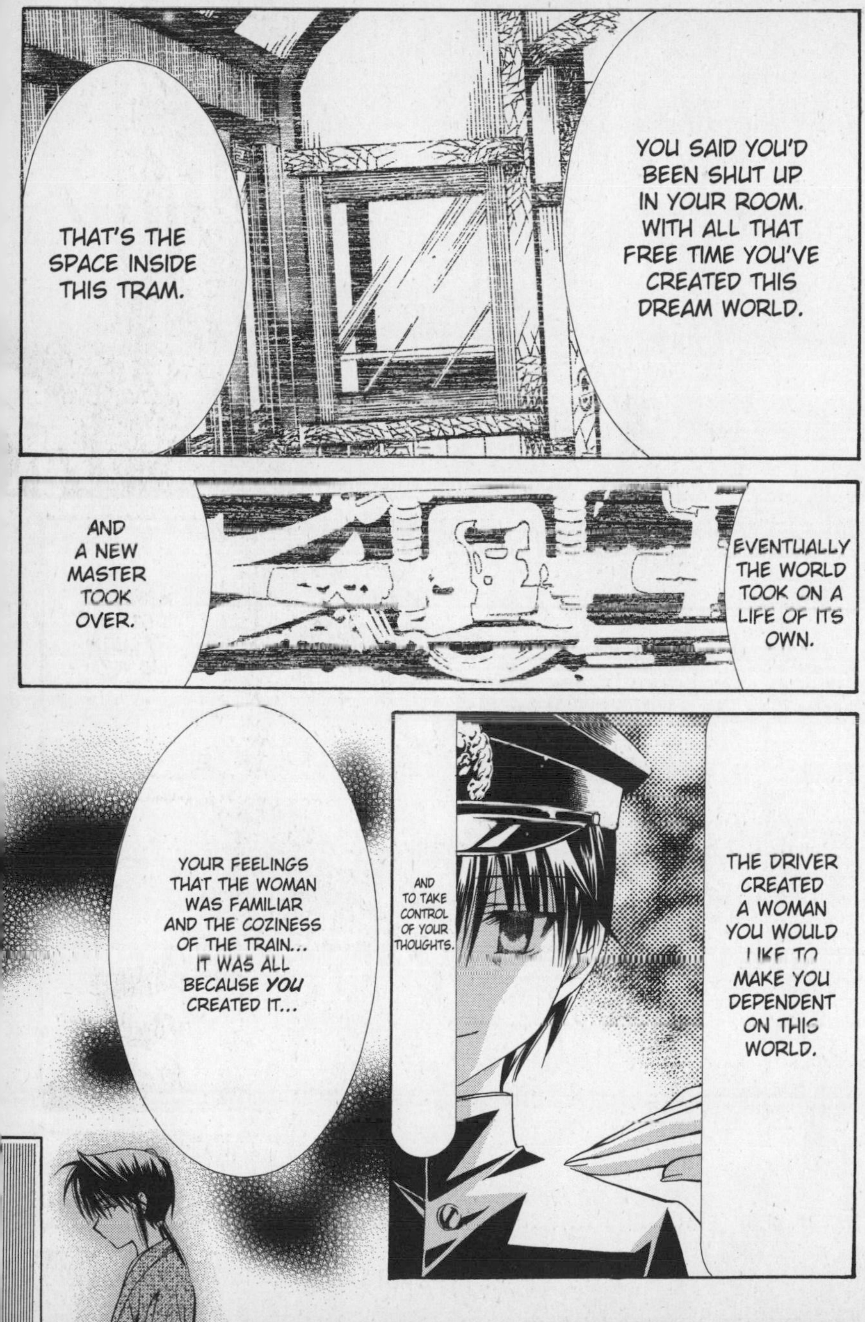
YOU SAID YOU'D BEEN SHUT UP IN YOUR ROOM. WITH ALL THAT FREE TIME YOU'VE CREATED THIS DREAM WORLD.
THAT'S THE SPACE INSIDE THIS TRAM.
EVENTUALLY THE WORLD TOOK ON A LIFE OF ITS OWN.
AND A NEW MASTER TOOK OVER.
THE DRIVER CREATED A WOMAN YOU WOULD LIKE TO MAKE YOU DEPENDENT ON THIS WORLD.
AND TO TAKE CONTROL OF YOUR THOUGHTS.
YOUR FEELINGS THAT THE WOMAN WAS FAMILIAR AND THE COZINESS OF THE TRAIN... IT WAS ALL BECAUSE *YOU* CREATED IT...

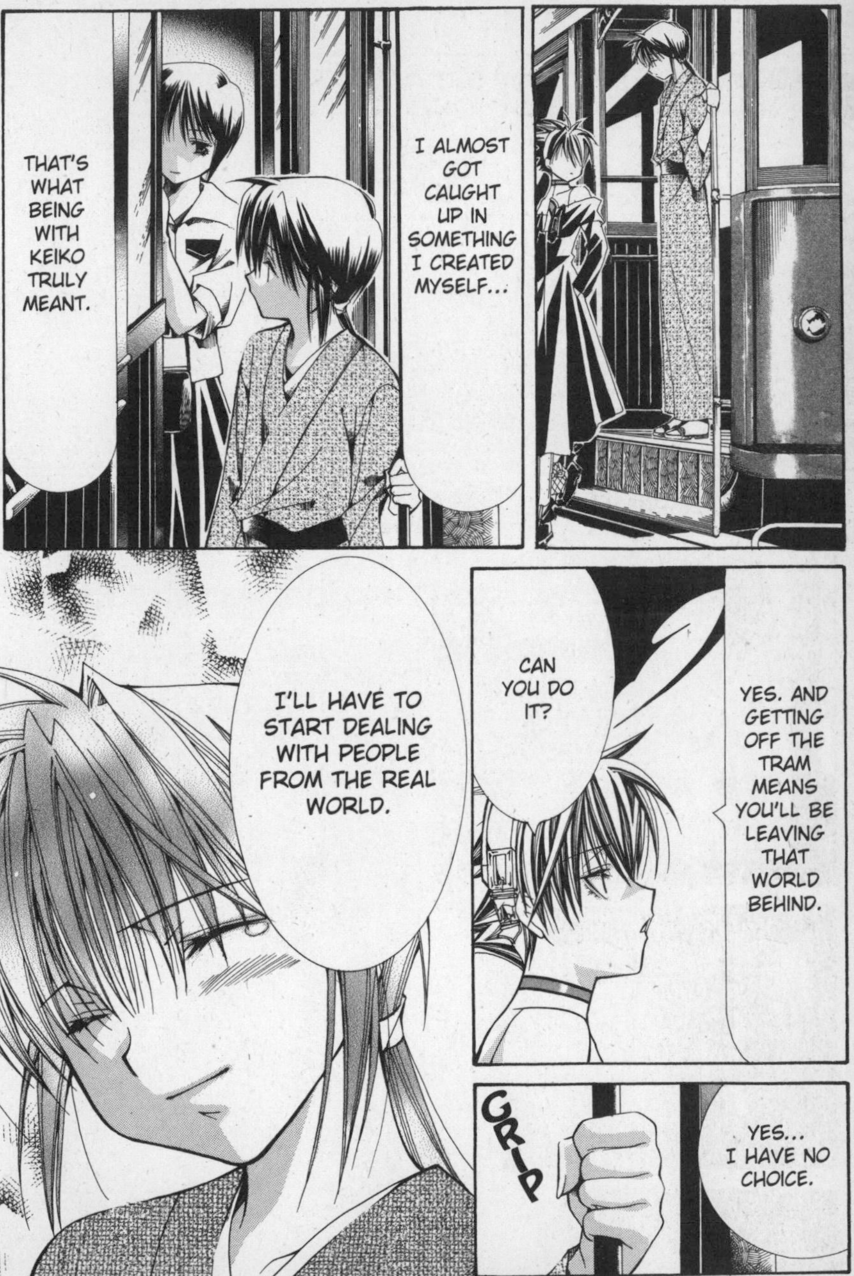
I ALMOST GOT CAUGHT UP IN SOMETHING I CREATED MYSELF...
THAT'S WHAT BEING WITH KEIKO TRULY MEANT.
YES. AND GETTING OFF THE TRAM MEANS YOU'LL BE LEAVING THAT WORLD BEHIND.
CAN YOU DO IT?
YES... I HAVE NO CHOICE.
GRIP
I'LL HAVE TO START DEALING WITH PEOPLE FROM THE REAL WORLD.

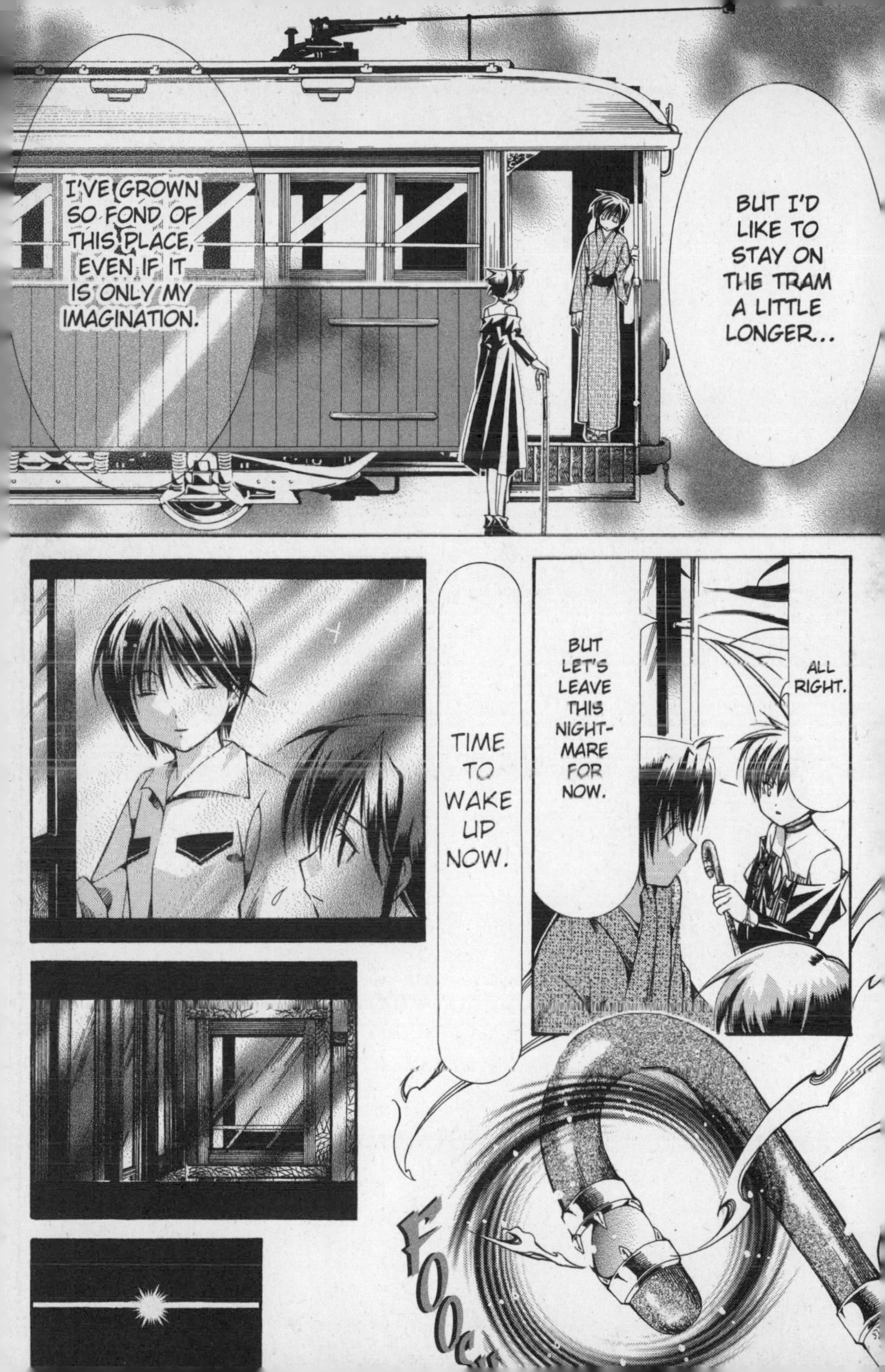
BUT I'D LIKE TO STAY ON THE TRAM A LITTLE LONGER...
I'VE GROWN SO FOND OF THIS PLACE, EVEN IF IT IS ONLY MY IMAGINATION.
ALL RIGHT.
BUT LET'S LEAVE THIS NIGHT-MARE FOR NOW.
TIME TO WAKE UP NOW.

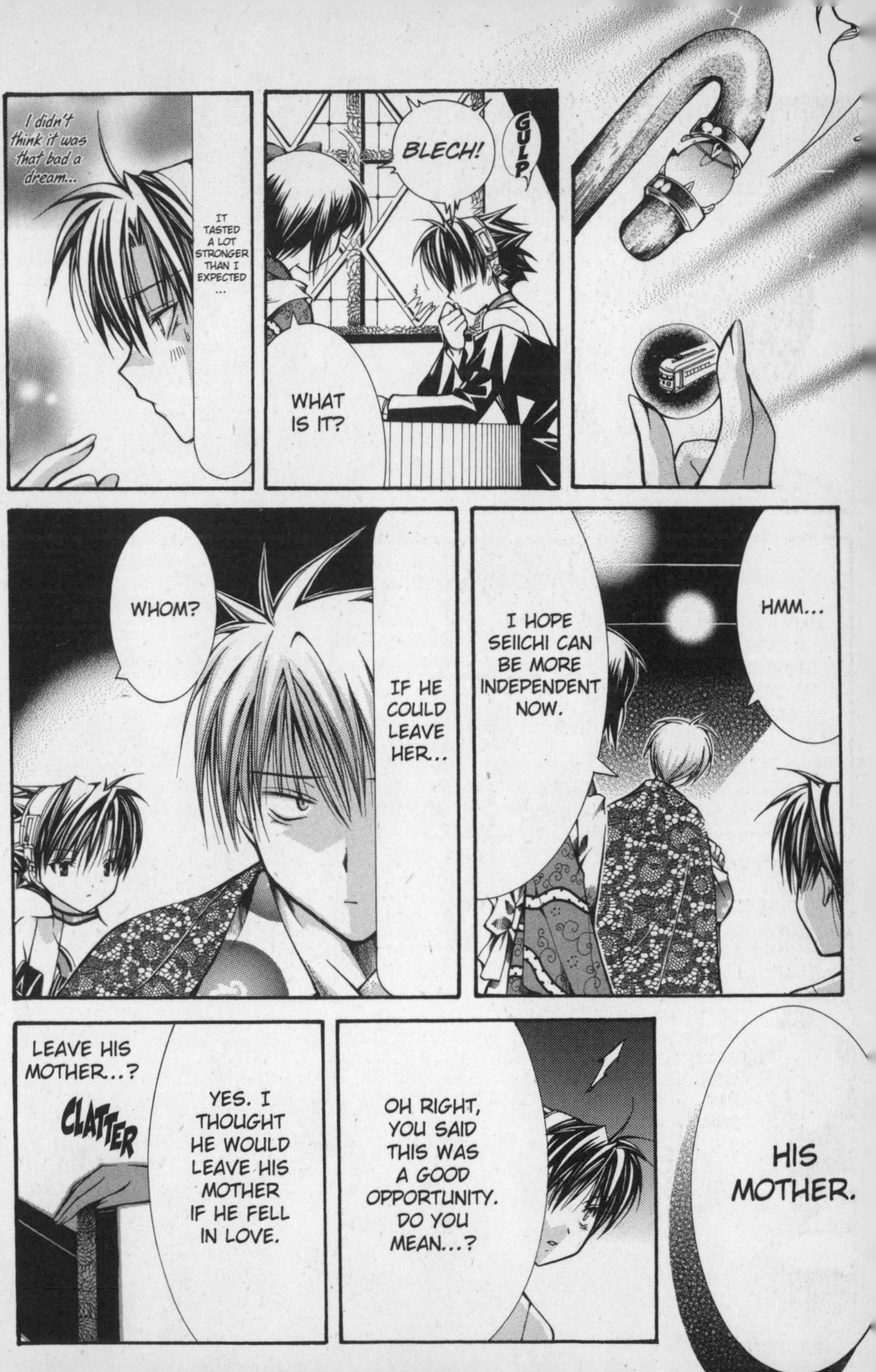
GULP
BLECH!
WHAT IS IT?
IT TASTED A LOT STRONGER THAN I EXPECTED ...
I didn't think it was that bad a dream...
HMM...
I HOPE SEIICHI CAN BE MORE INDEPENDENT NOW.
IF HE COULD LEAVE HER...
WHOM?
HIS MOTHER.
OH RIGHT, YOU SAID THIS WAS A GOOD OPPORTUNITY. DO YOU MEAN...?
YES. I THOUGHT HE WOULD LEAVE HIS MOTHER IF HE FELL IN LOVE.
LEAVE HIS MOTHER...?
CLATTER

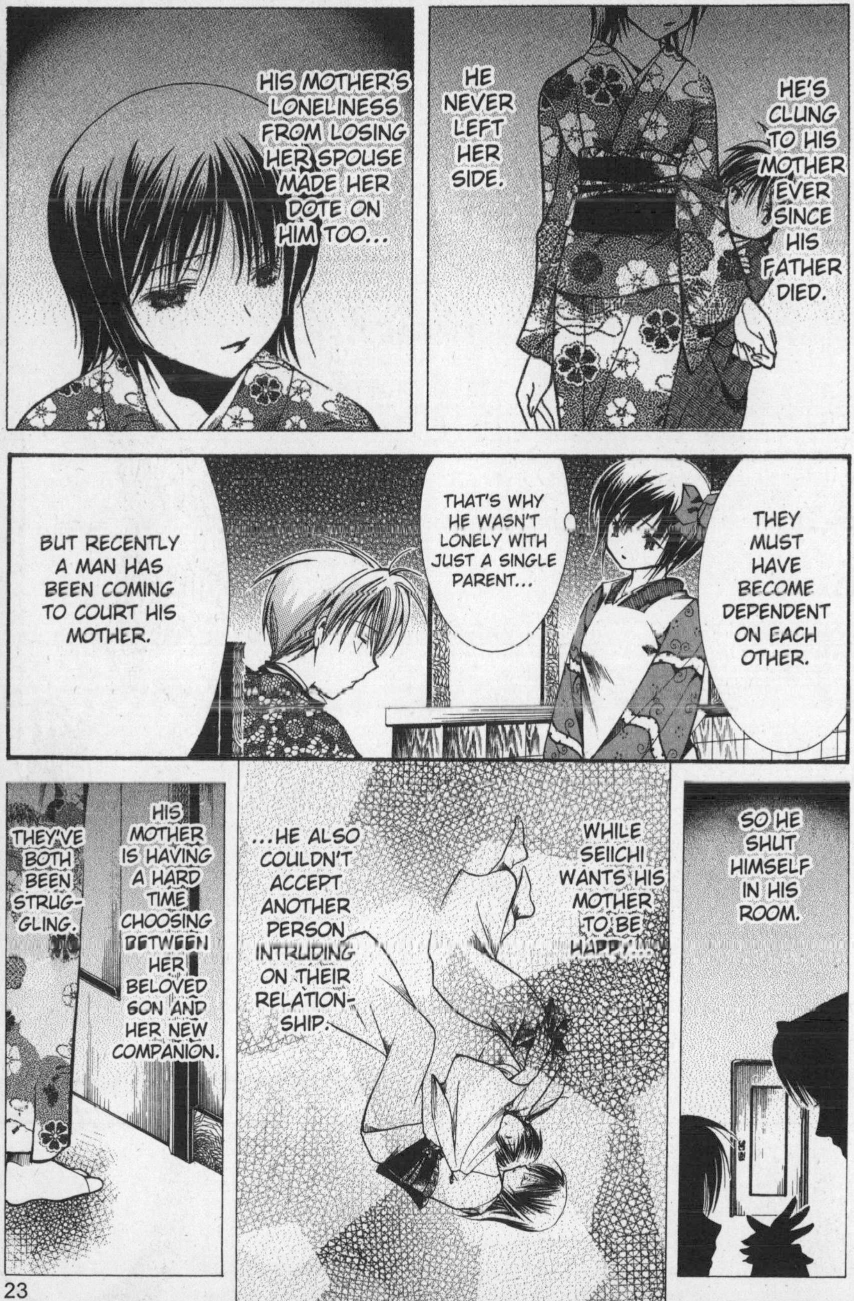
HE'S CLUNG TO HIS MOTHER EVER SINCE HIS FATHER DIED.
HE NEVER LEFT HER SIDE.
HIS MOTHER'S LONELINESS FROM LOSING HER SPOUSE MADE HER DOTE ON HIM TOO...
THEY MUST HAVE BECOME DEPENDENT ON EACH OTHER.
THAT'S WHY HE WASN'T LONELY WITH JUST A SINGLE PARENT...
BUT RECENTLY A MAN HAS BEEN COMING TO COURT HIS MOTHER.
SO HE SHUT HIMSELF IN HIS ROOM.
WHILE SEIICHI WANTS HIS MOTHER TO BE HAPPY...
...HE ALSO COULDN'T ACCEPT ANOTHER PERSON INTRUDING ON THEIR RELATIONSHIP.
HIS MOTHER IS HAVING A HARD TIME CHOOSING BETWEEN HER BELOVED SON AND HER NEW COMPANION.
THEY'VE BOTH BEEN STRUG-GLING.

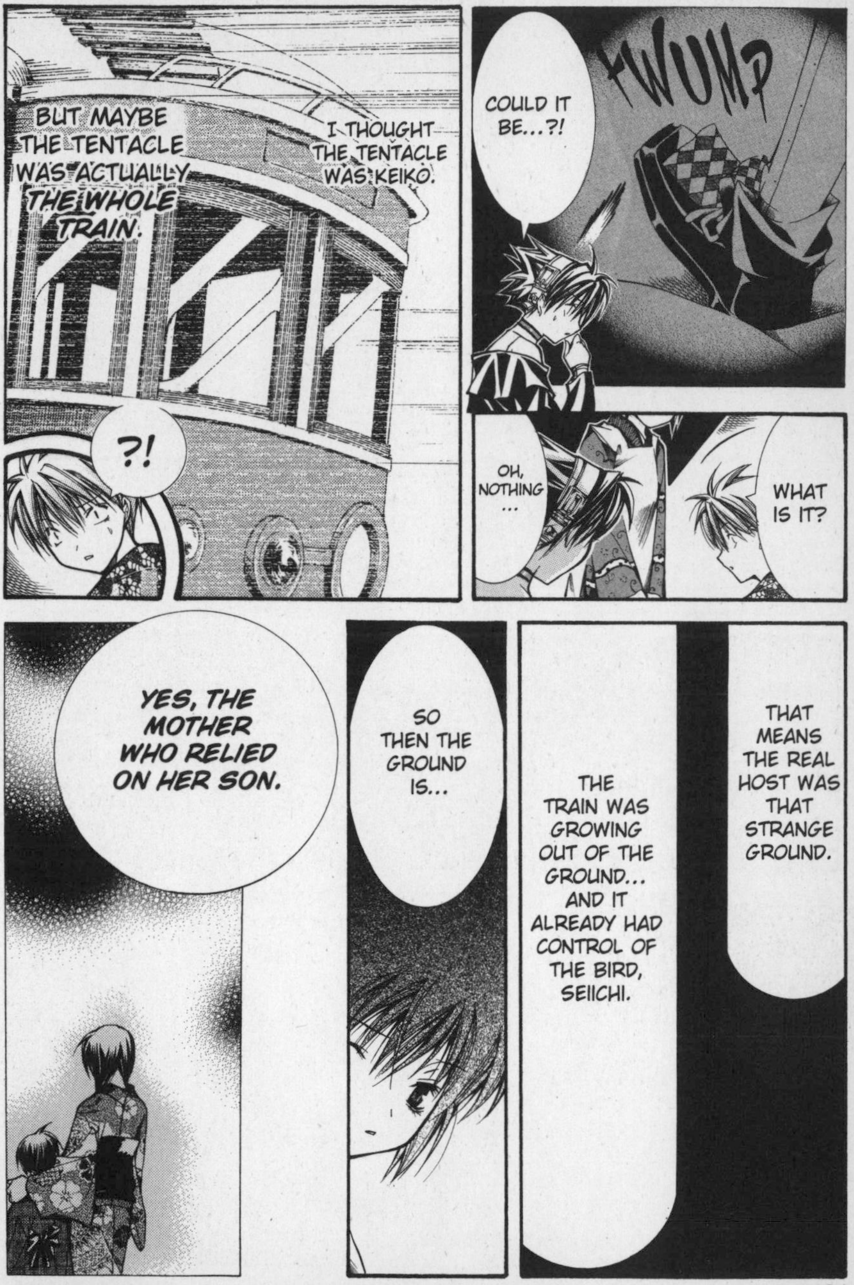
FWUMP
COULD IT BE...?!
WHAT IS IT?
OH, NOTHING...
I THOUGHT THE TENTACLE WAS KEIKO.
BUT MAYBE THE TENTACLE WAS ACTUALLY *THE WHOLE TRAIN*.
?!
THAT MEANS THE REAL HOST WAS THAT STRANGE GROUND.
THE TRAIN WAS GROWING OUT OF THE GROUND... AND IT ALREADY HAD CONTROL OF THE BIRD, SEIICHI.
SO THEN THE GROUND IS...
YES, THE MOTHER WHO RELIED ON HER SON.

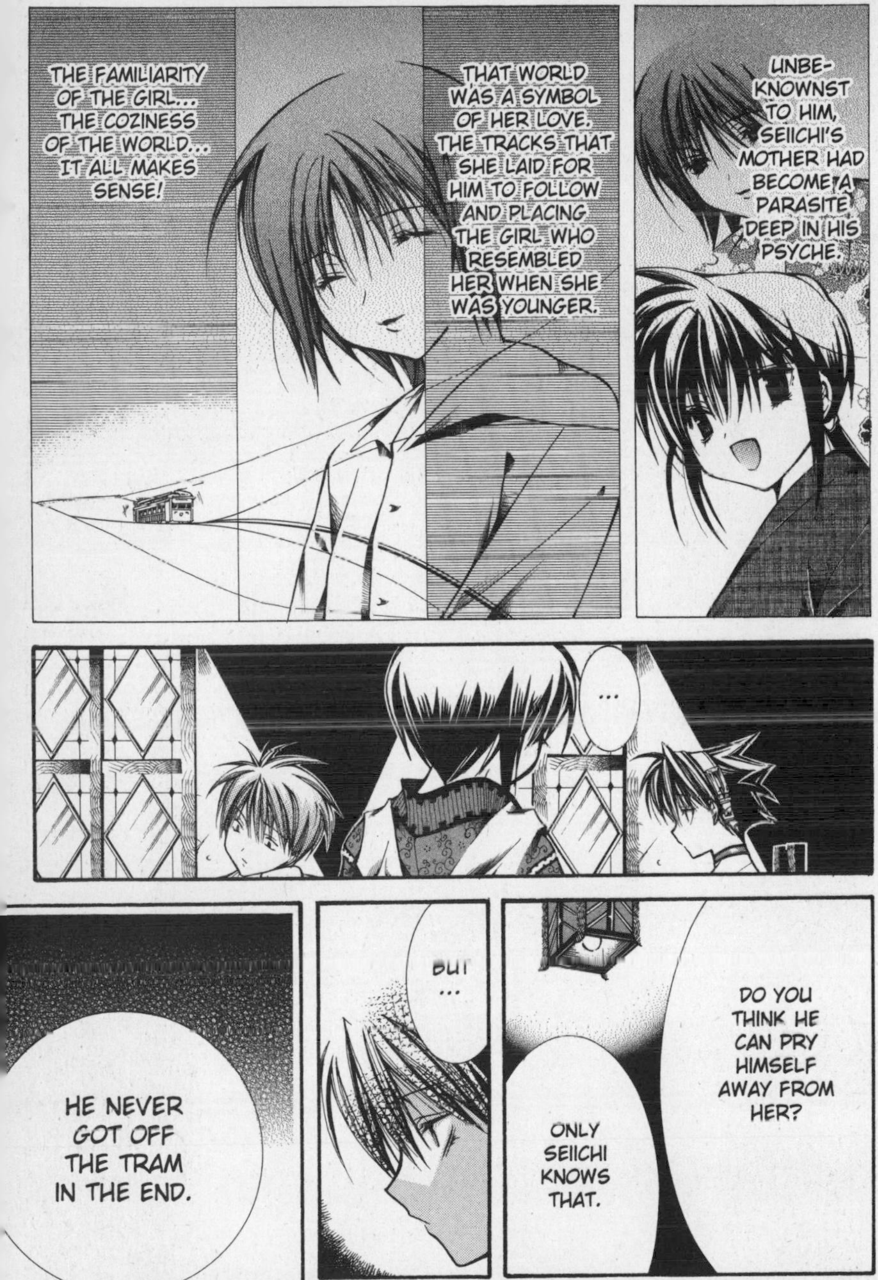
UNBE-KNOWNST TO HIM, SEIICHI'S MOTHER HAD BECOME A PARASITE DEEP IN HIS PSYCHE.
THAT WORLD WAS A SYMBOL OF HER LOVE. THE TRACKS THAT SHE LAID FOR HIM TO FOLLOW AND PLACING THE GIRL WHO RESEMBLED HER WHEN SHE WAS YOUNGER.
THE FAMILIARITY OF THE GIRL... THE COZINESS OF THE WORLD... IT ALL MAKES SENSE!
...
DO YOU THINK HE CAN PRY HIMSELF AWAY FROM HER?
ONLY SEIICHI KNOWS THAT.
BUT ...
HE NEVER GOT OFF THE TRAM IN THE END.

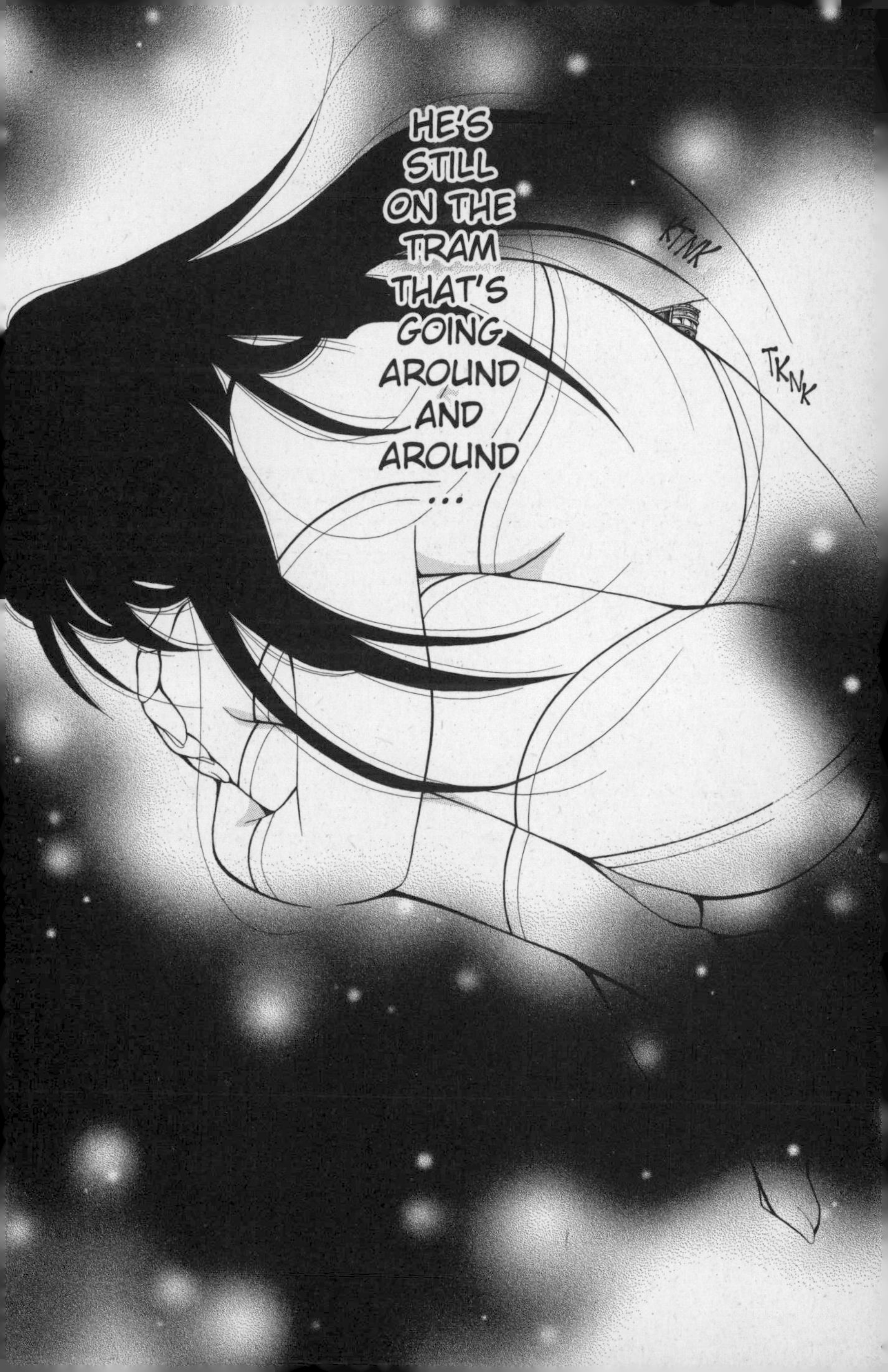
HE'S STILL ON THE TRAM THAT'S GOING AROUND AND AROUND...
KTNK
TKNK

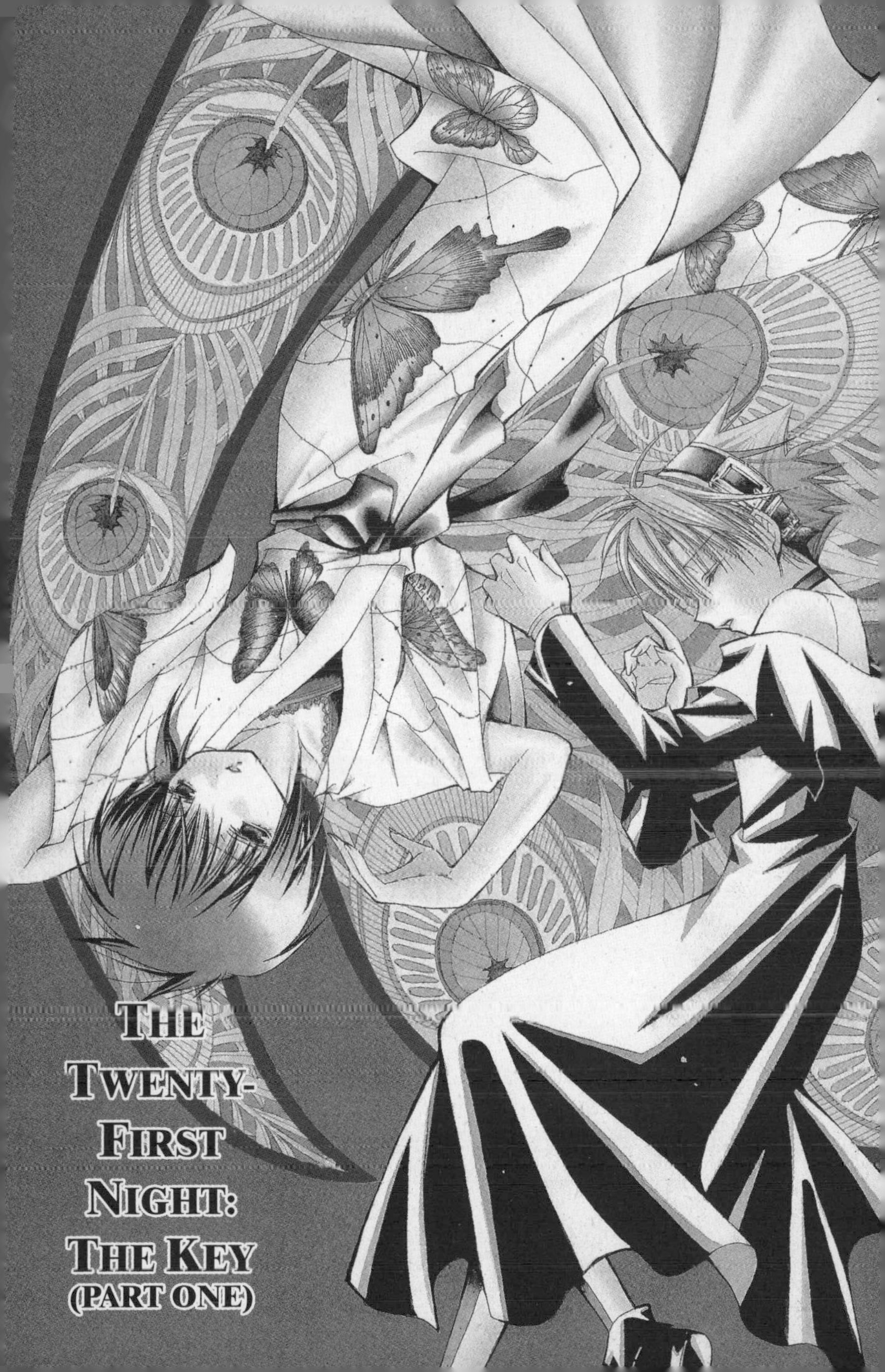
THE TWENTY-FIRST NIGHT: THE KEY
(PART ONE)

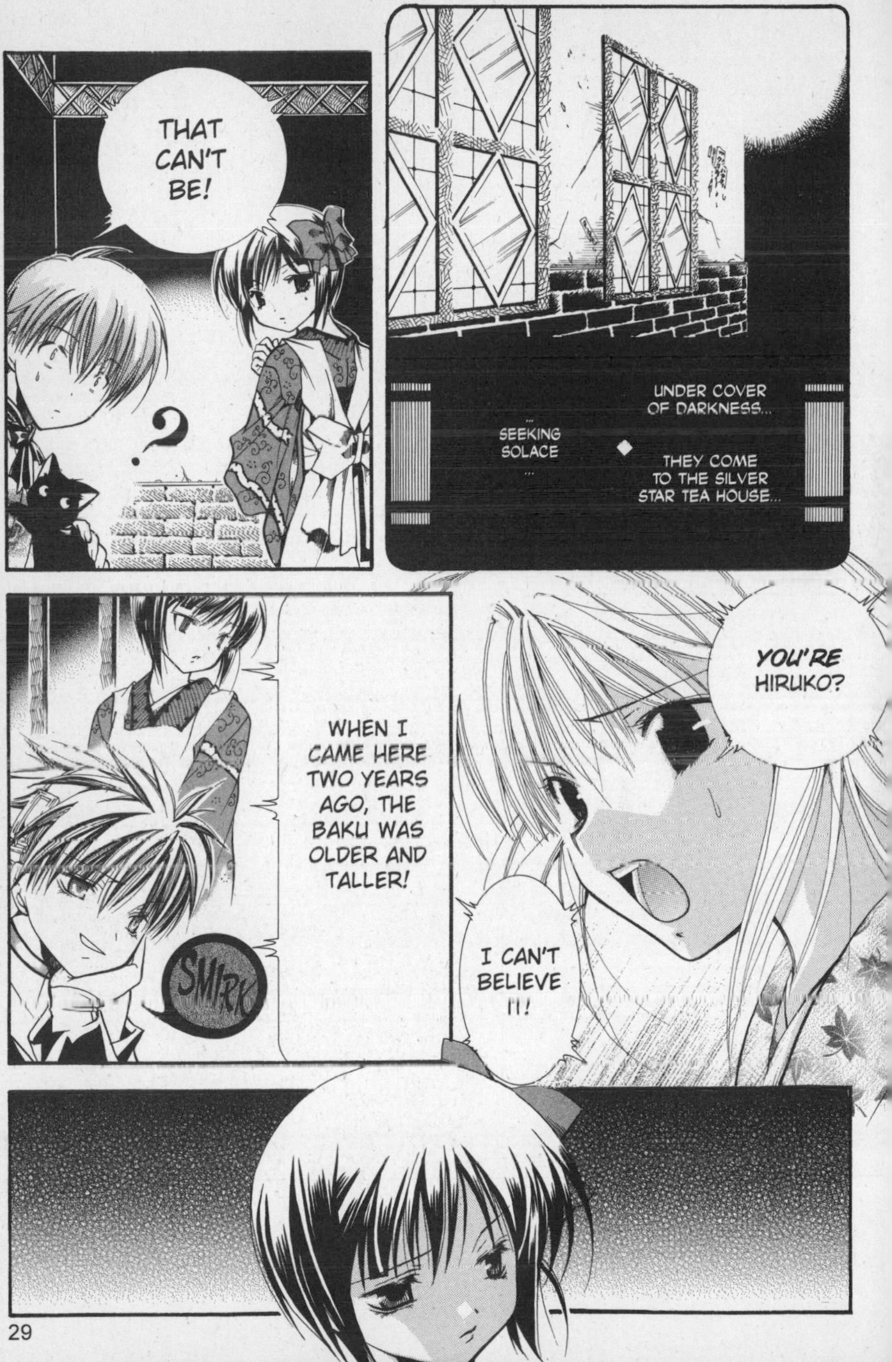
UNDER COVER OF DARKNESS...
THEY COME TO THE SILVER STAR TEA HOUSE...
...SEEKING SOLACE...
THAT CAN'T BE!
?
YOU'RE HIRUKO?
I CAN'T BELIEVE IT!
WHEN I CAME HERE TWO YEARS AGO, THE BAKU WAS OLDER AND TALLER!
SMIRK

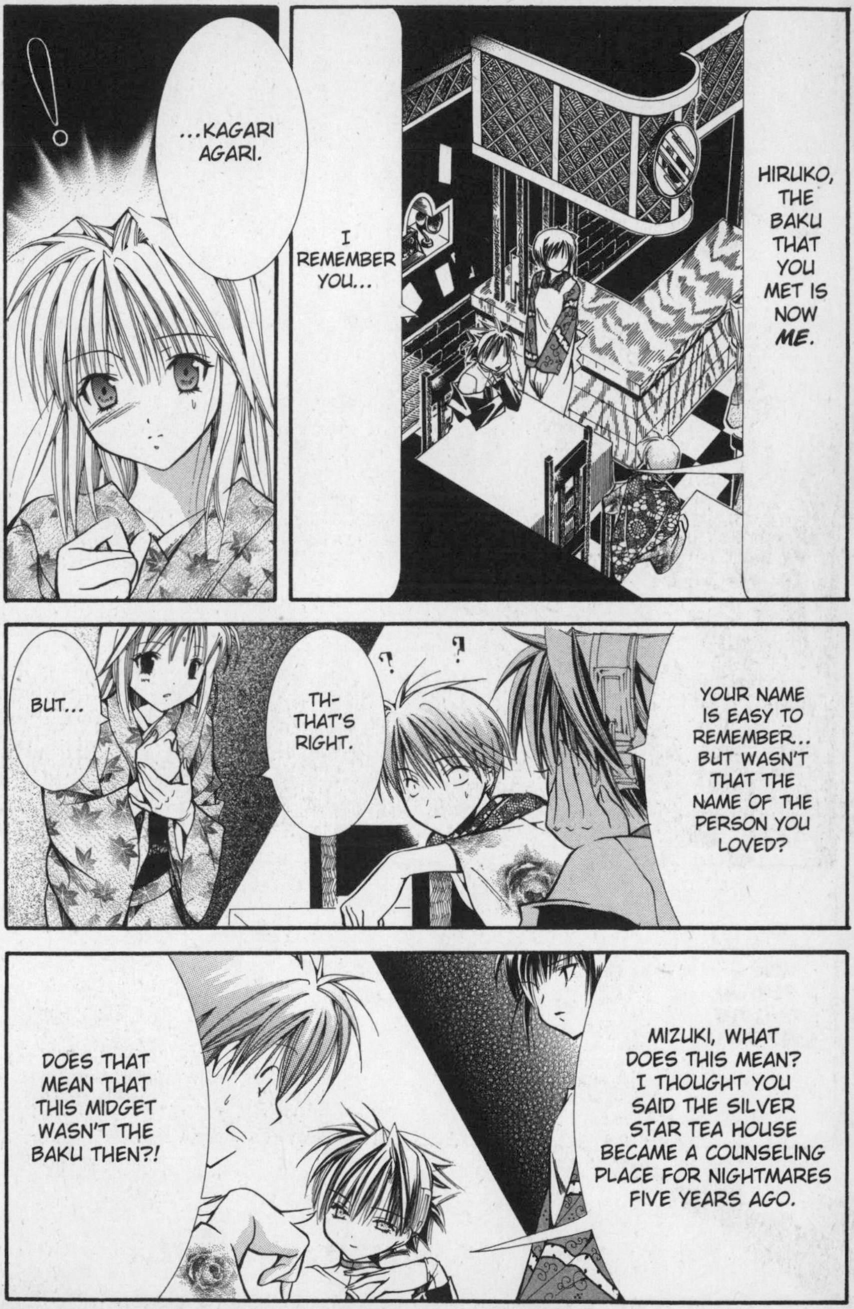
HIRUKO, THE BAKU THAT YOU MET IS NOW ***ME***.
I REMEMBER YOU...
!
...KAGARI AGARI.
YOUR NAME IS EASY TO REMEMBER... BUT WASN'T THAT THE NAME OF THE PERSON YOU LOVED?
?
?
TH-THAT'S RIGHT.
BUT...
MIZUKI, WHAT DOES THIS MEAN? I THOUGHT YOU SAID THE SILVER STAR TEA HOUSE BECAME A COUNSELING PLACE FOR NIGHTMARES FIVE YEARS AGO.
DOES THAT MEAN THAT THIS MIDGET WASN'T THE BAKU THEN?!

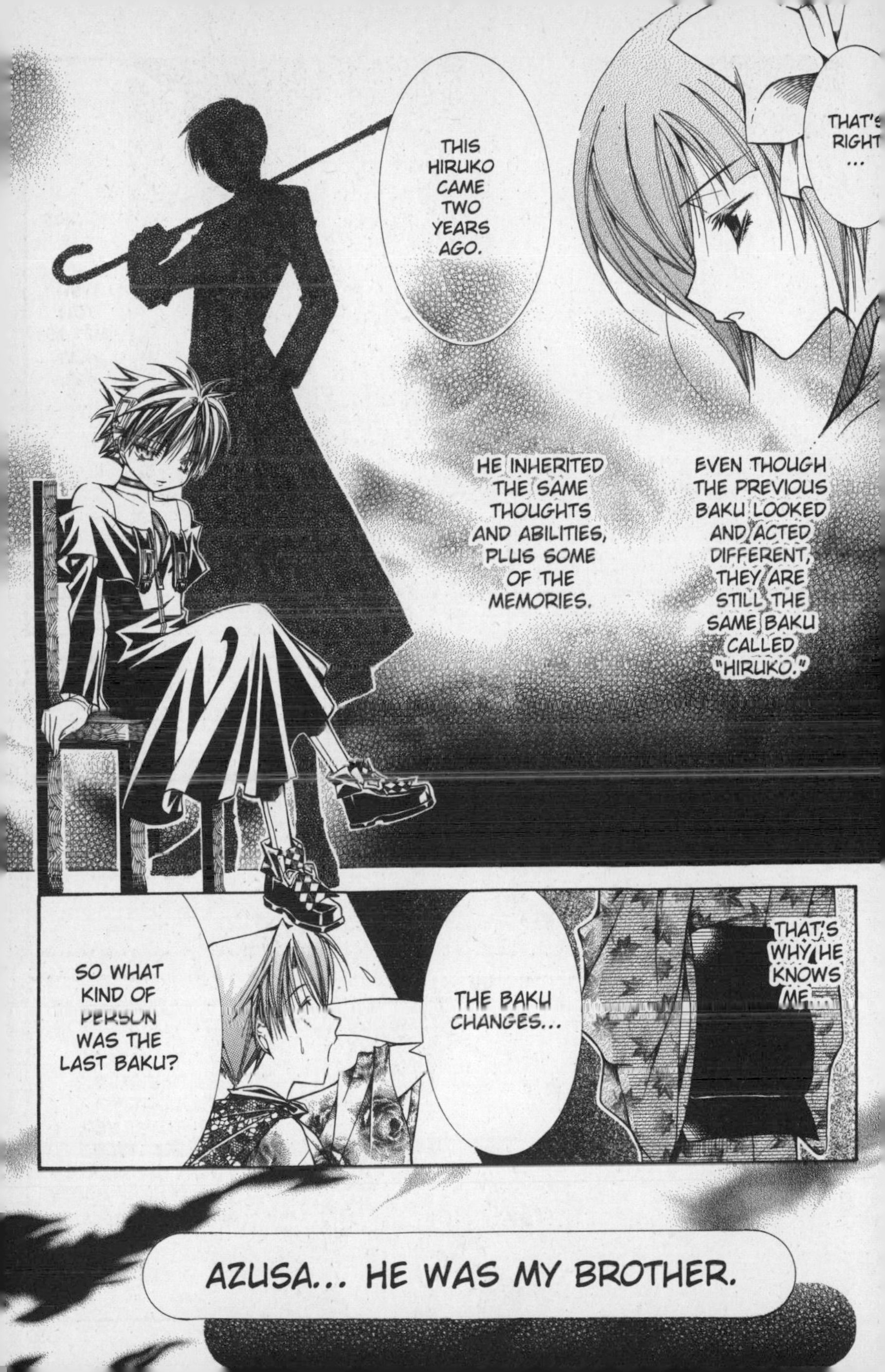
THAT'S RIGHT...
THIS HIRUKO CAME TWO YEARS AGO.
EVEN THOUGH THE PREVIOUS BAKU LOOKED AND ACTED DIFFERENT, THEY ARE STILL THE SAME BAKU CALLED "HIRUKO."
HE INHERITED THE SAME THOUGHTS AND ABILITIES, PLUS SOME OF THE MEMORIES.
THAT'S WHY HE KNOWS ME...
THE BAKU CHANGES...
SO WHAT KIND OF PERSON WAS THE LAST BAKU?
AZUSA... HE WAS MY BROTHER.

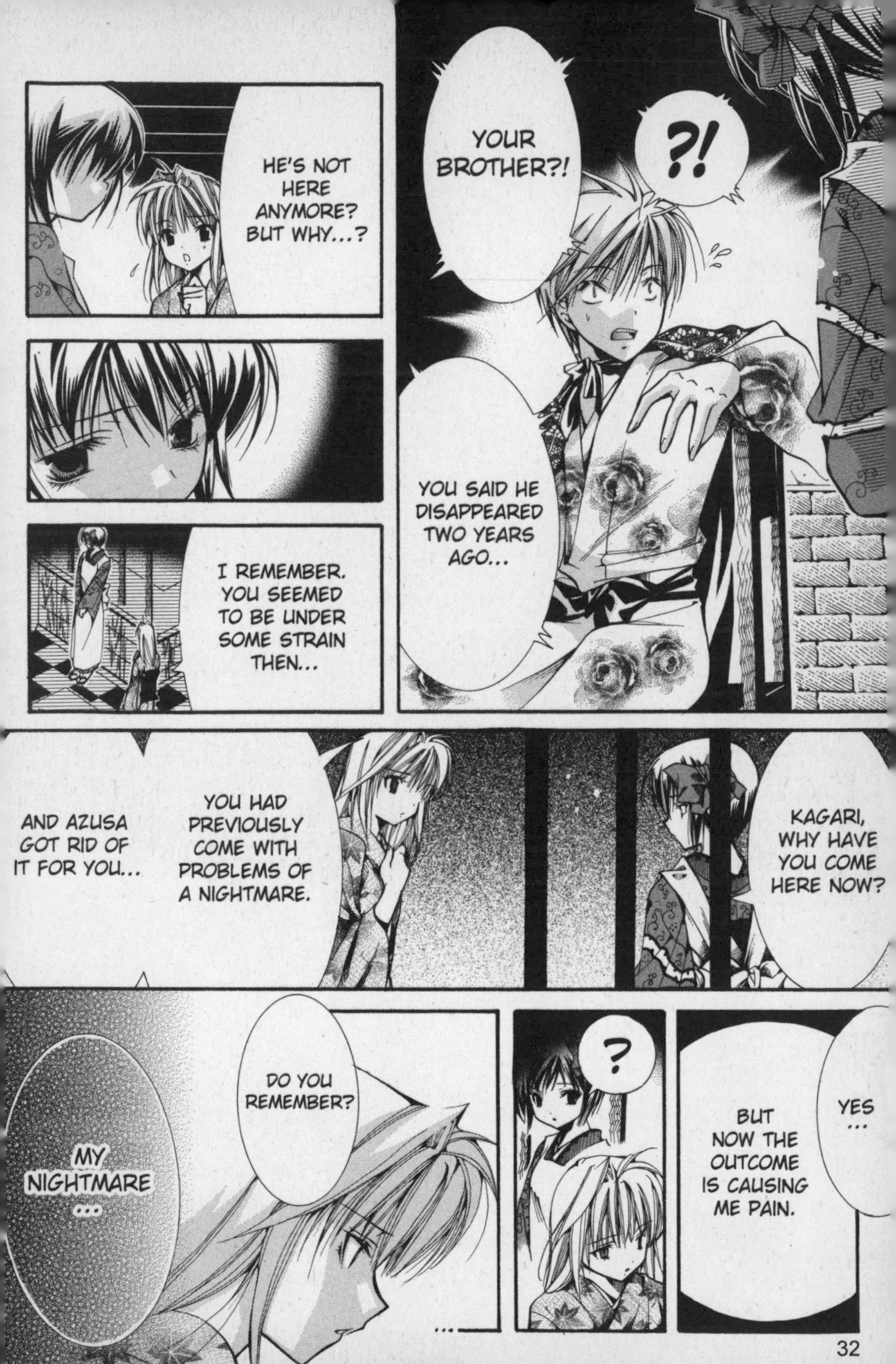
YOUR BROTHER?!
?!
YOU SAID HE DISAPPEARED TWO YEARS AGO...
HE'S NOT HERE ANYMORE? BUT WHY...?
I REMEMBER. YOU SEEMED TO BE UNDER SOME STRAIN THEN...
KAGARI, WHY HAVE YOU COME HERE NOW?
YOU HAD PREVIOUSLY COME WITH PROBLEMS OF A NIGHTMARE.
AND AZUSA GOT RID OF IT FOR YOU...
YES...
BUT NOW THE OUTCOME IS CAUSING ME PAIN.
?
...
DO YOU REMEMBER?
MY NIGHTMARE...

MY NAME IS KAGARI AGARI.

THAT'S ALL I KNOW.

I HAVE NO ME-MORIES OF MY PAST.

I DON'T KNOW IF THIS MEANS ANYTHING, BUT I'VE BEEN HAVING THIS NIGHTMARE.

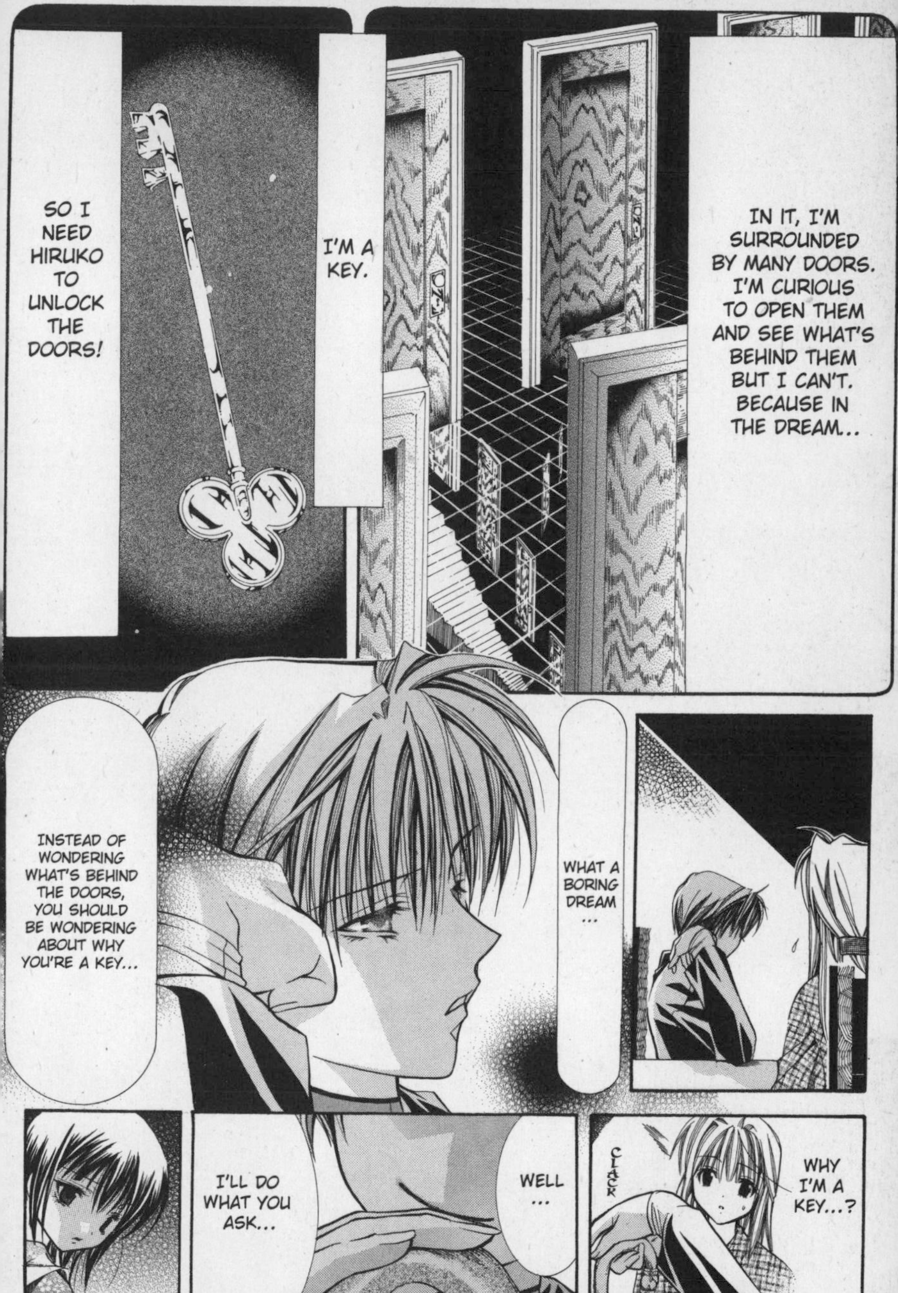
IN IT, I'M SURROUNDED BY MANY DOORS. I'M CURIOUS TO OPEN THEM AND SEE WHAT'S BEHIND THEM BUT I CAN'T. BECAUSE IN THE DREAM...
I'M A KEY.
SO I NEED HIRUKO TO UNLOCK THE DOORS!
WHAT A BORING DREAM...
INSTEAD OF WONDERING WHAT'S BEHIND THE DOORS, YOU SHOULD BE WONDERING ABOUT WHY YOU'RE A KEY...
WHY I'M A KEY...?
CLACK
WELL...
I'LL DO WHAT YOU ASK...

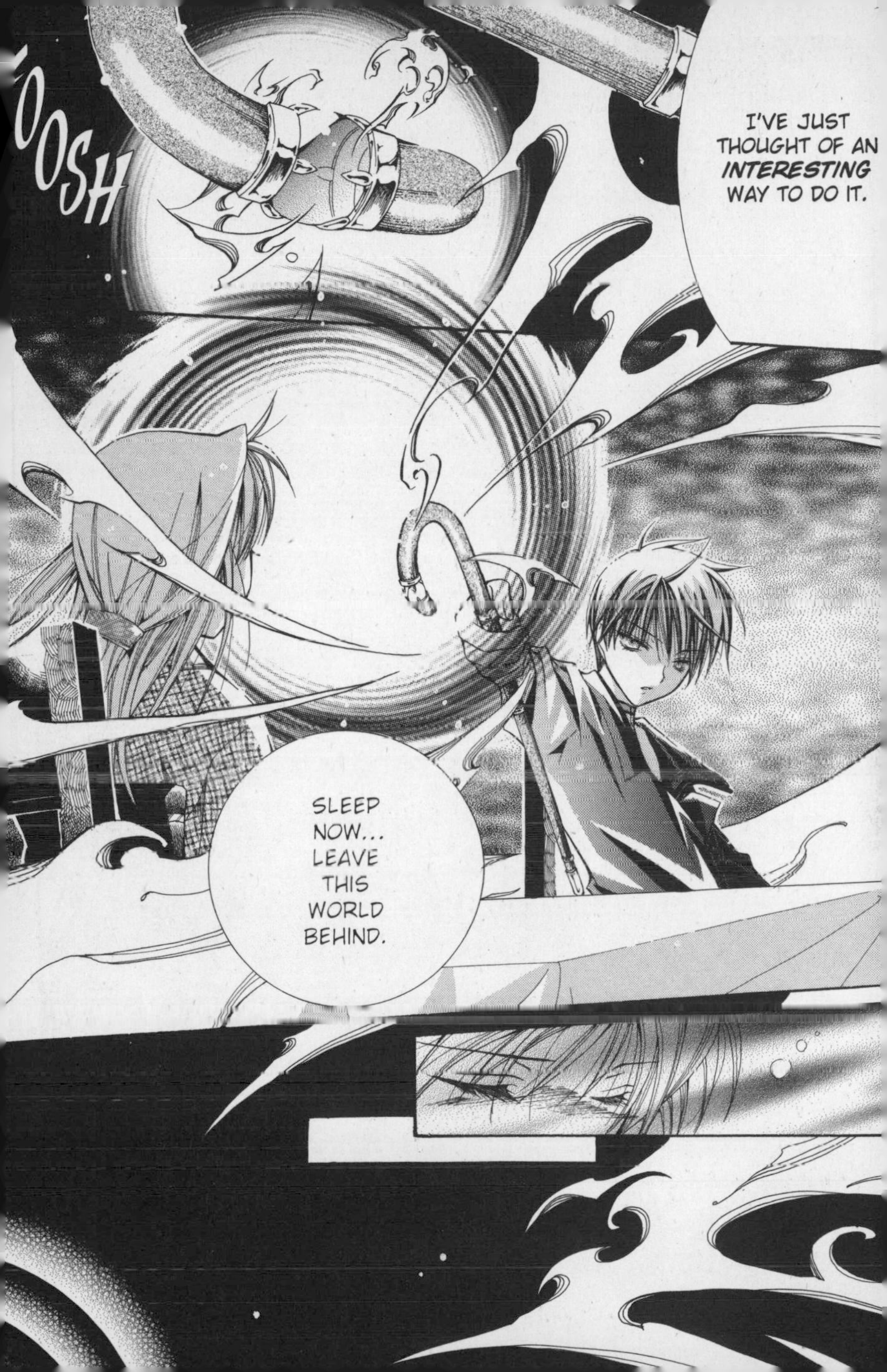
I'VE JUST THOUGHT OF AN ***INTERESTING*** WAY TO DO IT.
OOSH
SLEEP NOW... LEAVE THIS WORLD BEHIND.

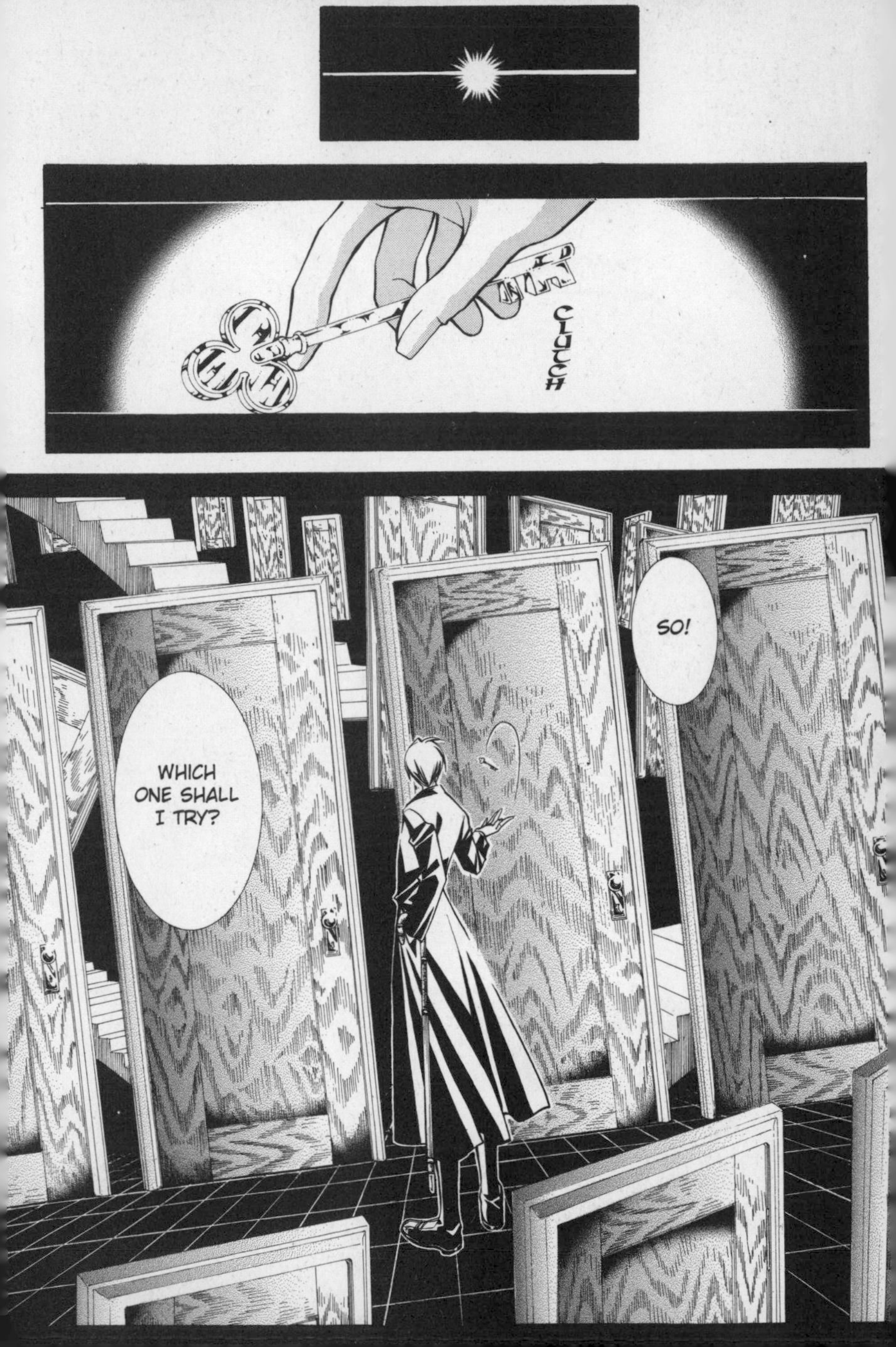
CLUTCH
SO!
WHICH ONE SHALL I TRY?

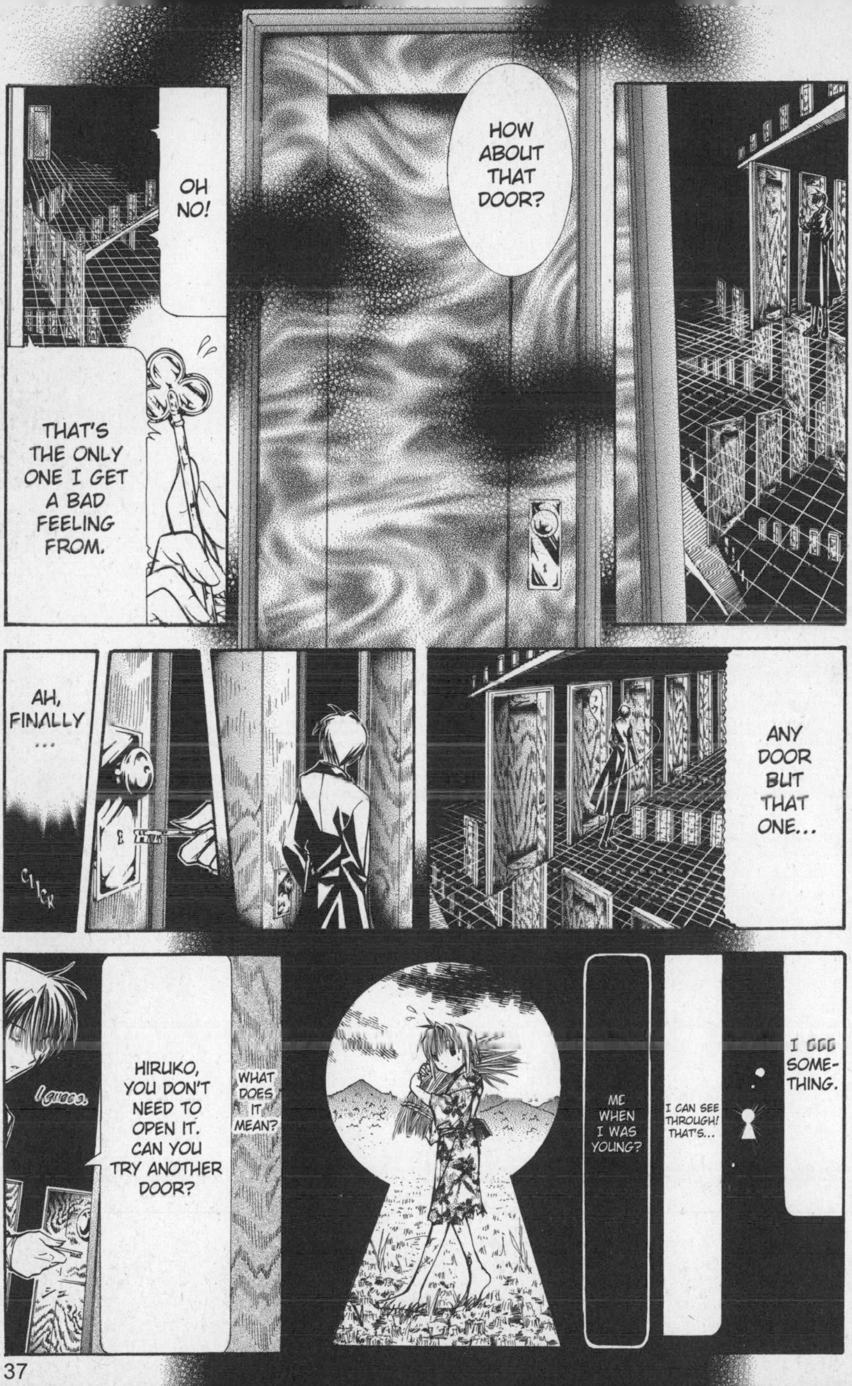
HOW ABOUT THAT DOOR?
OH NO!
THAT'S THE ONLY ONE I GET A BAD FEELING FROM.
ANY DOOR BUT THAT ONE...
AH, FINALLY ...
CLICK
I SOMETHING.
I CAN SEE THROUGH! THAT'S...
ME WHEN I WAS YOUNG?
WHAT DOES IT MEAN?
HIRUKO, YOU DON'T NEED TO OPEN IT. CAN YOU TRY ANOTHER DOOR?
I guess.

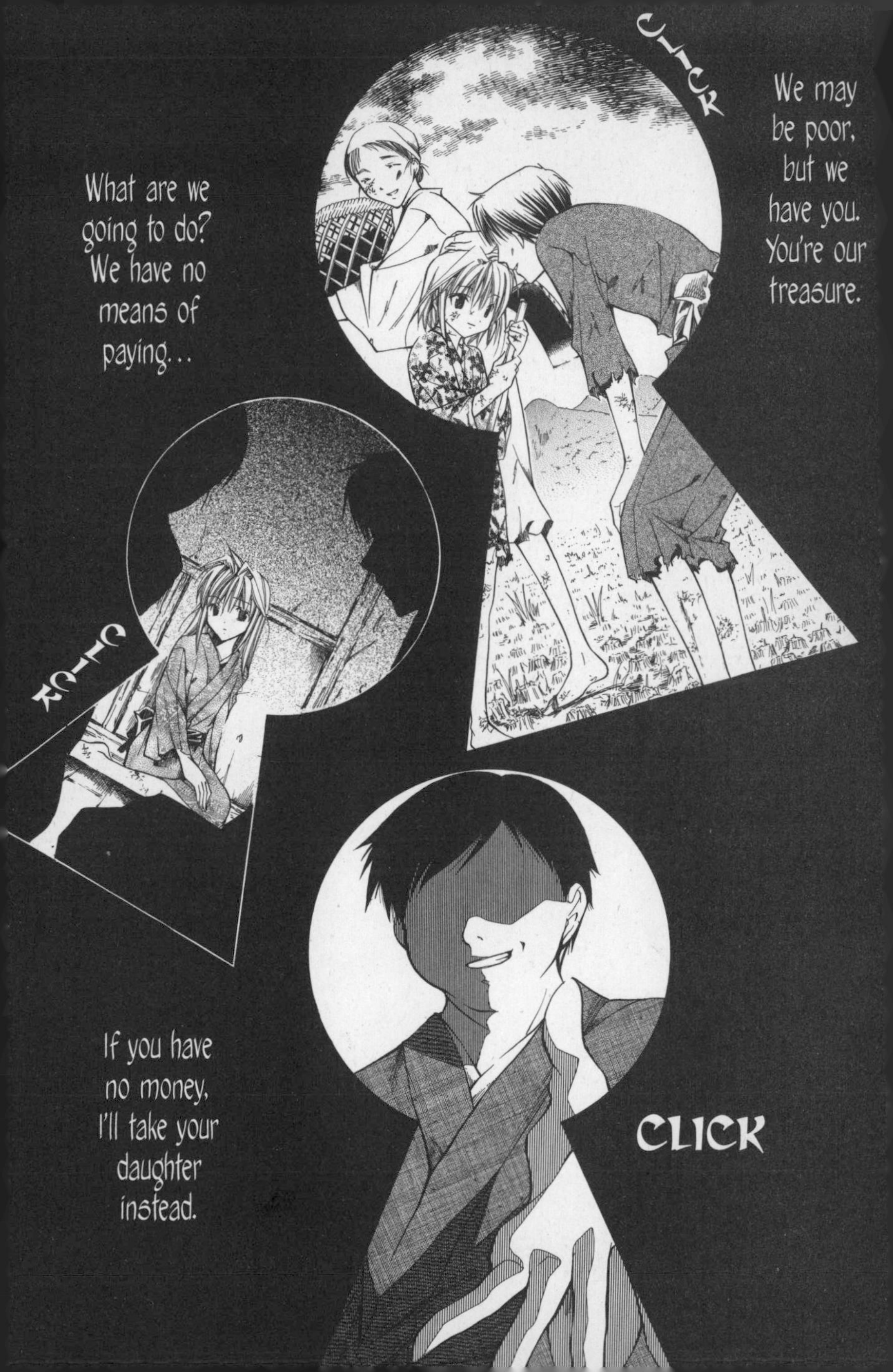
CLICK
We may be poor, but we have you. You're our treasure.
What are we going to do? We have no means of paying...
CLICK
CLICK
If you have no money, I'll take your daughter instead.

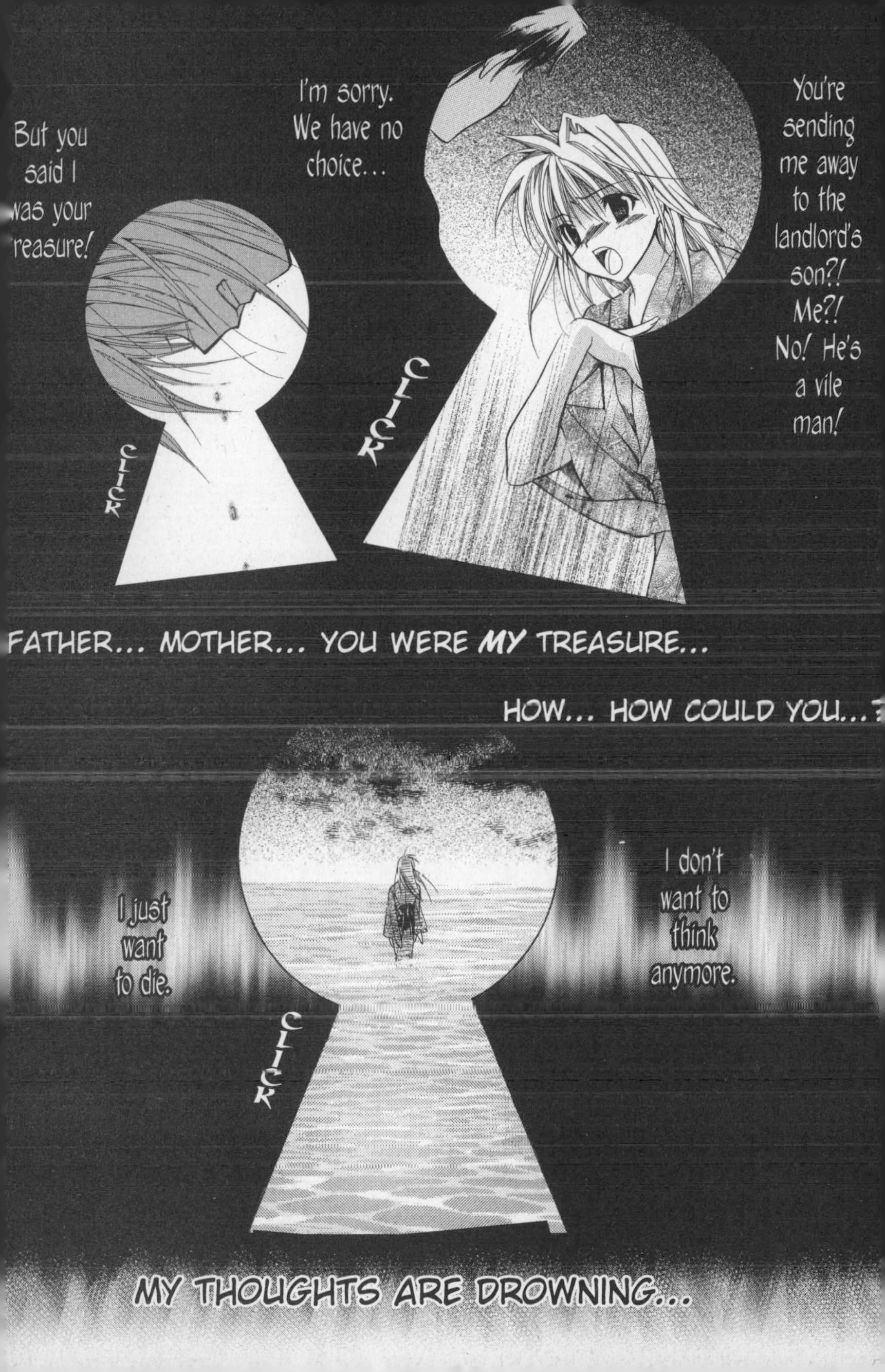
You're sending me away to the landlord's son?! Me?! No! He's a vile man!
I'm sorry. We have no choice...
But you said I was your treasure!
CLICK
CLICK
FATHER... MOTHER... YOU WERE *MY* TREASURE...
HOW... HOW COULD YOU...?
I don't want to think anymore.
I just want to die.
CLICK
MY THOUGHTS ARE DROWNING...

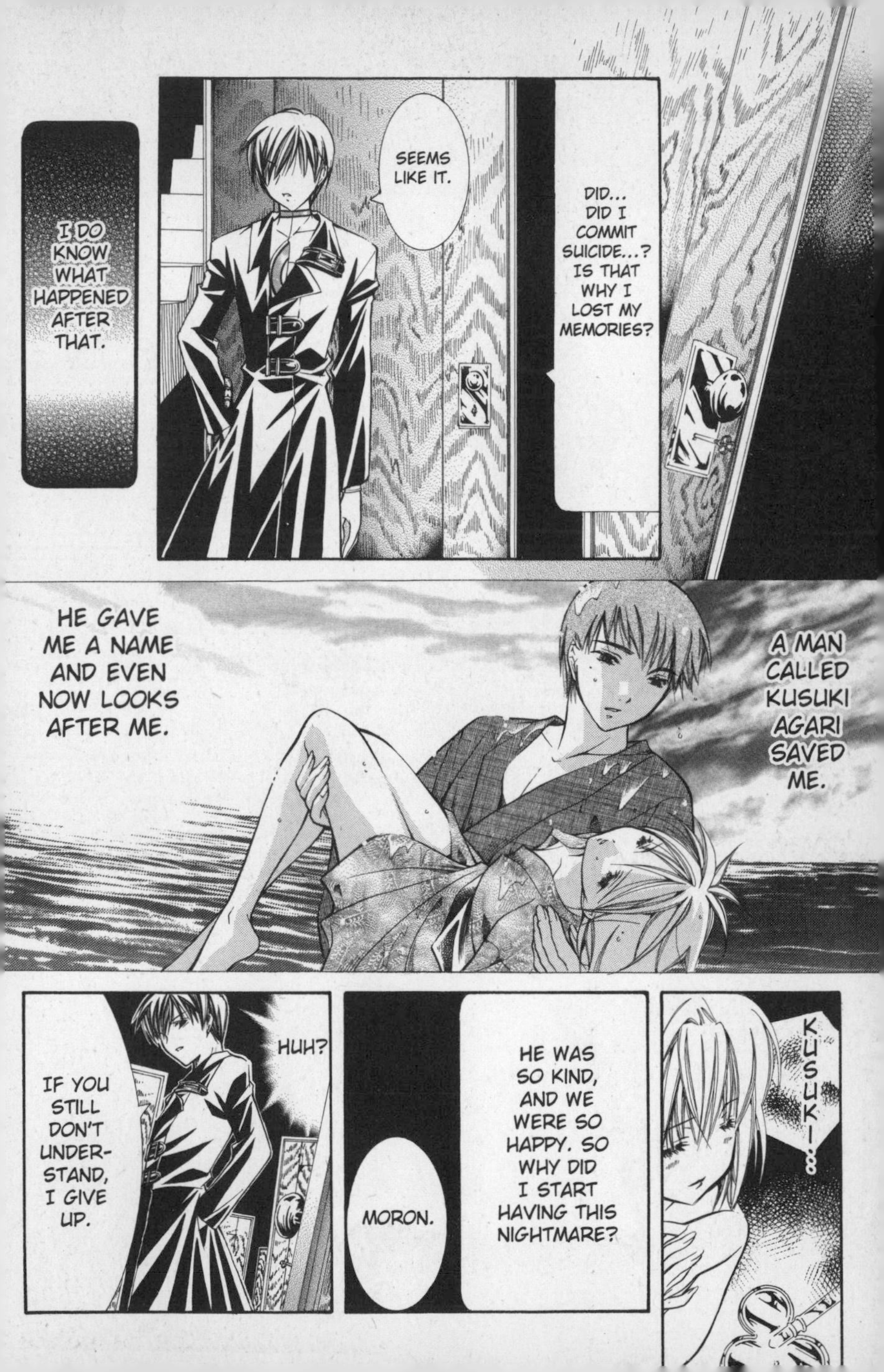
DID... DID I COMMIT SUICIDE...? IS THAT WHY I LOST MY MEMORIES?
SEEMS LIKE IT.
I DO KNOW WHAT HAPPENED AFTER THAT.
A MAN CALLED KUSUKI AGARI SAVED ME.
HE GAVE ME A NAME AND EVEN NOW LOOKS AFTER ME.
KUSUKI...
HE WAS SO KIND, AND WE WERE SO HAPPY. SO WHY DID I START HAVING THIS NIGHTMARE?
MORON.
HUH?
IF YOU STILL DON'T UNDER-STAND, I GIVE UP.

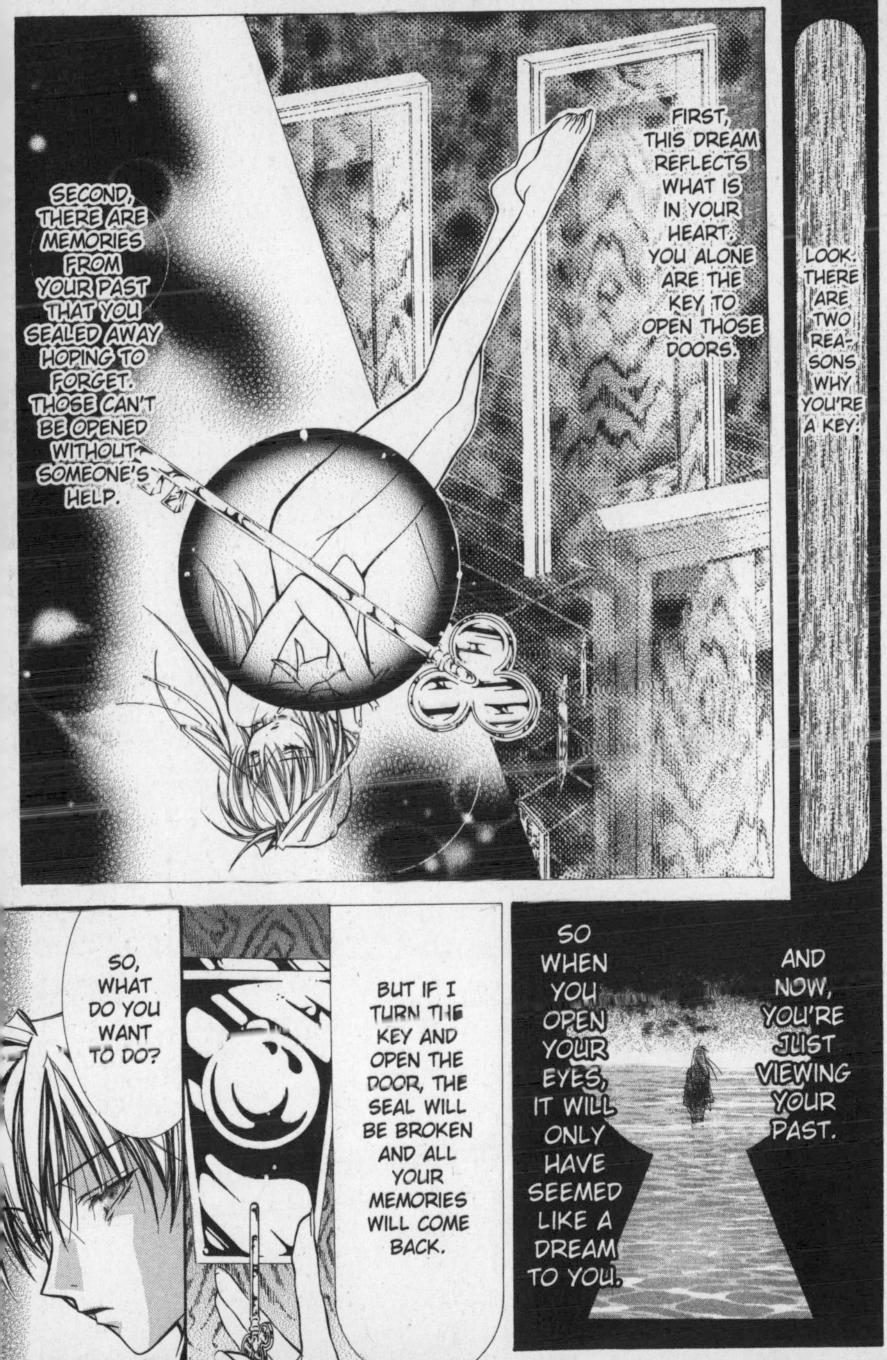
LOOK. THERE ARE TWO REASONS WHY YOU'RE A KEY.
FIRST, THIS DREAM REFLECTS WHAT IS IN YOUR HEART. YOU ALONE ARE THE KEY TO OPEN THOSE DOORS.
SECOND, THERE ARE MEMORIES FROM YOUR PAST THAT YOU SEALED AWAY HOPING TO FORGET. THOSE CAN'T BE OPENED WITHOUT SOMEONE'S HELP.
AND NOW, YOU'RE JUST VIEWING YOUR PAST.
SO WHEN YOU OPEN YOUR EYES, IT WILL ONLY HAVE SEEMED LIKE A DREAM TO YOU.
BUT IF I TURN THE KEY AND OPEN THE DOOR, THE SEAL WILL BE BROKEN AND ALL YOUR MEMORIES WILL COME BACK.
SO, WHAT DO YOU WANT TO DO?

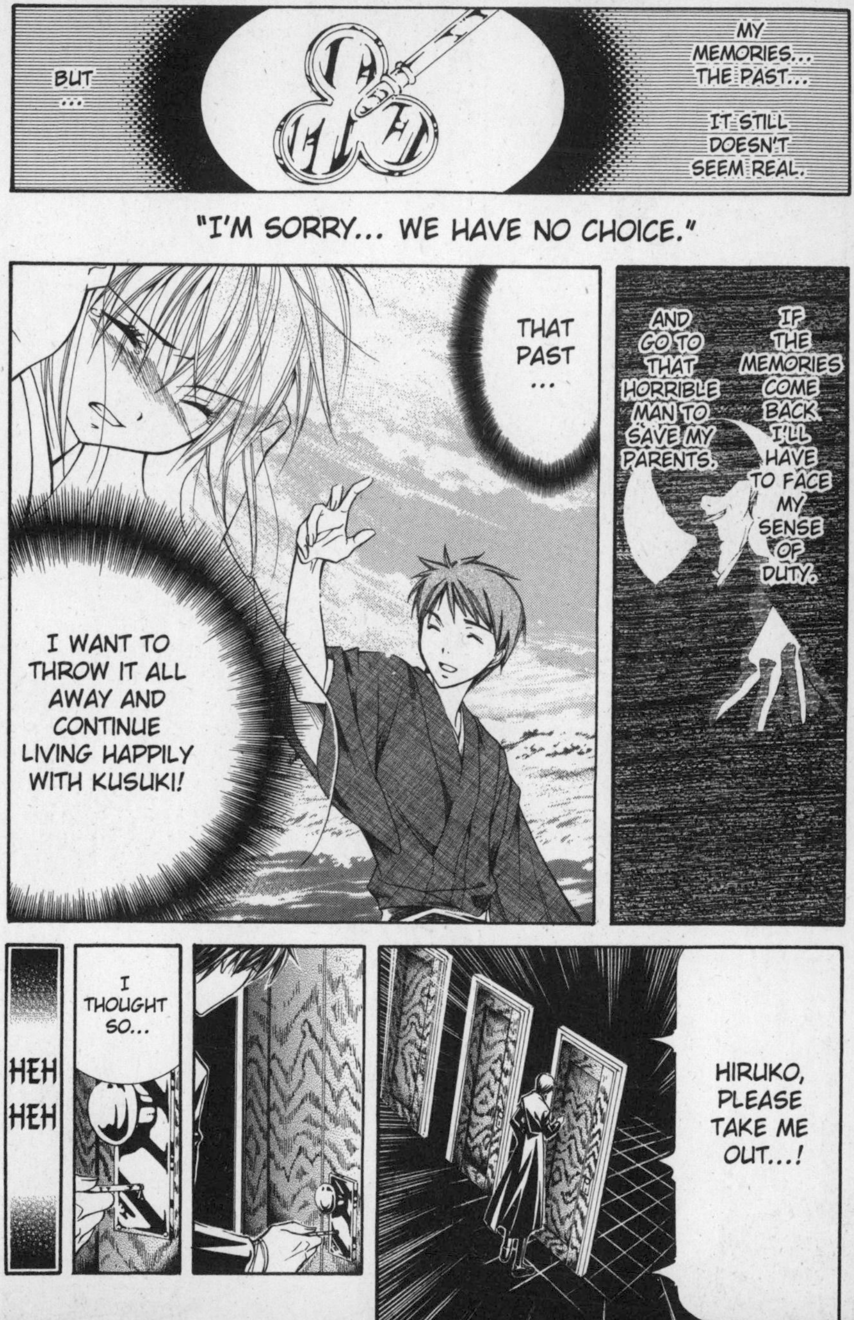
MY MEMORIES... THE PAST...
IT STILL DOESN'T SEEM REAL.
BUT ...
"I'M SORRY... WE HAVE NO CHOICE."
IF THE MEMORIES COME BACK I'LL HAVE TO FACE MY SENSE OF DUTY.
AND GO TO THAT HORRIBLE MAN TO SAVE MY PARENTS.
THAT PAST ...
I WANT TO THROW IT ALL AWAY AND CONTINUE LIVING HAPPILY WITH KUSUKI!
HIRUKO, PLEASE TAKE ME OUT...!
I THOUGHT SO...
HEH HEH

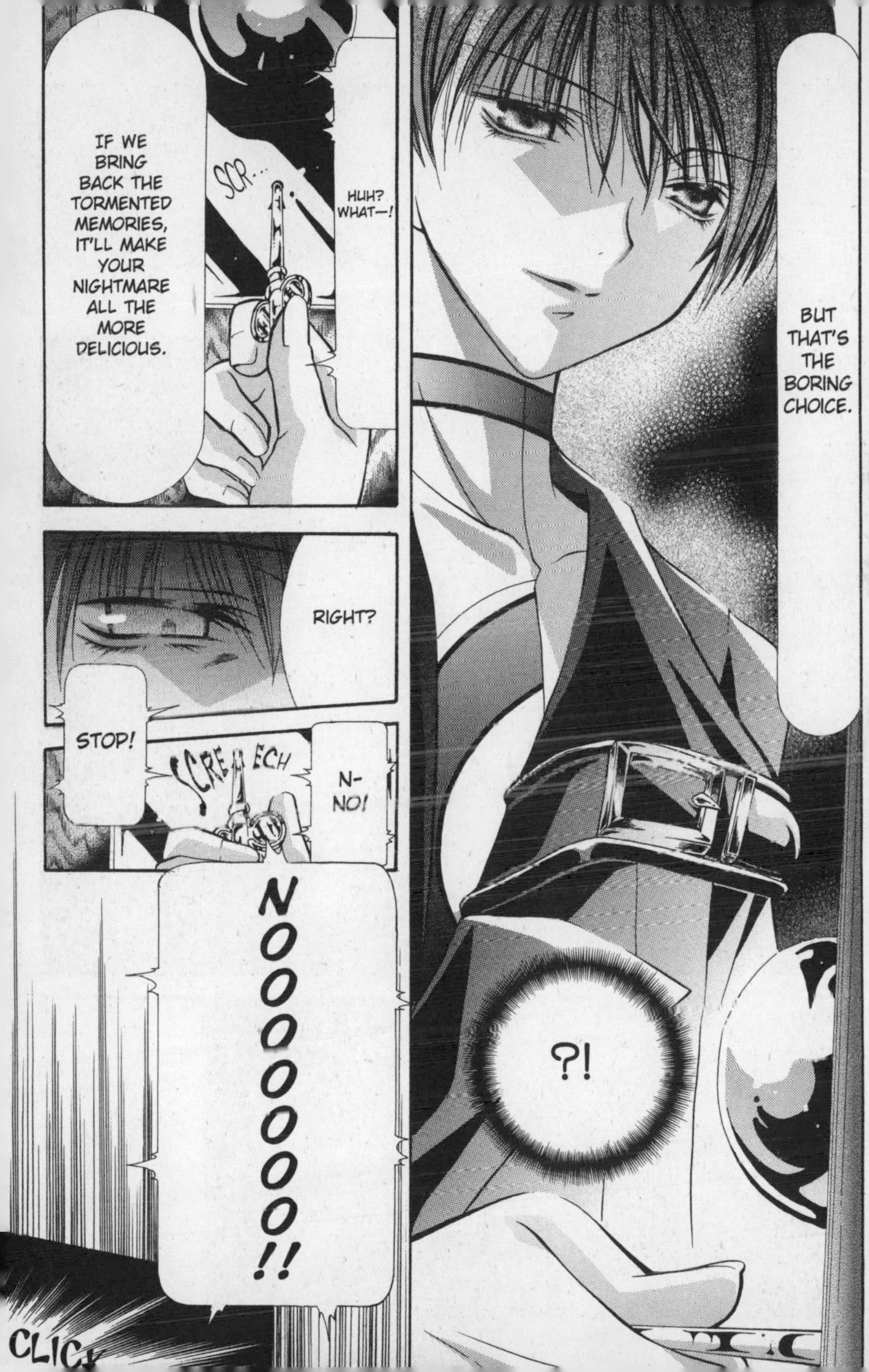
BUT THAT'S THE BORING CHOICE.
?!
HUH? WHAT—!
SCR...
IF WE BRING BACK THE TORMENTED MEMORIES, IT'LL MAKE YOUR NIGHTMARE ALL THE MORE DELICIOUS.
RIGHT?
N- NO!
SCREECH
STOP!
NOOOOOOOOOO!!
CLIC

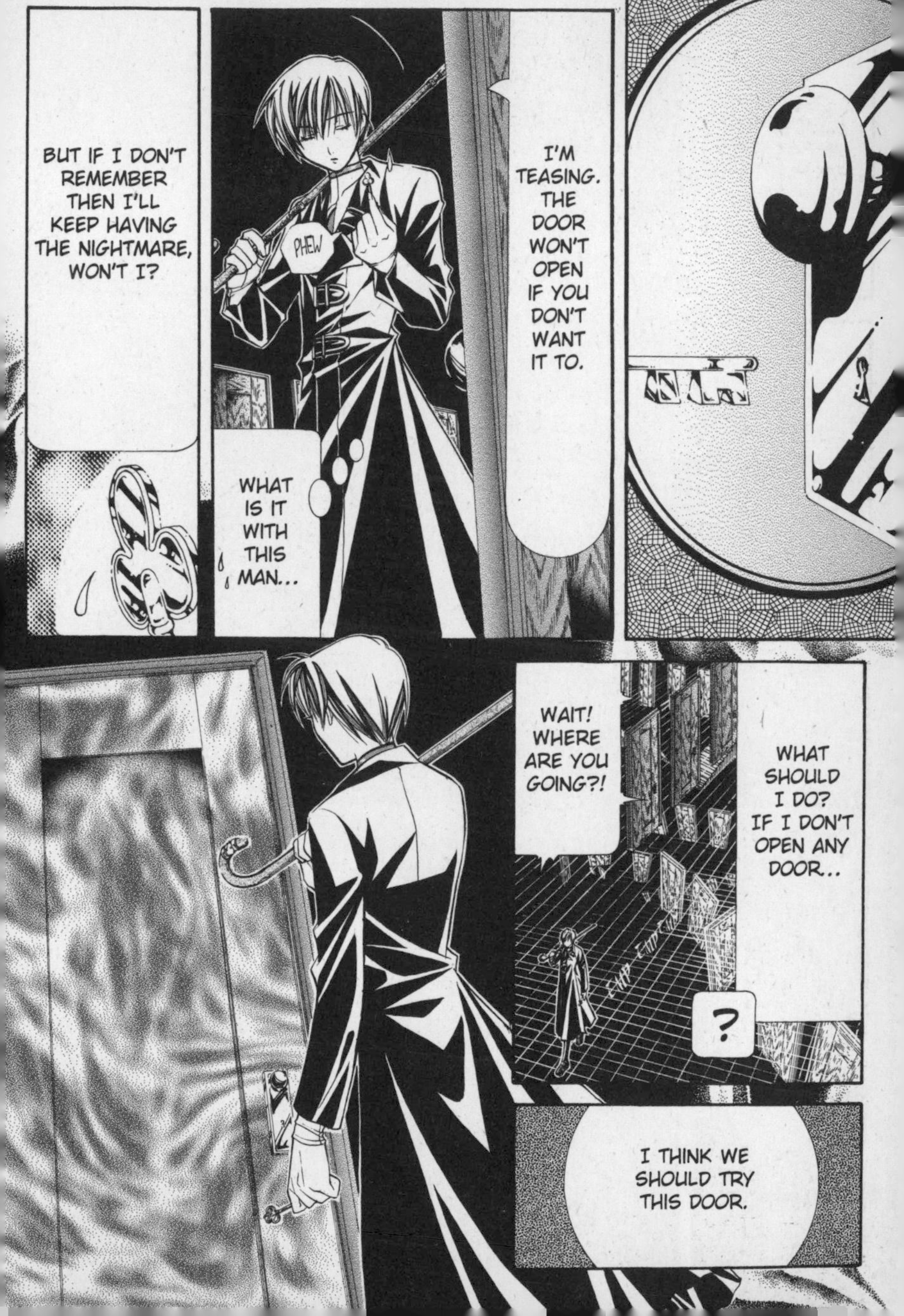
I'M TEASING. THE DOOR WON'T OPEN IF YOU DON'T WANT IT TO.
PHEW
WHAT IS IT WITH THIS MAN...
BUT IF I DON'T REMEMBER THEN I'LL KEEP HAVING THE NIGHTMARE, WON'T I?
WHAT SHOULD I DO? IF I DON'T OPEN ANY DOOR...
WAIT! WHERE ARE YOU GOING?!
?
I THINK WE SHOULD TRY THIS DOOR.

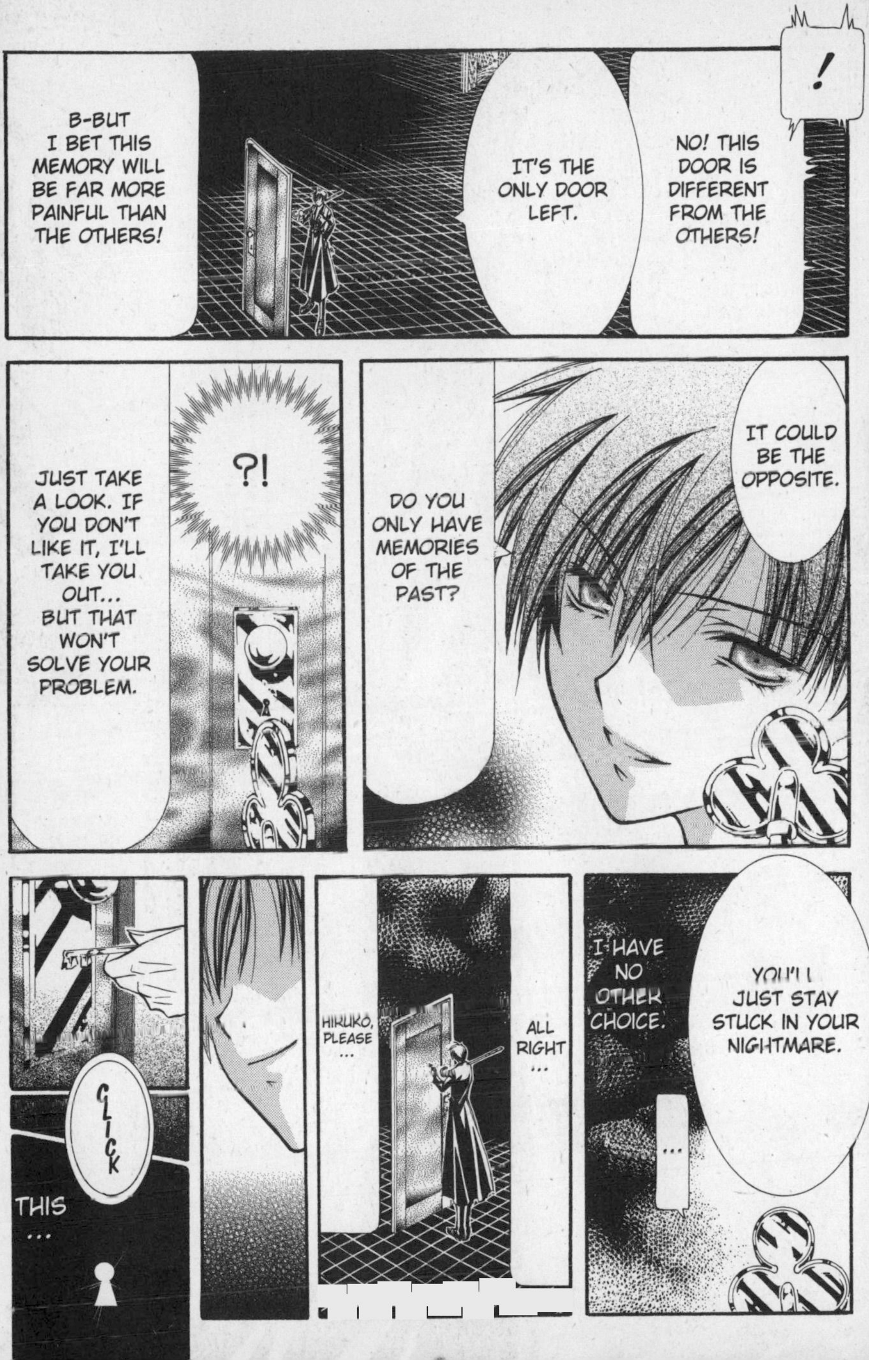
!
NO! THIS DOOR IS DIFFERENT FROM THE OTHERS!
IT'S THE ONLY DOOR LEFT.
B-BUT I BET THIS MEMORY WILL BE FAR MORE PAINFUL THAN THE OTHERS!
IT COULD BE THE OPPOSITE.
DO YOU ONLY HAVE MEMORIES OF THE PAST?
?!
JUST TAKE A LOOK. IF YOU DON'T LIKE IT, I'LL TAKE YOU OUT... BUT THAT WON'T SOLVE YOUR PROBLEM.
YOU'LL JUST STAY STUCK IN YOUR NIGHTMARE.
I HAVE NO OTHER CHOICE.
...
ALL RIGHT...
HIRUKO, PLEASE...
CLICK
THIS...

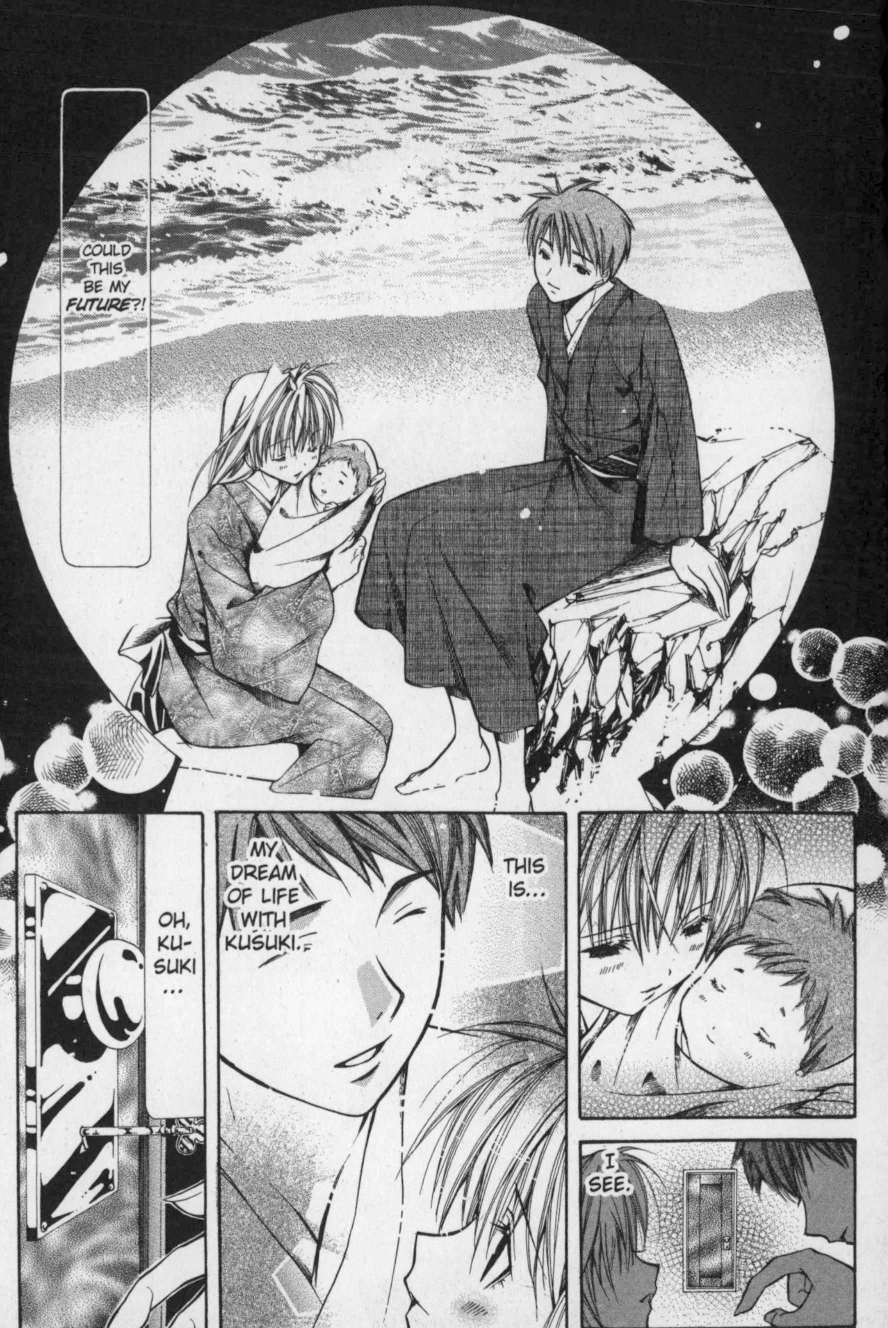
COULD THIS BE MY *FUTURE*?!
I SEE.
THIS IS...
MY DREAM OF LIFE WITH KUSUKI...
OH, KU-SUKI ...

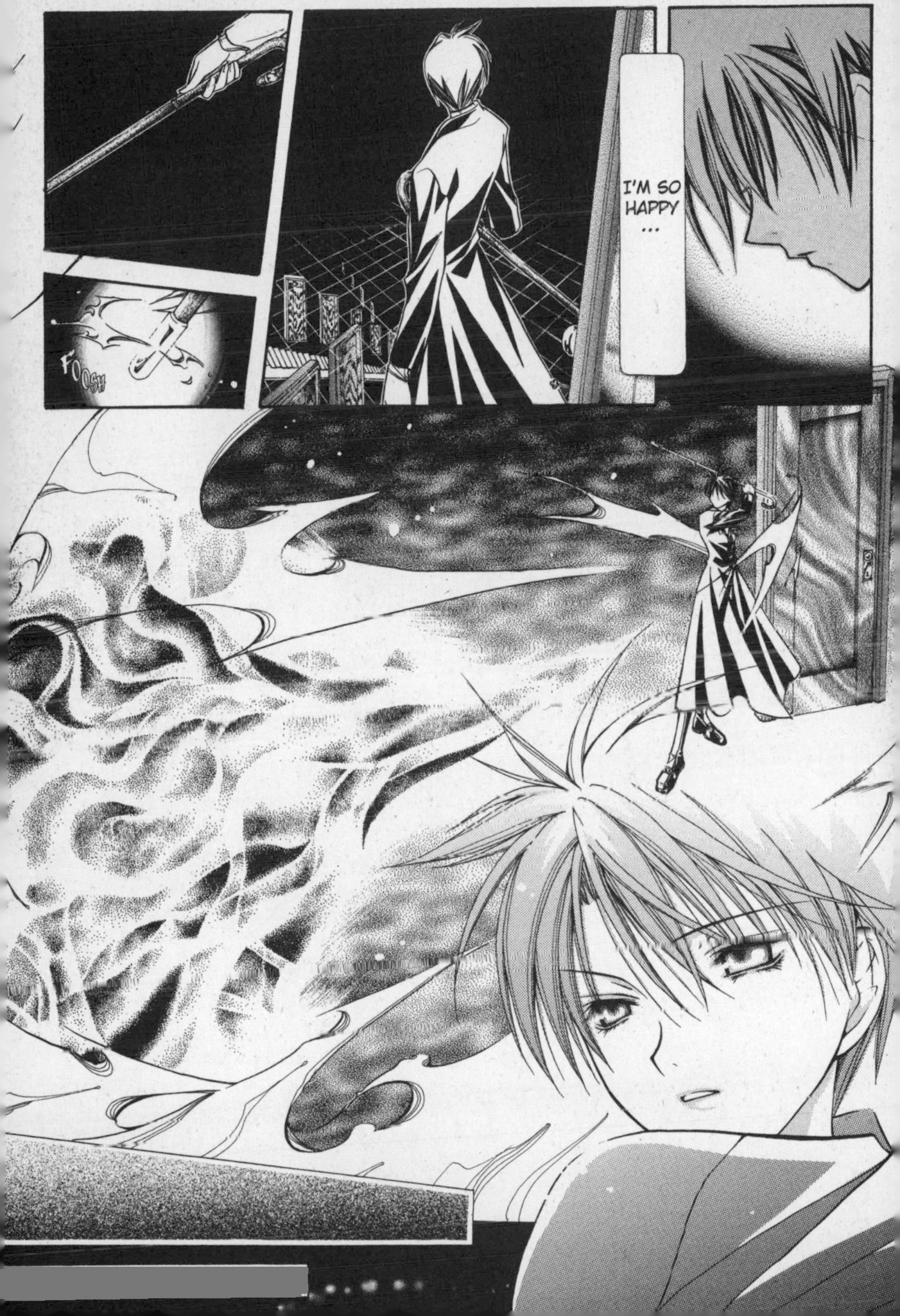
I'M SO HAPPY ...
FOOSH

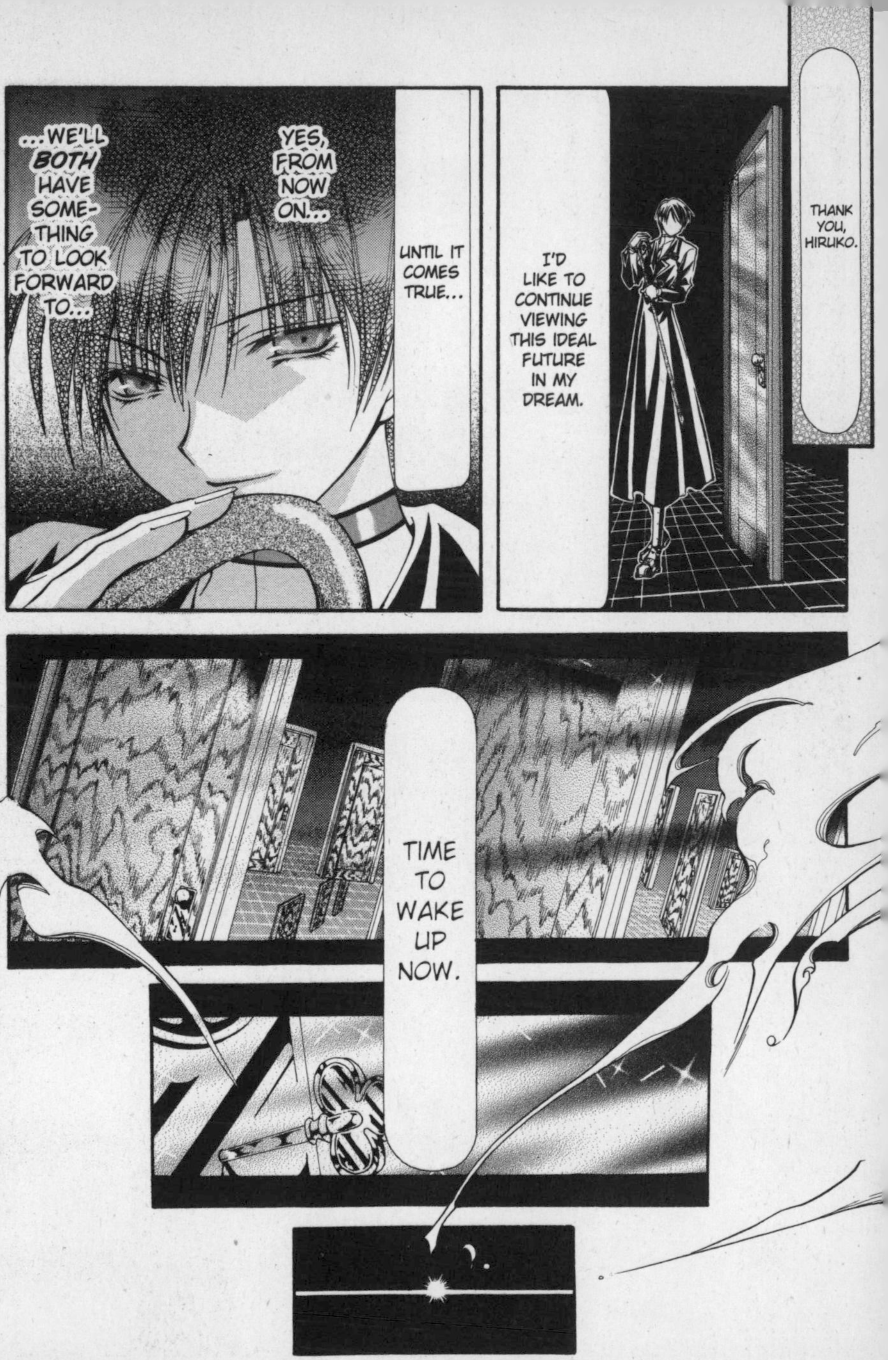
THANK YOU, HIRUKO.
I'D LIKE TO CONTINUE VIEWING THIS IDEAL FUTURE IN MY DREAM.
UNTIL IT COMES TRUE...
YES, FROM NOW ON...
...WE'LL *BOTH* HAVE SOME-THING TO LOOK FORWARD TO...
TIME TO WAKE UP NOW.

The Twenty-Second Night: The Key (Part Two)

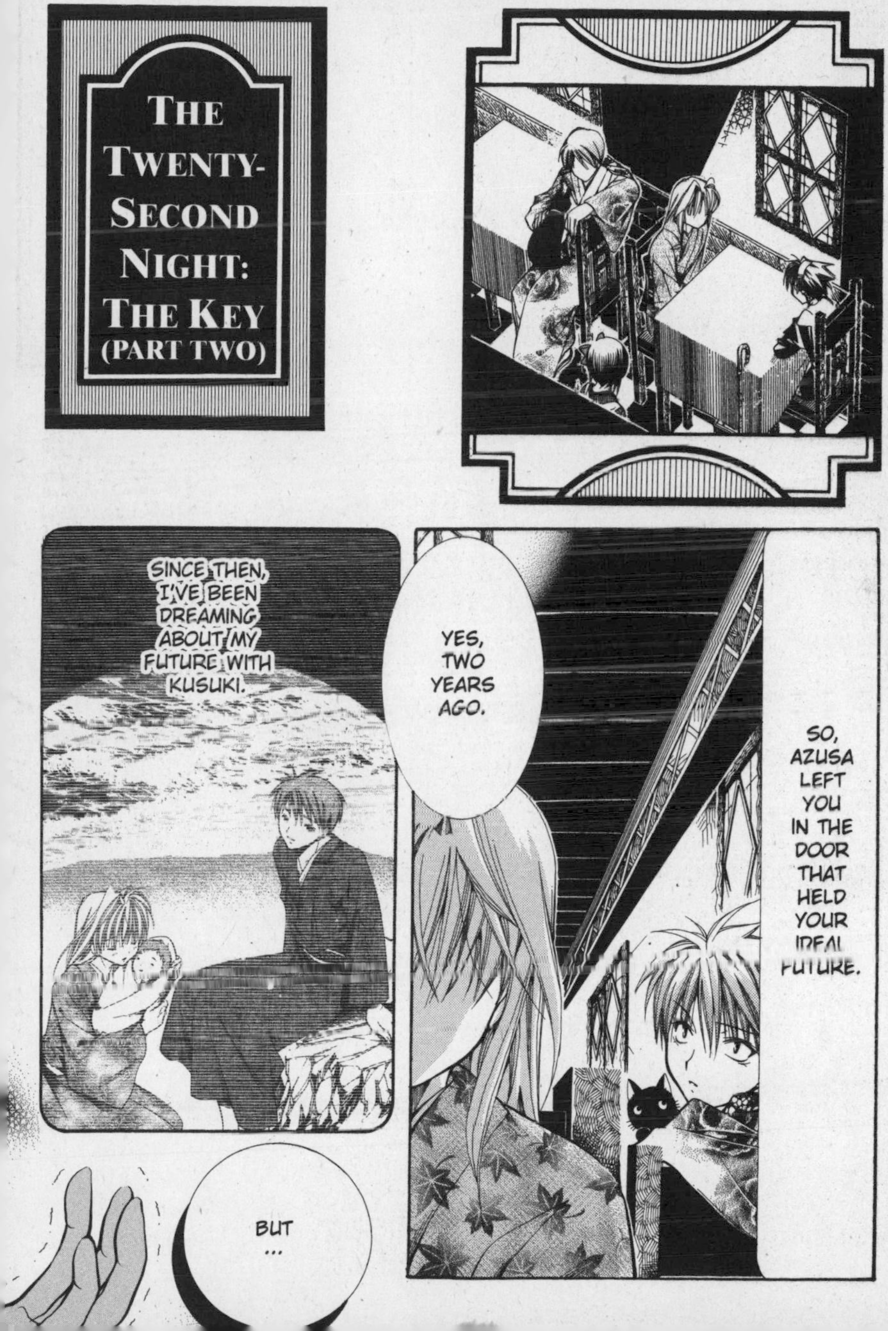
So, Azusa left you in the door that held your ideal future.
Yes, two years ago.
Since then, I've been dreaming about my future with Kusuki.
But ...

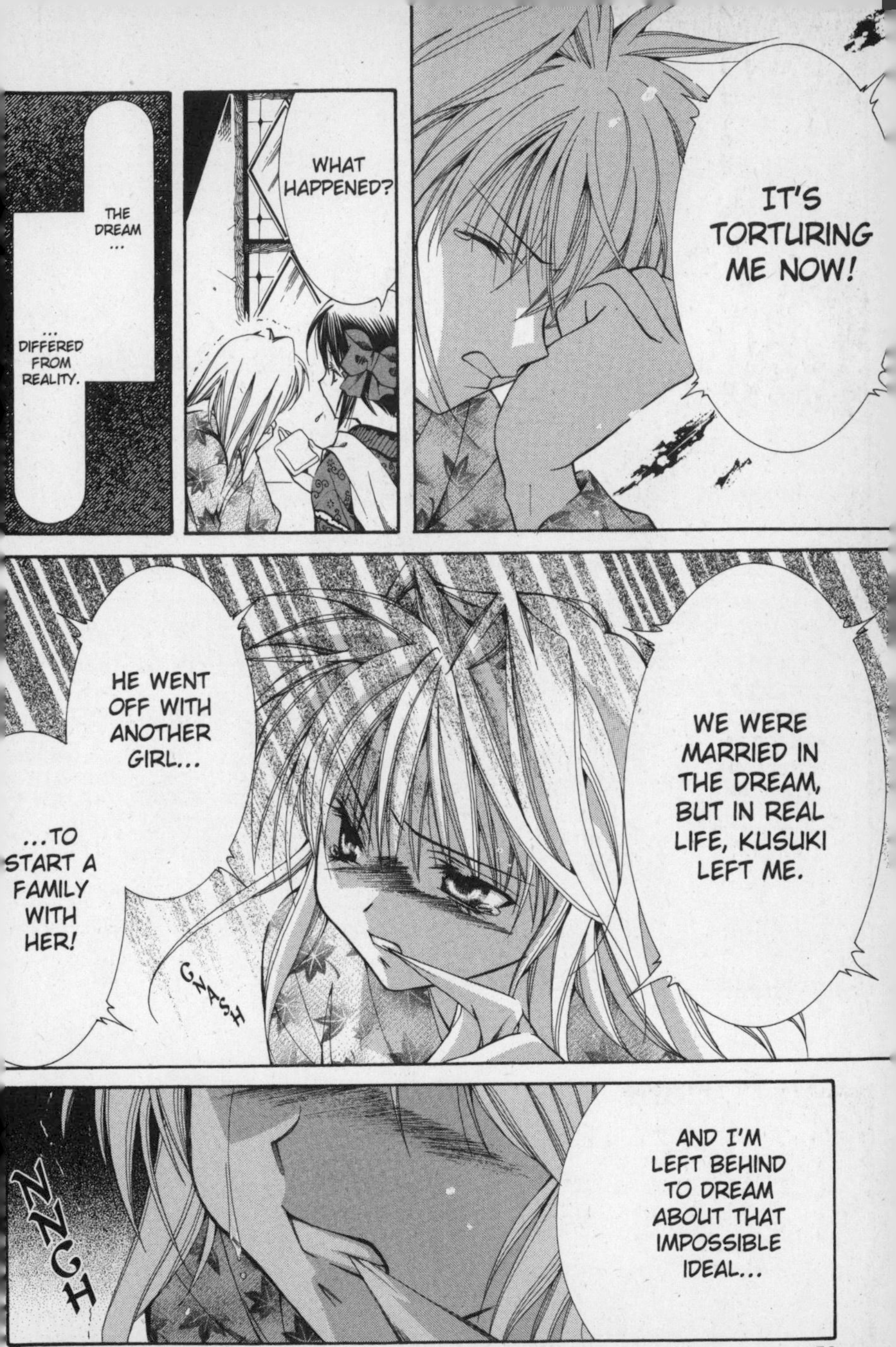
IT'S TORTURING ME NOW!
WHAT HAPPENED?
THE DREAM...
...DIFFERED FROM REALITY.
WE WERE MARRIED IN THE DREAM, BUT IN REAL LIFE, KUSUKI LEFT ME.
HE WENT OFF WITH ANOTHER GIRL...
...TO START A FAMILY WITH HER!
GNASH
AND I'M LEFT BEHIND TO DREAM ABOUT THAT IMPOSSIBLE IDEAL...
NNGH

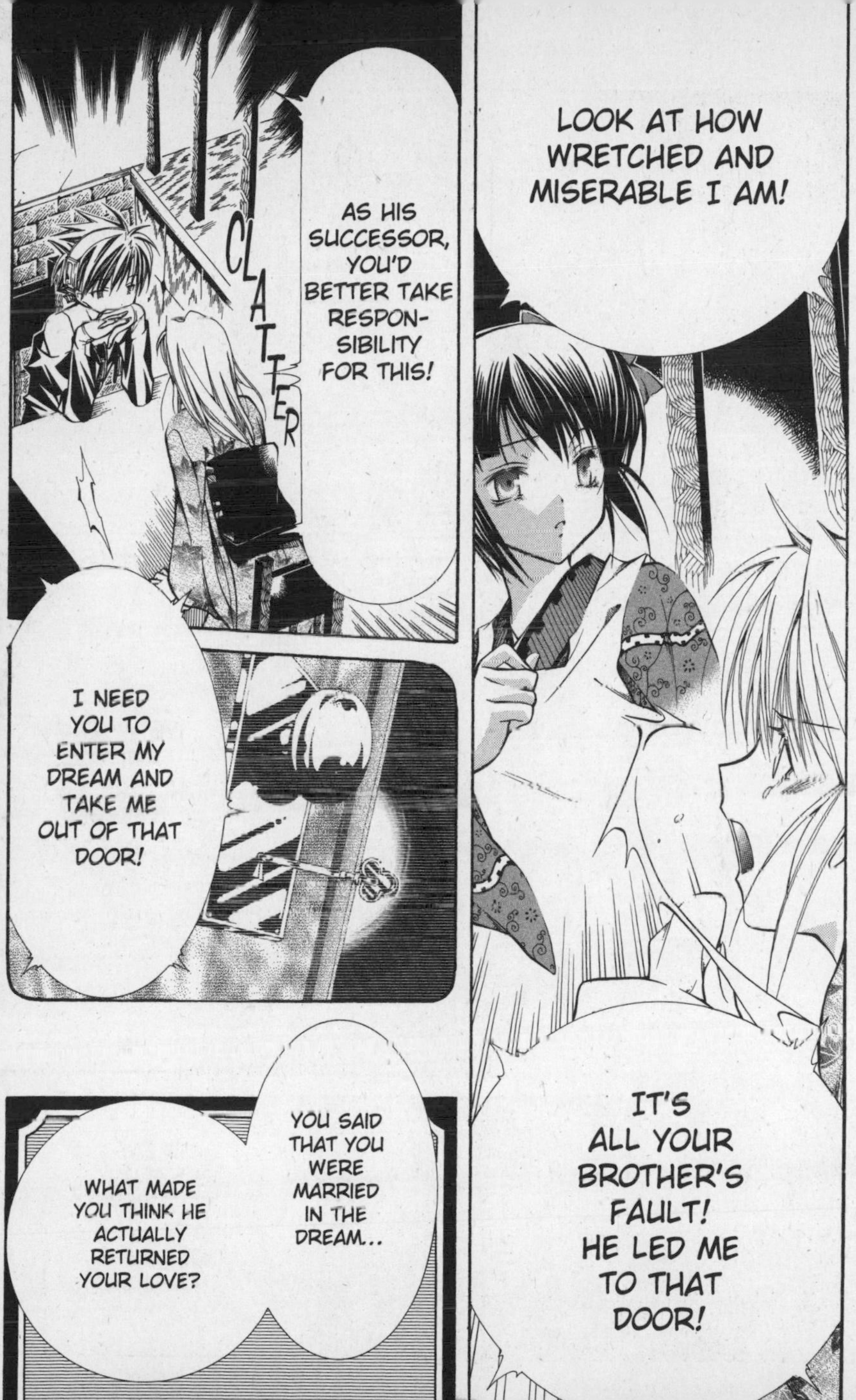
LOOK AT HOW WRETCHED AND MISERABLE I AM!
IT'S ALL YOUR BROTHER'S FAULT! HE LED ME TO THAT DOOR!
AS HIS SUCCESSOR, YOU'D BETTER TAKE RESPON-SIBILITY FOR THIS!
CLATTER
I NEED YOU TO ENTER MY DREAM AND TAKE ME OUT OF THAT DOOR!
YOU SAID THAT YOU WERE MARRIED IN THE DREAM...
WHAT MADE YOU THINK HE ACTUALLY RETURNED YOUR LOVE?

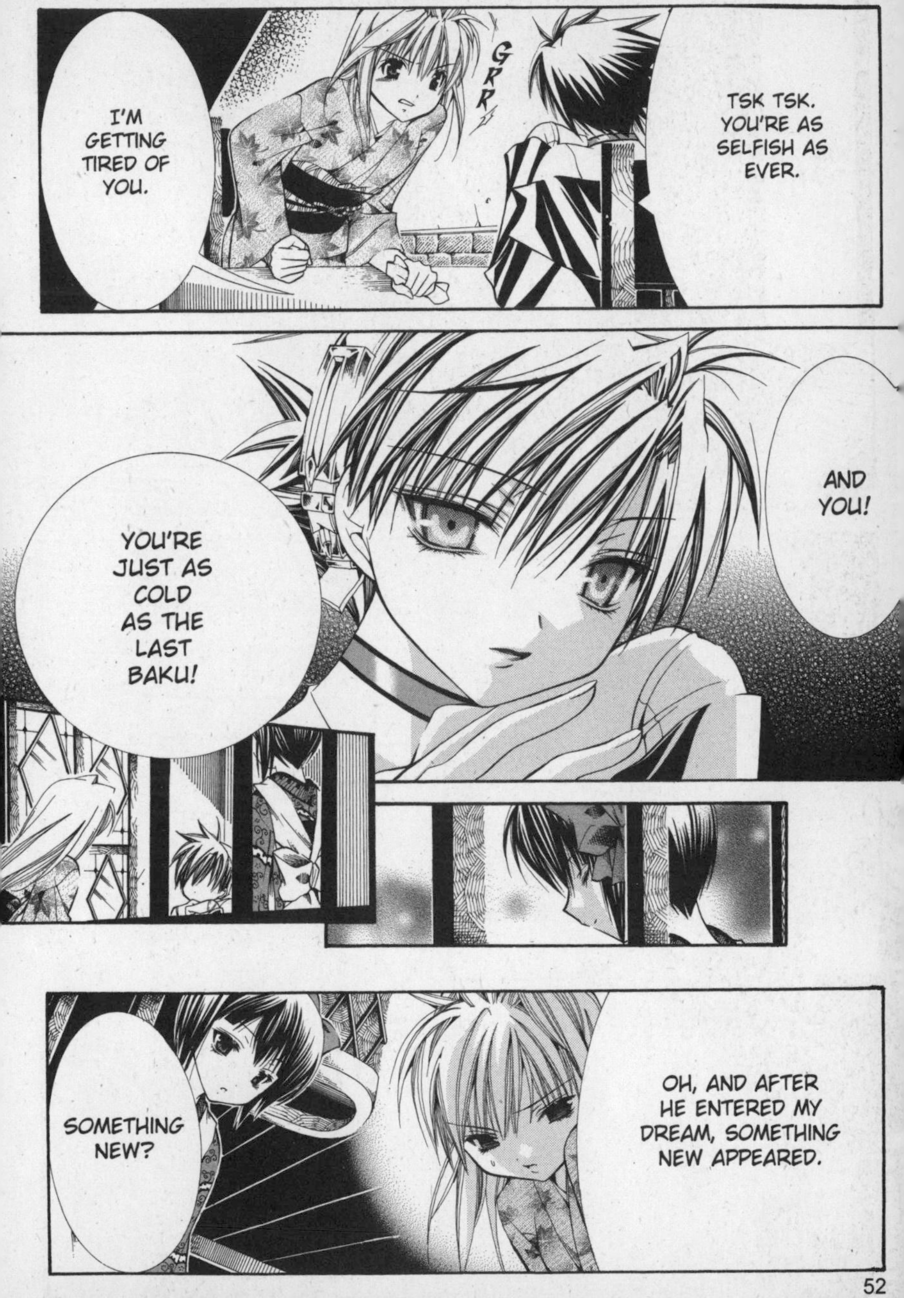
TSK TSK. YOU'RE AS SELFISH AS EVER.
GRR
I'M GETTING TIRED OF YOU.
AND YOU!
YOU'RE JUST AS COLD AS THE LAST BAKU!
OH, AND AFTER HE ENTERED MY DREAM, SOMETHING NEW APPEARED.
SOMETHING NEW?

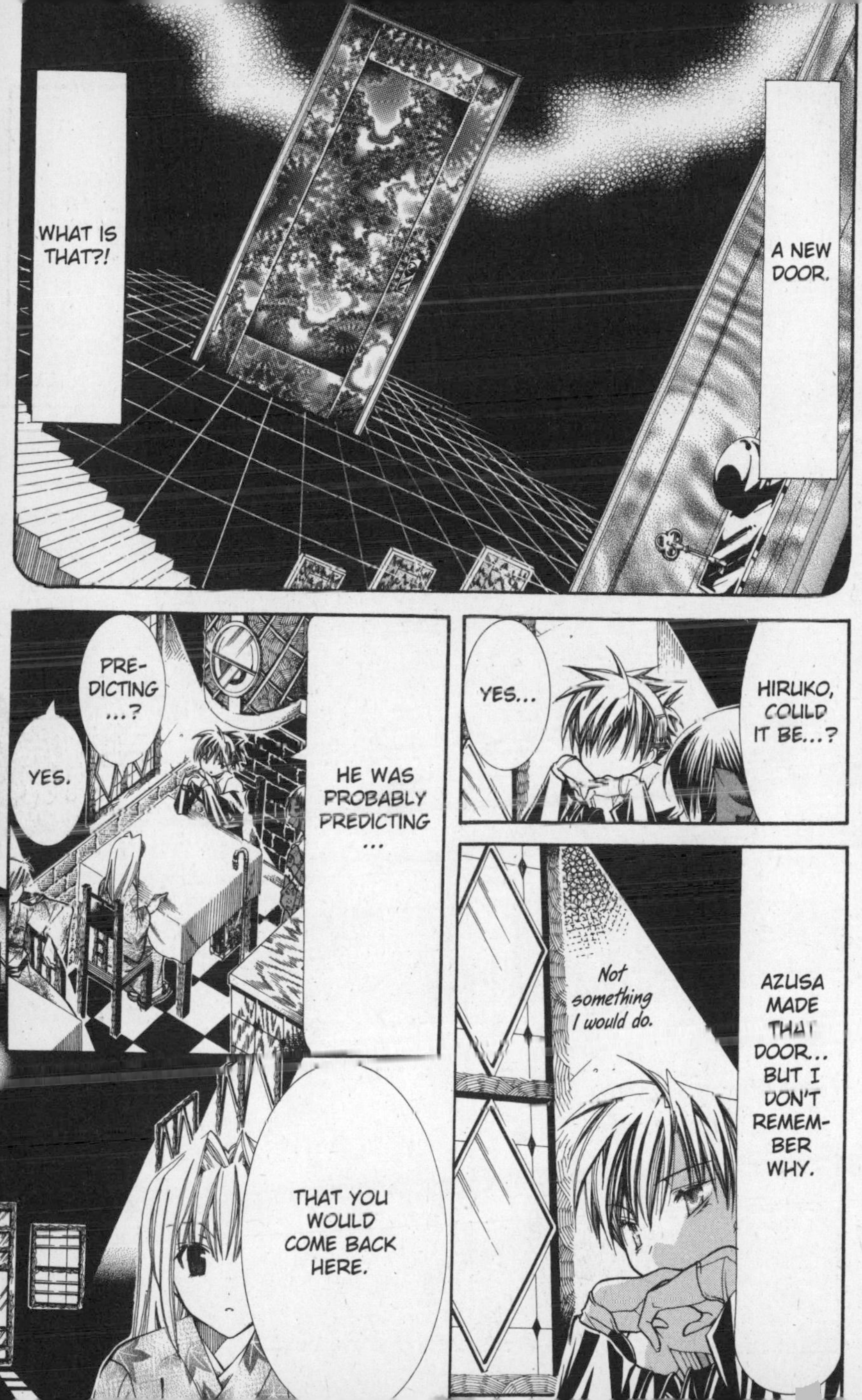
A NEW DOOR.
WHAT IS THAT?!
HIRUKO, COULD IT BE...?
YES...
AZUSA MADE THAT DOOR... BUT I DON'T REMEMBER WHY.
Not something I would do.
HE WAS PROBABLY PREDICTING...
PRE-DICTING...?
YES.
THAT YOU WOULD COME BACK HERE.

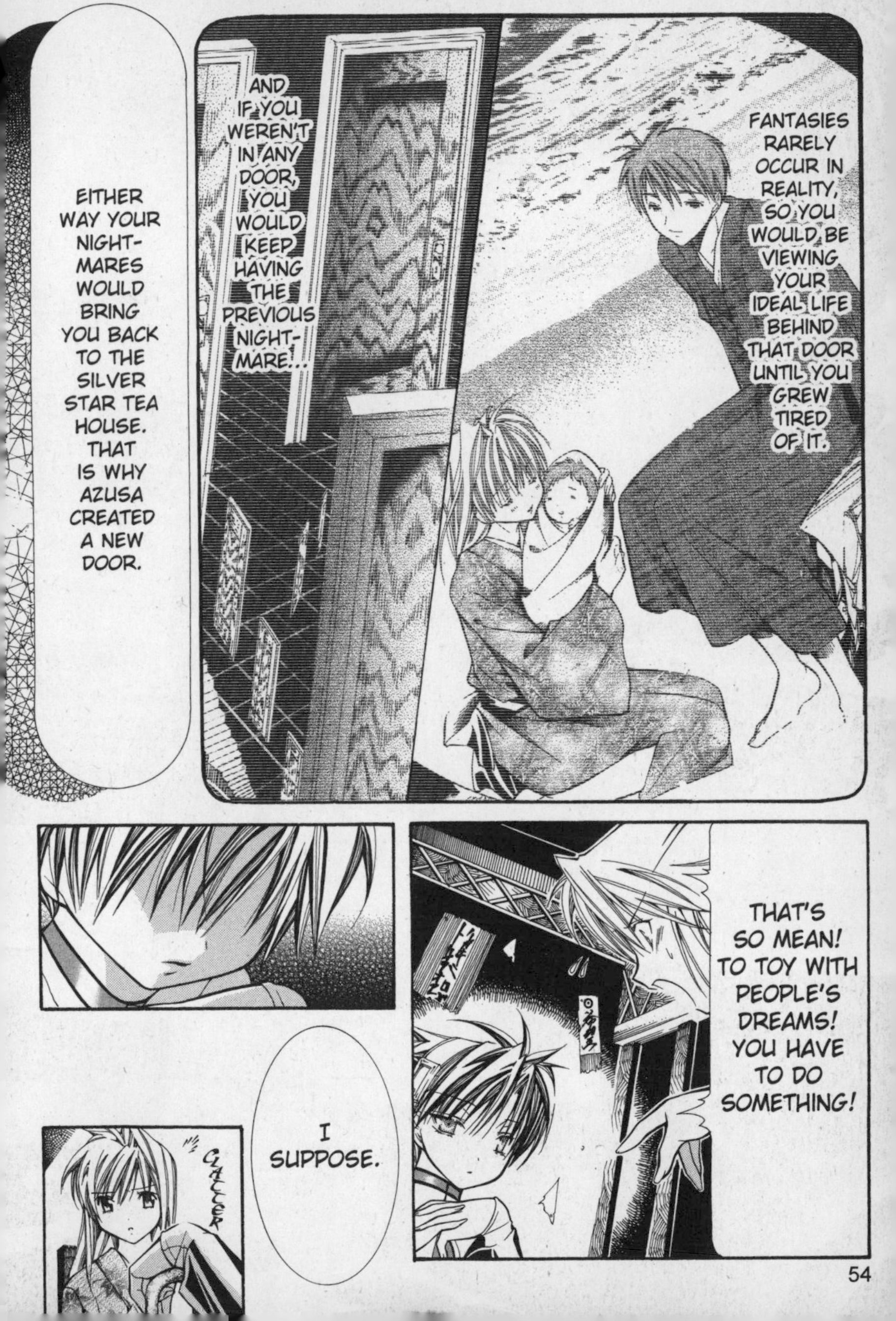
FANTASIES RARELY OCCUR IN REALITY, SO YOU WOULD BE VIEWING YOUR IDEAL LIFE BEHIND THAT DOOR UNTIL YOU GREW TIRED OF IT.
AND IF YOU WEREN'T IN ANY DOOR, YOU WOULD KEEP HAVING THE PREVIOUS NIGHTMARE...
EITHER WAY YOUR NIGHTMARES WOULD BRING YOU BACK TO THE SILVER STAR TEA HOUSE. THAT IS WHY AZUSA CREATED A NEW DOOR.
THAT'S SO MEAN! TO TOY WITH PEOPLE'S DREAMS! YOU HAVE TO DO SOMETHING!
I SUPPOSE.
CLACCER

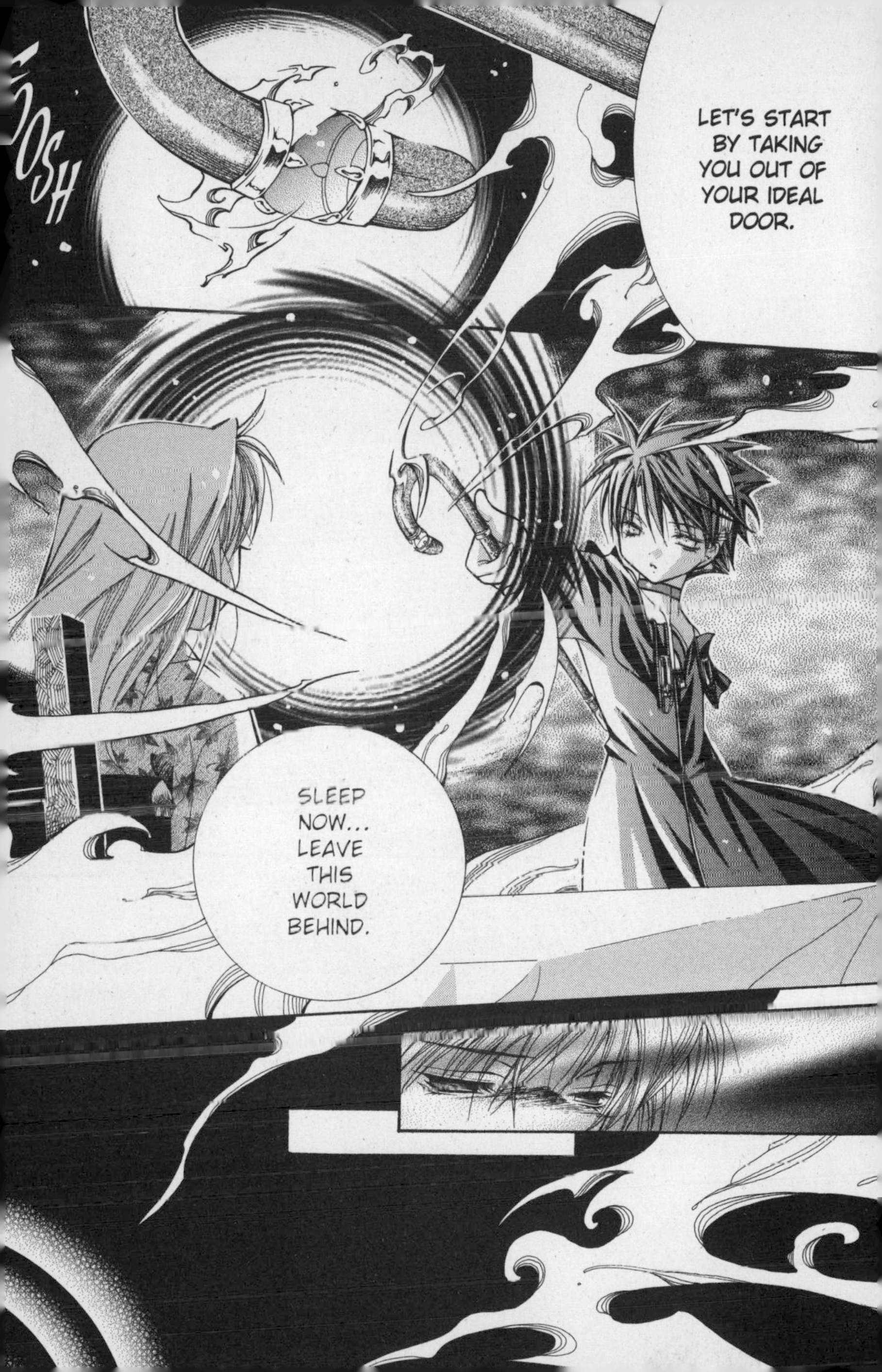
LET'S START BY TAKING YOU OUT OF YOUR IDEAL DOOR.
OOSH
SLEEP NOW... LEAVE THIS WORLD BEHIND.

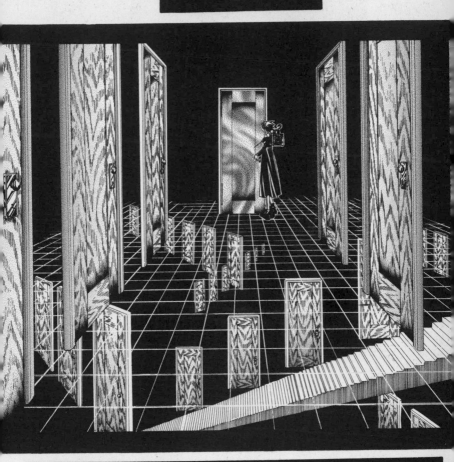

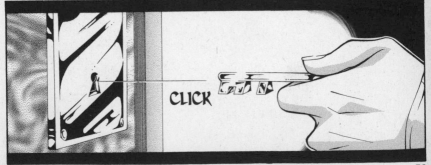

CLICK

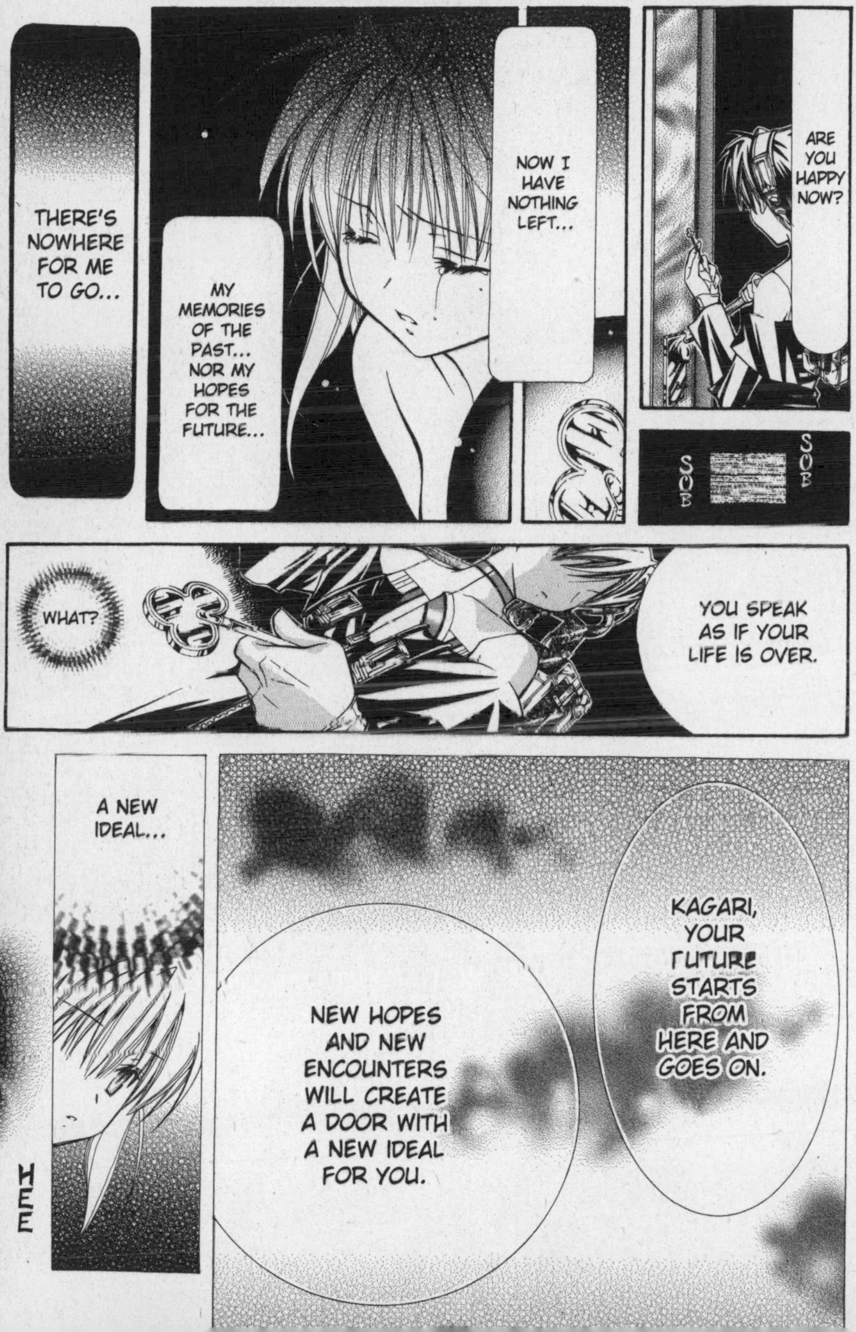
ARE YOU HAPPY NOW?
SOB
SOB
NOW I HAVE NOTHING LEFT...
MY MEMORIES OF THE PAST... NOR MY HOPES FOR THE FUTURE...
THERE'S NOWHERE FOR ME TO GO...
YOU SPEAK AS IF YOUR LIFE IS OVER.
WHAT?
KAGARI, YOUR FUTURE STARTS FROM HERE AND GOES ON.
NEW HOPES AND NEW ENCOUNTERS WILL CREATE A DOOR WITH A NEW IDEAL FOR YOU.
A NEW IDEAL...
HEE

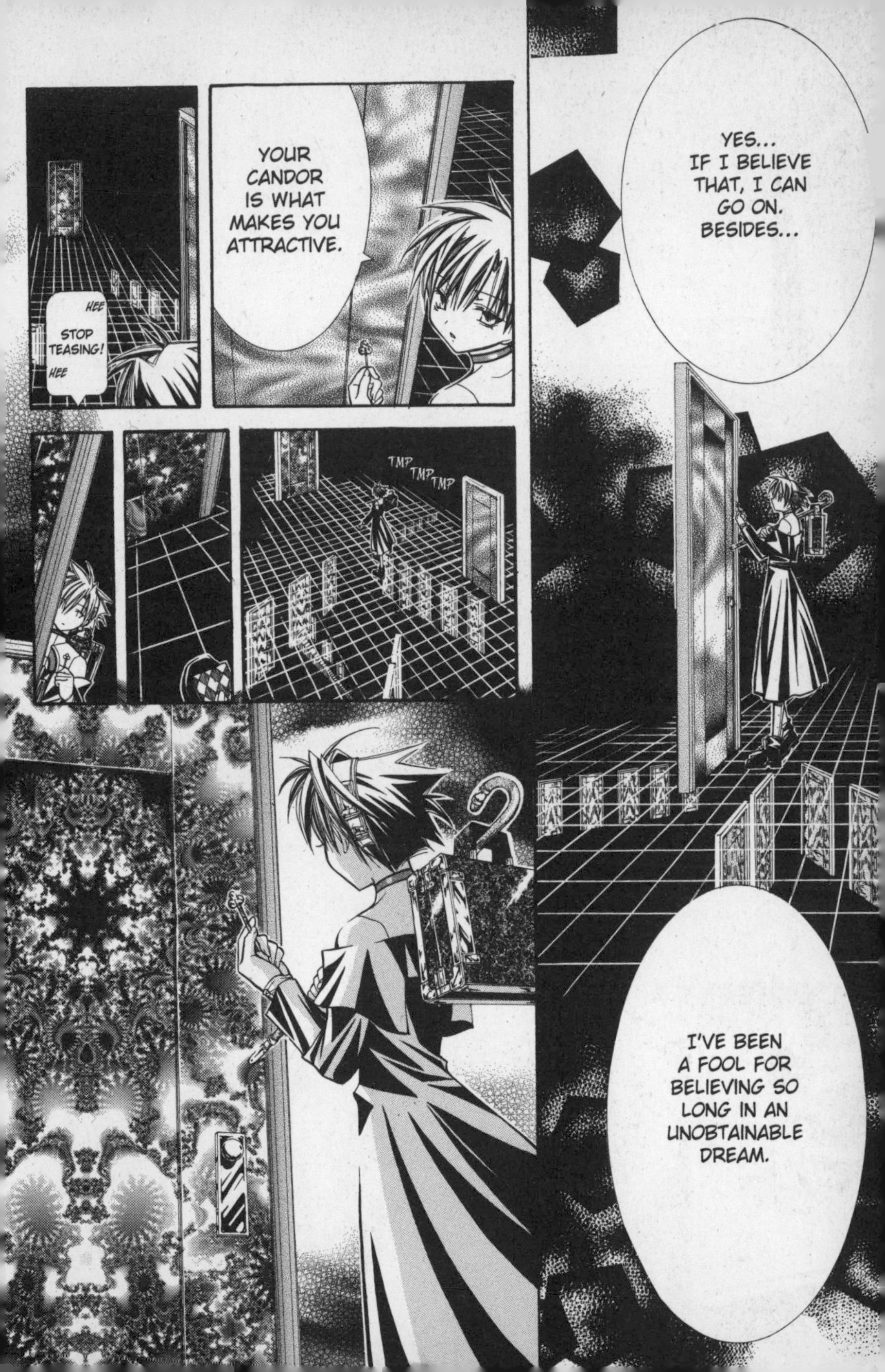
YES... IF I BELIEVE THAT, I CAN GO ON. BESIDES...
I'VE BEEN A FOOL FOR BELIEVING SO LONG IN AN UNOBTAINABLE DREAM.
YOUR CANDOR IS WHAT MAKES YOU ATTRACTIVE.
HEE
STOP TEASING!
HEE
TMP TMP TMP

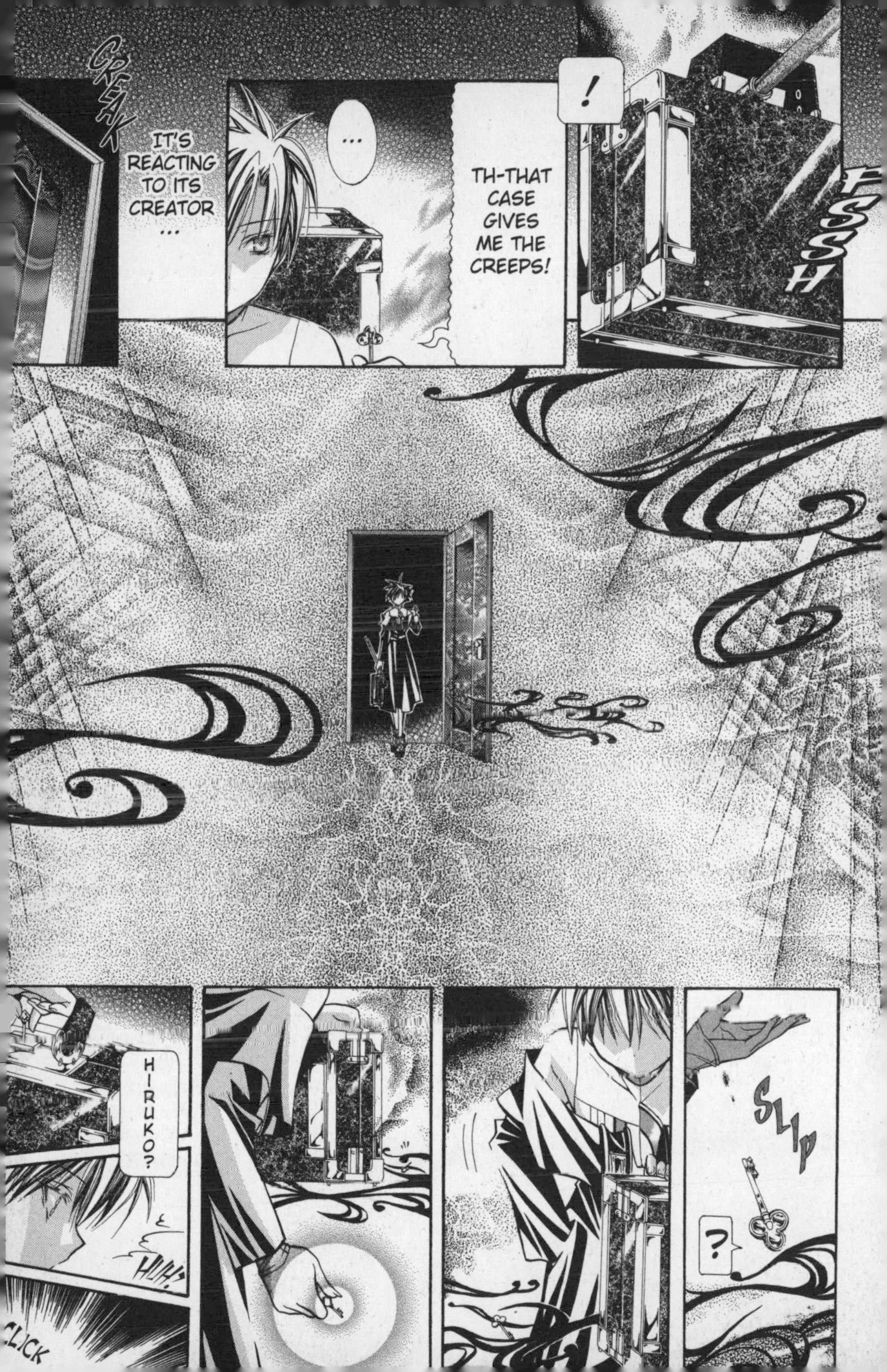
!
FSSH
...
TH-THAT CASE GIVES ME THE CREEPS!
CREAK
IT'S REACTING TO ITS CREATOR ...
SLIP
?
HIRUKO?
HUH!
CLICK

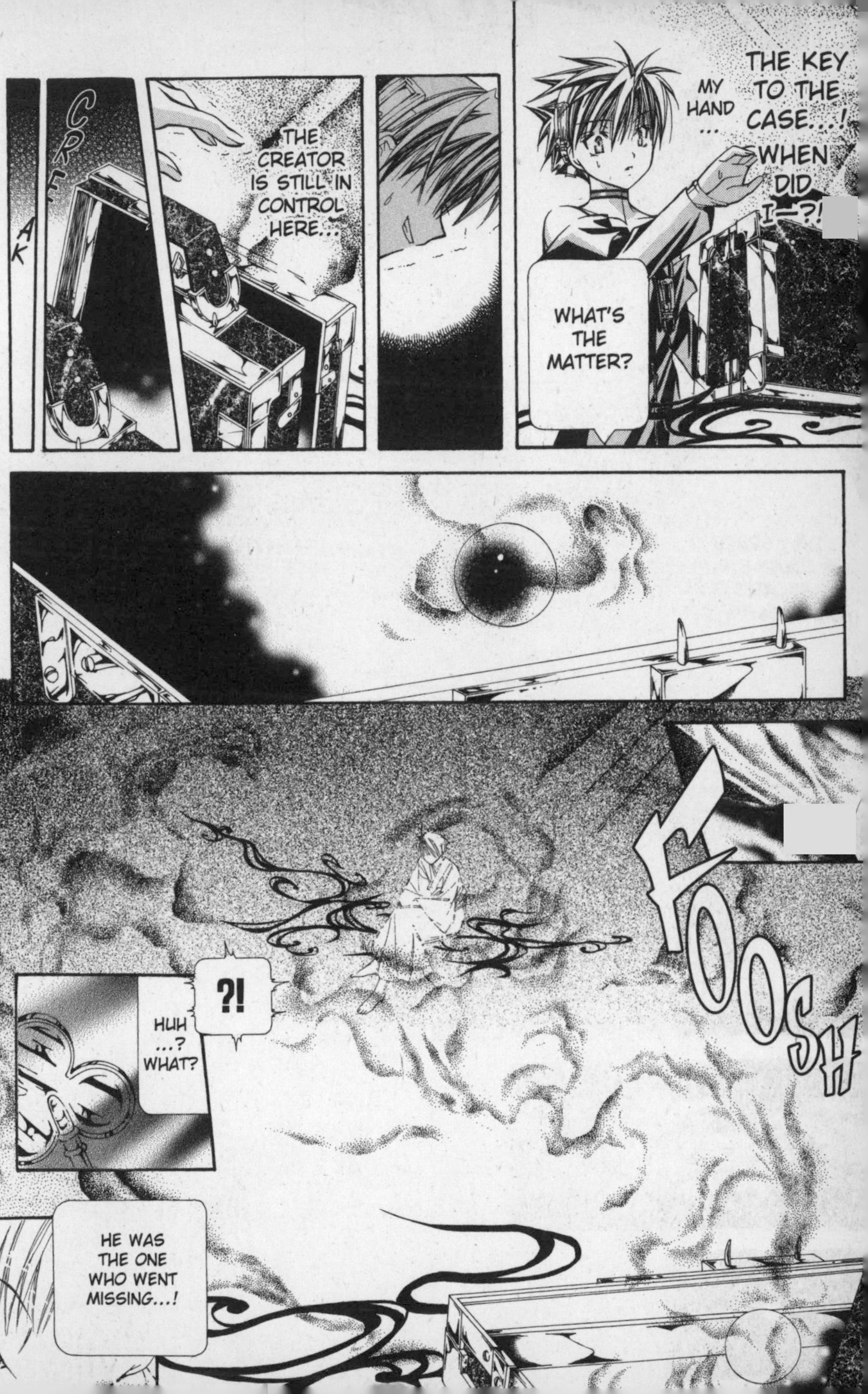
THE KEY TO THE CASE...! WHEN DID I—?!
MY HAND...
WHAT'S THE MATTER?
THE CREATOR IS STILL IN CONTROL HERE...
CREAK
FOOSH
?!
HUH...? WHAT?
HE WAS THE ONE WHO WENT MISSING...!

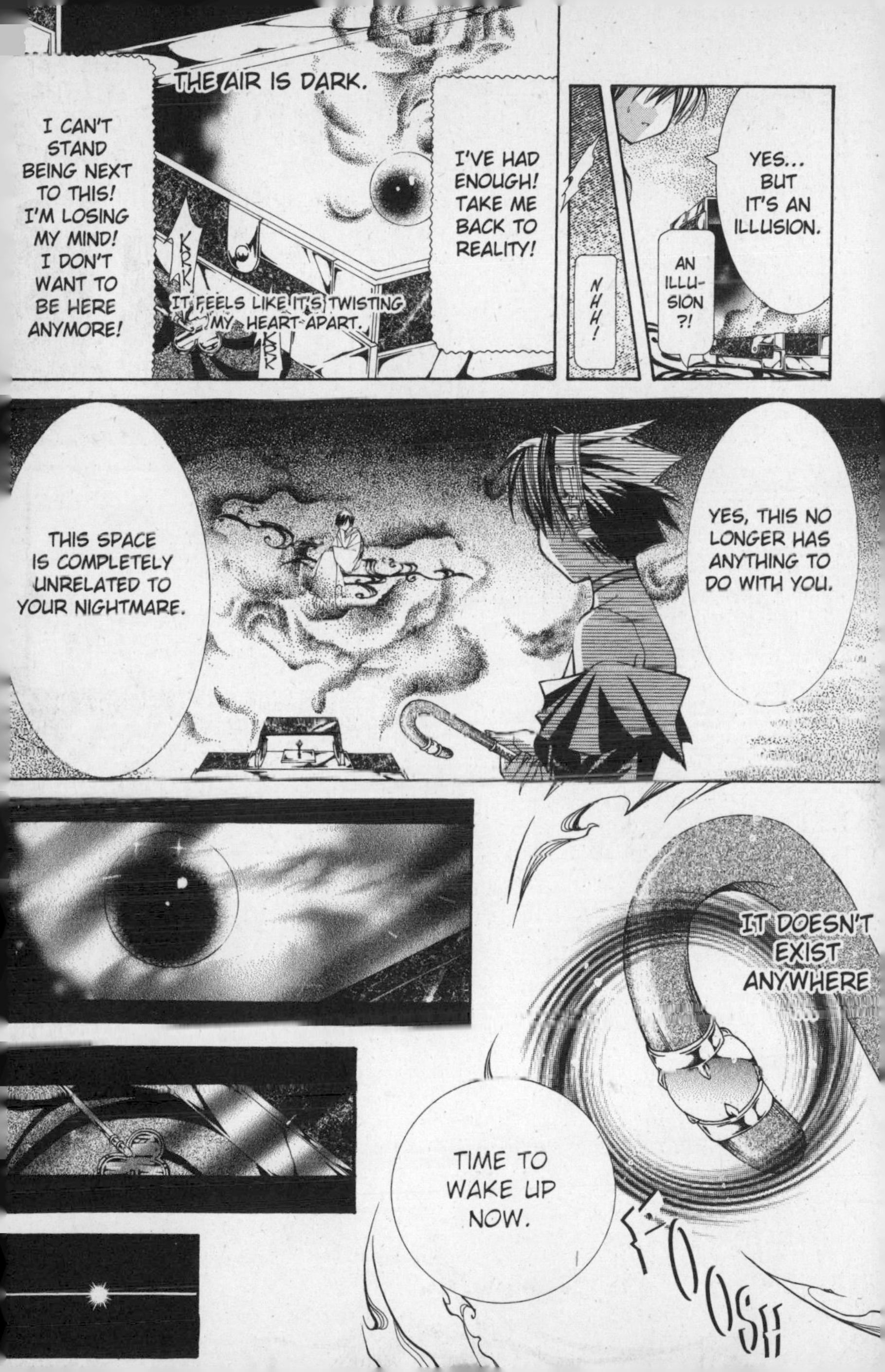
YES... BUT IT'S AN ILLUSION.
AN ILLUSION?!
NHH!
I'VE HAD ENOUGH! TAKE ME BACK TO REALITY!
THE AIR IS DARK.
I CAN'T STAND BEING NEXT TO THIS! I'M LOSING MY MIND! I DON'T WANT TO BE HERE ANYMORE!
KRK
IT FEELS LIKE IT'S TWISTING MY HEART APART.
KRK
YES, THIS NO LONGER HAS ANYTHING TO DO WITH YOU.
THIS SPACE IS COMPLETELY UNRELATED TO YOUR NIGHTMARE.
IT DOESN'T EXIST ANYWHERE
TIME TO WAKE UP NOW.
FOOSH

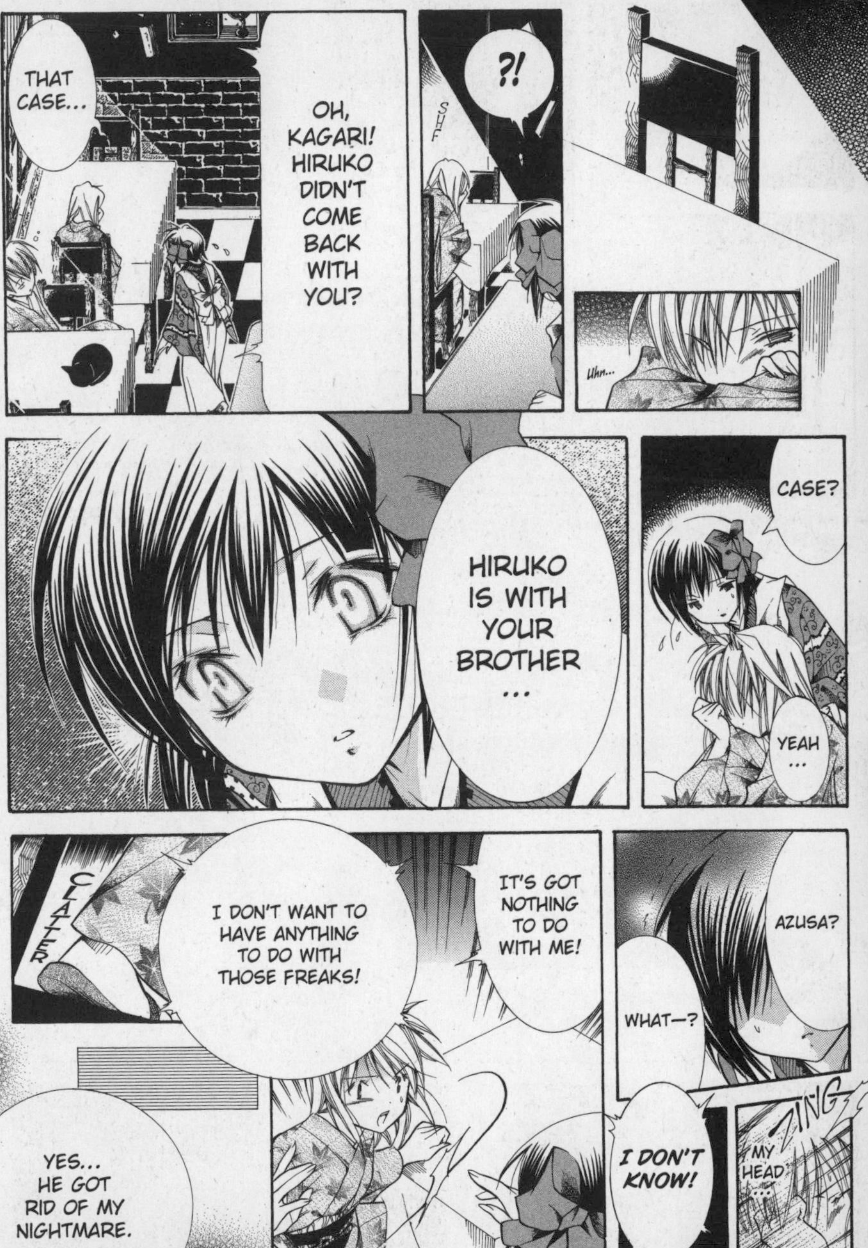
Uhn...
?!
SHF
OH, KAGARI! HIRUKO DIDN'T COME BACK WITH YOU?
THAT CASE...
CASE?
YEAH...
HIRUKO IS WITH YOUR BROTHER...
AZUSA?
WHAT—?
IT'S GOT NOTHING TO DO WITH ME!
I DON'T WANT TO HAVE ANYTHING TO DO WITH THOSE FREAKS!
CLATTER
ZING
MY HEAD...
I DON'T KNOW!
YES... HE GOT RID OF MY NIGHTMARE.

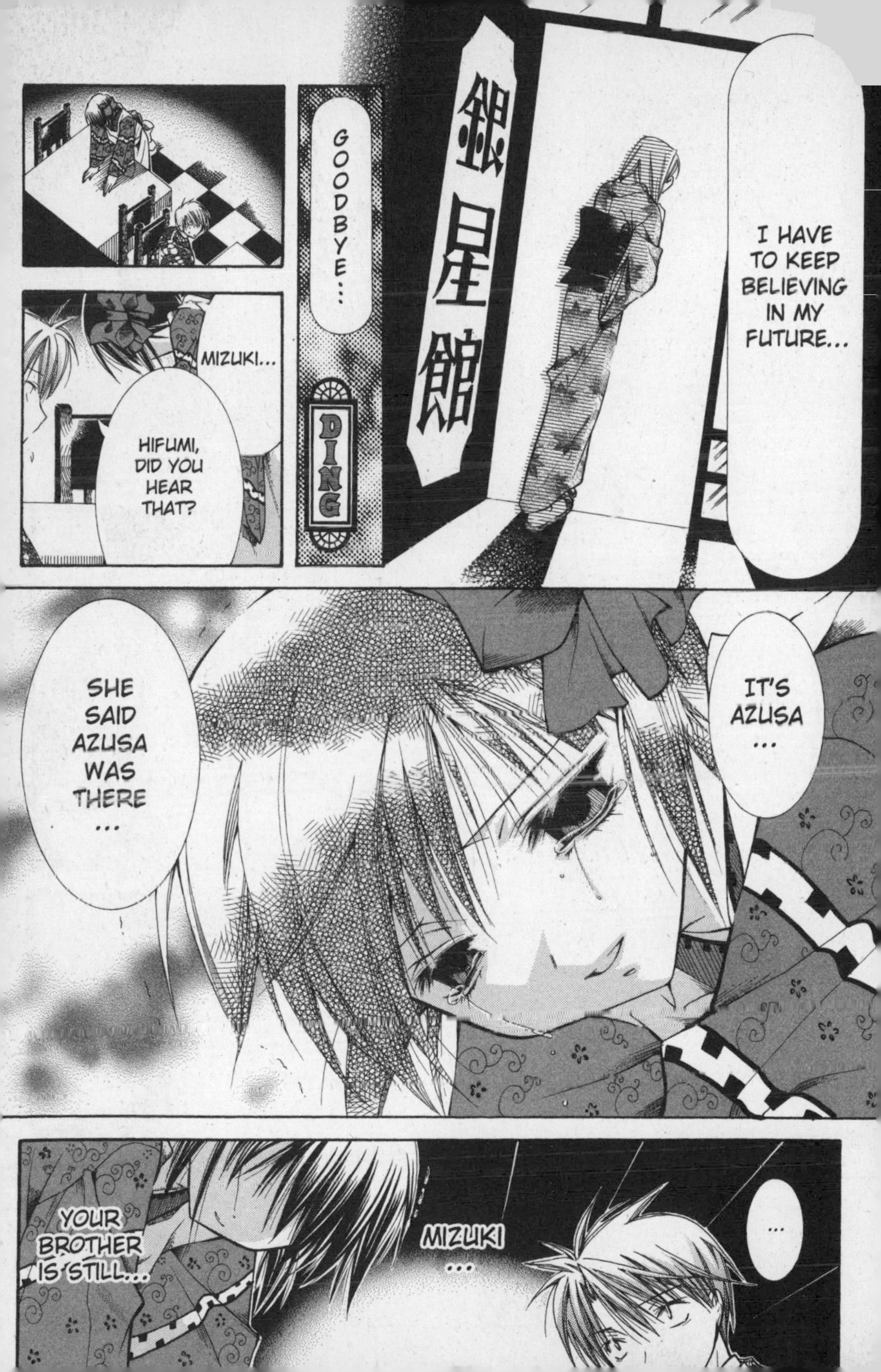
I HAVE TO KEEP BELIEVING IN MY FUTURE...
銀星館
GOODBYE...
DING
MIZUKI...
HIFUMI, DID YOU HEAR THAT?
IT'S AZUSA...
SHE SAID AZUSA WAS THERE...
...
MIZUKI...
YOUR BROTHER IS STILL...

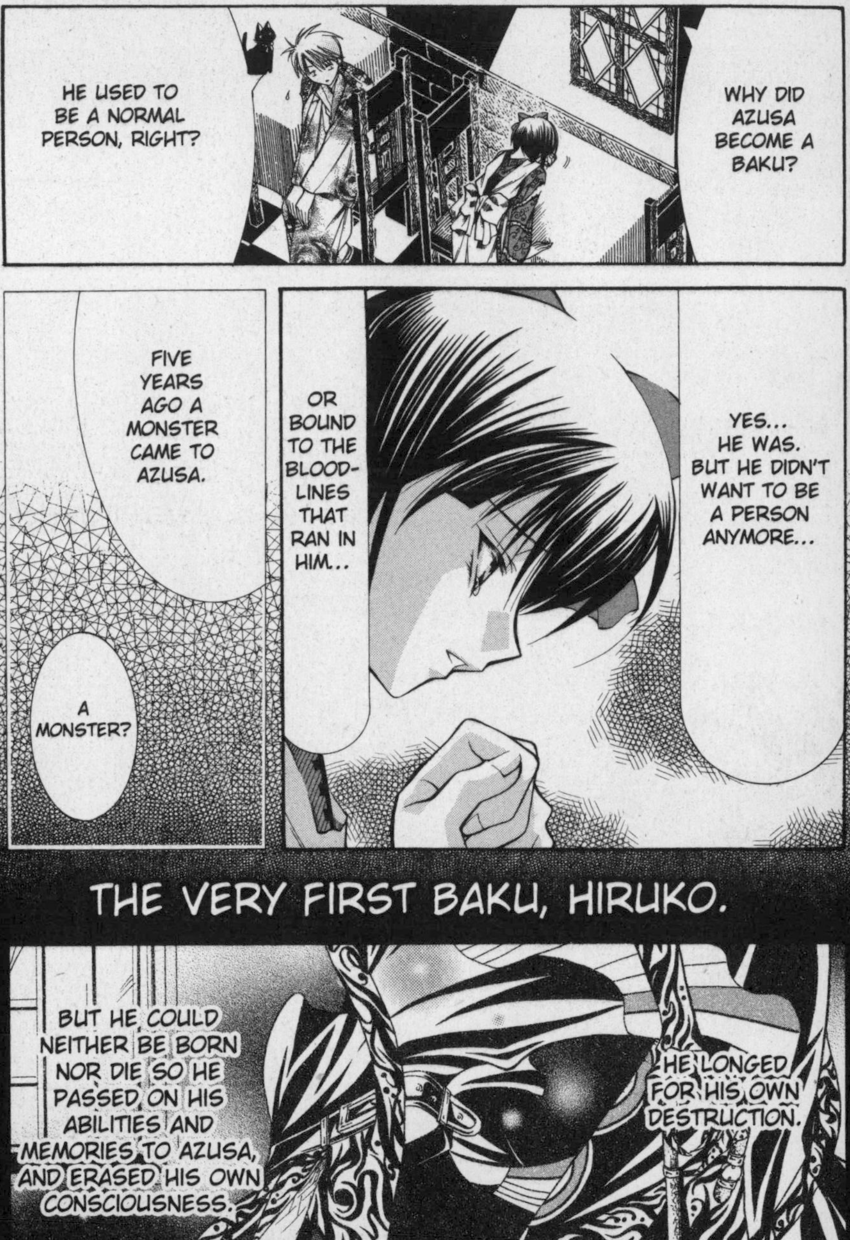
WHY DID AZUSA BECOME A BAKU?
HE USED TO BE A NORMAL PERSON, RIGHT?
YES... HE WAS. BUT HE DIDN'T WANT TO BE A PERSON ANYMORE...
OR BOUND TO THE BLOODLINES THAT RAN IN HIM...
FIVE YEARS AGO A MONSTER CAME TO AZUSA.
A MONSTER?
THE VERY FIRST BAKU, HIRUKO.
HE LONGED FOR HIS OWN DESTRUCTION.
BUT HE COULD NEITHER BE BORN NOR DIE SO HE PASSED ON HIS ABILITIES AND MEMORIES TO AZUSA, AND ERASED HIS OWN CONSCIOUSNESS.

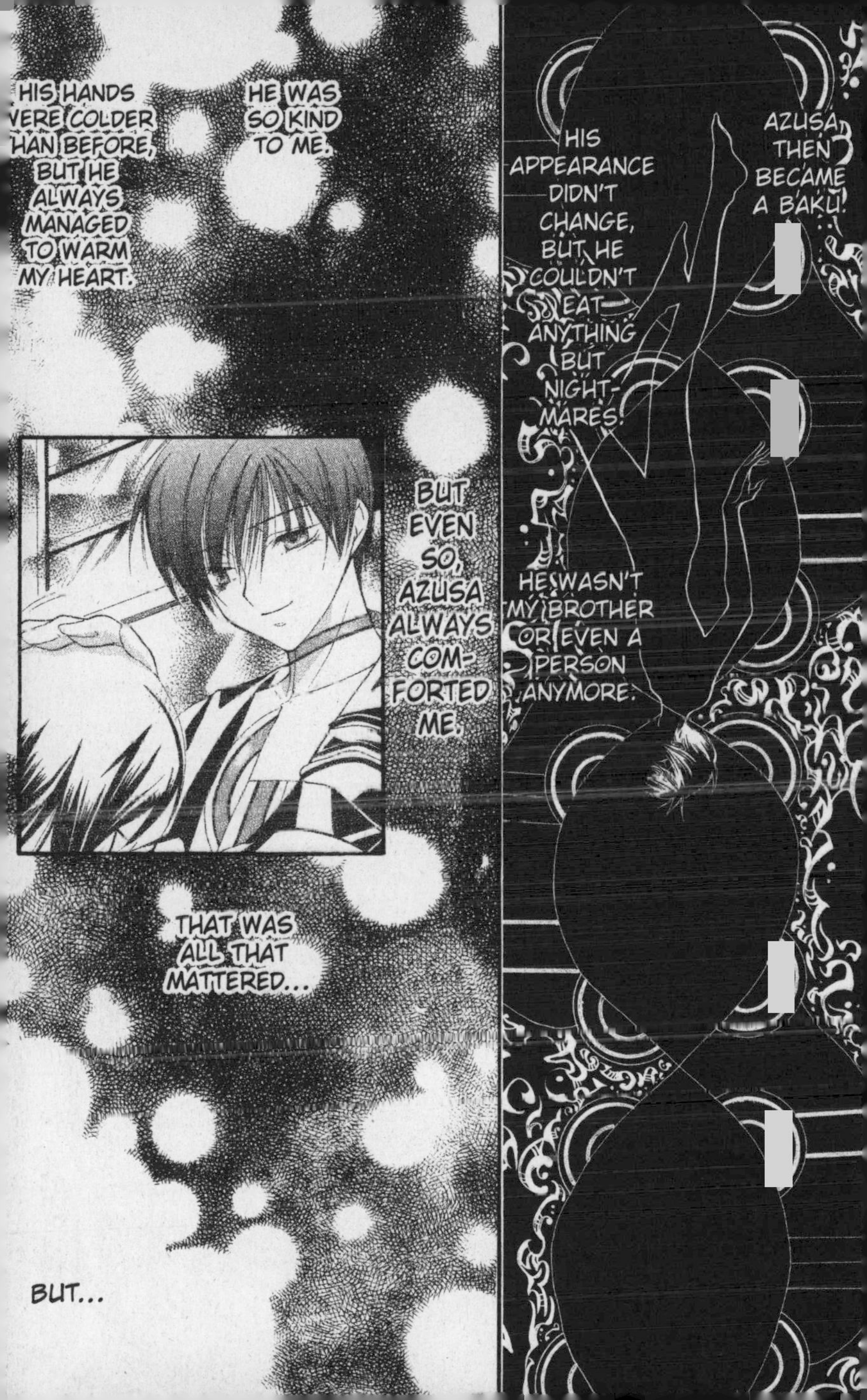
AZUSA THEN BECAME A BAKU.
HIS APPEARANCE DIDN'T CHANGE, BUT HE COULDN'T EAT ANYTHING BUT NIGHTMARES.
HE WASN'T MY BROTHER OR EVEN A PERSON ANYMORE.
HE WAS SO KIND TO ME.
HIS HANDS WERE COLDER THAN BEFORE, BUT HE ALWAYS MANAGED TO WARM MY HEART.
BUT EVEN SO, AZUSA ALWAYS COMFORTED ME.
THAT WAS ALL THAT MATTERED...
BUT...

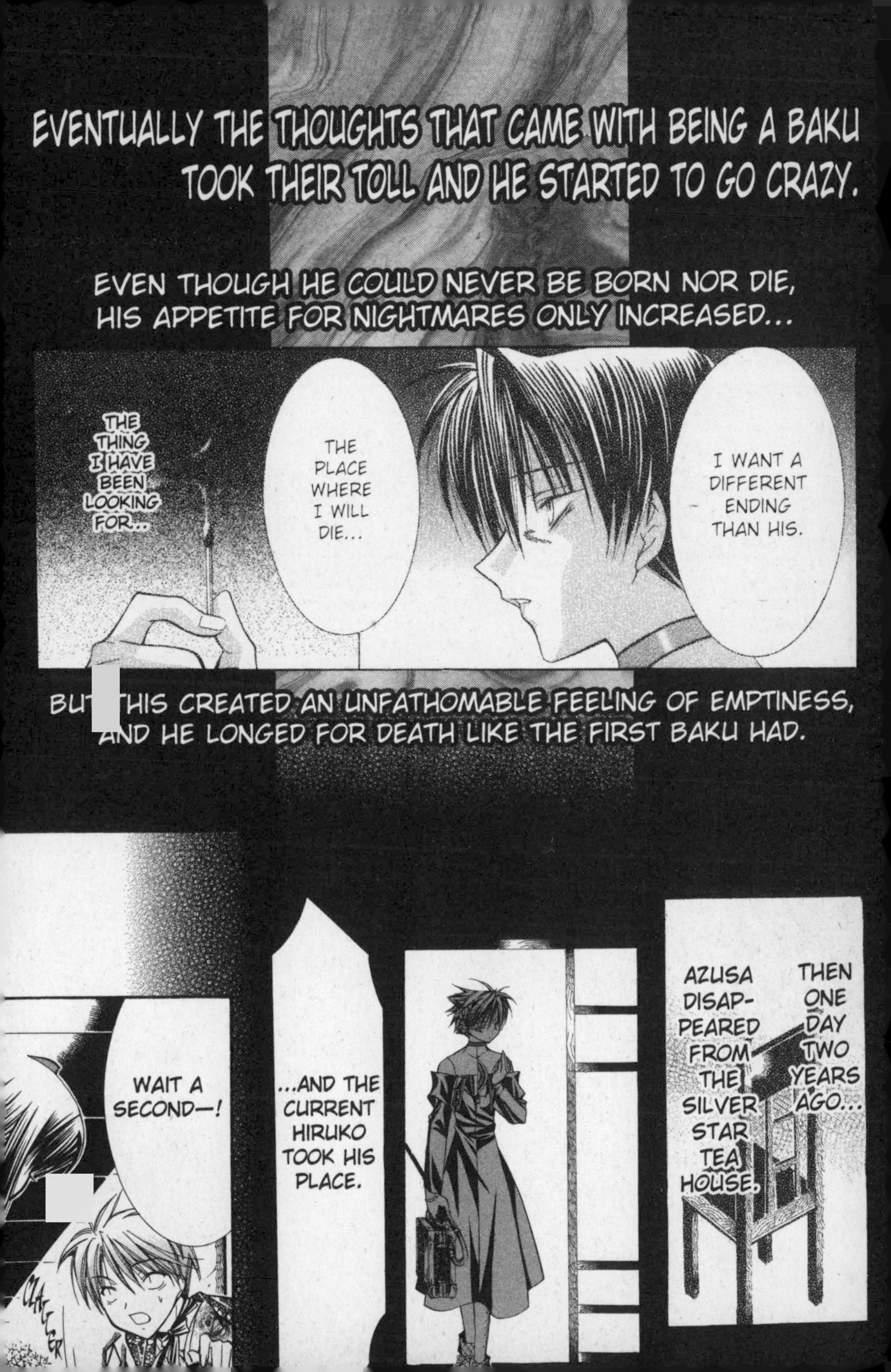
EVENTUALLY THE THOUGHTS THAT CAME WITH BEING A BAKU TOOK THEIR TOLL AND HE STARTED TO GO CRAZY.
EVEN THOUGH HE COULD NEVER BE BORN NOR DIE, HIS APPETITE FOR NIGHTMARES ONLY INCREASED...
I WANT A DIFFERENT ENDING THAN HIS.
THE PLACE WHERE I WILL DIE...
THE THING I HAVE BEEN LOOKING FOR...
BUT THIS CREATED AN UNFATHOMABLE FEELING OF EMPTINESS, AND HE LONGED FOR DEATH LIKE THE FIRST BAKU HAD.
THEN ONE DAY TWO YEARS AGO...
AZUSA DISAPPEARED FROM THE SILVER STAR TEA HOUSE.
...AND THE CURRENT HIRUKO TOOK HIS PLACE.
WAIT A SECOND—!
CLATTER

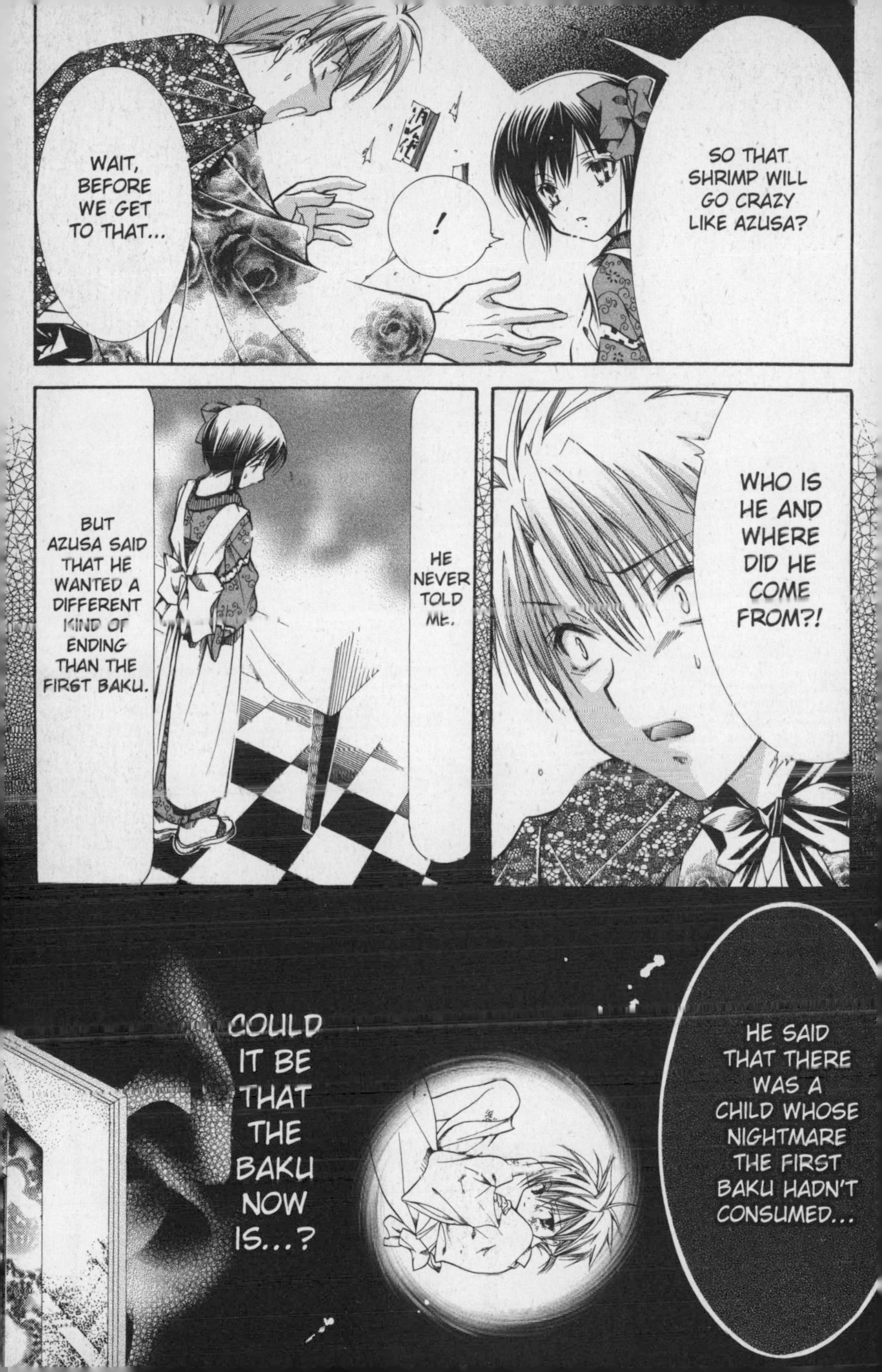
SO THAT SHRIMP WILL GO CRAZY LIKE AZUSA?
!
WAIT, BEFORE WE GET TO THAT...
WHO IS HE AND WHERE DID HE COME FROM?!
HE NEVER TOLD ME.
BUT AZUSA SAID THAT HE WANTED A DIFFERENT KIND OF ENDING THAN THE FIRST BAKU.
HE SAID THAT THERE WAS A CHILD WHOSE NIGHTMARE THE FIRST BAKU HADN'T CONSUMED...
COULD IT BE THAT THE BAKU NOW IS...?

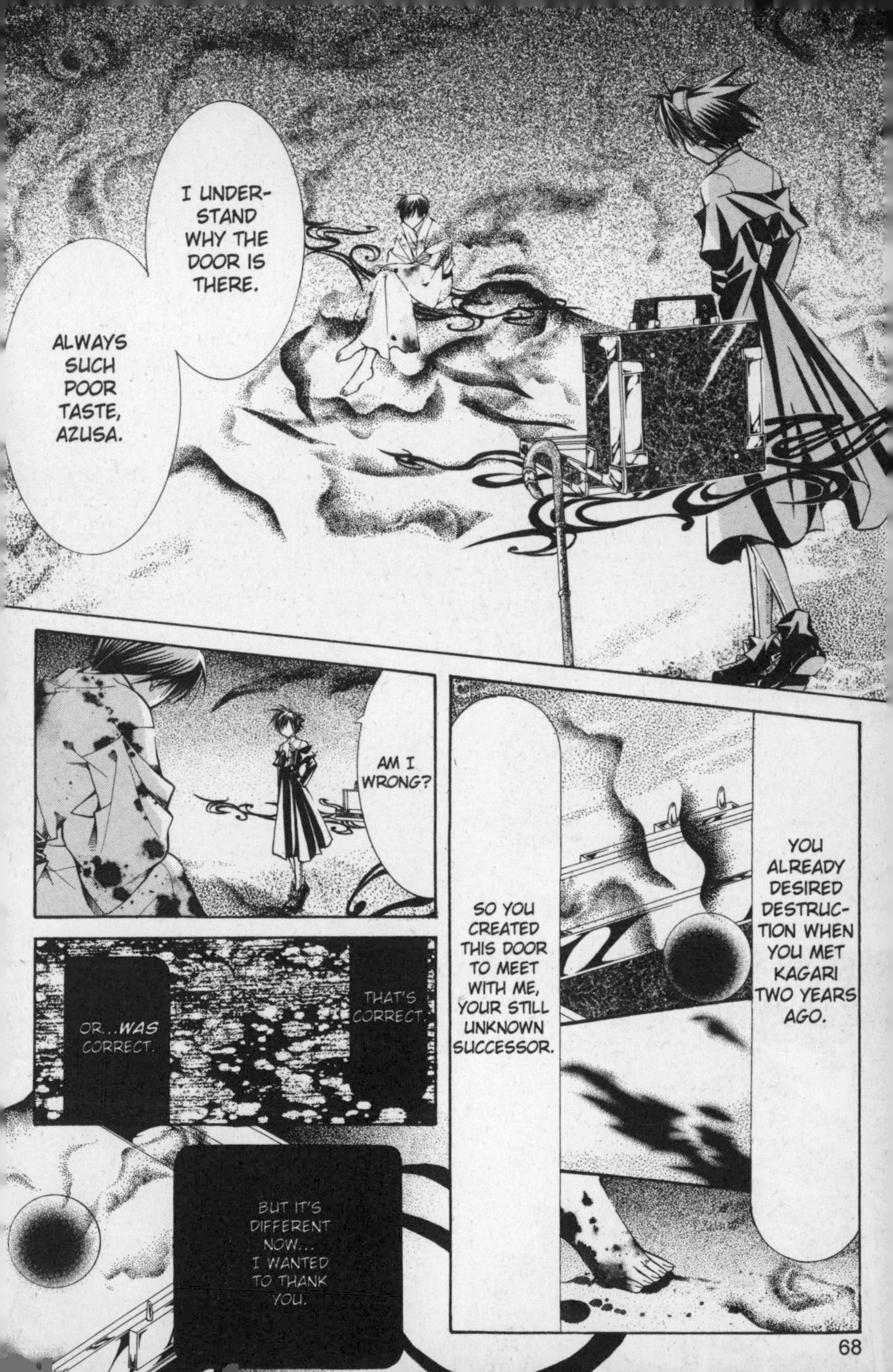
I UNDER-STAND WHY THE DOOR IS THERE.
ALWAYS SUCH POOR TASTE, AZUSA.
YOU ALREADY DESIRED DESTRUC-TION WHEN YOU MET KAGARI TWO YEARS AGO.
SO YOU CREATED THIS DOOR TO MEET WITH ME, YOUR STILL UNKNOWN SUCCESSOR.
AM I WRONG?
THAT'S CORRECT.
OR...*WAS* CORRECT.
BUT IT'S DIFFERENT NOW... I WANTED TO THANK YOU.

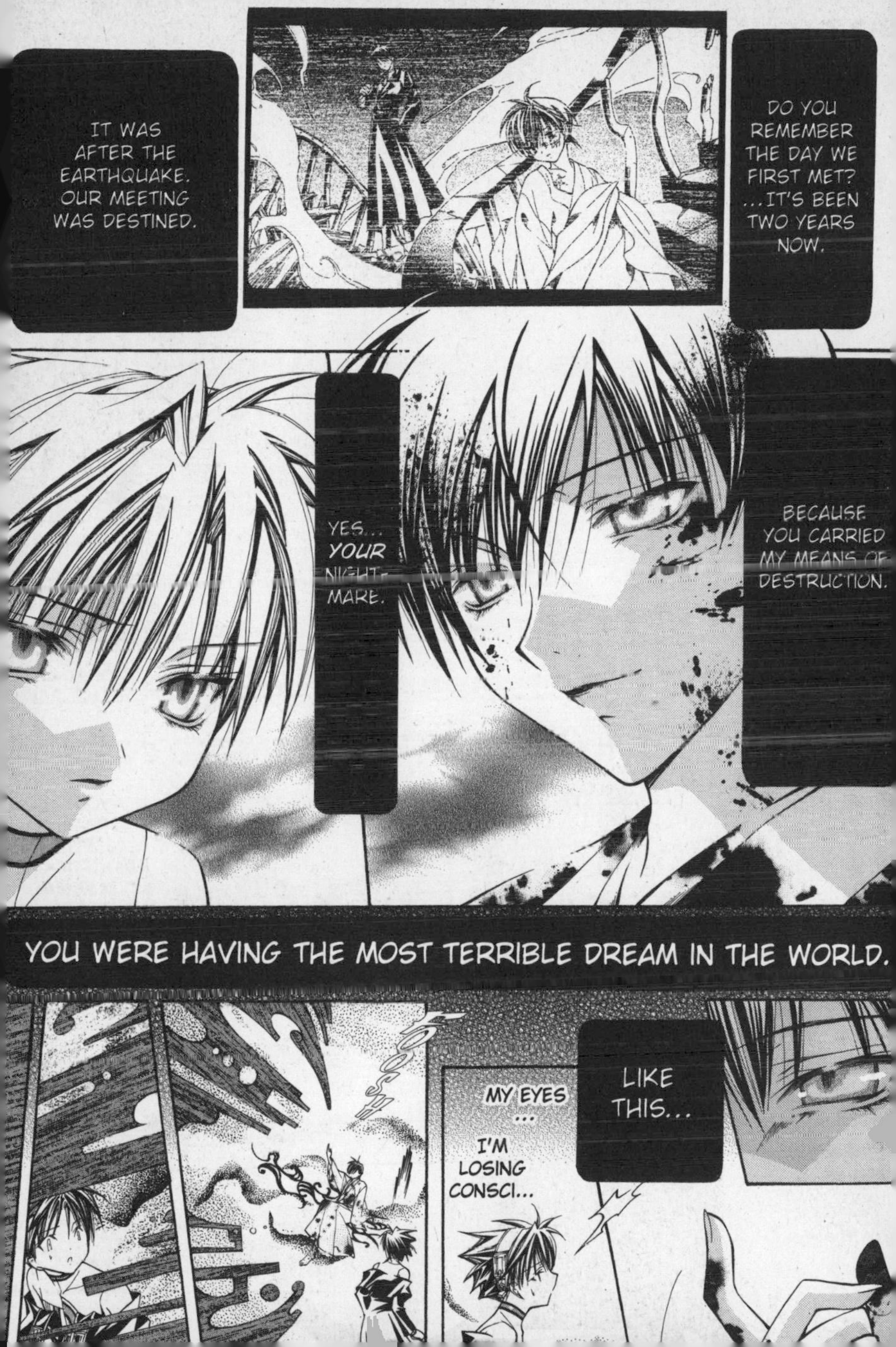
DO YOU REMEMBER THE DAY WE FIRST MET? ...IT'S BEEN TWO YEARS NOW.
IT WAS AFTER THE EARTHQUAKE. OUR MEETING WAS DESTINED.
BECAUSE YOU CARRIED MY MEANS OF DESTRUCTION.
YES... YOUR NIGHTMARE.
YOU WERE HAVING THE MOST TERRIBLE DREAM IN THE WORLD.
LIKE THIS...
MY EYES ...
I'M LOSING CONSCI...
FOOOSH

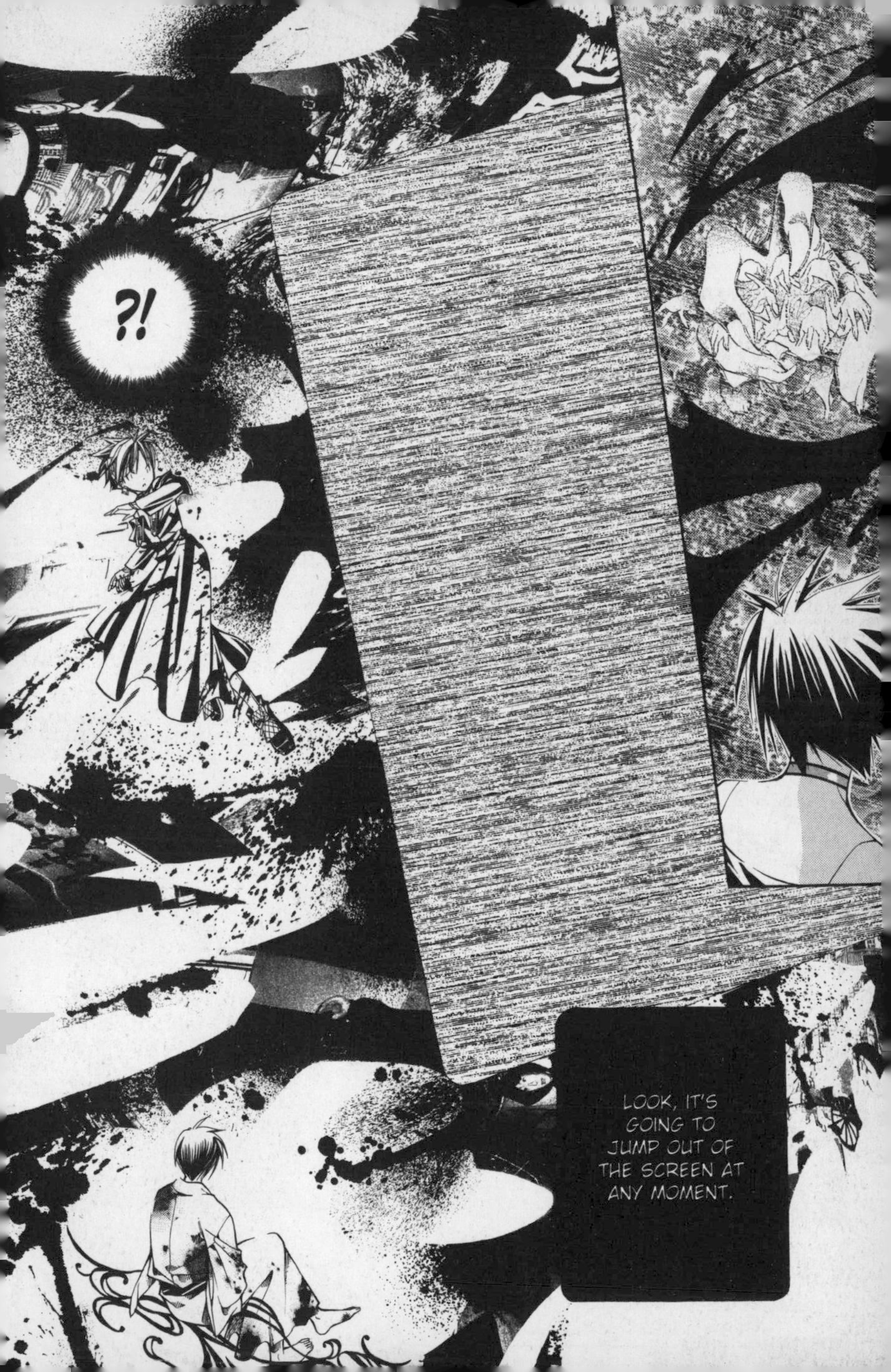
?!
LOOK, IT'S GOING TO JUMP OUT OF THE SCREEN AT ANY MOMENT.

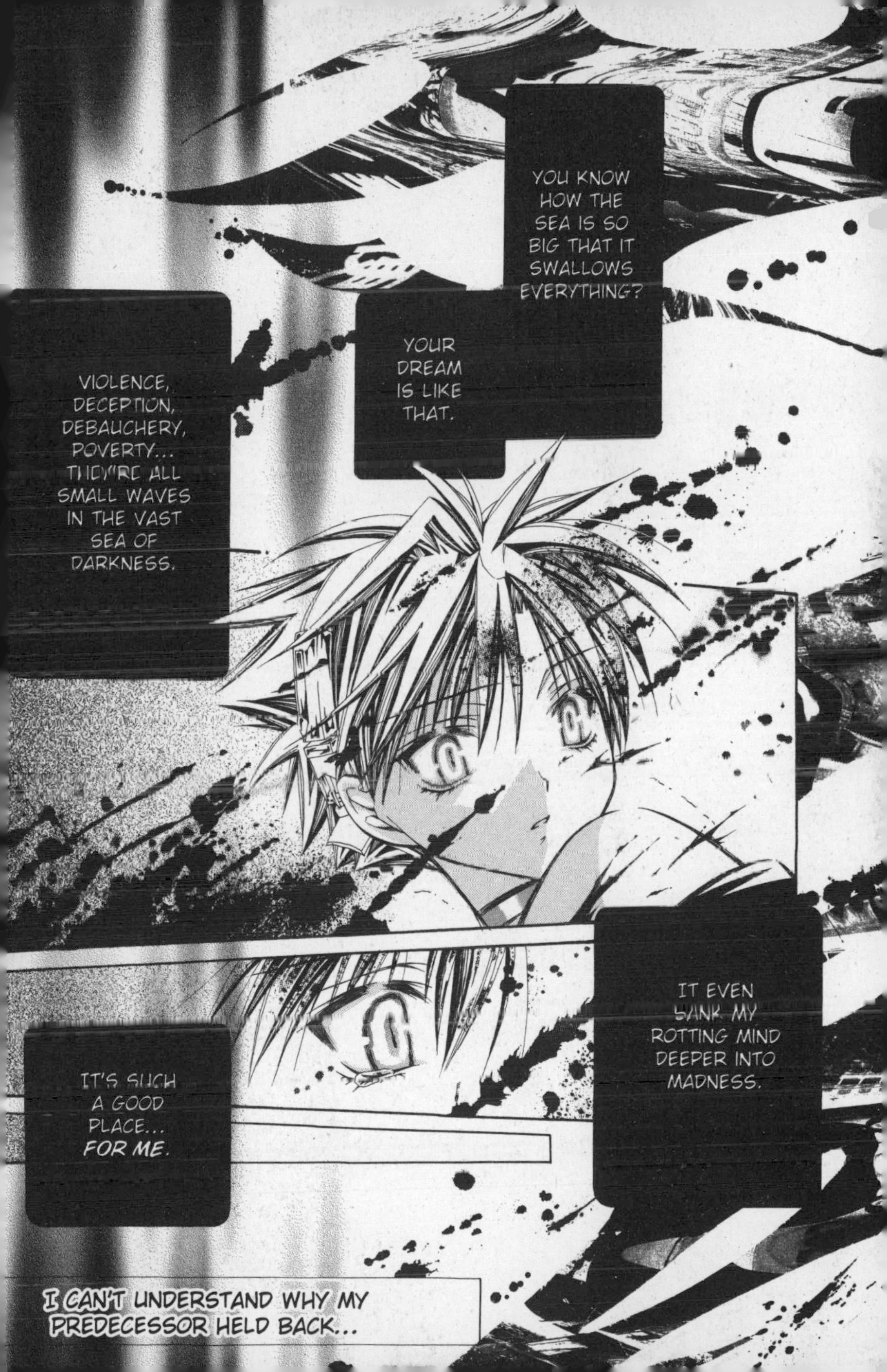
YOU KNOW HOW THE SEA IS SO BIG THAT IT SWALLOWS EVERYTHING?
YOUR DREAM IS LIKE THAT.
VIOLENCE, DECEPTION, DEBAUCHERY, POVERTY... THEY'RE ALL SMALL WAVES IN THE VAST SEA OF DARKNESS.
IT EVEN SANK MY ROTTING MIND DEEPER INTO MADNESS.
IT'S SUCH A GOOD PLACE... *FOR ME*.
I CAN'T UNDERSTAND WHY MY PREDECESSOR HELD BACK...

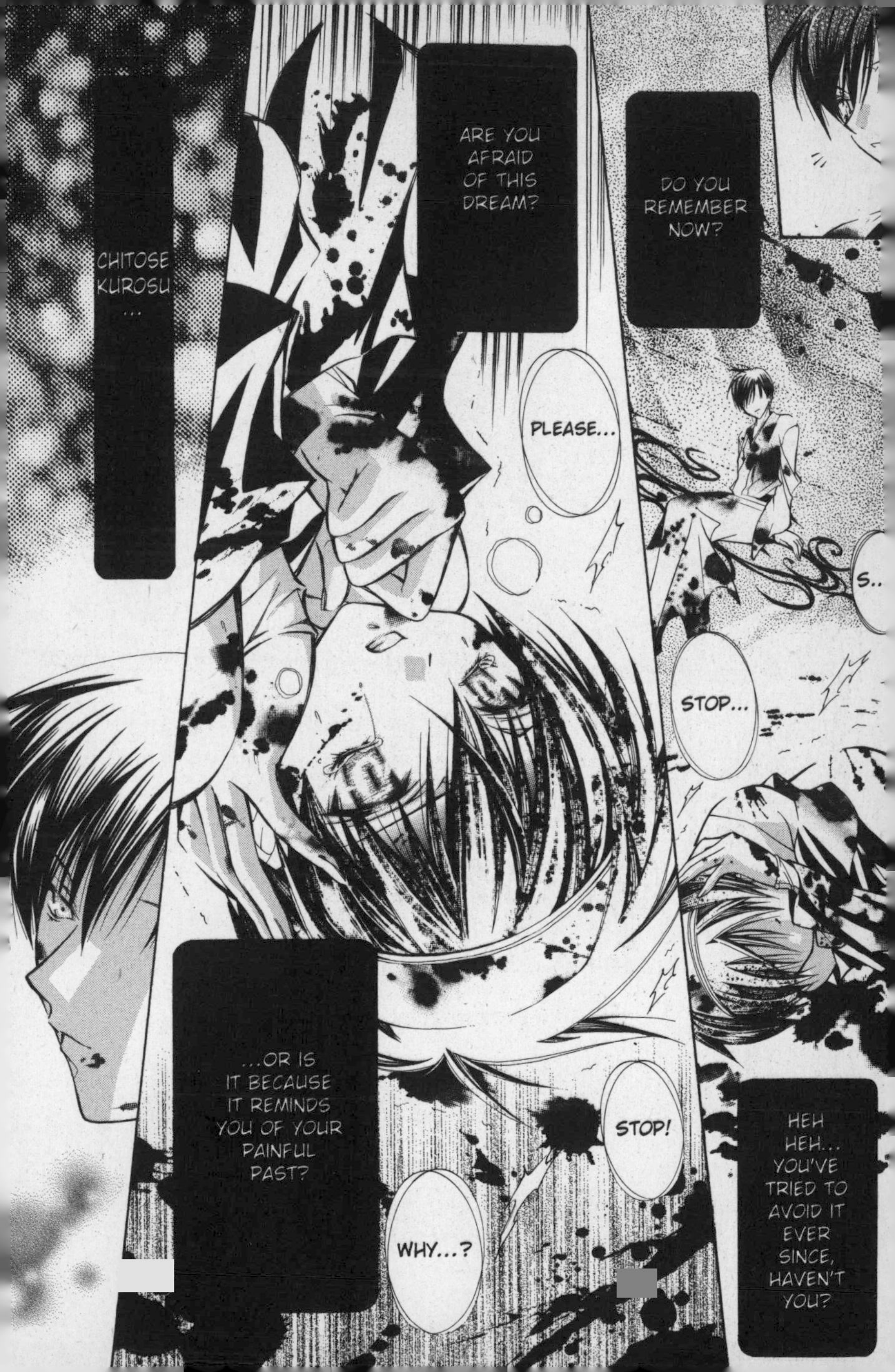
DO YOU REMEMBER NOW?
S...
STOP...
HEH HEH... YOU'VE TRIED TO AVOID IT EVER SINCE, HAVEN'T YOU?
ARE YOU AFRAID OF THIS DREAM?
PLEASE...
STOP!
WHY...?
...OR IS IT BECAUSE IT REMINDS YOU OF YOUR PAINFUL PAST?
CHITOSE KUROSU ...

POOR CHITOSE...
LONG, BLESSED LIFE. YOUR NAME REALLY DOESN'T SUIT YOU.
HEH HEH... SORRY. I MADE YOU REMEMBER TOO MUCH. I ONLY WANTED TO THANK YOU.
WHY DON'T WE GO NOW? AS YOU SAID, THIS PLACE IS USELESS.
YOU HAVE SOMEWHERE TO RETURN TO, AS DO I...

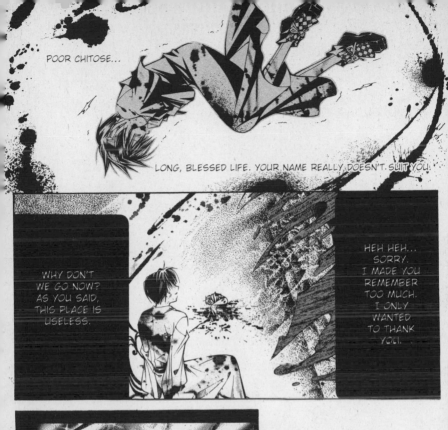

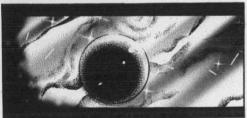

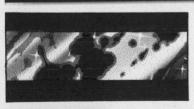

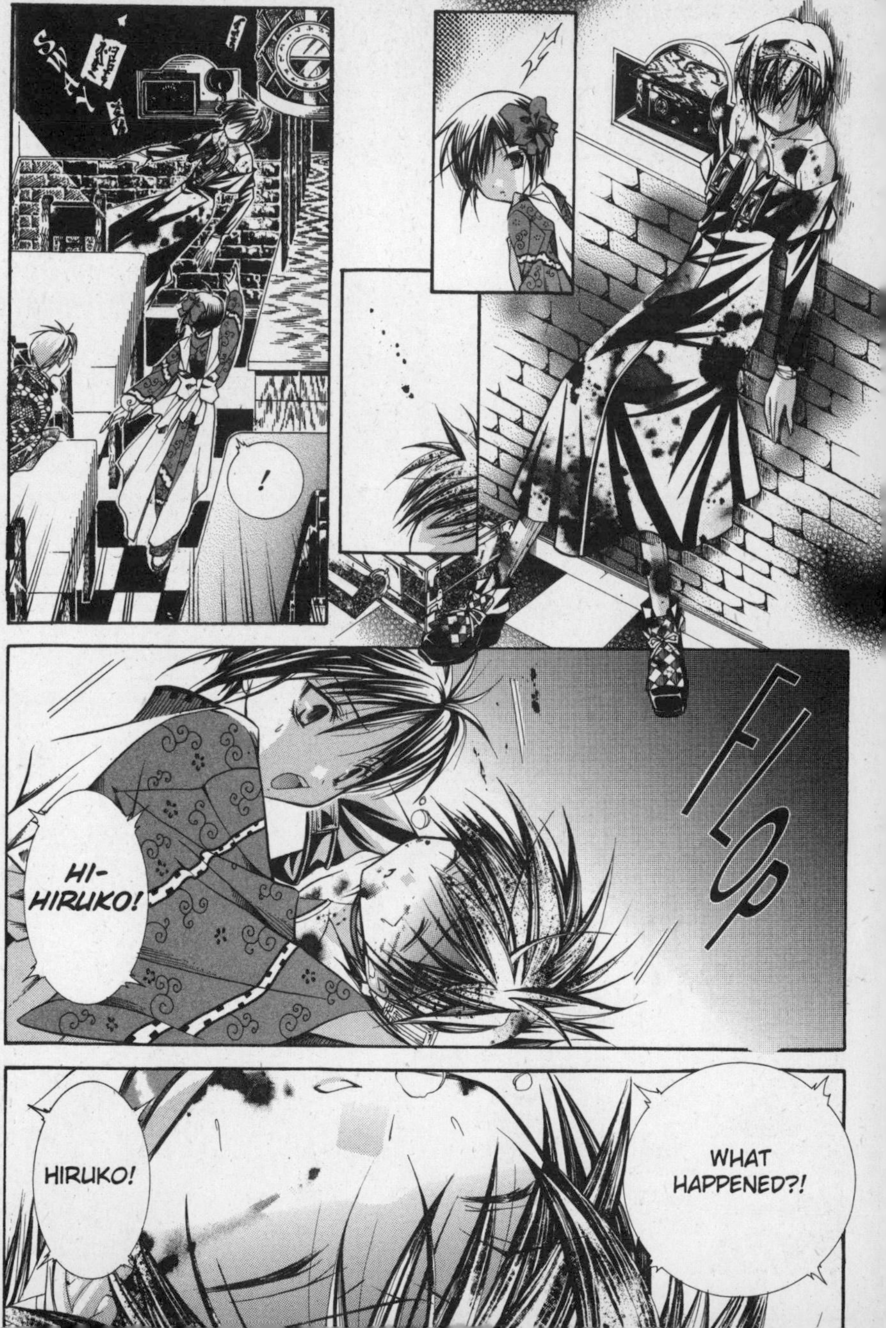
SWAY
!
FLOP
HI-
HIRUKO!
WHAT
HAPPENED?!
HIRUKO!

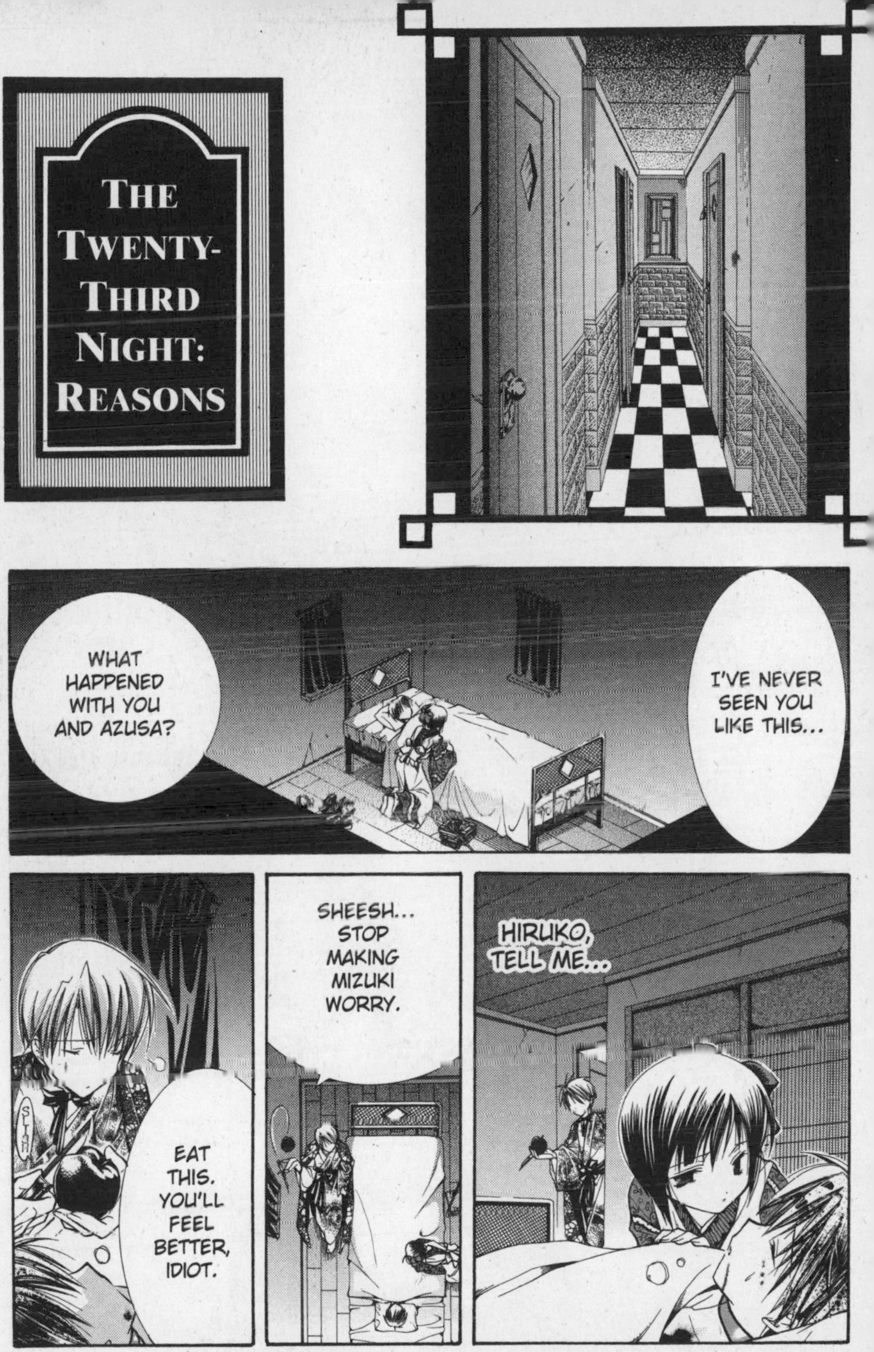
THE TWENTY-THIRD NIGHT: REASONS
I'VE NEVER SEEN YOU LIKE THIS...
WHAT HAPPENED WITH YOU AND AZUSA?
HIRUKO, TELL ME...
SHEESH... STOP MAKING MIZUKI WORRY.
SLISH
EAT THIS. YOU'LL FEEL BETTER, IDIOT.

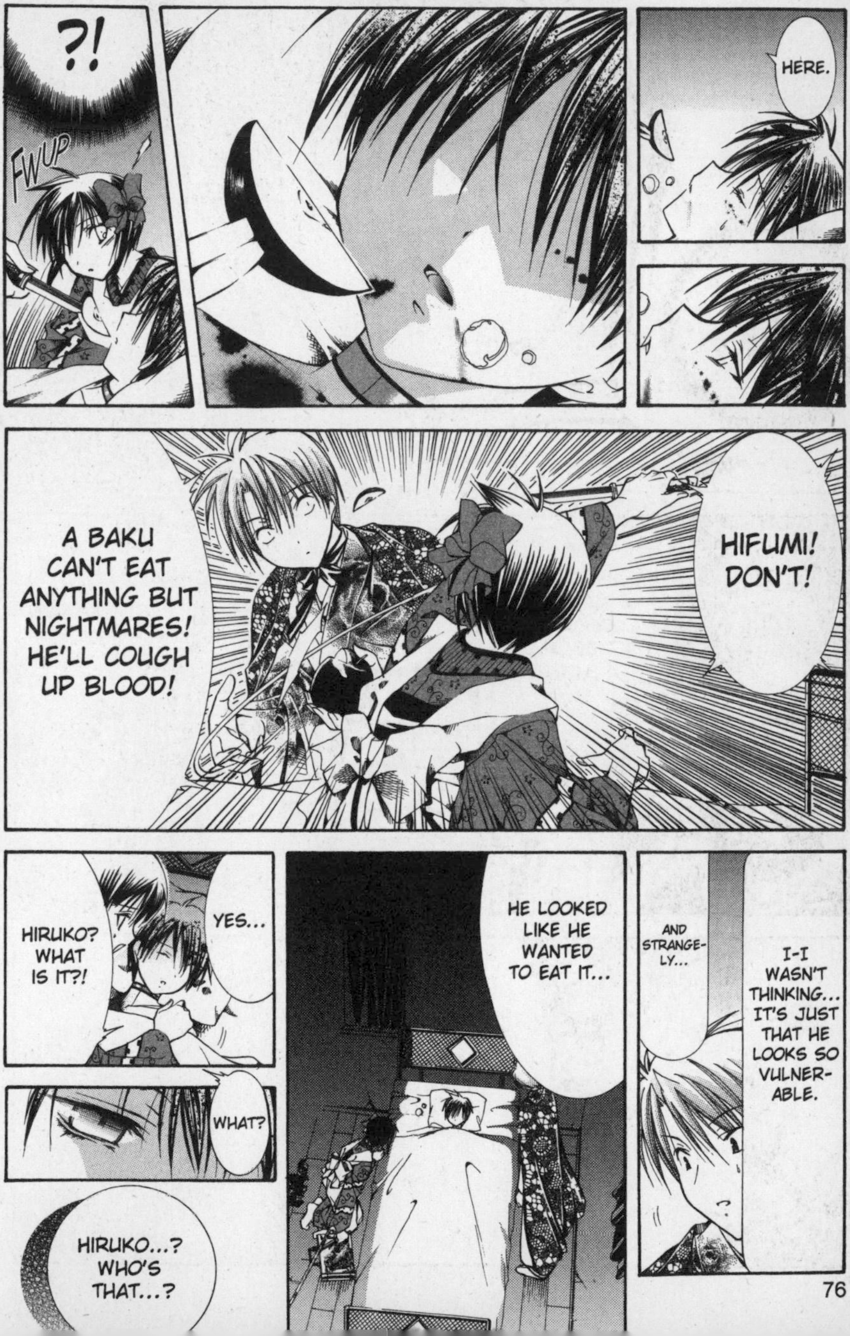
HERE.
?!
FWUP
HIFUMI! DON'T!
A BAKU CAN'T EAT ANYTHING BUT NIGHTMARES! HE'LL COUGH UP BLOOD!
I-I WASN'T THINKING... IT'S JUST THAT HE LOOKS SO VULNER-ABLE.
AND STRANGE-LY...
HE LOOKED LIKE HE WANTED TO EAT IT...
YES...
HIRUKO? WHAT IS IT?!
WHAT?
HIRUKO...? WHO'S THAT...?

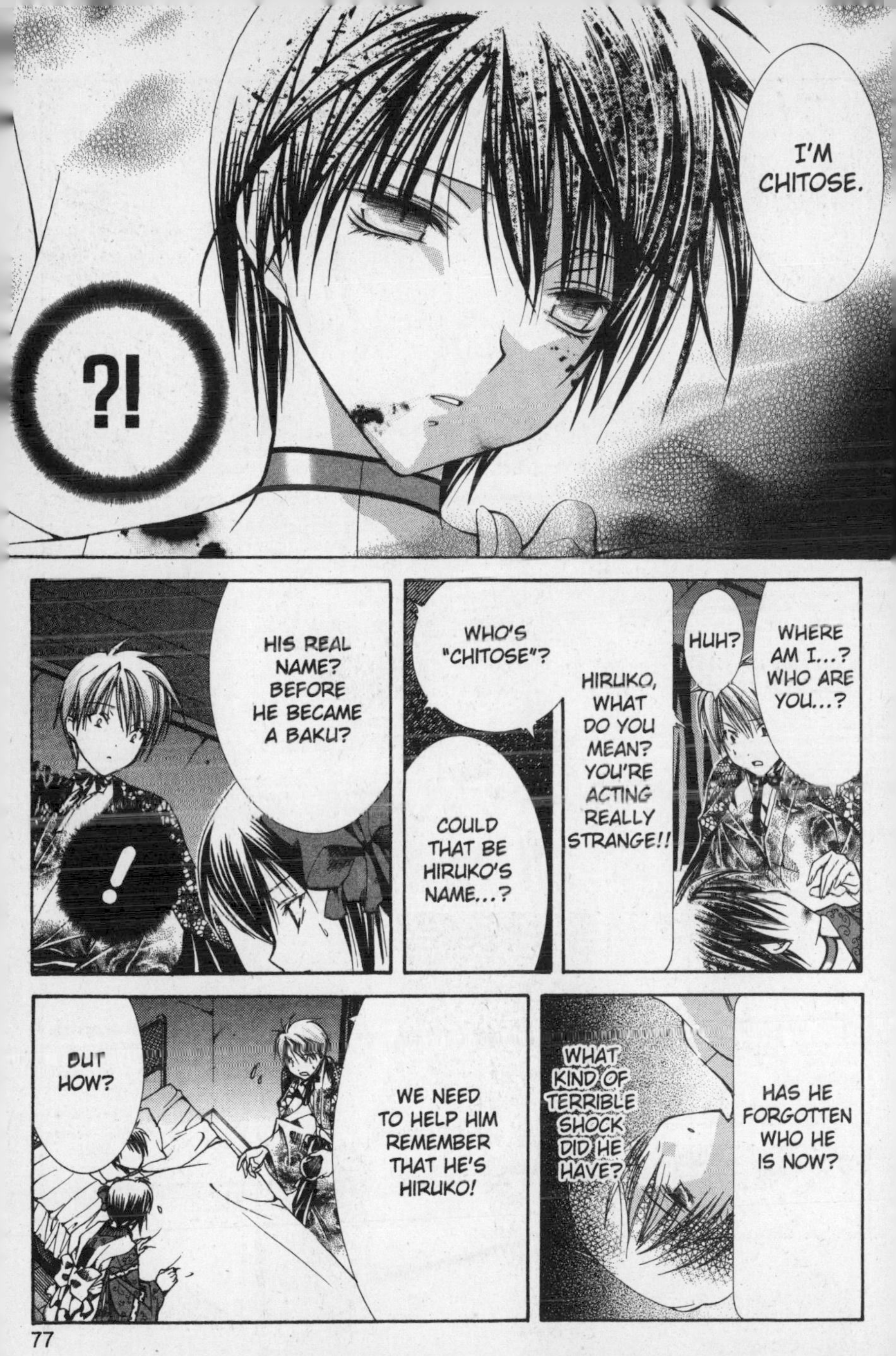
I'M CHITOSE.
?!
WHERE AM I...? WHO ARE YOU...?
HUH?
HIRUKO, WHAT DO YOU MEAN? YOU'RE ACTING REALLY STRANGE!!
WHO'S "CHITOSE"?
COULD THAT BE HIRUKO'S NAME...?
HIS REAL NAME? BEFORE HE BECAME A BAKU?
!
HAS HE FORGOTTEN WHO HE IS NOW?
WHAT KIND OF TERRIBLE SHOCK DID HE HAVE?
WE NEED TO HELP HIM REMEMBER THAT HE'S HIRUKO!
BUT HOW?

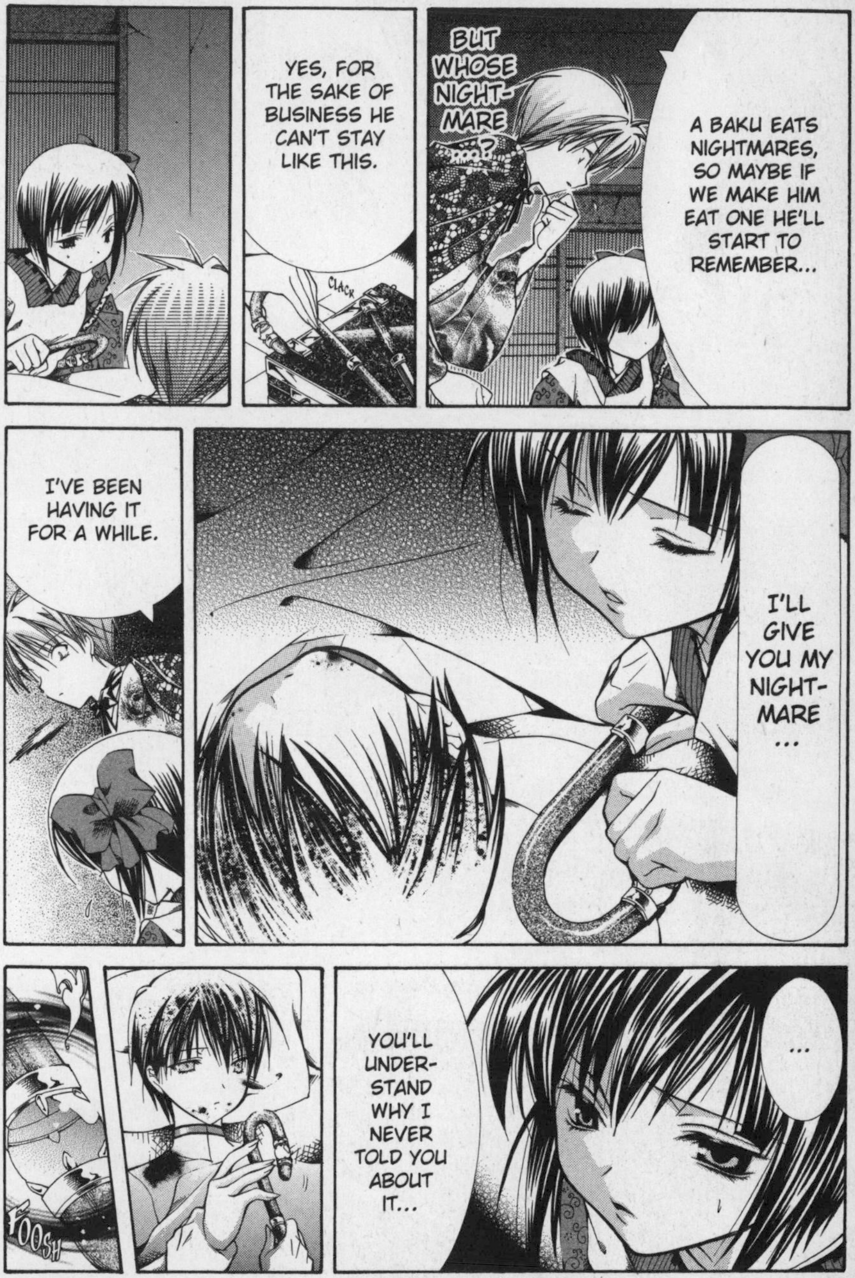
A BAKU EATS NIGHTMARES, SO MAYBE IF WE MAKE HIM EAT ONE HE'LL START TO REMEMBER...
BUT WHOSE NIGHTMARE?
YES, FOR THE SAKE OF BUSINESS HE CAN'T STAY LIKE THIS.
CLACK
I'LL GIVE YOU MY NIGHTMARE...
I'VE BEEN HAVING IT FOR A WHILE.
...
YOU'LL UNDERSTAND WHY I NEVER TOLD YOU ABOUT IT...
FOOSH

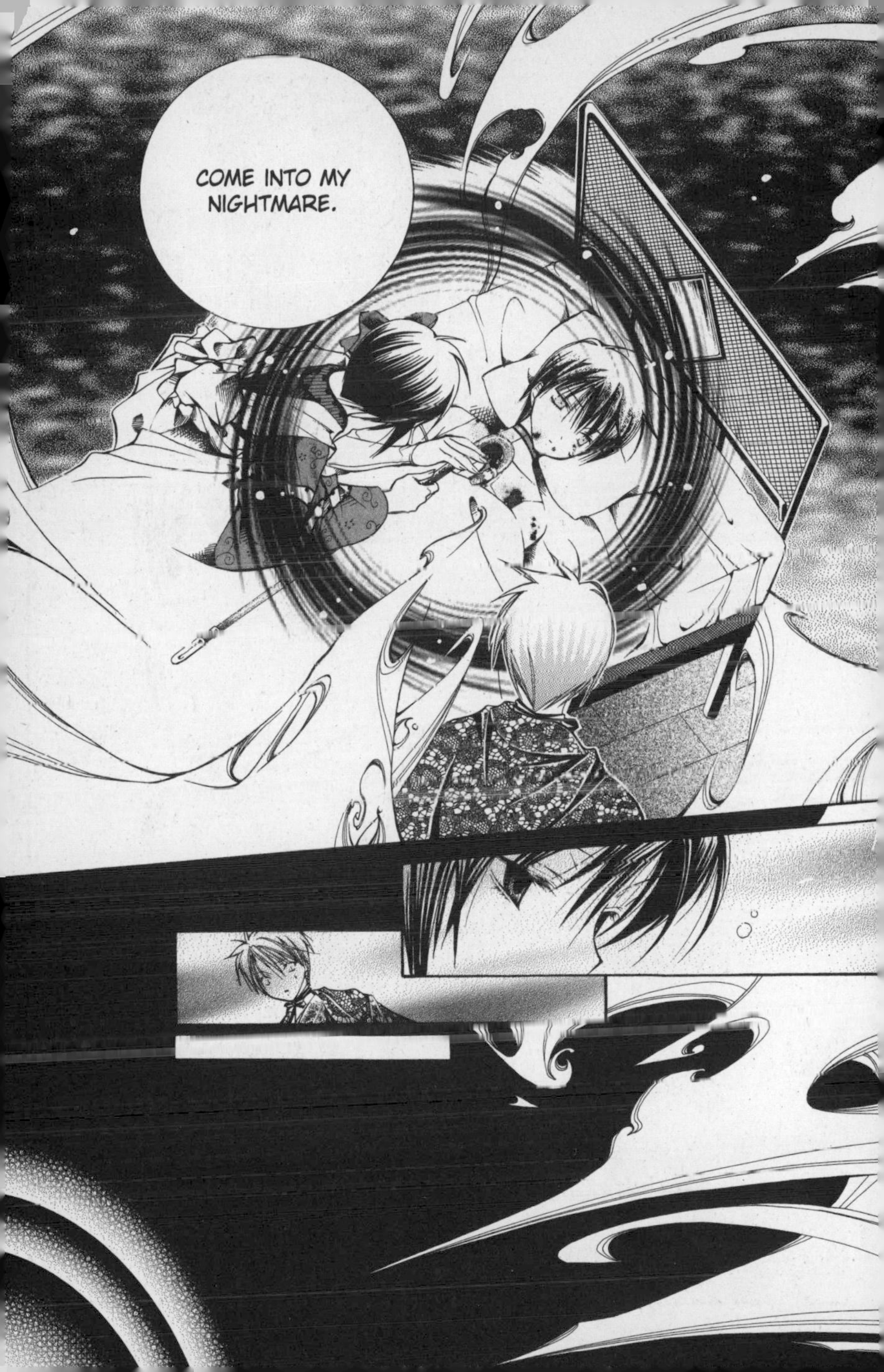
COME INTO MY NIGHTMARE.

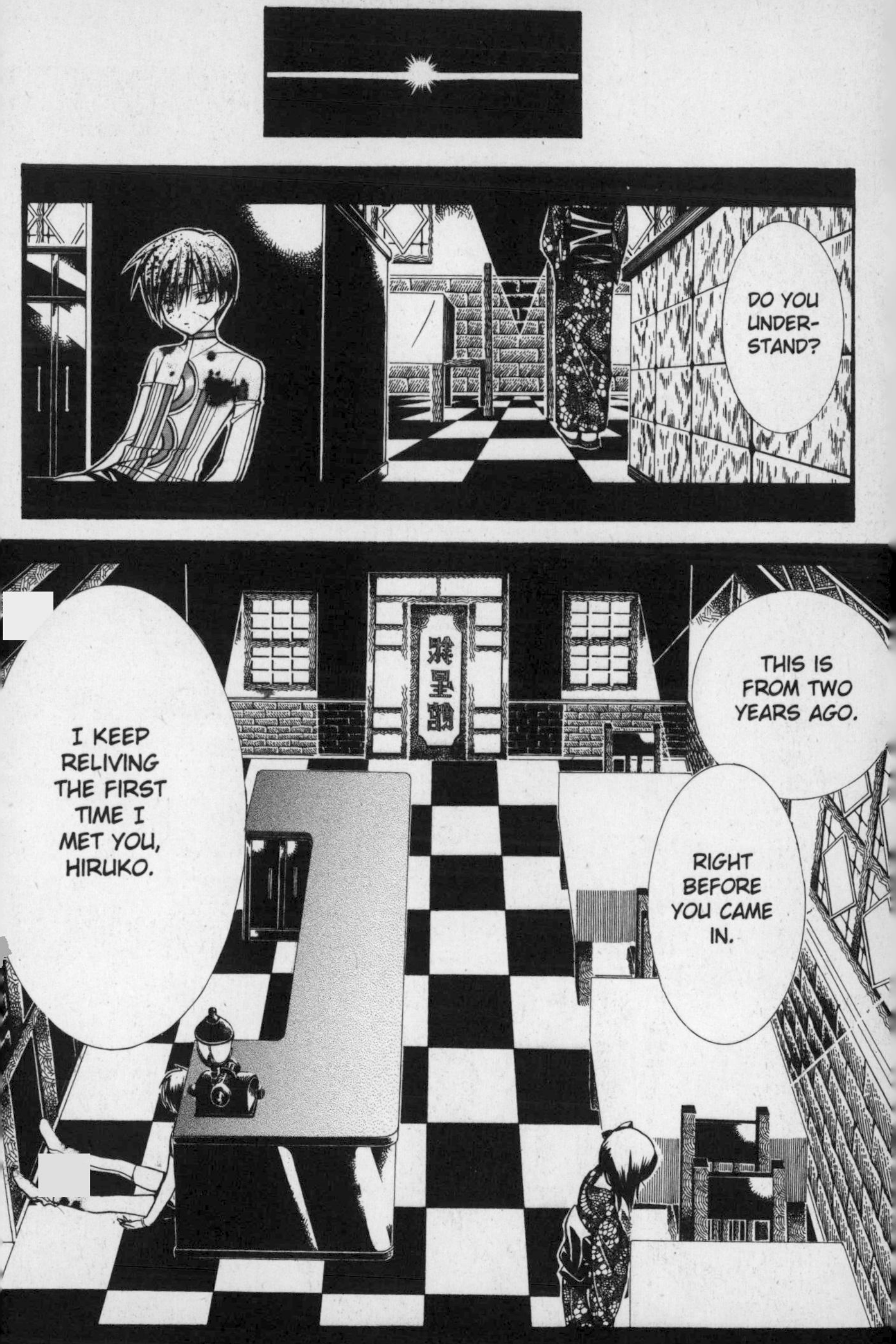
DO YOU UNDERSTAND?
THIS IS FROM TWO YEARS AGO.
RIGHT BEFORE YOU CAME IN.
I KEEP RELIVING THE FIRST TIME I MET YOU, HIRUKO.

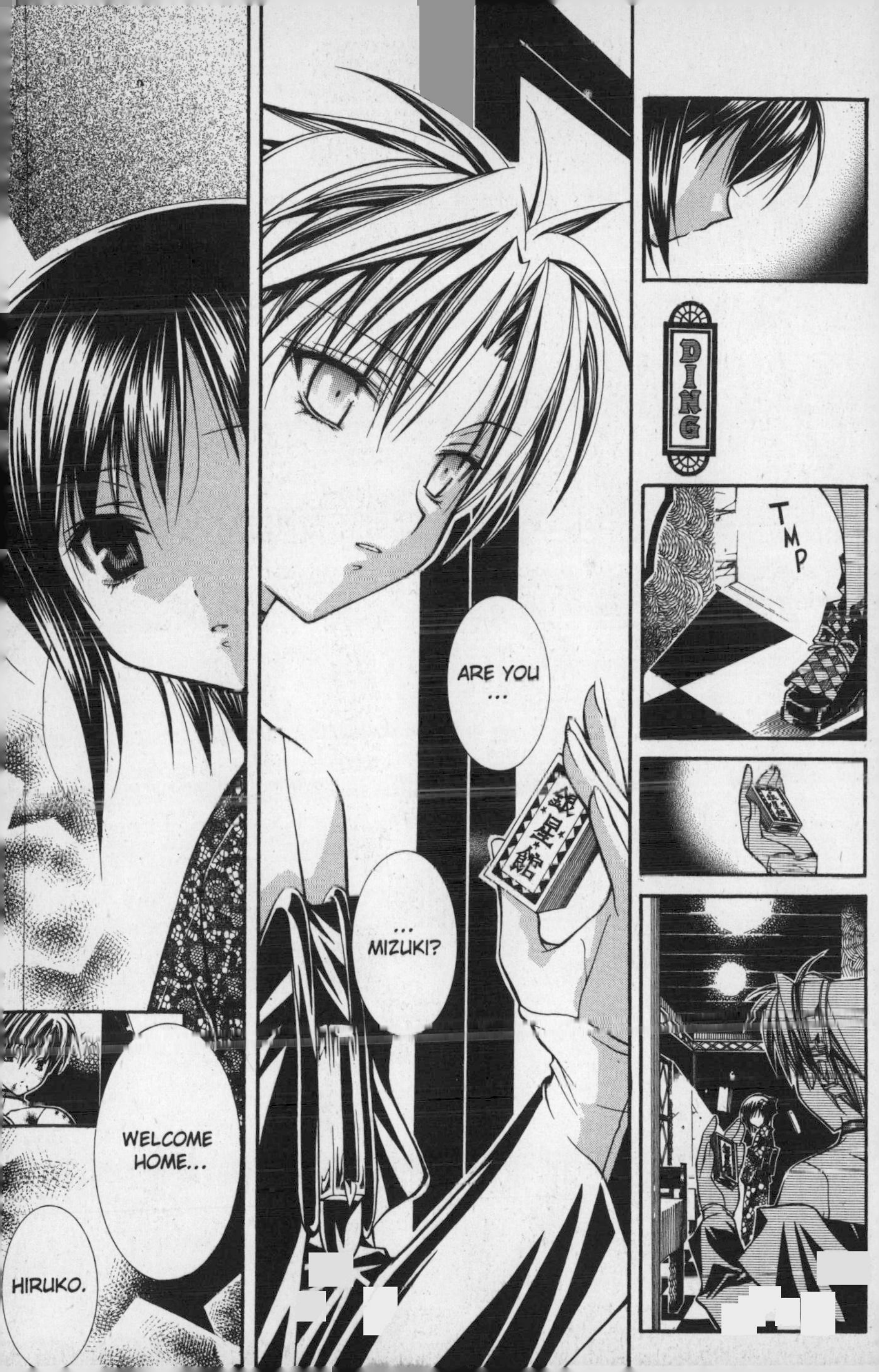
DING
TMP
ARE YOU ...
... MIZUKI?
銀星館
WELCOME HOME...
HIRUKO.

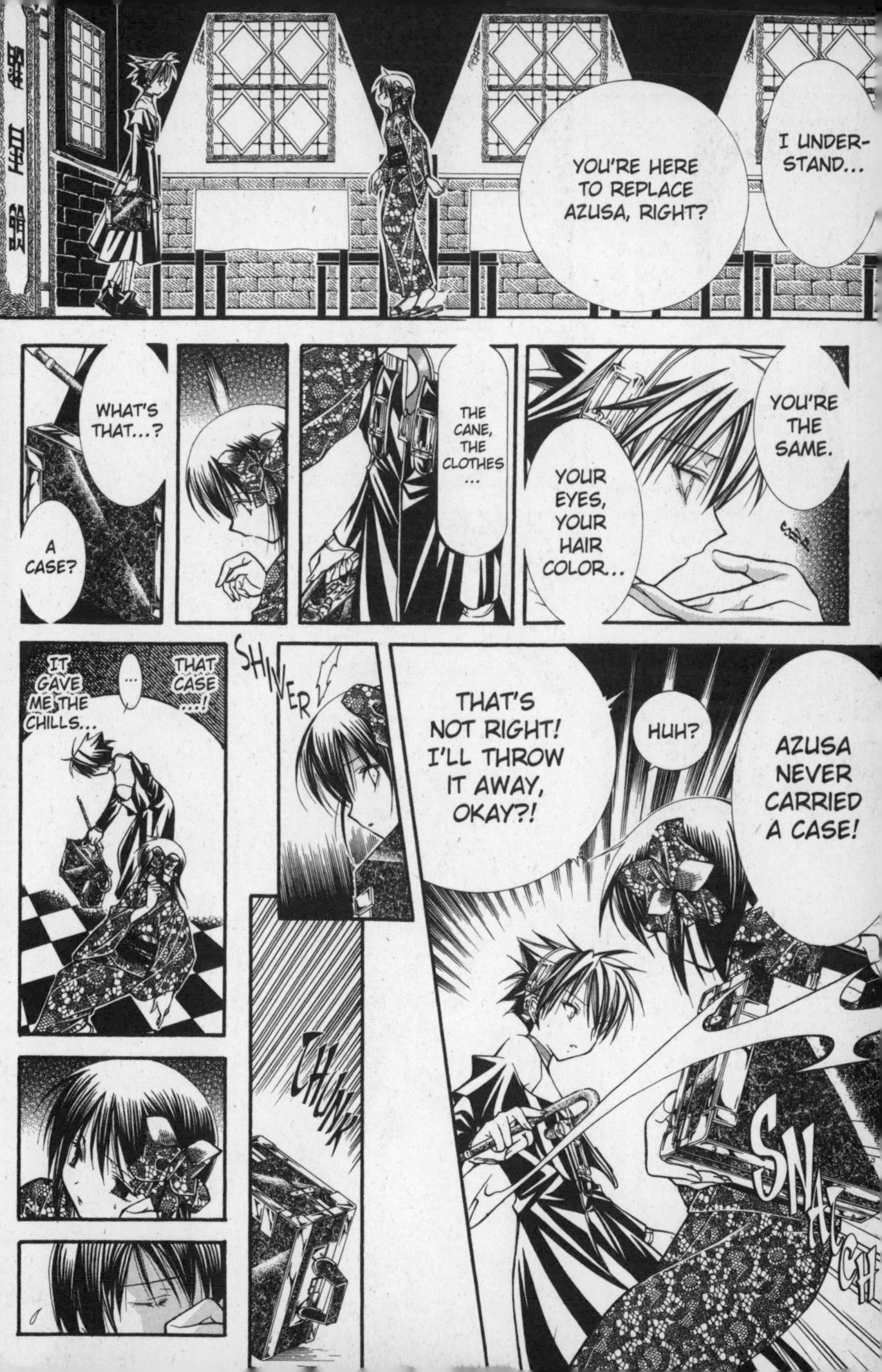

I UNDER-STAND...
YOU'RE HERE TO REPLACE AZUSA, RIGHT?
YOU'RE THE SAME.
YOUR EYES, YOUR HAIR COLOR...
THE CANE, THE CLOTHES ...
WHAT'S THAT...?
A CASE?
AZUSA NEVER CARRIED A CASE!
HUH?
THAT'S NOT RIGHT! I'LL THROW IT AWAY, OKAY?!
SNATCH
SHIVER
CHUNK
THAT CASE ...!
...
IT GAVE ME THE CHILLS...

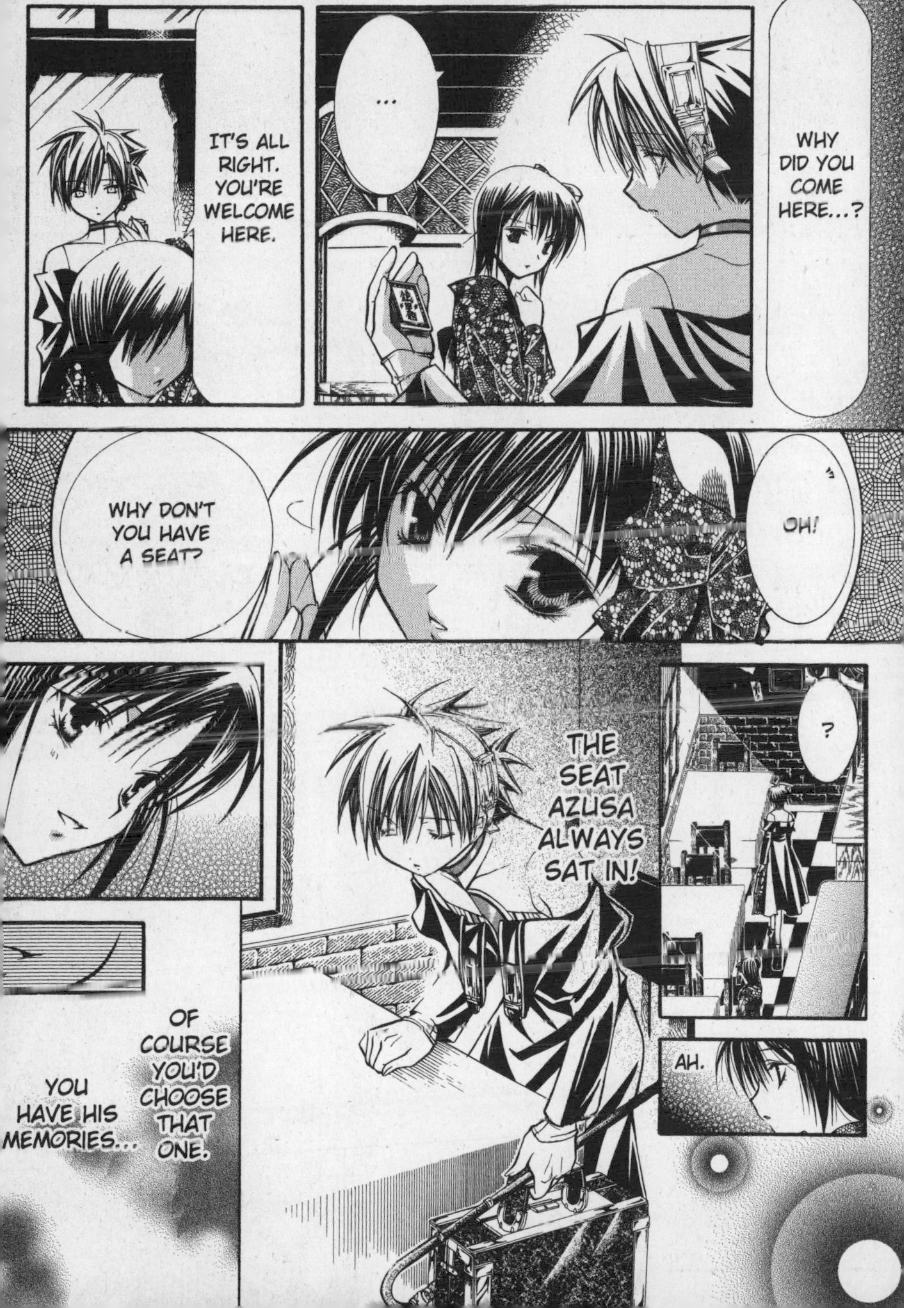
WHY DID YOU COME HERE...?
...
IT'S ALL RIGHT. YOU'RE WELCOME HERE.
OH!
WHY DON'T YOU HAVE A SEAT?
?
AH.
THE SEAT AZUSA ALWAYS SAT IN!
OF COURSE YOU'D CHOOSE THAT ONE.
YOU HAVE HIS MEMORIES...

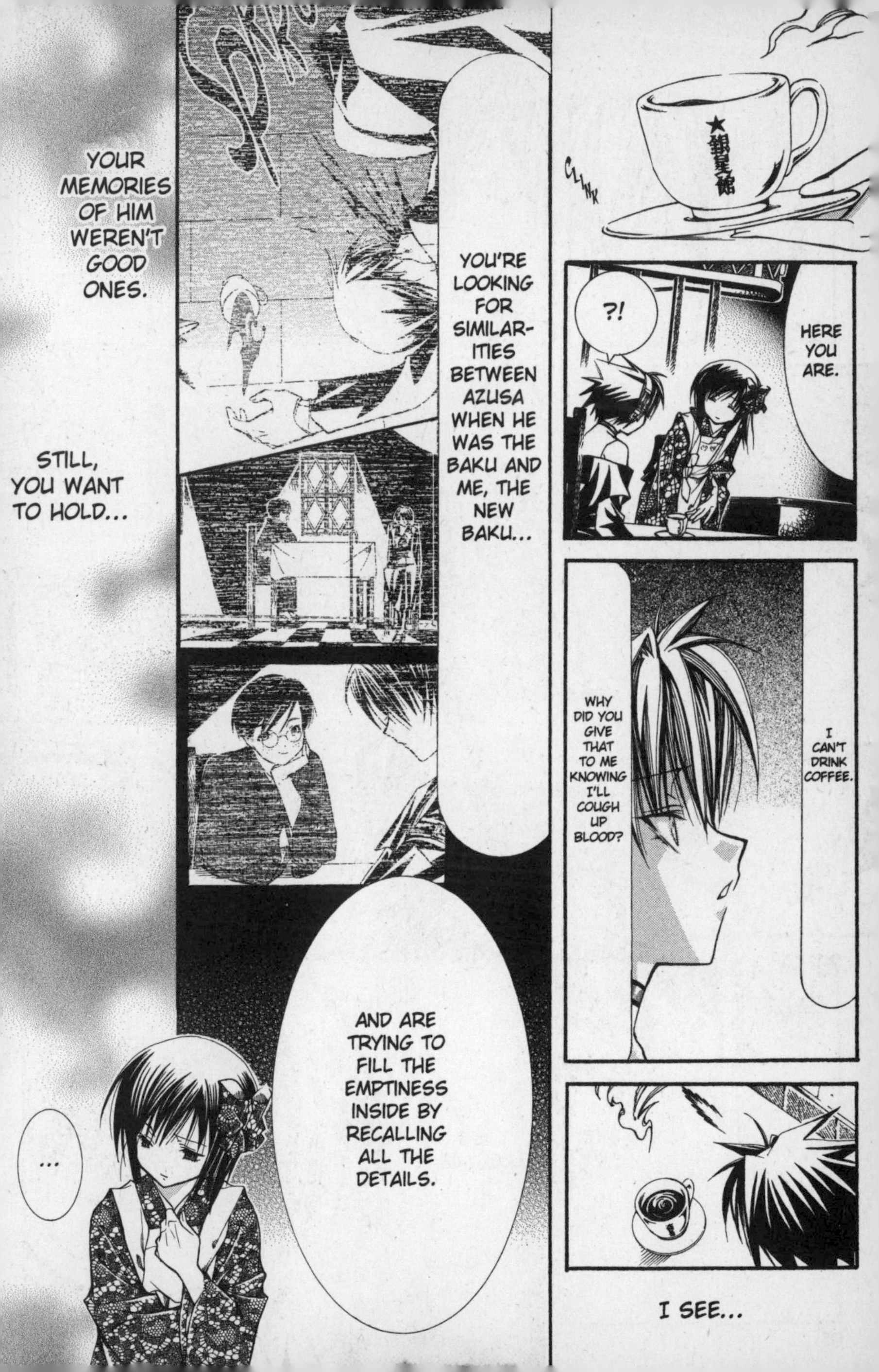
CLINK
?!
HERE YOU ARE.
I CAN'T DRINK COFFEE.
WHY DID YOU GIVE THAT TO ME KNOWING I'LL COUGH UP BLOOD?
I SEE...
YOU'RE LOOKING FOR SIMILAR-ITIES BETWEEN AZUSA WHEN HE WAS THE BAKU AND ME, THE NEW BAKU...
AND ARE TRYING TO FILL THE EMPTINESS INSIDE BY RECALLING ALL THE DETAILS.
YOUR MEMORIES OF HIM WEREN'T GOOD ONES.
STILL, YOU WANT TO HOLD...
...

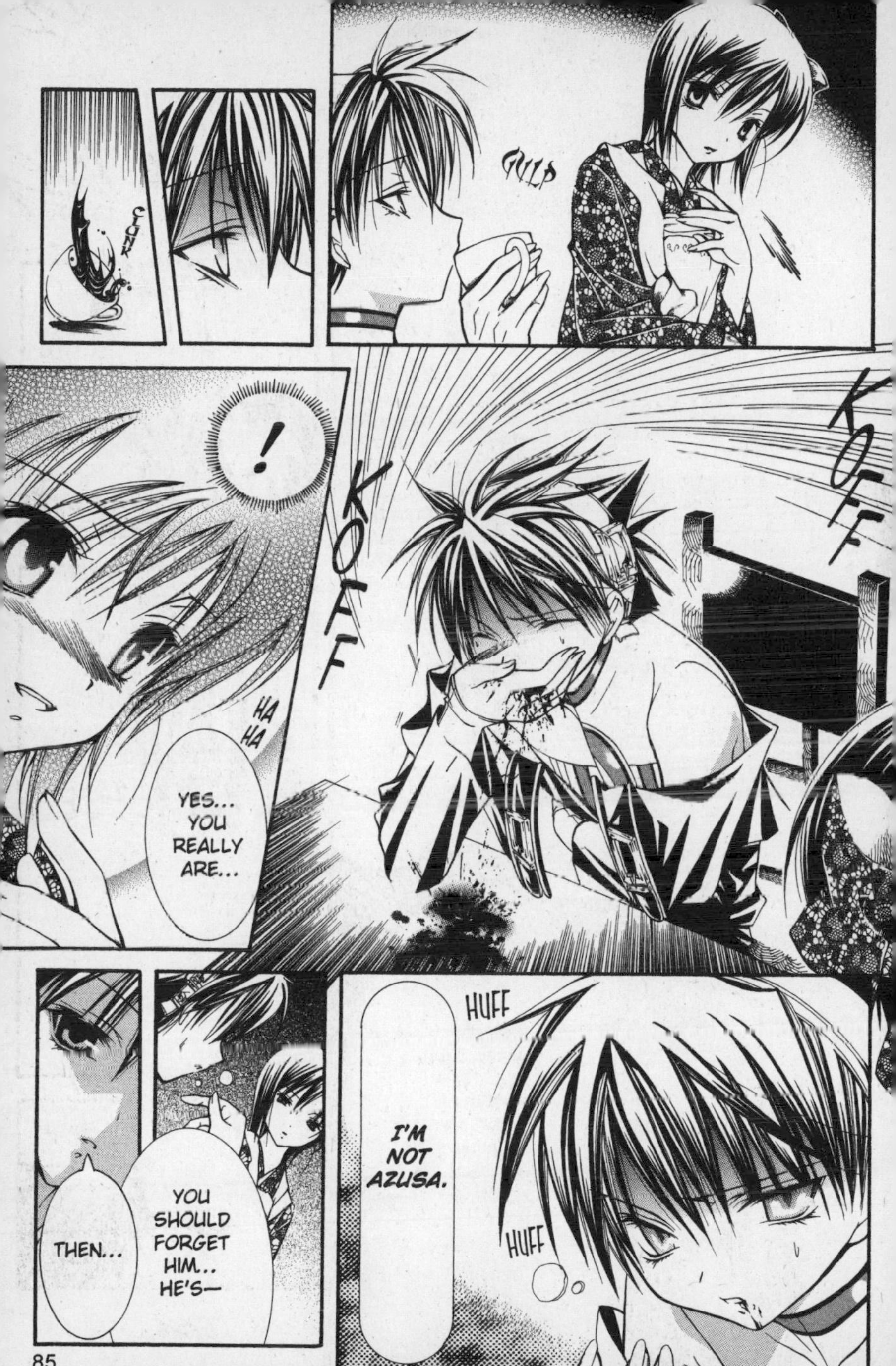
GULP
CLUNK
KOFF KOFF
KOFF KOFF
!
HA HA
YES... YOU REALLY ARE...
HUFF
I'M NOT AZUSA.
HUFF
YOU SHOULD FORGET HIM.. HE'S—
THEN...

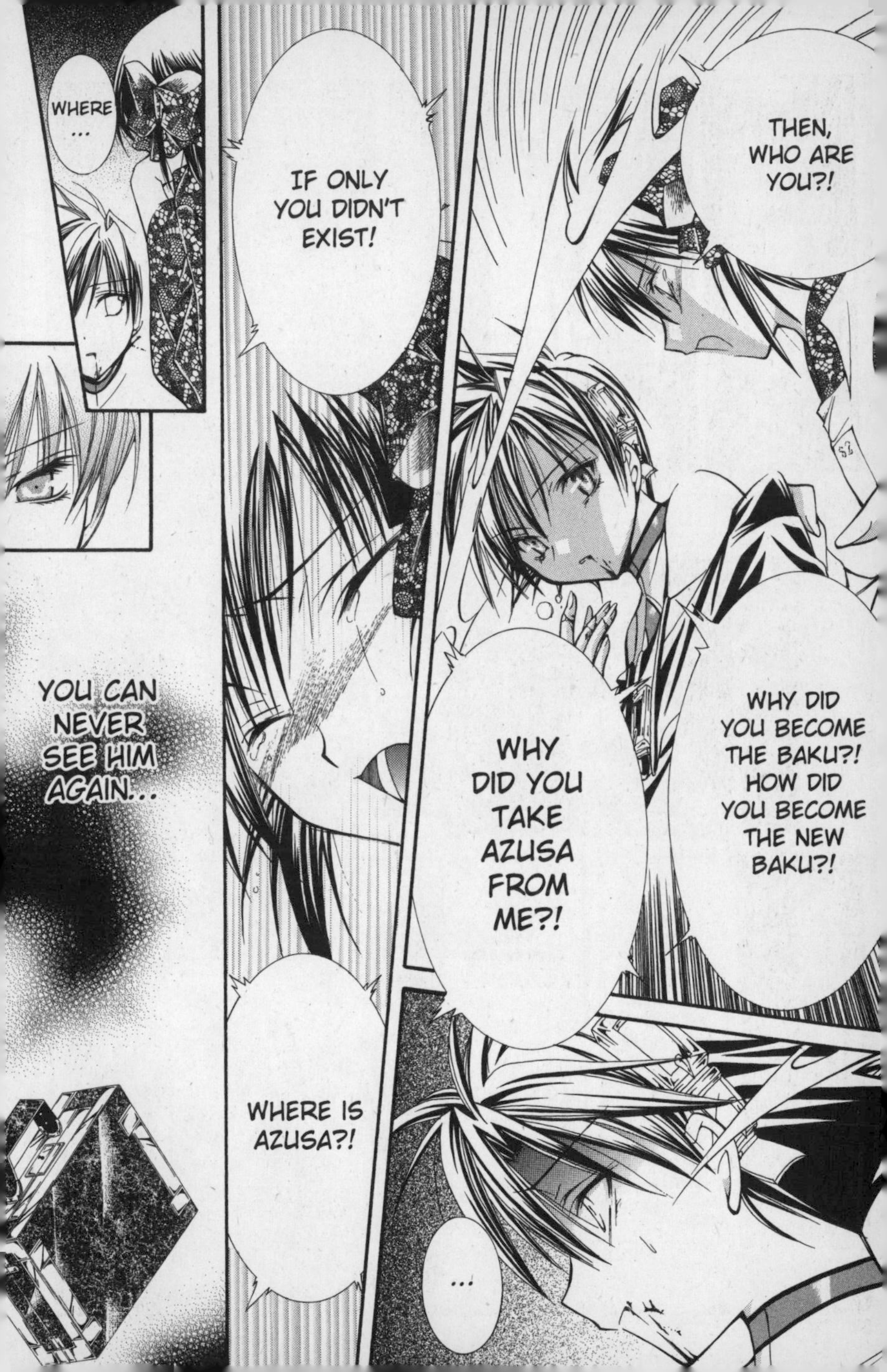
THEN, WHO ARE YOU?!
WHY DID YOU BECOME THE BAKU?! HOW DID YOU BECOME THE NEW BAKU?!
WHY DID YOU TAKE AZUSA FROM ME?!
IF ONLY YOU DIDN'T EXIST!
WHERE IS AZUSA?!
...
WHERE ...
YOU CAN NEVER SEE HIM AGAIN...

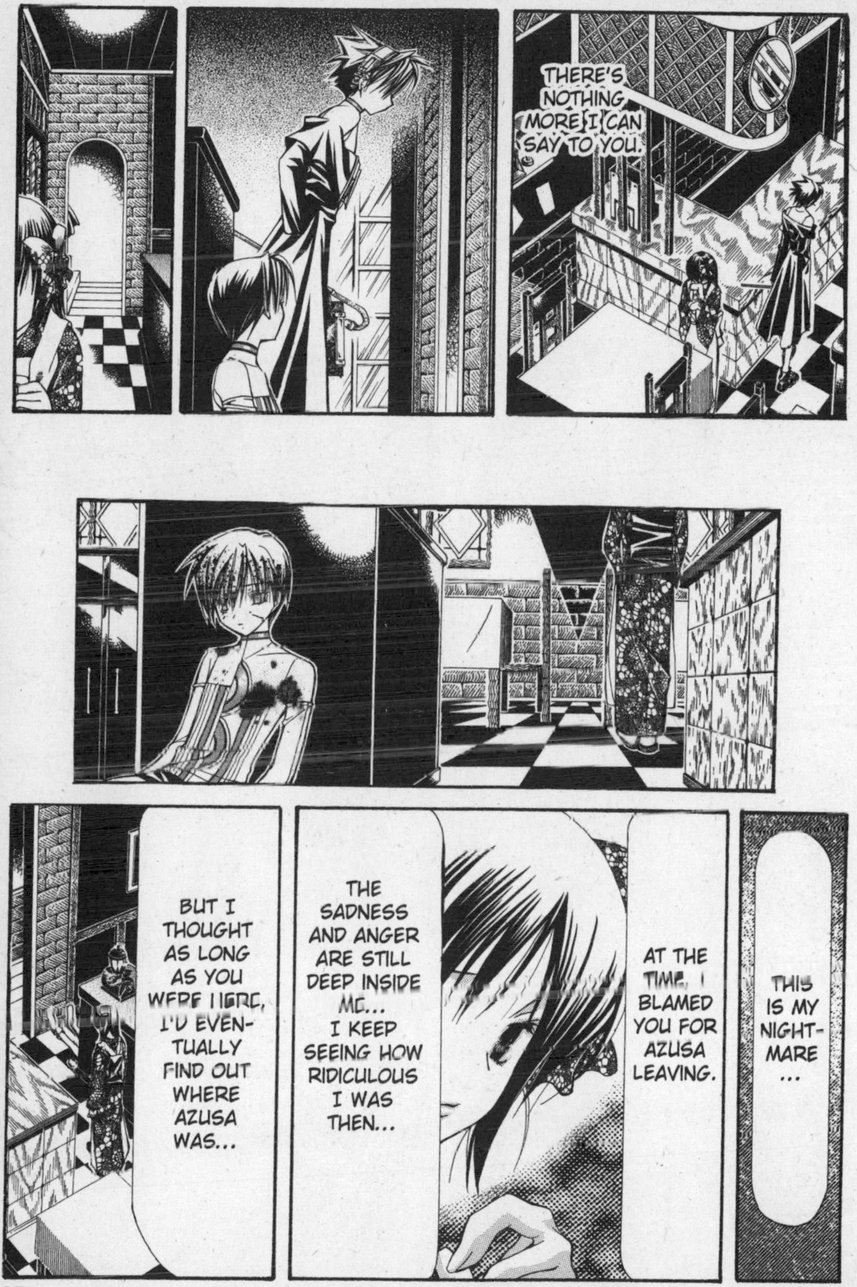
THERE'S NOTHING MORE I CAN SAY TO YOU.
THIS IS MY NIGHT-MARE ...
AT THE TIME, I BLAMED YOU FOR AZUSA LEAVING.
THE SADNESS AND ANGER ARE STILL DEEP INSIDE ME... I KEEP SEEING HOW RIDICULOUS I WAS THEN...
BUT I THOUGHT AS LONG AS YOU WERE HERE, I'D EVENTUALLY FIND OUT WHERE AZUSA WAS...

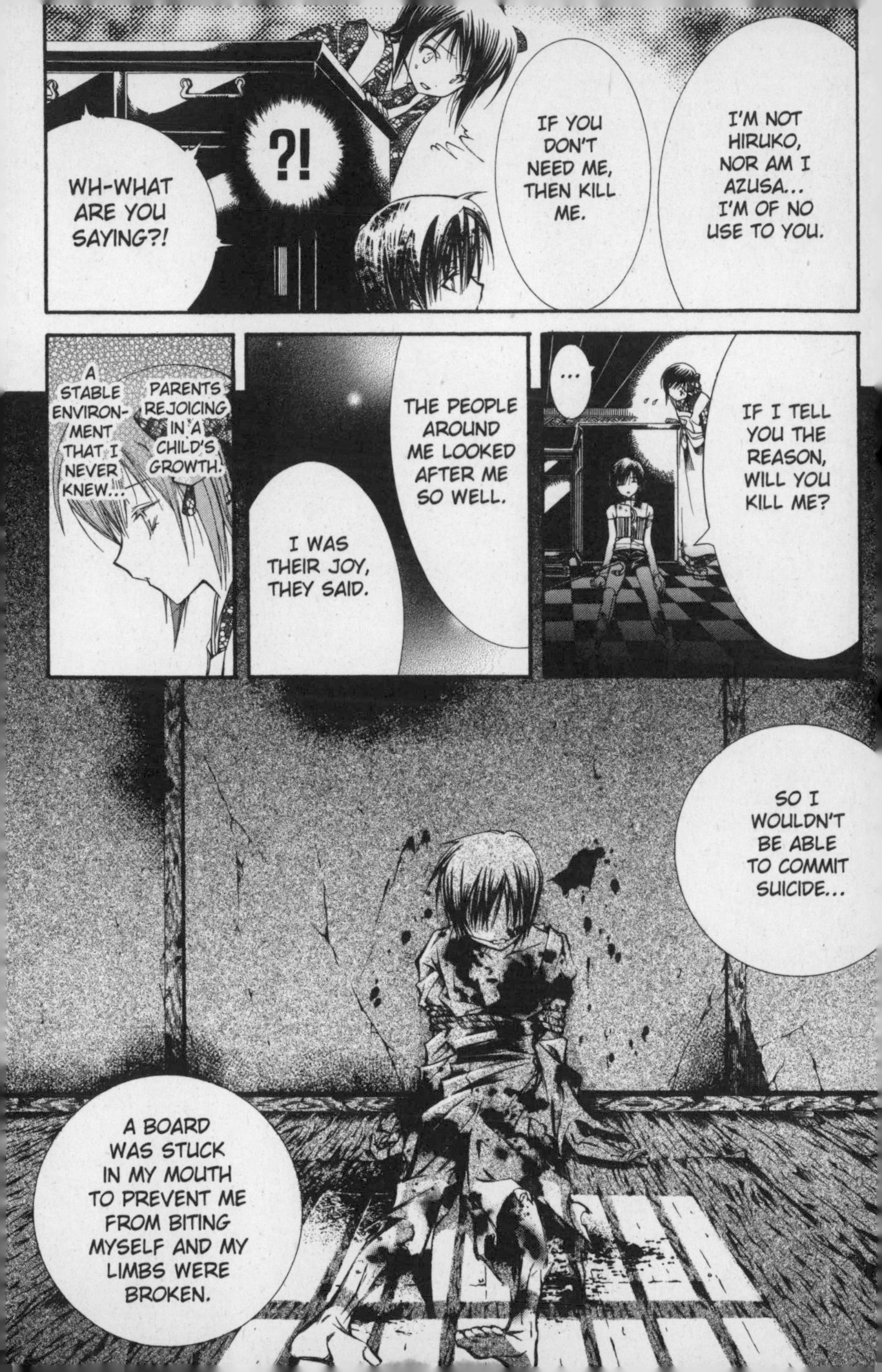
I'M NOT HIRUKO, NOR AM I AZUSA… I'M OF NO USE TO YOU.
IF YOU DON'T NEED ME, THEN KILL ME.
?!
WH-WHAT ARE YOU SAYING?!
IF I TELL YOU THE REASON, WILL YOU KILL ME?
…
THE PEOPLE AROUND ME LOOKED AFTER ME SO WELL.
I WAS THEIR JOY, THEY SAID.
PARENTS REJOICING IN A CHILD'S GROWTH.
A STABLE ENVIRONMENT THAT I NEVER KNEW…
SO I WOULDN'T BE ABLE TO COMMIT SUICIDE…
A BOARD WAS STUCK IN MY MOUTH TO PREVENT ME FROM BITING MYSELF AND MY LIMBS WERE BROKEN.

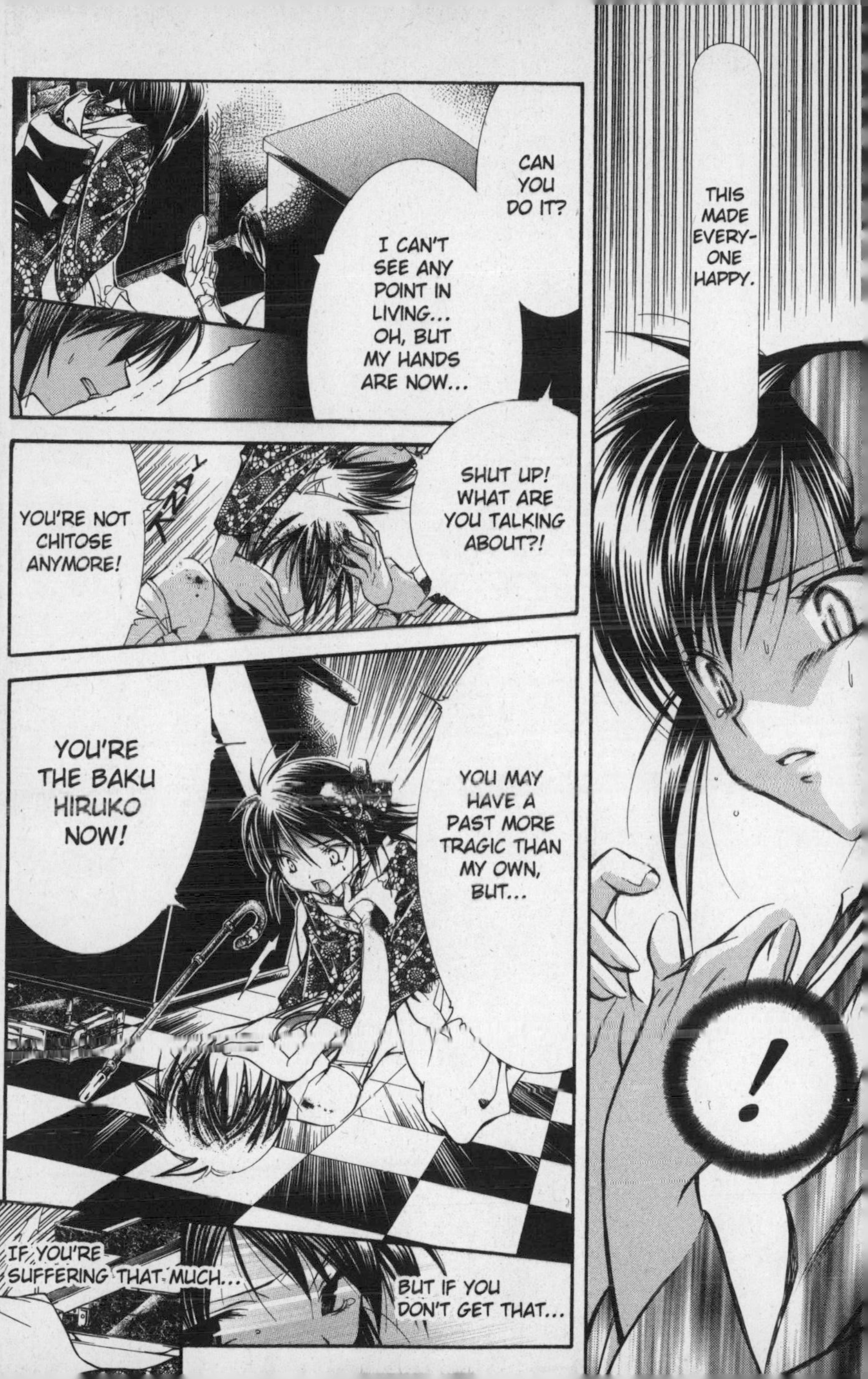
THIS MADE EVERY-ONE HAPPY.
!
CAN YOU DO IT?
I CAN'T SEE ANY POINT IN LIVING... OH, BUT MY HANDS ARE NOW...
SHUT UP! WHAT ARE YOU TALKING ABOUT?!
YOU'RE NOT CHITOSE ANYMORE!
YOU MAY HAVE A PAST MORE TRAGIC THAN MY OWN, BUT...
YOU'RE THE BAKU HIRUKO NOW!
BUT IF YOU DON'T GET THAT...
IF YOU'RE SUFFERING THAT MUCH...

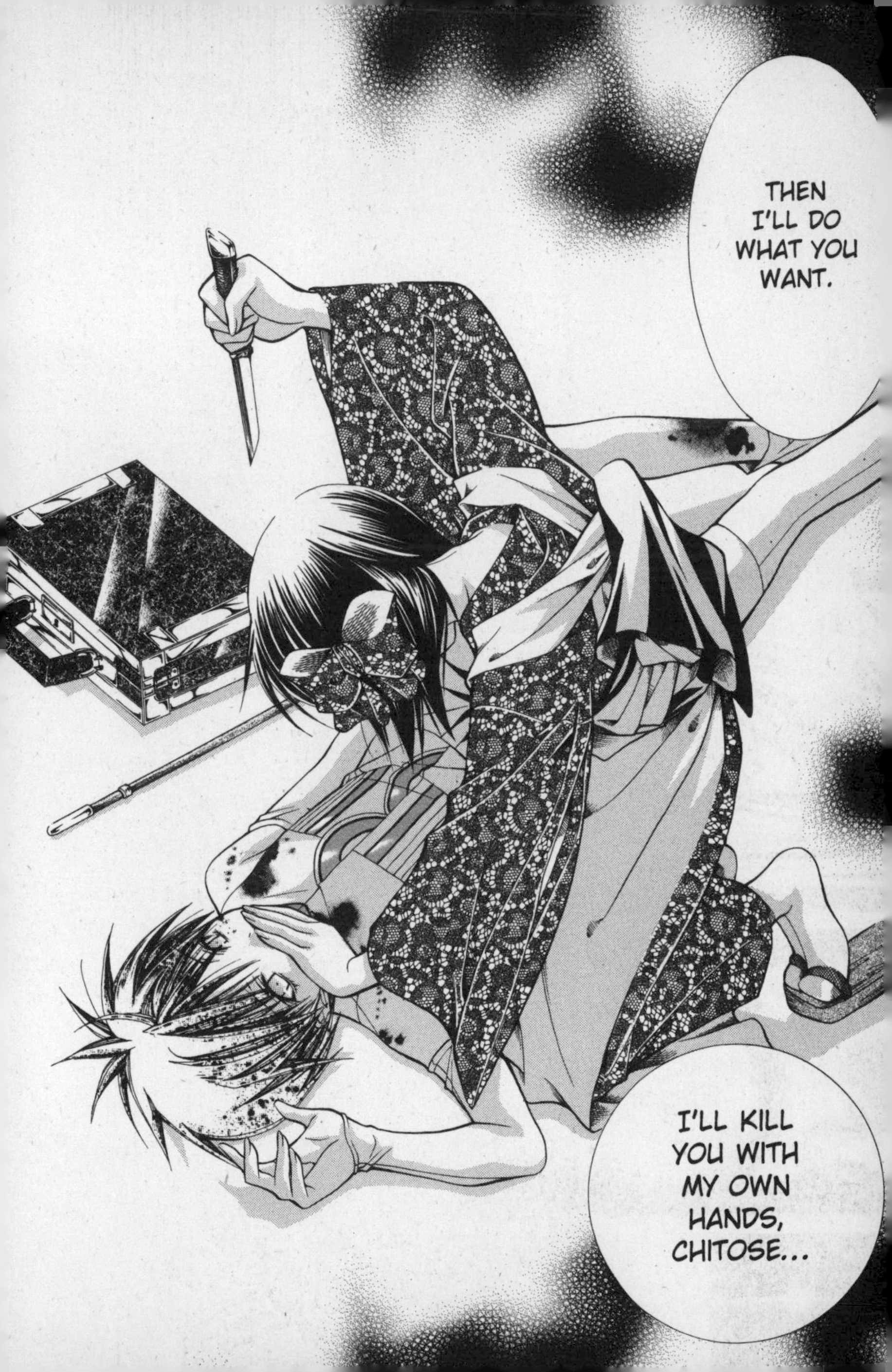
THEN I'LL DO WHAT YOU WANT.
I'LL KILL YOU WITH MY OWN HANDS, CHITOSE...

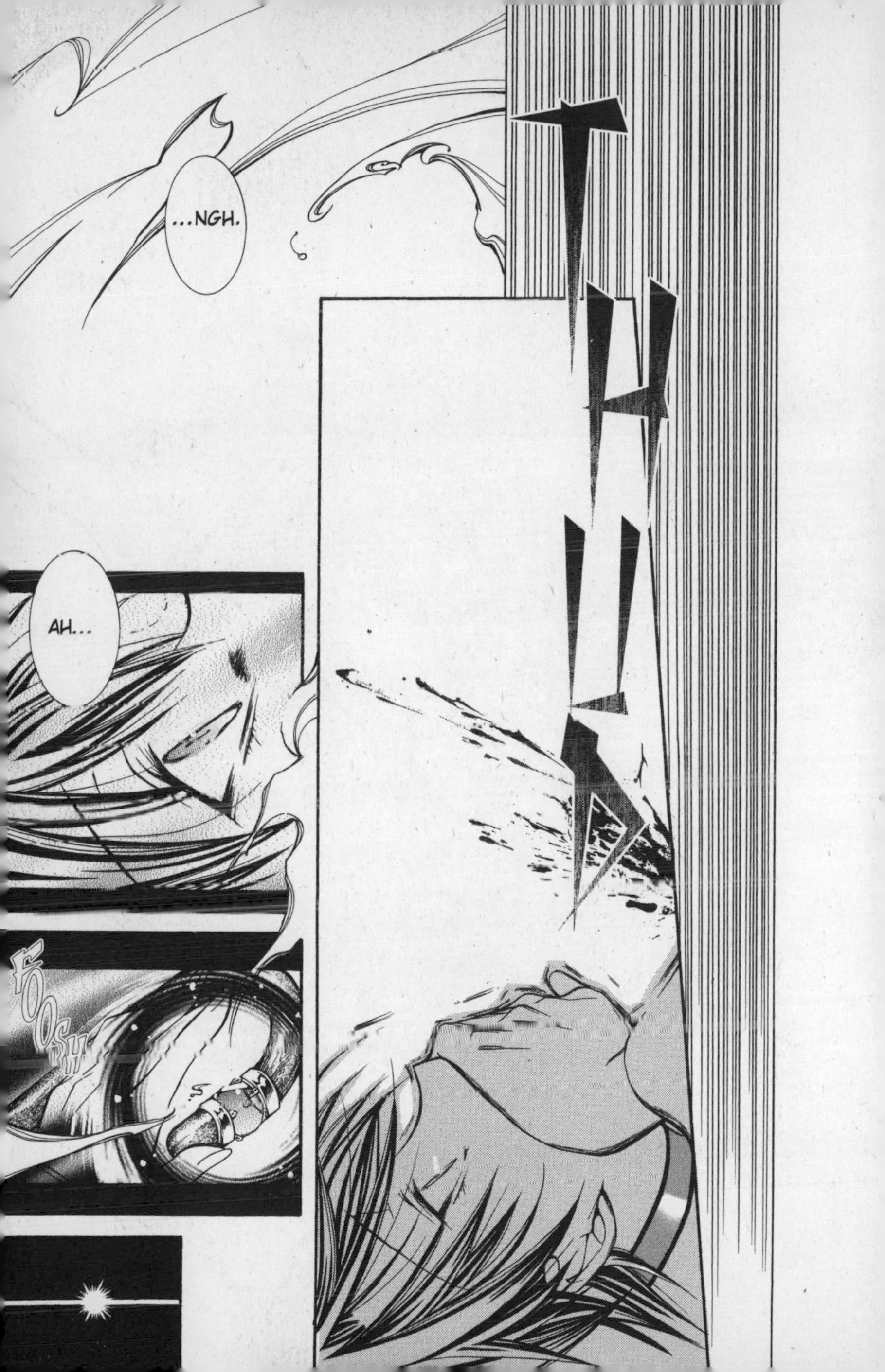
...NGH.
AH...
FOOSH

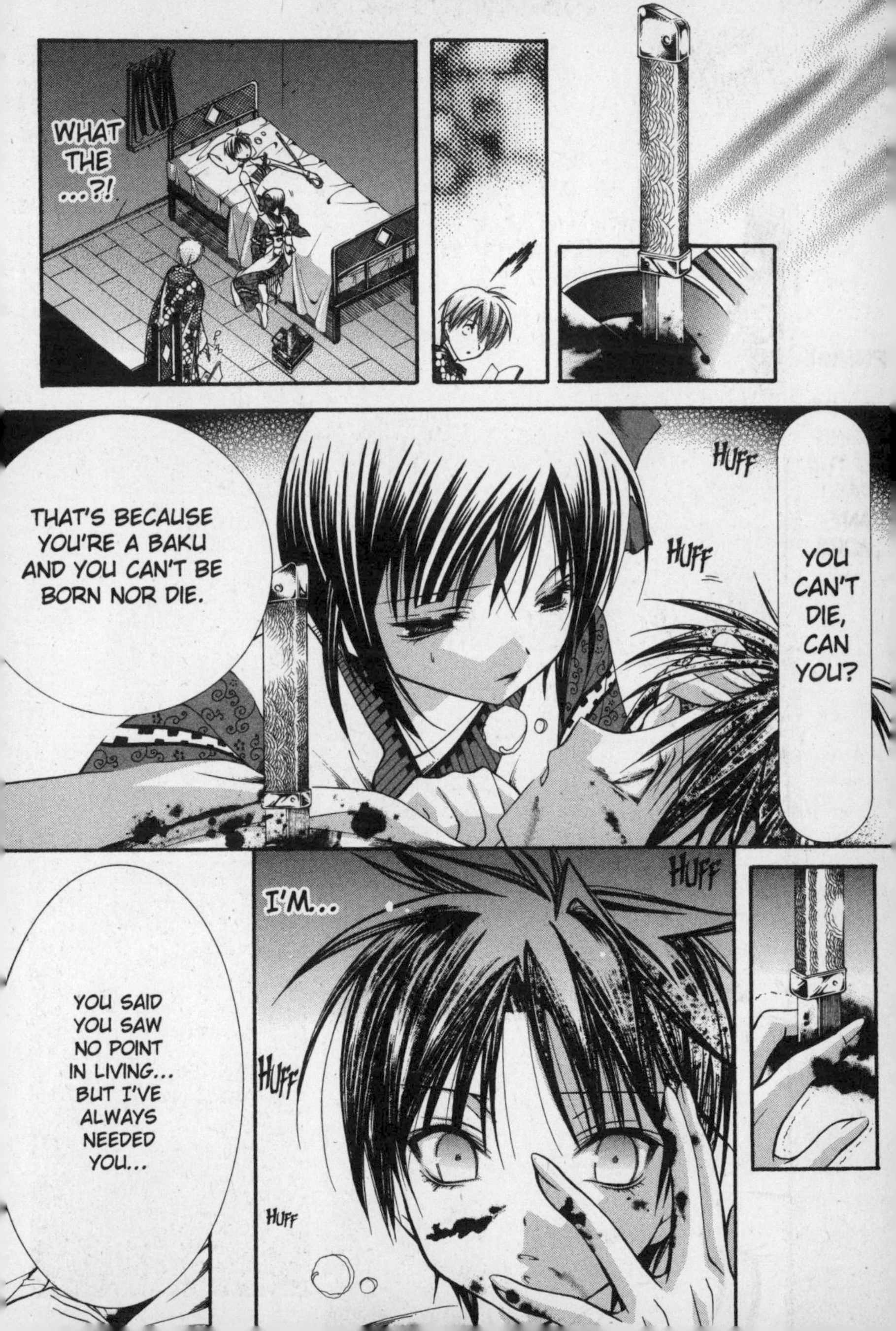
WHAT THE ...?!
HUFF
YOU CAN'T DIE, CAN YOU?
HUFF
THAT'S BECAUSE YOU'RE A BAKU AND YOU CAN'T BE BORN NOR DIE.
HUFF
I'M..
HUFF
HUFF
YOU SAID YOU SAW NO POINT IN LIVING... BUT I'VE ALWAYS NEEDED YOU...

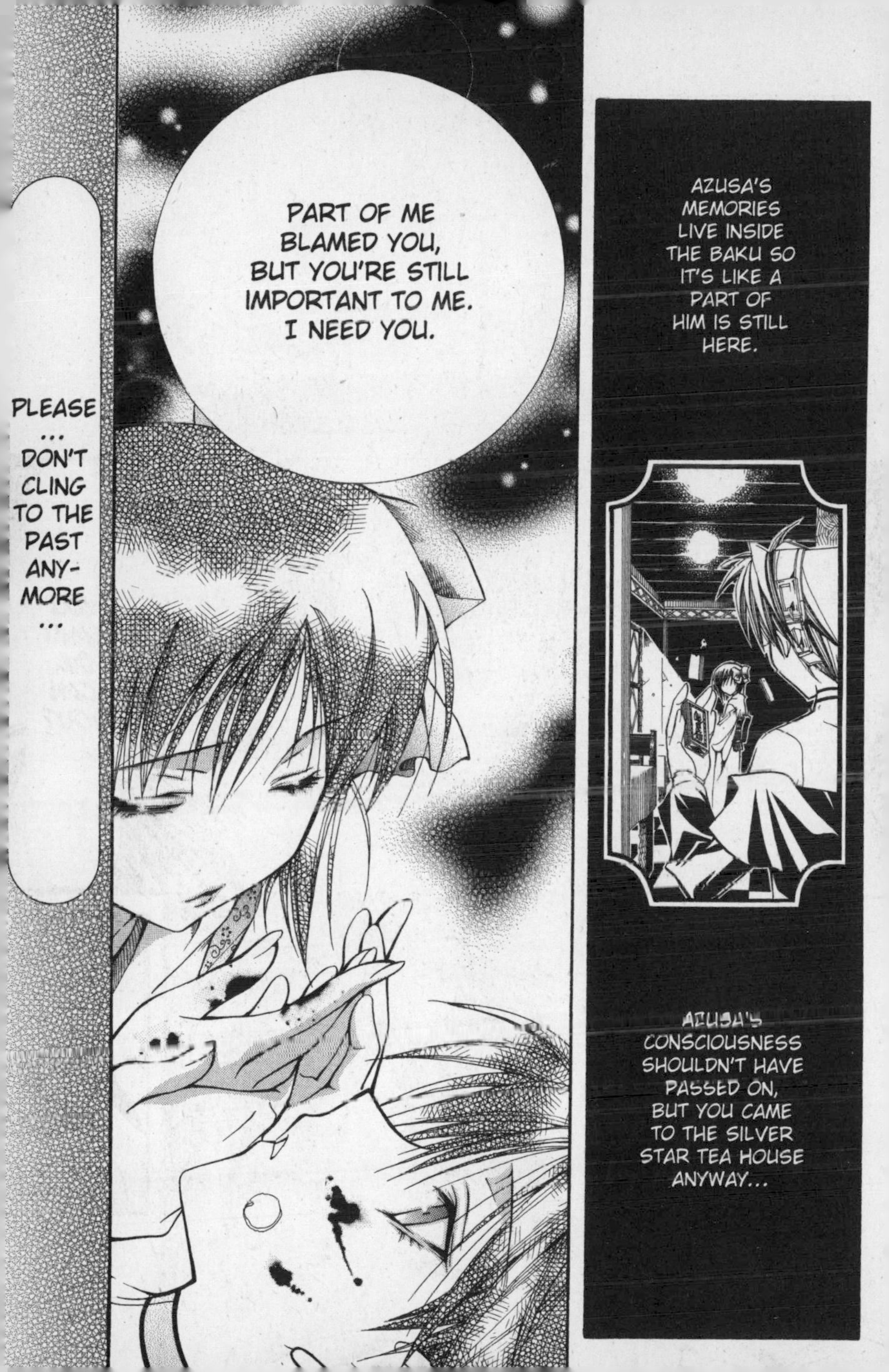
AZUSA'S MEMORIES LIVE INSIDE THE BAKU SO IT'S LIKE A PART OF HIM IS STILL HERE.
AZUSA'S CONSCIOUSNESS SHOULDN'T HAVE PASSED ON, BUT YOU CAME TO THE SILVER STAR TEA HOUSE ANYWAY...
PART OF ME BLAMED YOU, BUT YOU'RE STILL IMPORTANT TO ME. I NEED YOU.
PLEASE... DON'T CLING TO THE PAST ANYMORE...

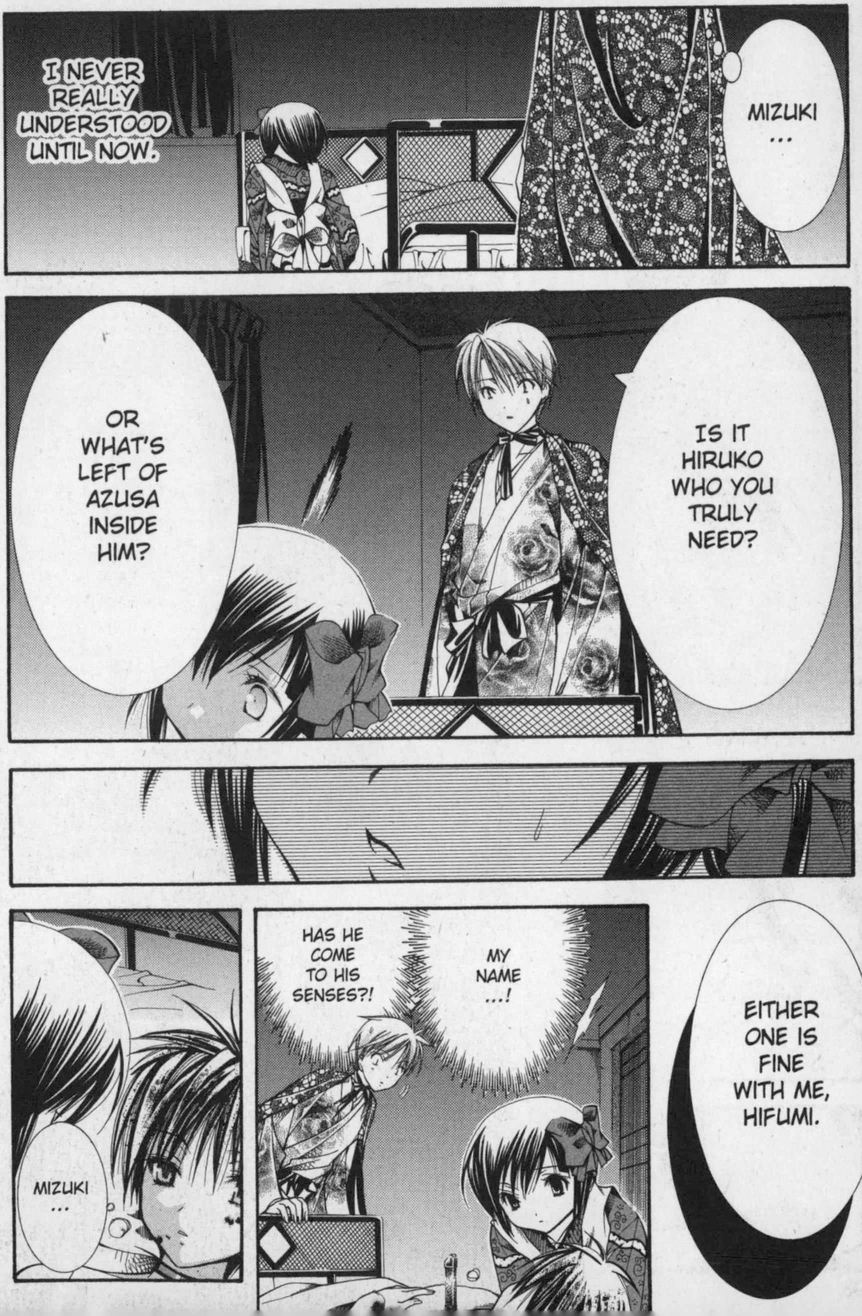
MIZUKI ...
I NEVER REALLY UNDERSTOOD UNTIL NOW.
IS IT HIRUKO WHO YOU TRULY NEED?
OR WHAT'S LEFT OF AZUSA INSIDE HIM?
EITHER ONE IS FINE WITH ME, HIFUMI.
MY NAME ...!
HAS HE COME TO HIS SENSES?!
MIZUKI ...

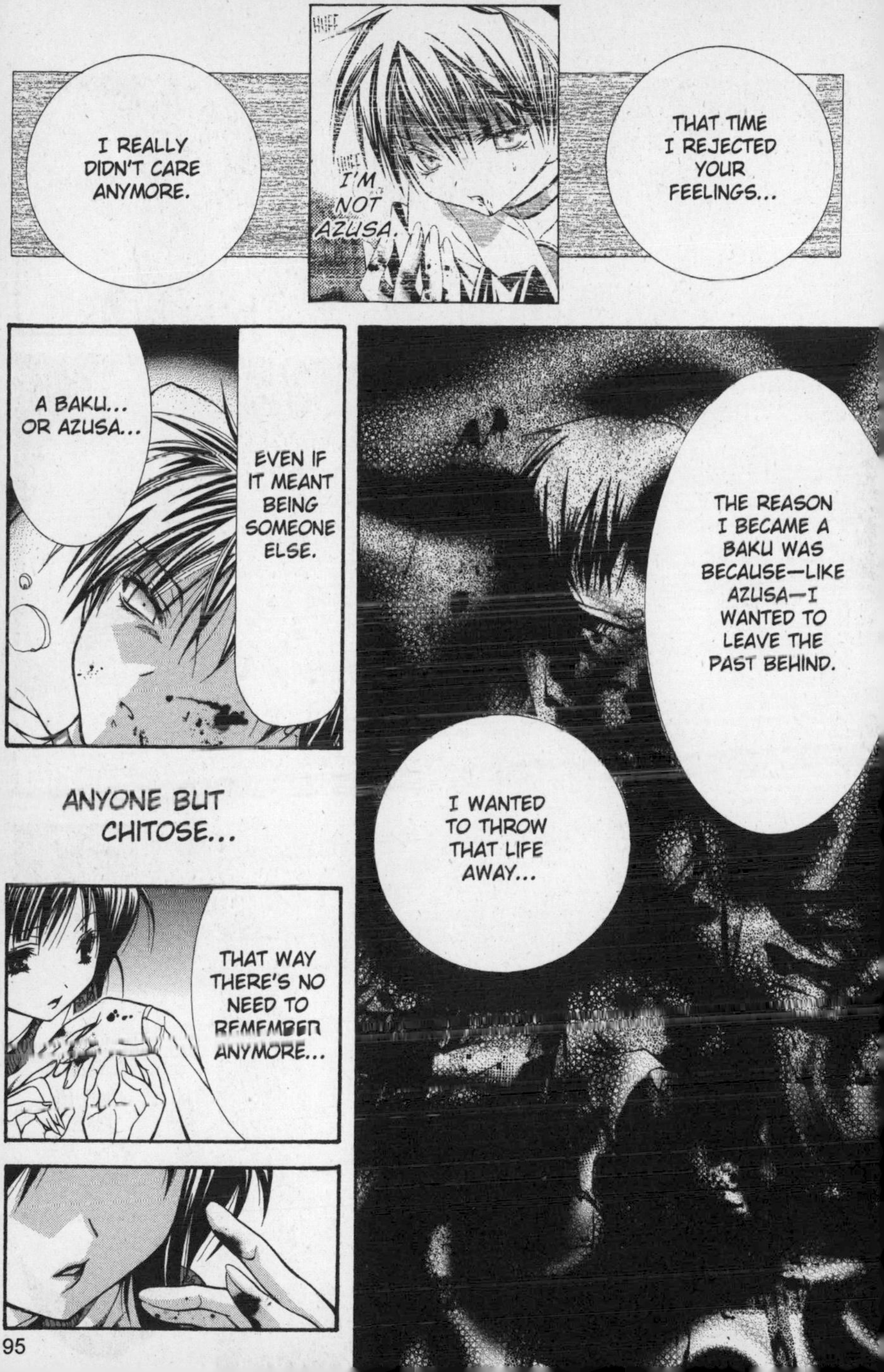
THAT TIME I REJECTED YOUR FEELINGS...
HUFF
HUFF
I'M NOT AZUSA.
I REALLY DIDN'T CARE ANYMORE.
THE REASON I BECAME A BAKU WAS BECAUSE—LIKE AZUSA—I WANTED TO LEAVE THE PAST BEHIND.
I WANTED TO THROW THAT LIFE AWAY...
EVEN IF IT MEANT BEING SOMEONE ELSE.
A BAKU... OR AZUSA...
ANYONE BUT CHITOSE...
THAT WAY THERE'S NO NEED TO REMEMBER ANYMORE...

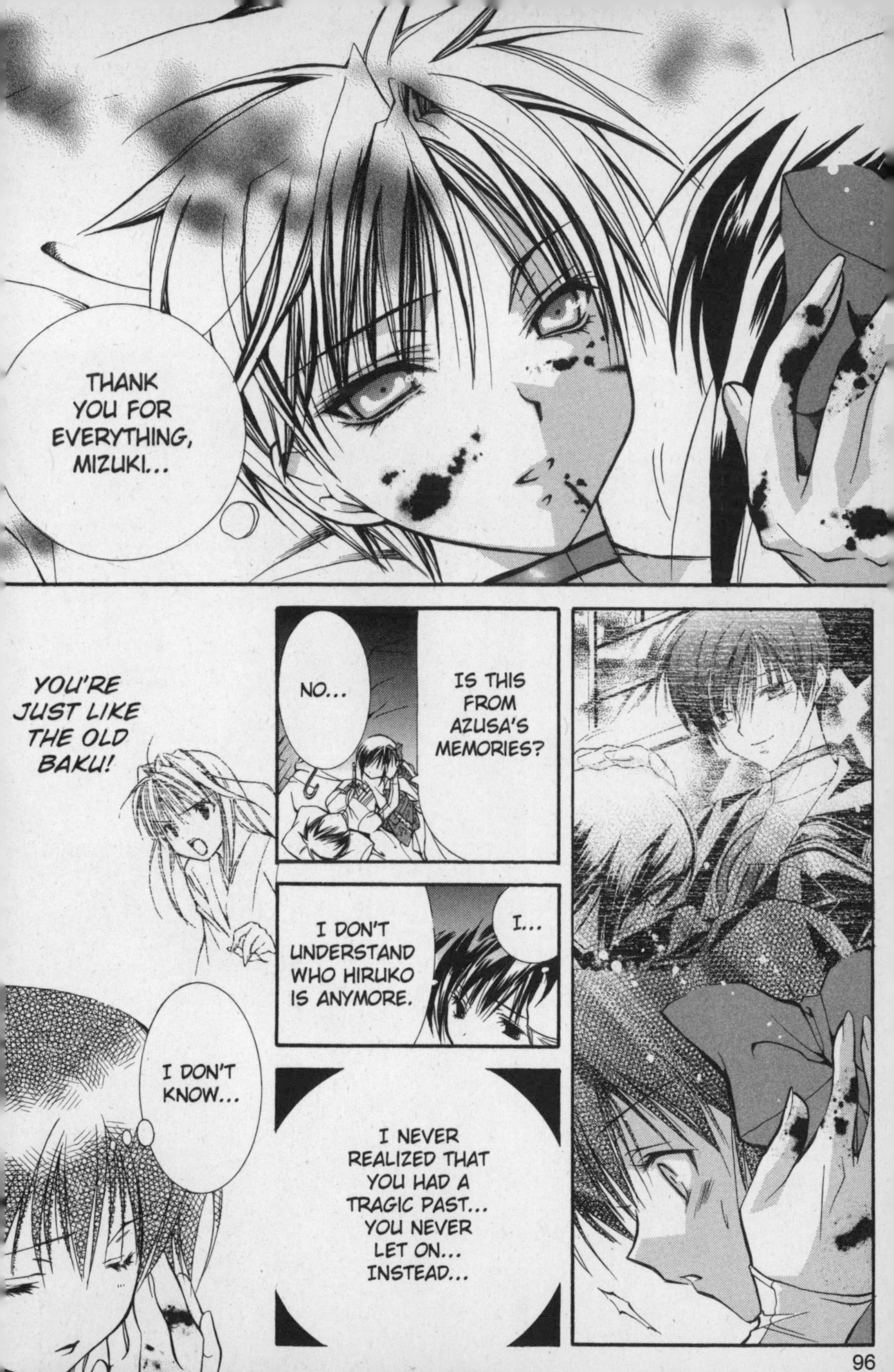
THANK YOU FOR EVERYTHING, MIZUKI...
IS THIS FROM AZUSA'S MEMORIES?
NO...
I...
I DON'T UNDERSTAND WHO HIRUKO IS ANYMORE.
I NEVER REALIZED THAT YOU HAD A TRAGIC PAST... YOU NEVER LET ON... INSTEAD...
YOU'RE JUST LIKE THE OLD BAKU!
I DON'T KNOW...

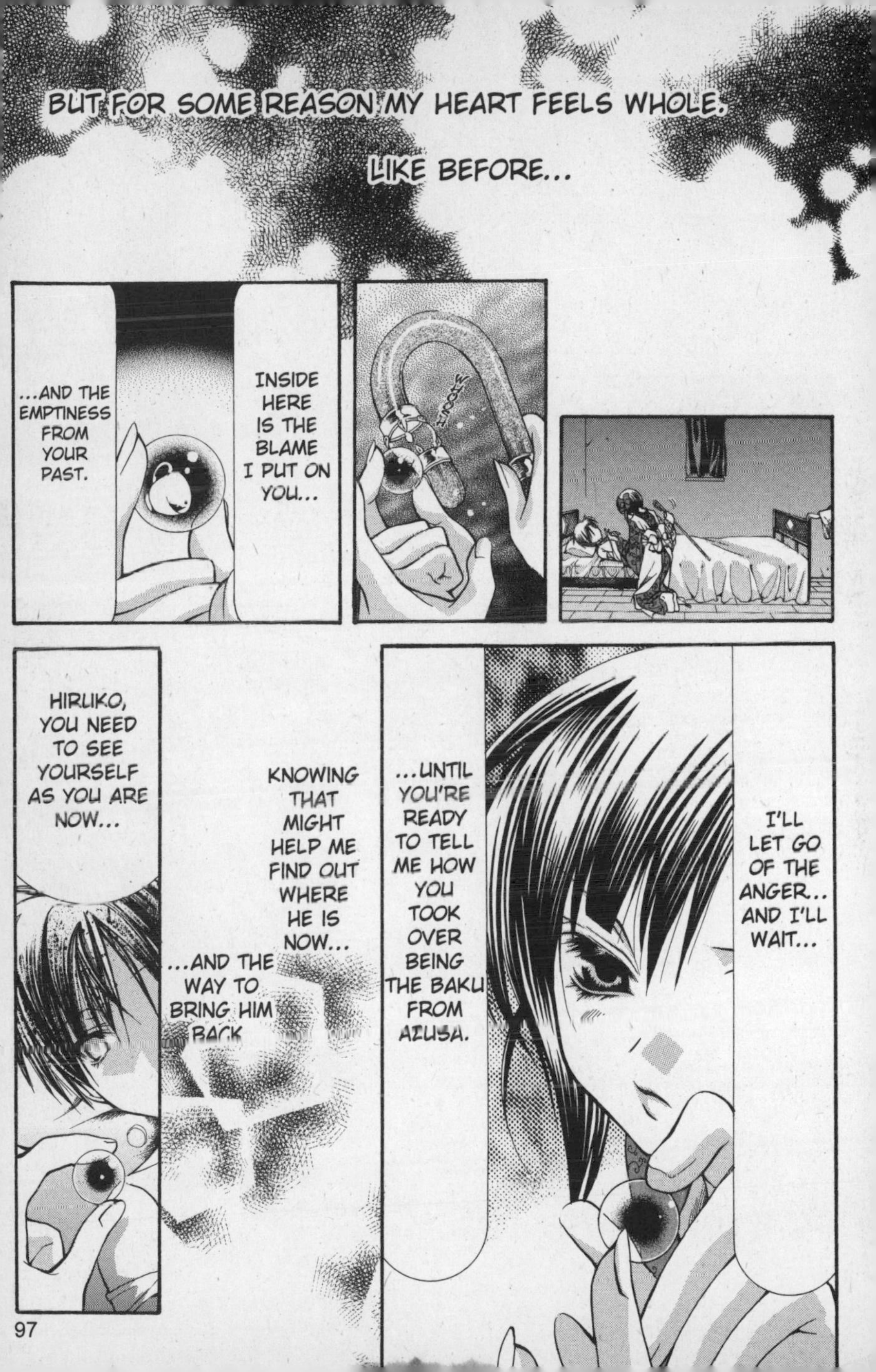
BUT FOR SOME REASON MY HEART FEELS WHOLE.
LIKE BEFORE...
INSIDE HERE IS THE BLAME I PUT ON YOU...
...AND THE EMPTINESS FROM YOUR PAST.
I'LL LET GO OF THE ANGER... AND I'LL WAIT...
...UNTIL YOU'RE READY TO TELL ME HOW YOU TOOK OVER BEING THE BAKU FROM AZUSA.
KNOWING THAT MIGHT HELP ME FIND OUT WHERE HE IS NOW...
...AND THE WAY TO BRING HIM BACK
HIRUKO, YOU NEED TO SEE YOURSELF AS YOU ARE NOW...

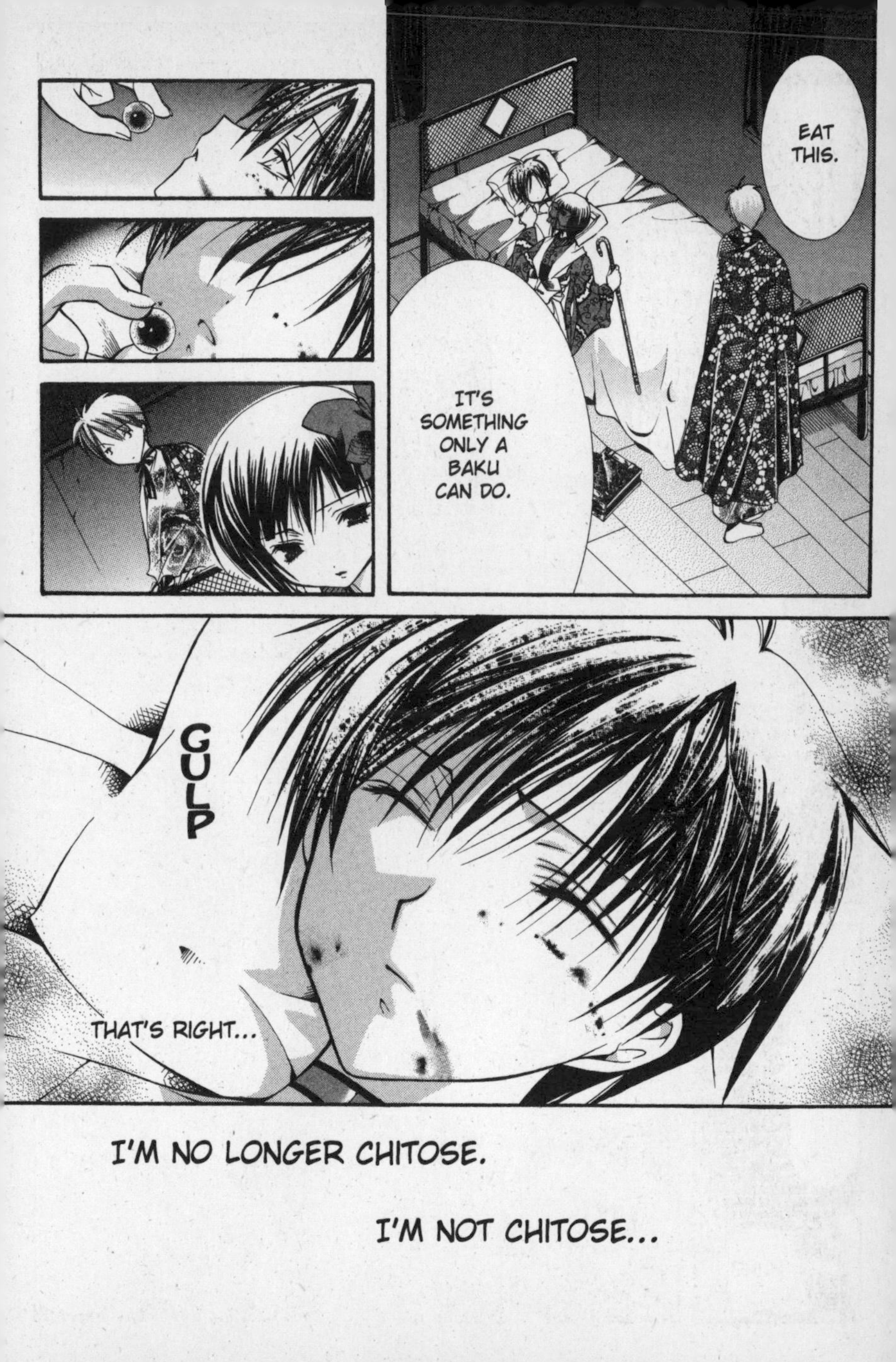
EAT THIS.
IT'S SOMETHING ONLY A BAKU CAN DO.
GULP
THAT'S RIGHT...
I'M NO LONGER CHITOSE.
I'M NOT CHITOSE...

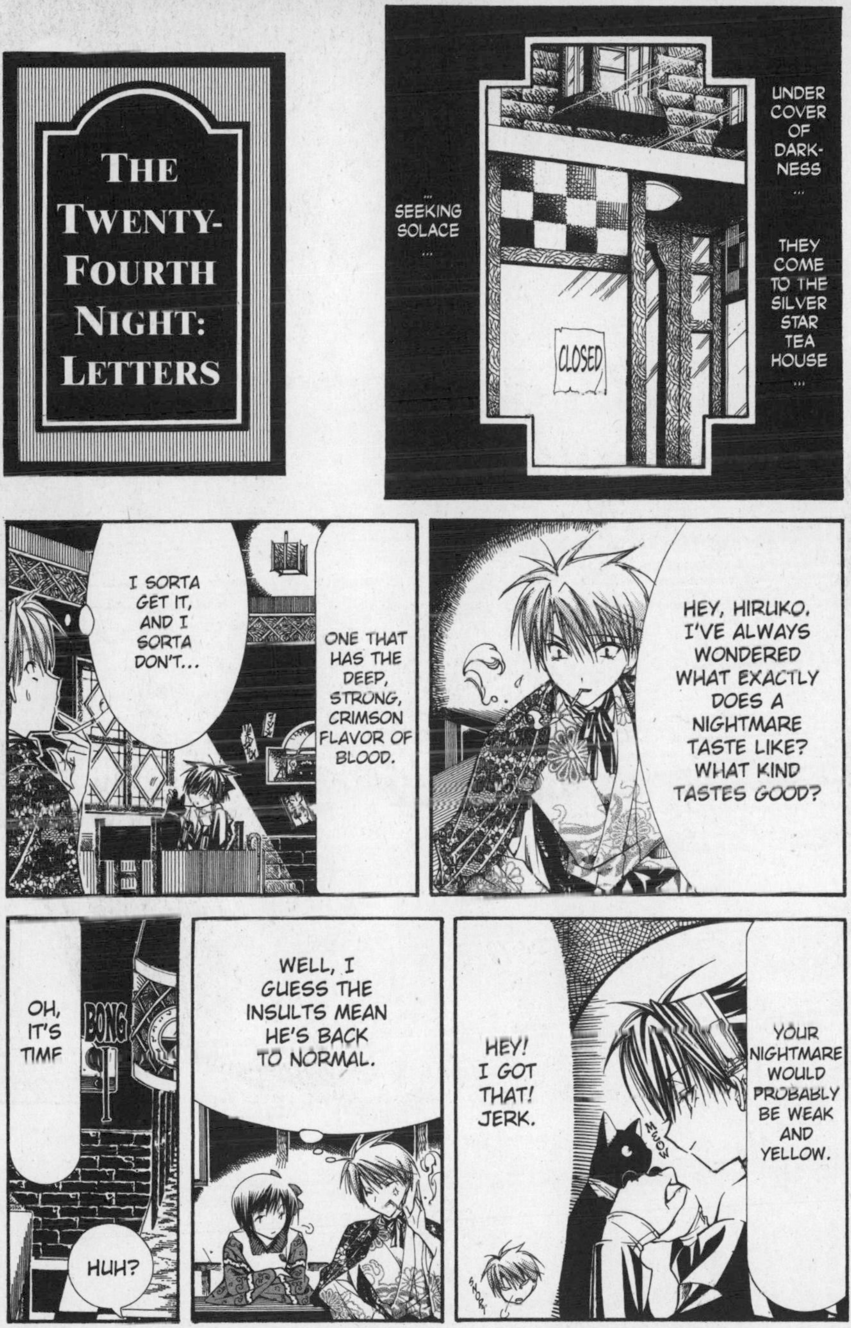
UNDER COVER OF DARKNESS...
THEY COME TO THE SILVER STAR TEA HOUSE...
CLOSED
...SEEKING SOLACE...
THE TWENTY-FOURTH NIGHT: LETTERS
HEY, HIRUKO. I'VE ALWAYS WONDERED WHAT EXACTLY DOES A NIGHTMARE TASTE LIKE? WHAT KIND TASTES GOOD?
ONE THAT HAS THE DEEP, STRONG, CRIMSON FLAVOR OF BLOOD.
I SORTA GET IT, AND I SORTA DON'T...
YOUR NIGHTMARE WOULD PROBABLY BE WEAK AND YELLOW.
MEOW
HEY! I GOT THAT! JERK.
SNORT
WELL, I GUESS THE INSULTS MEAN HE'S BACK TO NORMAL.
BONG
OH, IT'S TIME
HUH?

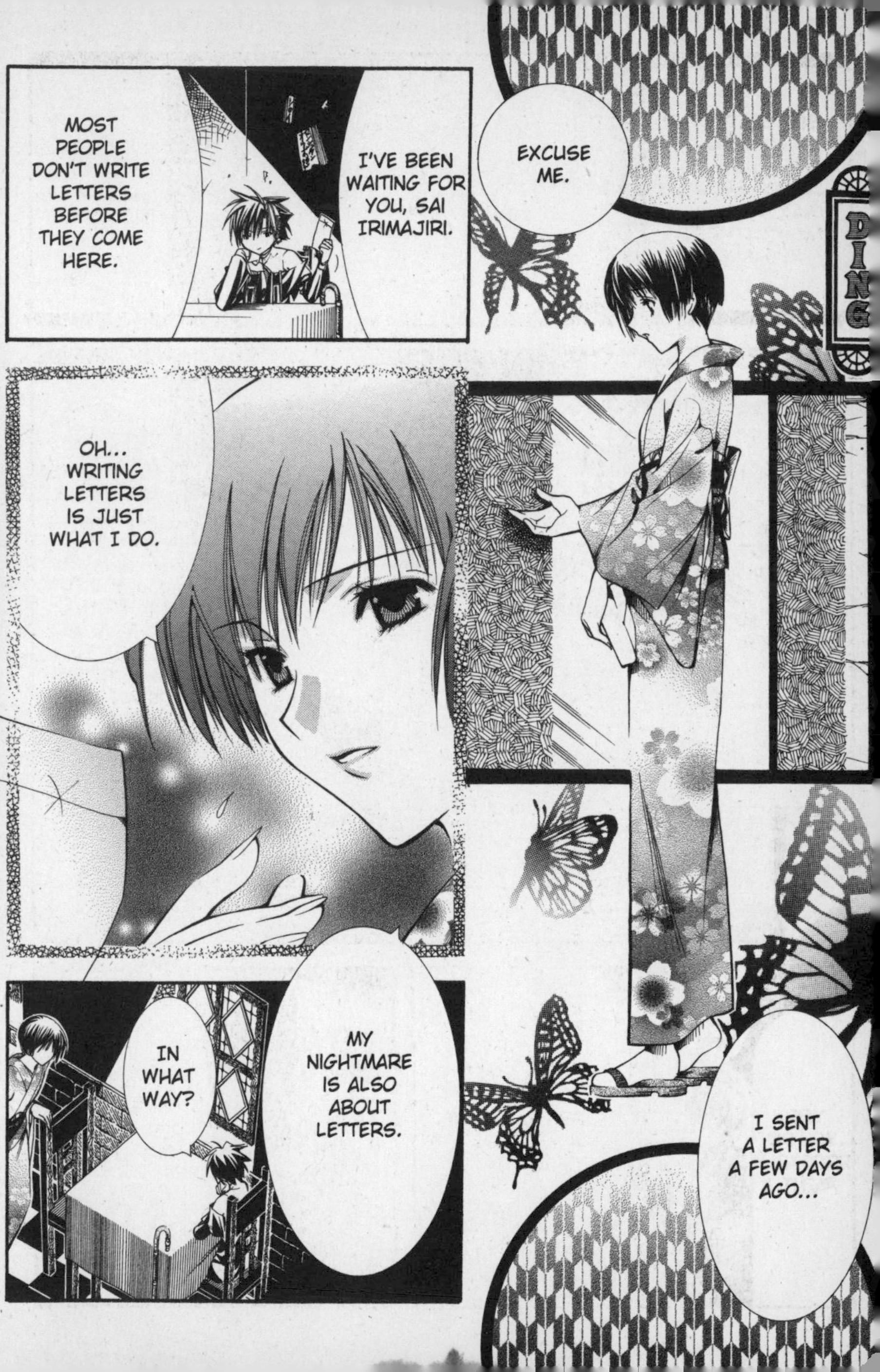
EXCUSE ME.
DING
I SENT A LETTER A FEW DAYS AGO...
I'VE BEEN WAITING FOR YOU, SAI IRIMAJIRI.
MOST PEOPLE DON'T WRITE LETTERS BEFORE THEY COME HERE.
OH... WRITING LETTERS IS JUST WHAT I DO.
MY NIGHTMARE IS ALSO ABOUT LETTERS.
IN WHAT WAY?

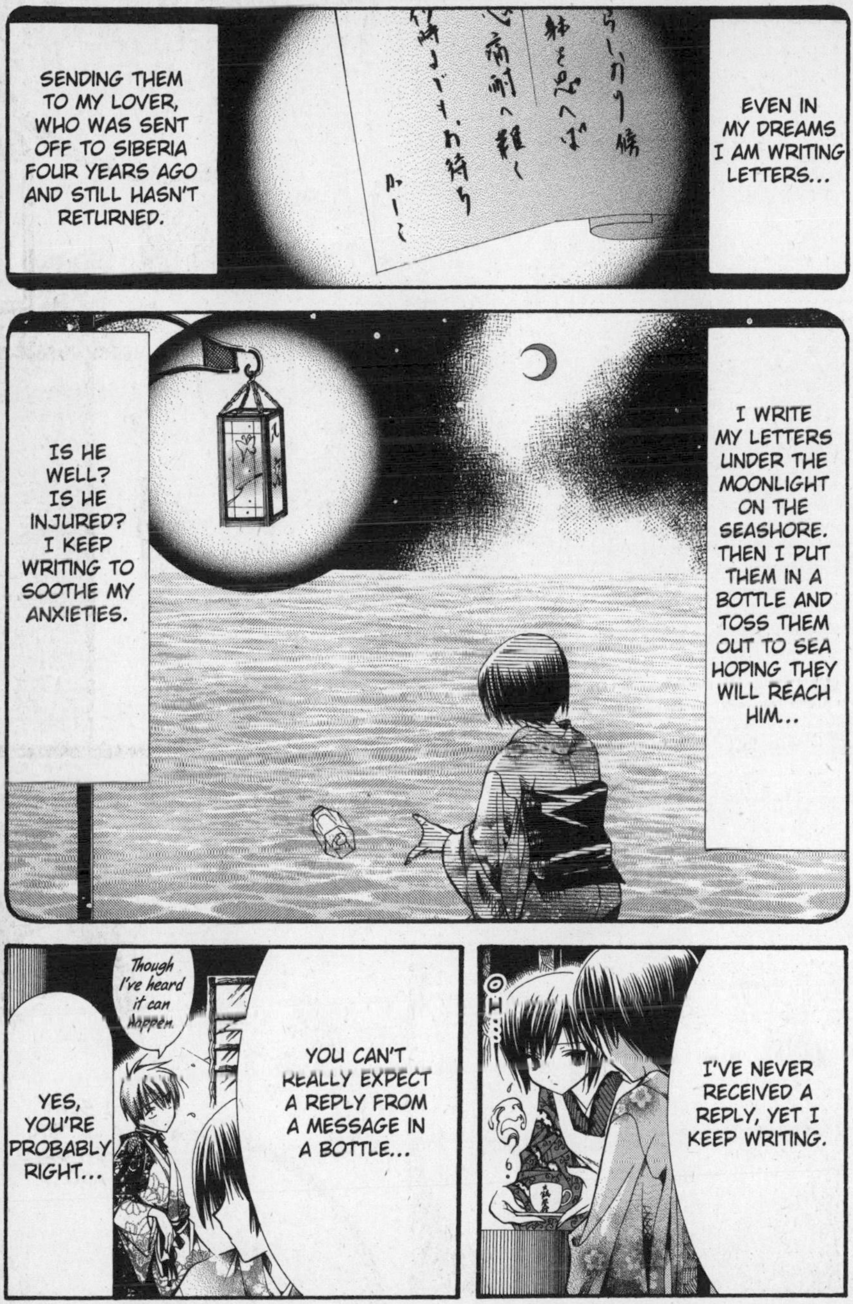
EVEN IN MY DREAMS I AM WRITING LETTERS...
SENDING THEM TO MY LOVER, WHO WAS SENT OFF TO SIBERIA FOUR YEARS AGO AND STILL HASN'T RETURNED.
I WRITE MY LETTERS UNDER THE MOONLIGHT ON THE SEASHORE. THEN I PUT THEM IN A BOTTLE AND TOSS THEM OUT TO SEA HOPING THEY WILL REACH HIM..
IS HE WELL? IS HE INJURED? I KEEP WRITING TO SOOTHE MY ANXIETIES.
I'VE NEVER RECEIVED A REPLY, YET I KEEP WRITING.
YOU CAN'T REALLY EXPECT A REPLY FROM A MESSAGE IN A BOTTLE...
Though I've heard it can happen.
YES, YOU'RE PROBABLY RIGHT...

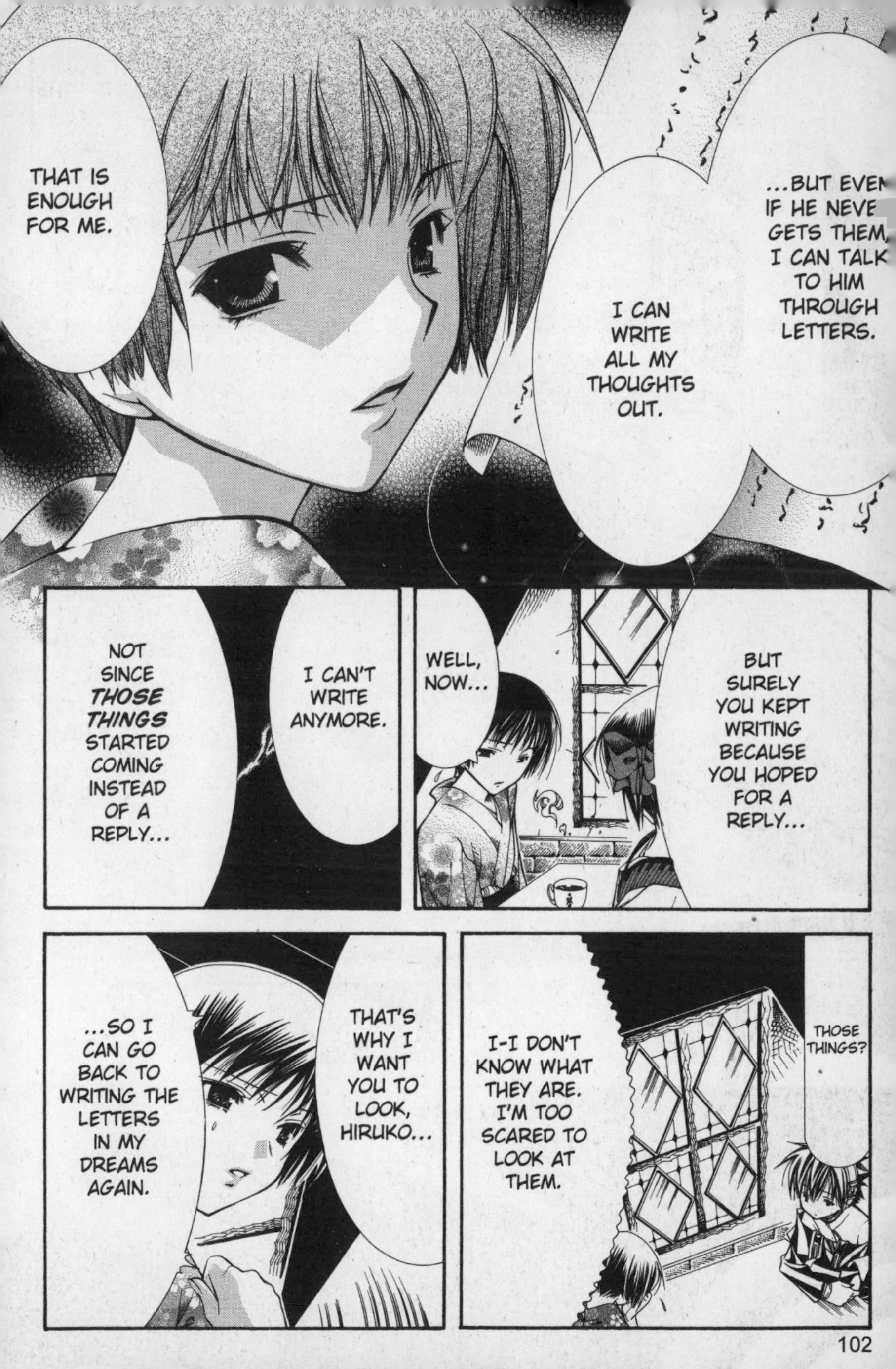
...BUT EVEN IF HE NEVE GETS THEM, I CAN TALK TO HIM THROUGH LETTERS.
I CAN WRITE ALL MY THOUGHTS OUT.
THAT IS ENOUGH FOR ME.
BUT SURELY YOU KEPT WRITING BECAUSE YOU HOPED FOR A REPLY...
WELL, NOW...
I CAN'T WRITE ANYMORE.
NOT SINCE *THOSE THINGS* STARTED COMING INSTEAD OF A REPLY...
THOSE THINGS?
I-I DON'T KNOW WHAT THEY ARE. I'M TOO SCARED TO LOOK AT THEM.
THAT'S WHY I WANT YOU TO LOOK, HIRUKO...
...SO I CAN GO BACK TO WRITING THE LETTERS IN MY DREAMS AGAIN.

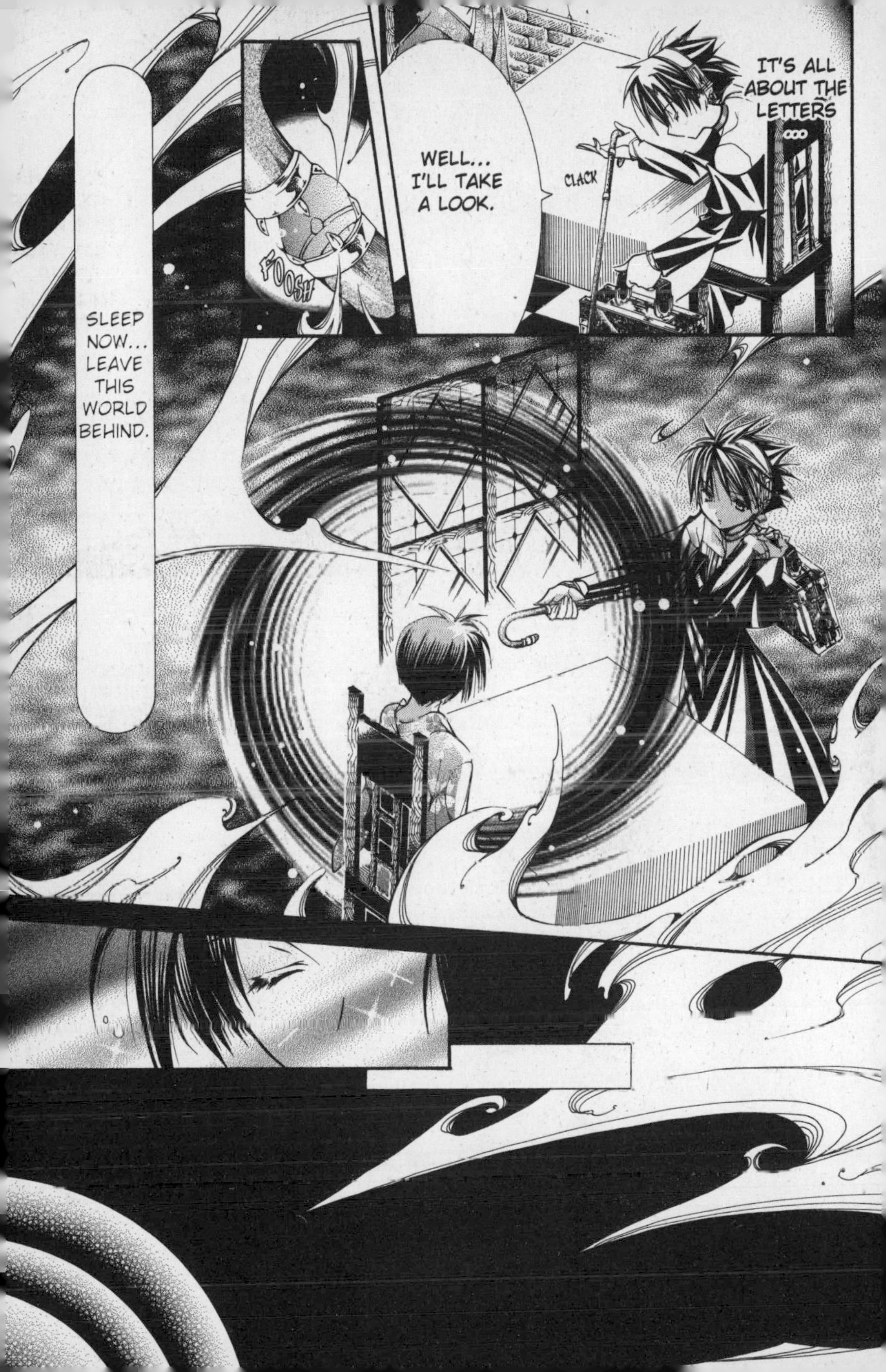
IT'S ALL ABOUT THE LETTERS...
CLACK
WELL... I'LL TAKE A LOOK.
FOOSH
SLEEP NOW... LEAVE THIS WORLD BEHIND.

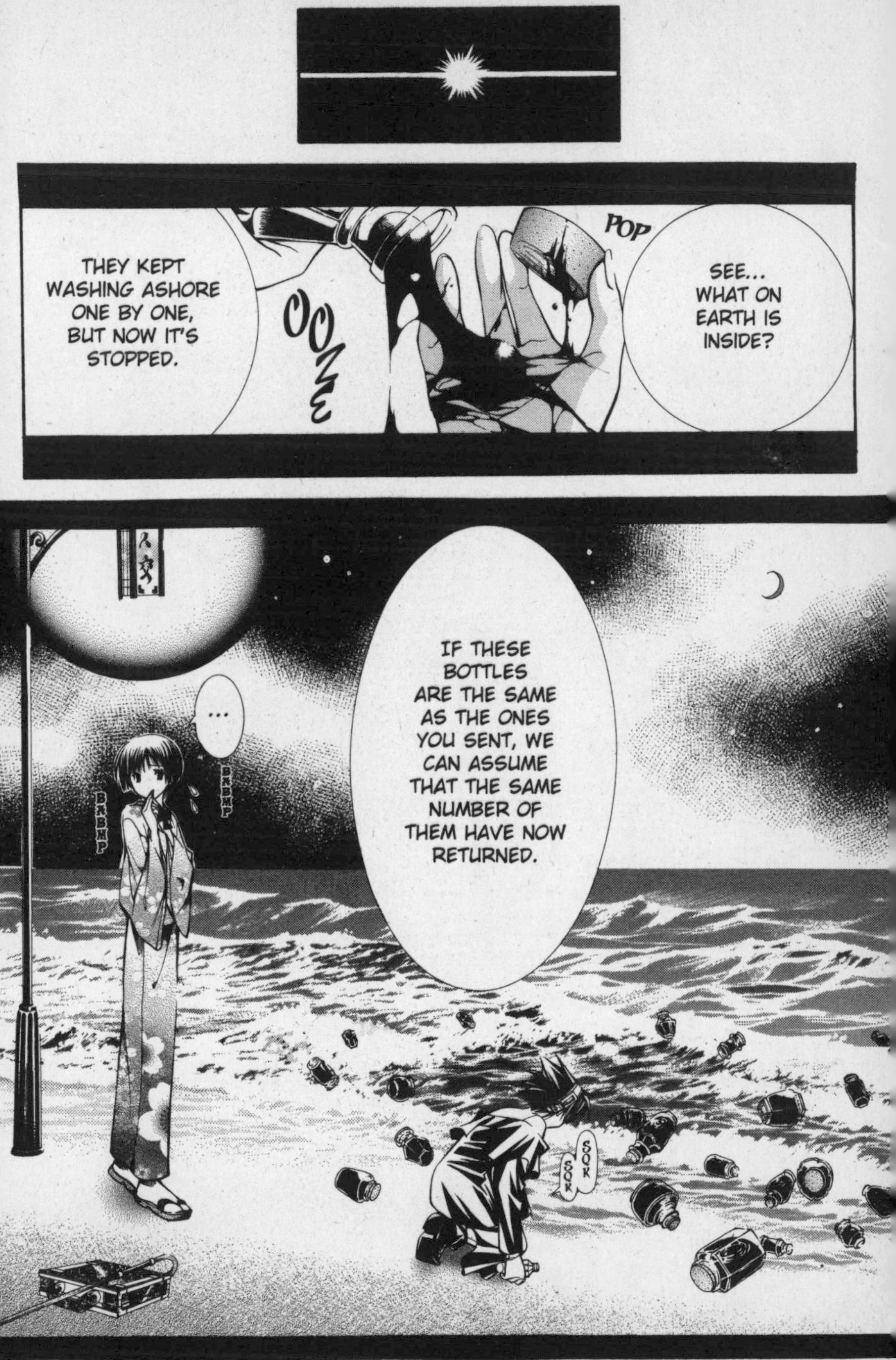
POP
SEE... WHAT ON EARTH IS INSIDE?
OOZE
THEY KEPT WASHING ASHORE ONE BY ONE, BUT NOW IT'S STOPPED.
IF THESE BOTTLES ARE THE SAME AS THE ONES YOU SENT, WE CAN ASSUME THAT THE SAME NUMBER OF THEM HAVE NOW RETURNED.
...
BABMP
BABMP
SQK
SQK

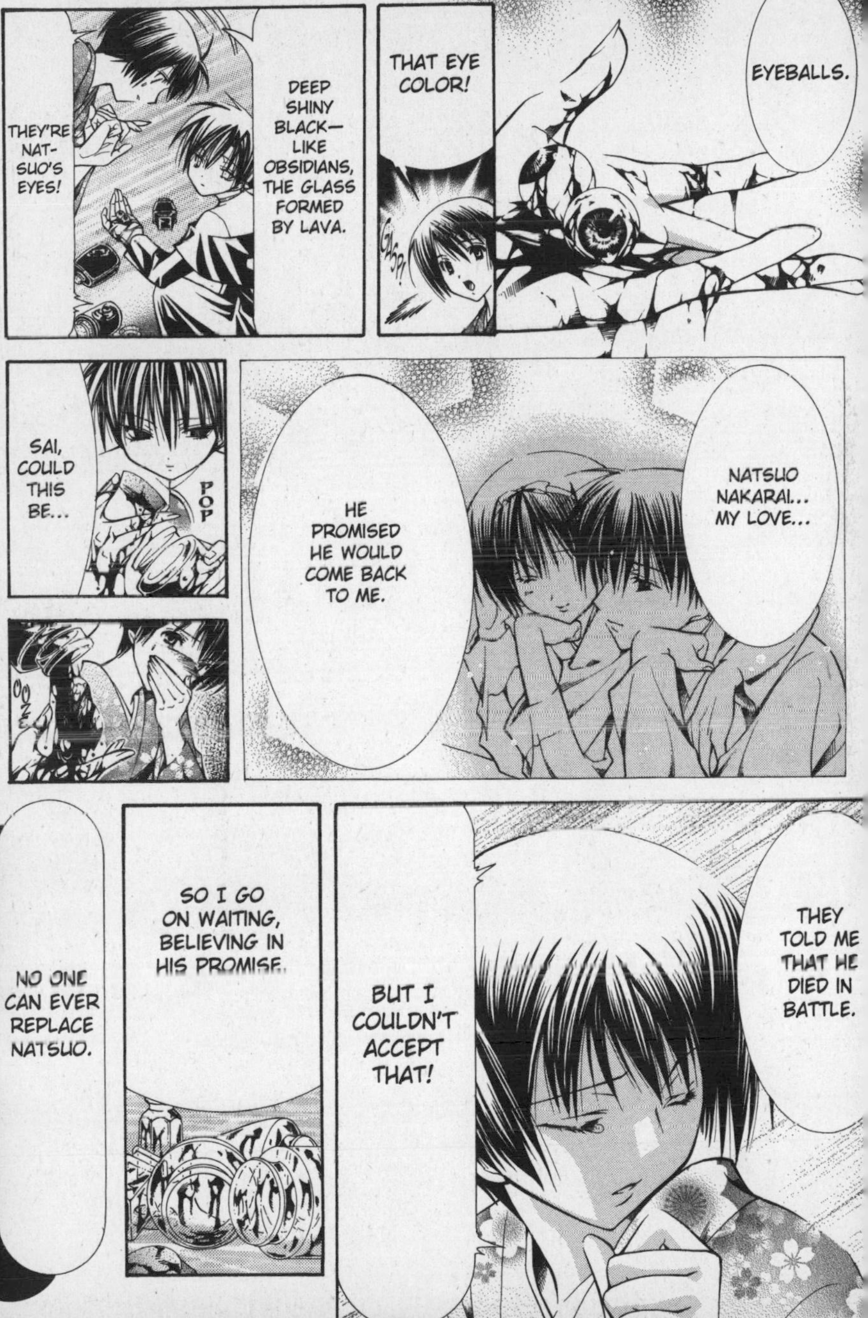
EYEBALLS.
THAT EYE COLOR!
GASP!
DEEP SHINY BLACK—LIKE OBSIDIANS, THE GLASS FORMED BY LAVA.
THEY'RE NATSUO'S EYES!
NATSUO NAKARAI... MY LOVE...
HE PROMISED HE WOULD COME BACK TO ME.
SAI, COULD THIS BE...
POP
OOZE
THEY TOLD ME THAT HE DIED IN BATTLE.
BUT I COULDN'T ACCEPT THAT!
SO I GO ON WAITING, BELIEVING IN HIS PROMISE.
NO ONE CAN EVER REPLACE NATSUO.

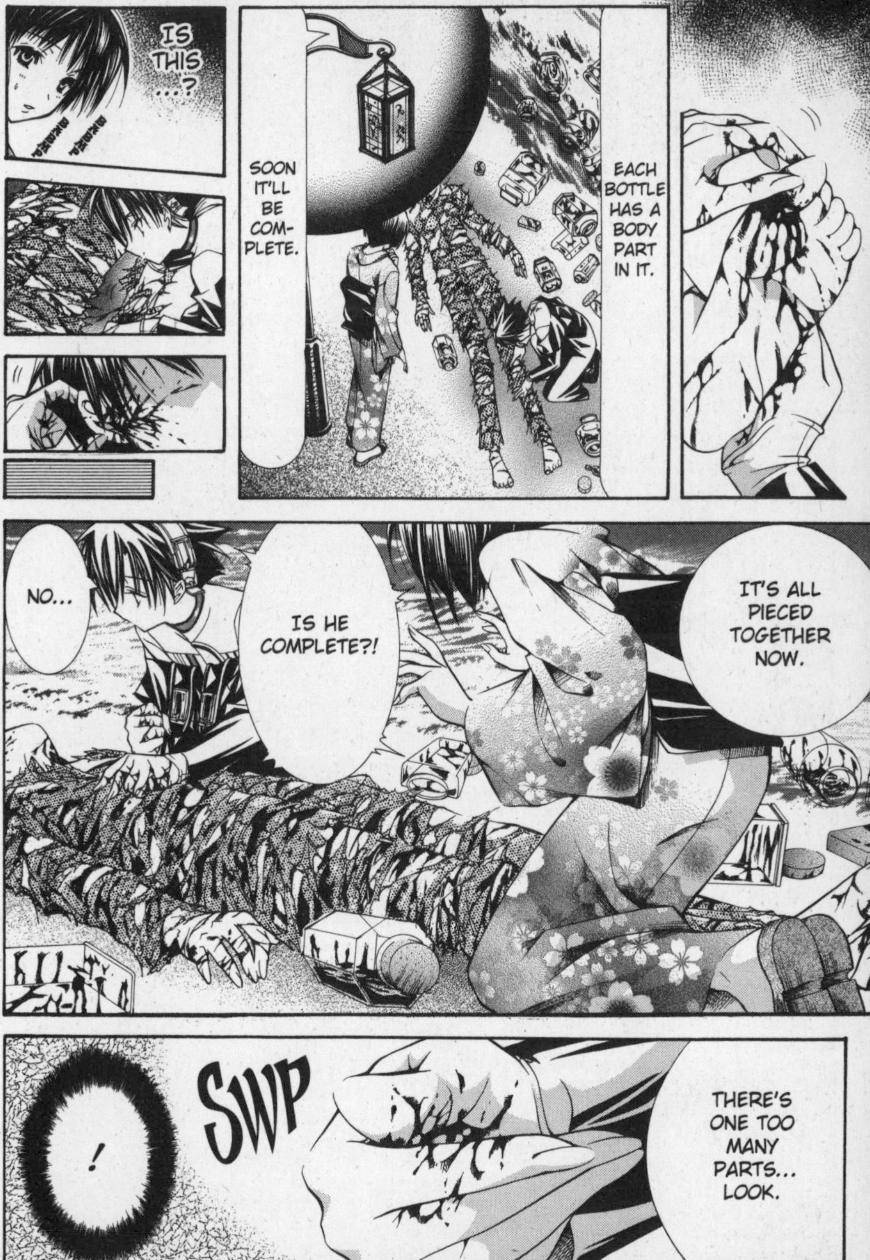
EACH BOTTLE HAS A BODY PART IN IT.
SOON IT'LL BE COM- PLETE.
IS THIS ...?
IT'S ALL PIECED TOGETHER NOW.
IS HE COMPLETE?!
NO...
THERE'S ONE TOO MANY PARTS... LOOK.
SWP
!

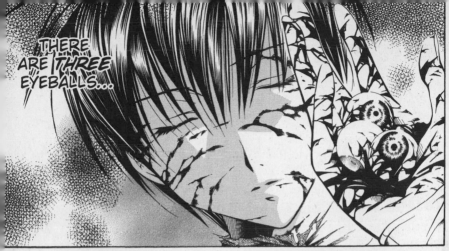

THERE ARE THREE EYEBALLS...
THAT'S STRANGE.
ONE OF THEM IS CLOUDED.
IT WAS IN A DIFFERENT BOTTLE FROM THE OTHER TWO.
IS IT FAMILIAR?
NO!
IT ISN'T NATSUO'S!
THIS EYEBALL HAS NOTHING TO DO WITH NATSUO!
THE EYES THAT I LOVE SHINE LIKE OBSIDIANS.

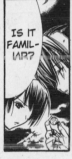

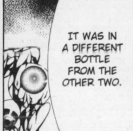

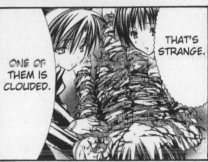

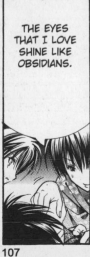

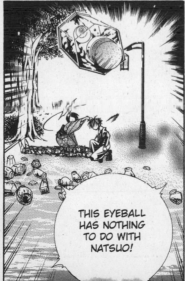

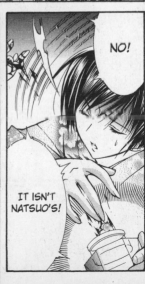

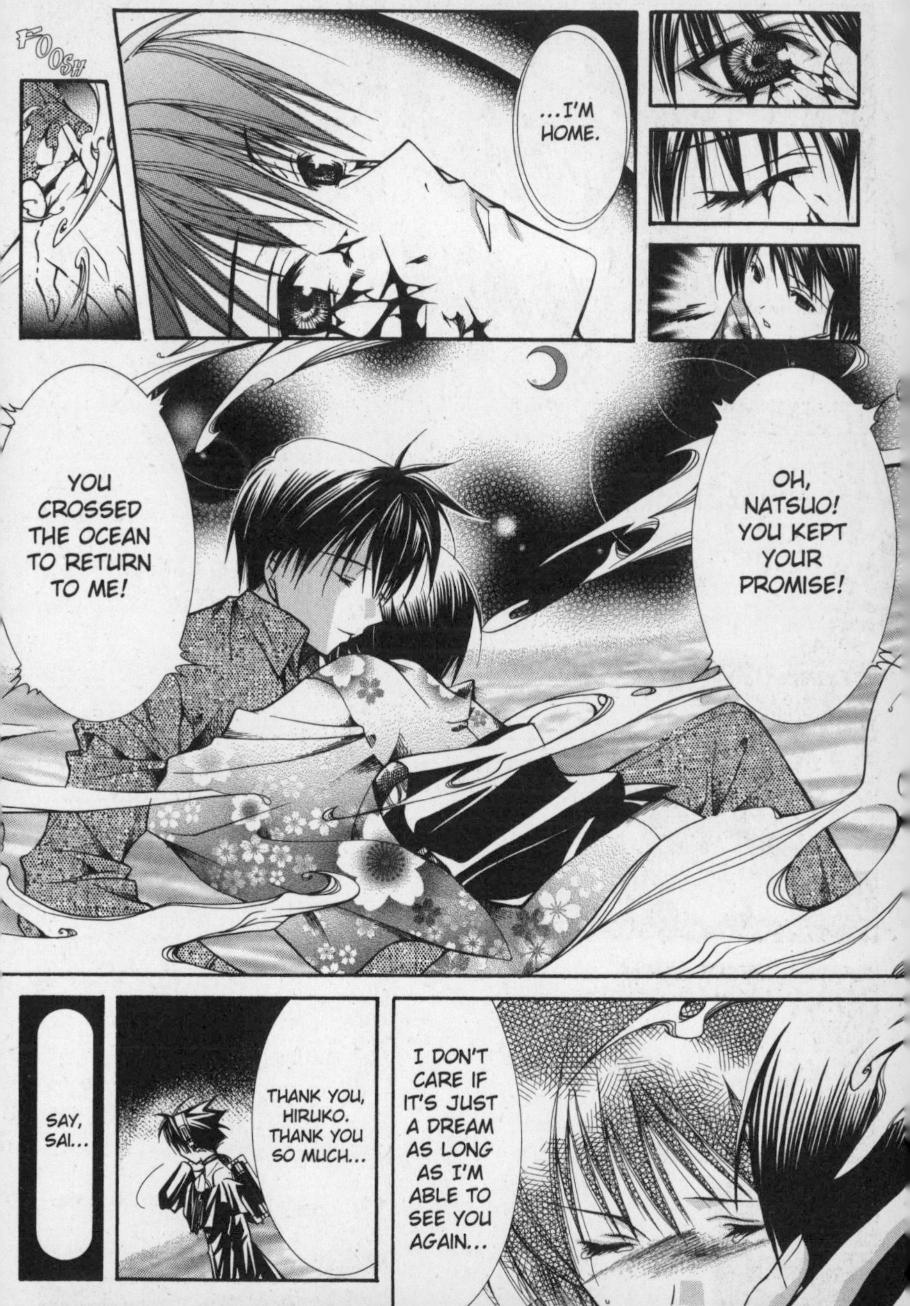
...I'M HOME.
FOOSH
OH, NATSUO! YOU KEPT YOUR PROMISE!
YOU CROSSED THE OCEAN TO RETURN TO ME!
I DON'T CARE IF IT'S JUST A DREAM AS LONG AS I'M ABLE TO SEE YOU AGAIN...
THANK YOU, HIRUKO. THANK YOU SO MUCH...
SAY, SAI...

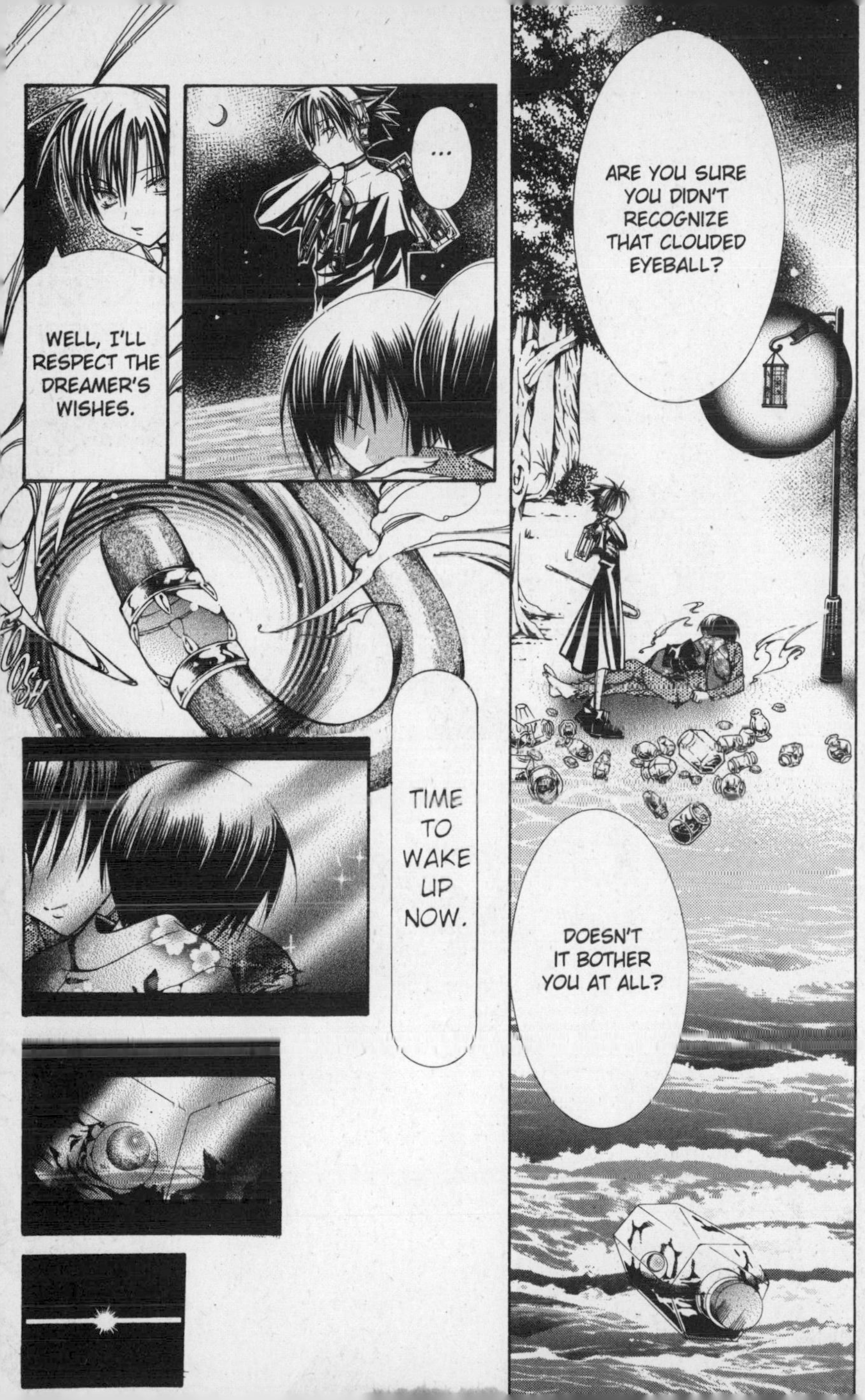
ARE YOU SURE YOU DIDN'T RECOGNIZE THAT CLOUDED EYEBALL?
DOESN'T IT BOTHER YOU AT ALL?
...
WELL, I'LL RESPECT THE DREAMER'S WISHES.
TIME TO WAKE UP NOW.

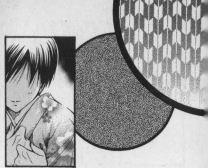

It was so-so.

I'M HAPPY FOR YOU, SAI.

I GUESS THE ANXIOUS FEELINGS IN YOUR LETTERS SOMEHOW TURNED INTO HIS BODY...

...TO REUNITE YOU WITH A LOVED ONE WHO IS NO LONGER ALIVE.

!

DING

EXCUSE ME...

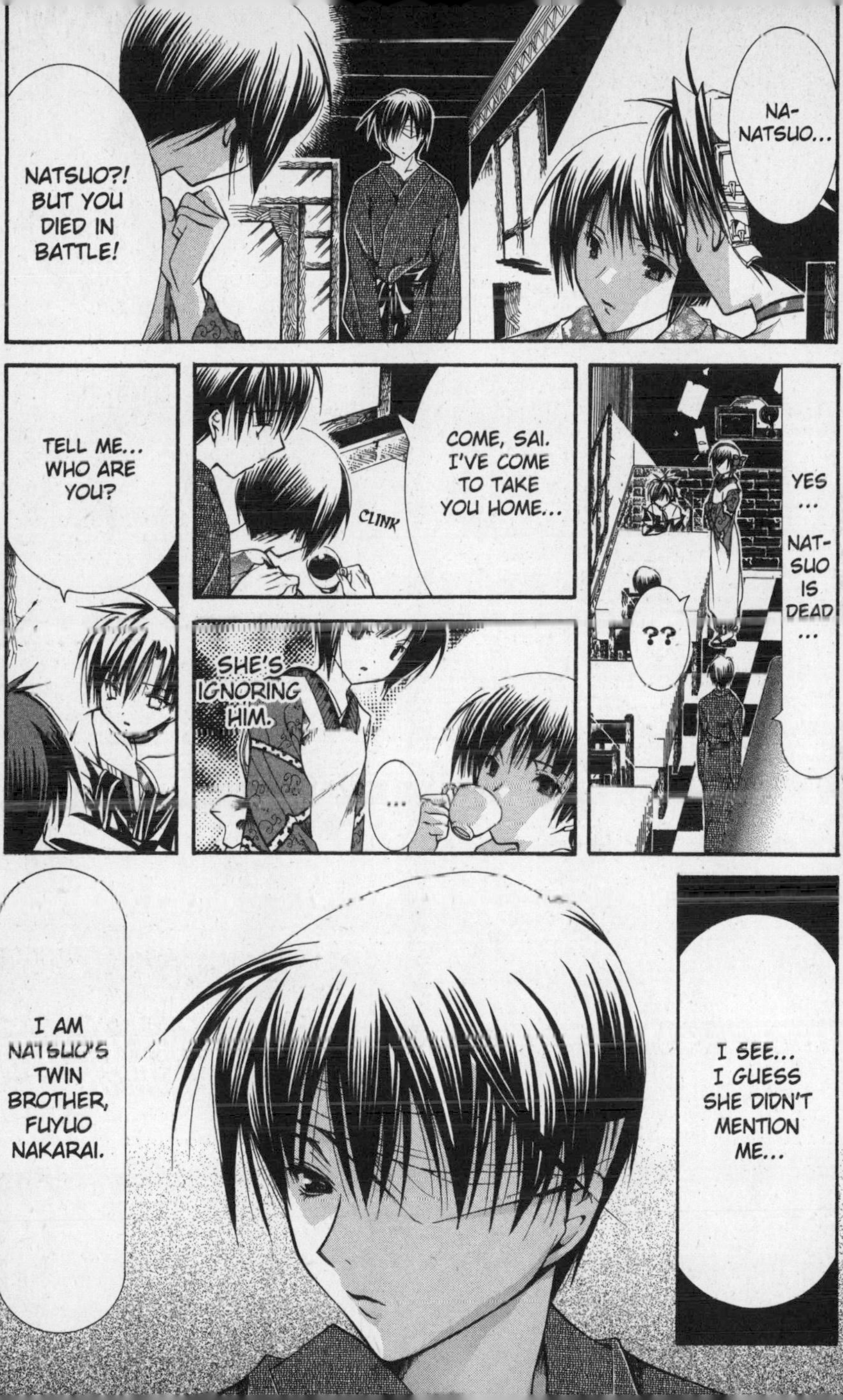
NA-NATSUO...
NATSUO?! BUT YOU DIED IN BATTLE!
YES... NATSUO IS DEAD...
??
COME, SAI. I'VE COME TO TAKE YOU HOME...
CLINK
SHE'S IGNORING HIM.
...
TELL ME... WHO ARE YOU?
I SEE... I GUESS SHE DIDN'T MENTION ME...
I AM NATSUO'S TWIN BROTHER, FUYUO NAKARAI.

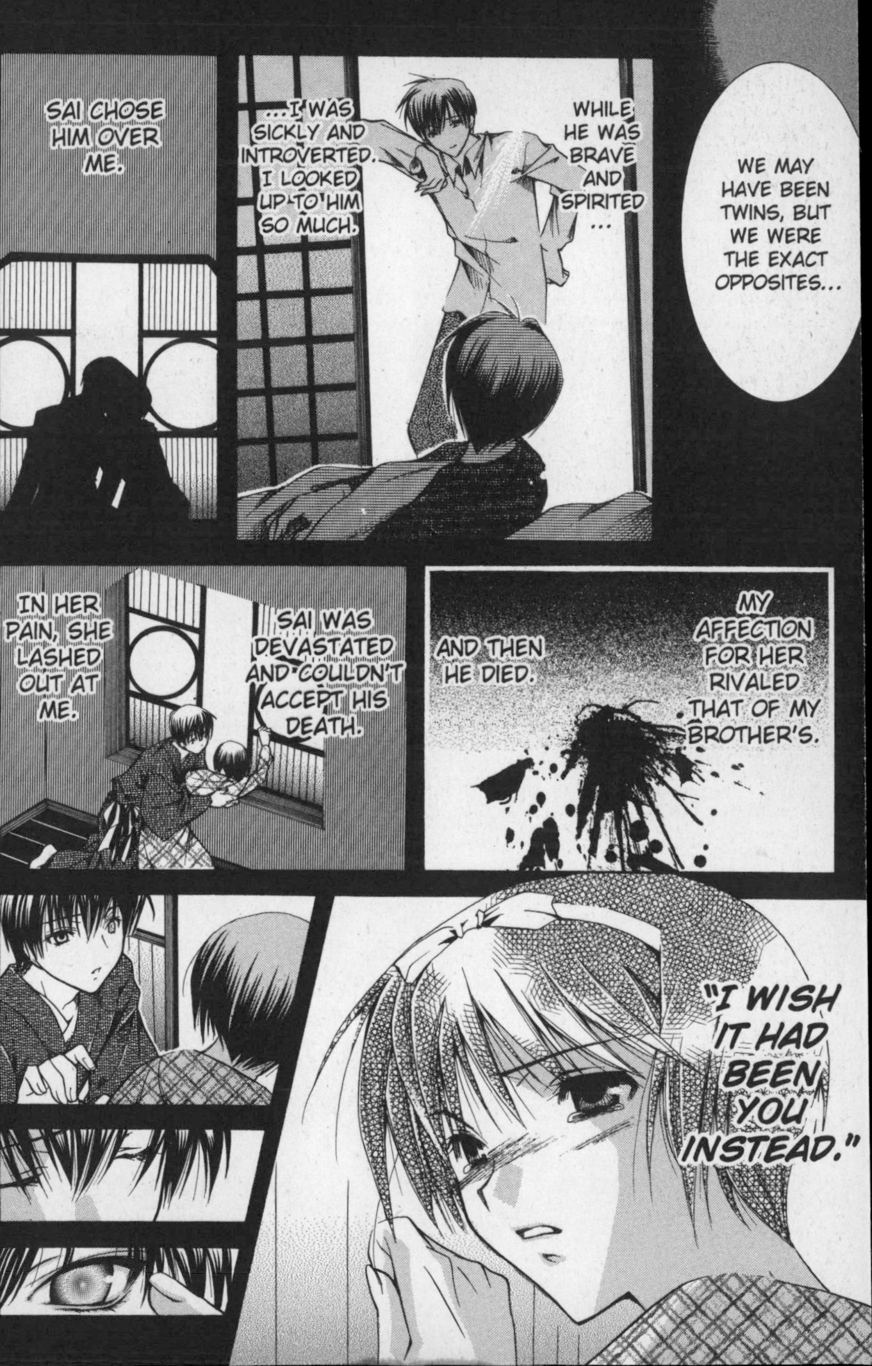
WE MAY HAVE BEEN TWINS, BUT WE WERE THE EXACT OPPOSITES...
WHILE HE WAS BRAVE AND SPIRITED...
...I WAS SICKLY AND INTROVERTED. I LOOKED UP TO HIM SO MUCH.
SAI CHOSE HIM OVER ME.
MY AFFECTION FOR HER RIVALED THAT OF MY BROTHER'S.
AND THEN HE DIED.
SAI WAS DEVASTATED AND COULDN'T ACCEPT HIS DEATH.
IN HER PAIN, SHE LASHED OUT AT ME.
"I WISH IT HAD BEEN YOU INSTEAD."

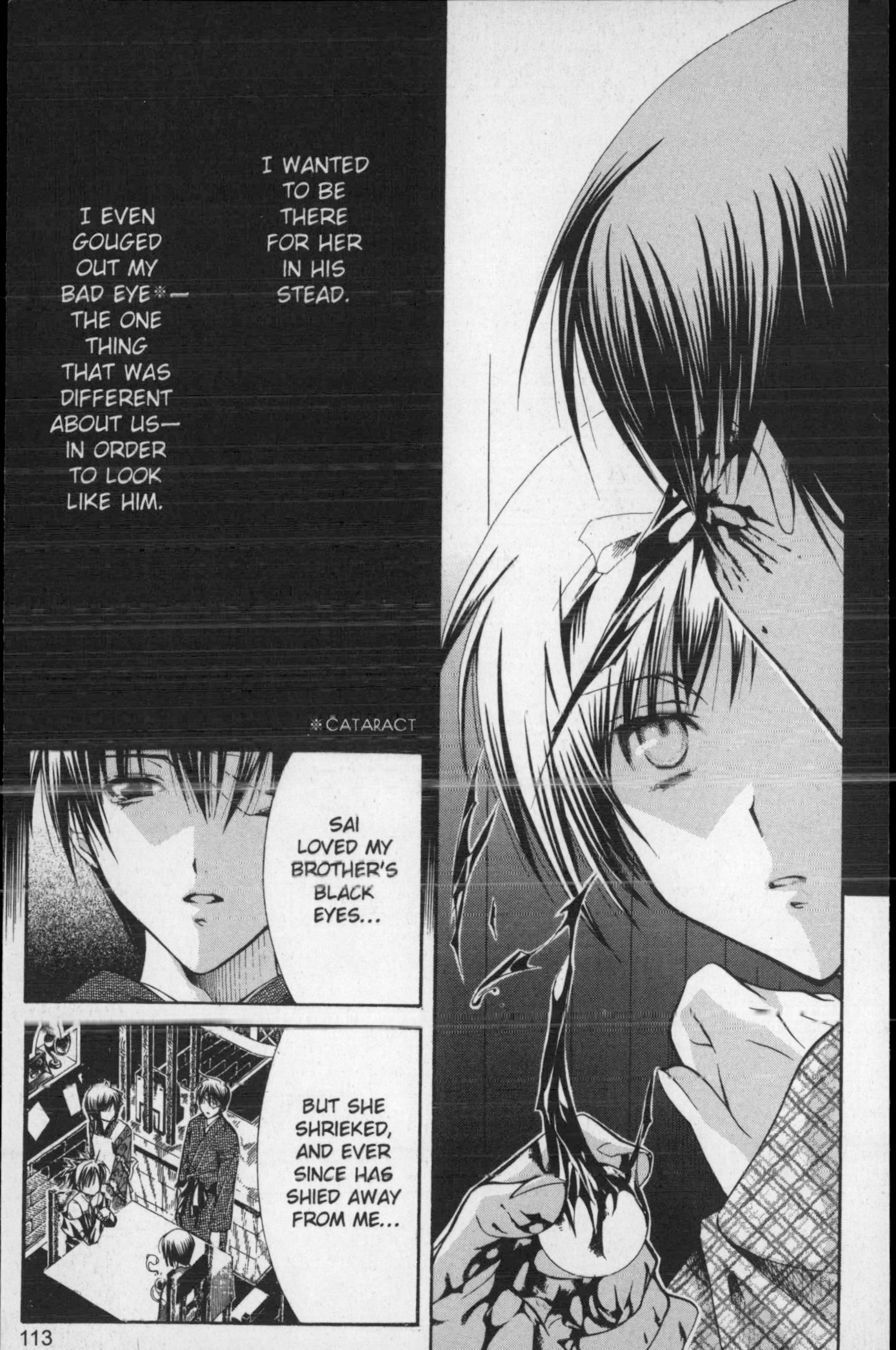
I WANTED TO BE THERE FOR HER IN HIS STEAD.
I EVEN GOUGED OUT MY BAD EYE※— THE ONE THING THAT WAS DIFFERENT ABOUT US— IN ORDER TO LOOK LIKE HIM.
※CATARACT
SAI LOVED MY BROTHER'S BLACK EYES...
BUT SHE SHRIEKED, AND EVER SINCE HAS SHIED AWAY FROM ME...

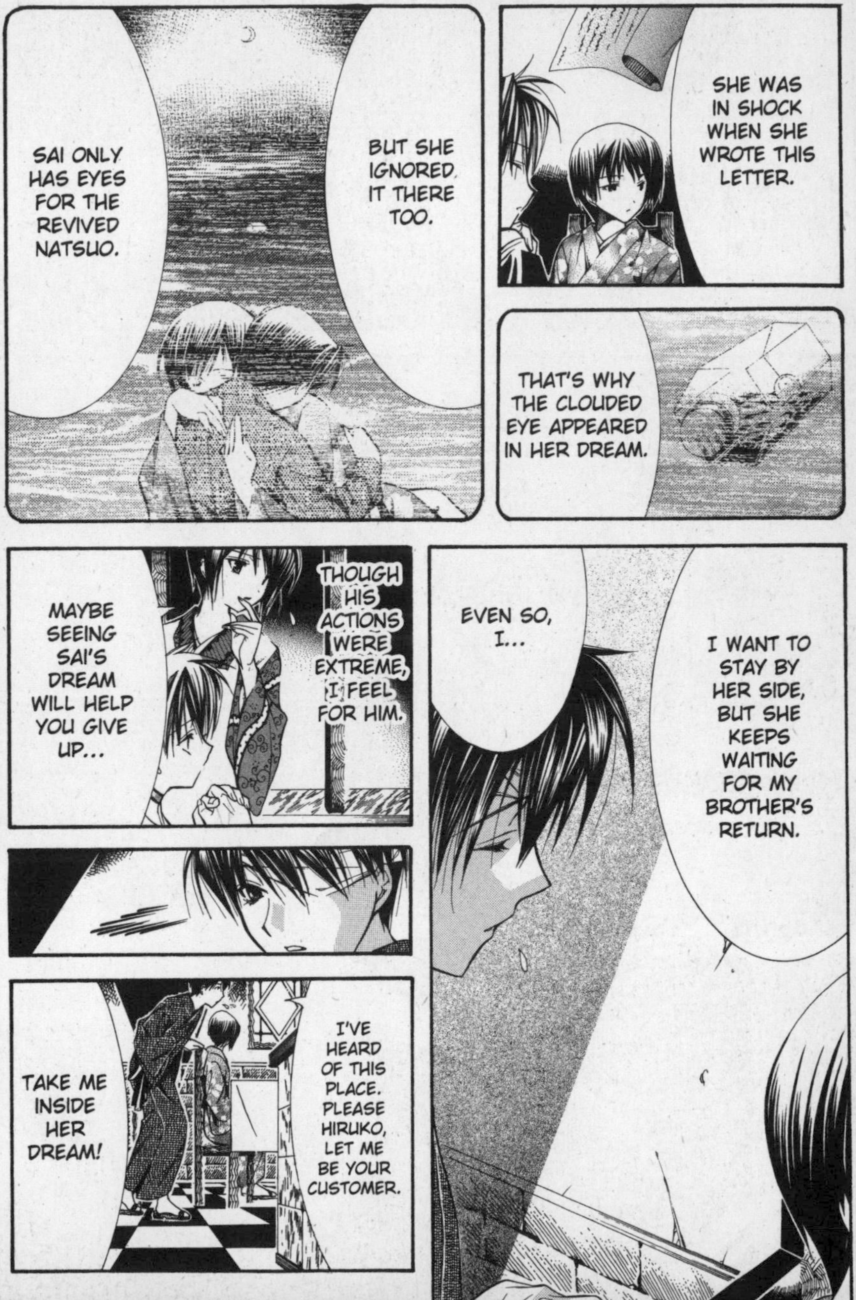

SHE WAS IN SHOCK WHEN SHE WROTE THIS LETTER.
THAT'S WHY THE CLOUDED EYE APPEARED IN HER DREAM.
BUT SHE IGNORED IT THERE TOO.
SAI ONLY HAS EYES FOR THE REVIVED NATSUO.
I WANT TO STAY BY HER SIDE, BUT SHE KEEPS WAITING FOR MY BROTHER'S RETURN.
EVEN SO, I...
THOUGH HIS ACTIONS WERE EXTREME, I FEEL FOR HIM.
MAYBE SEEING SAI'S DREAM WILL HELP YOU GIVE UP...
I'VE HEARD OF THIS PLACE. PLEASE HIRUKO, LET ME BE YOUR CUSTOMER.
TAKE ME INSIDE HER DREAM!

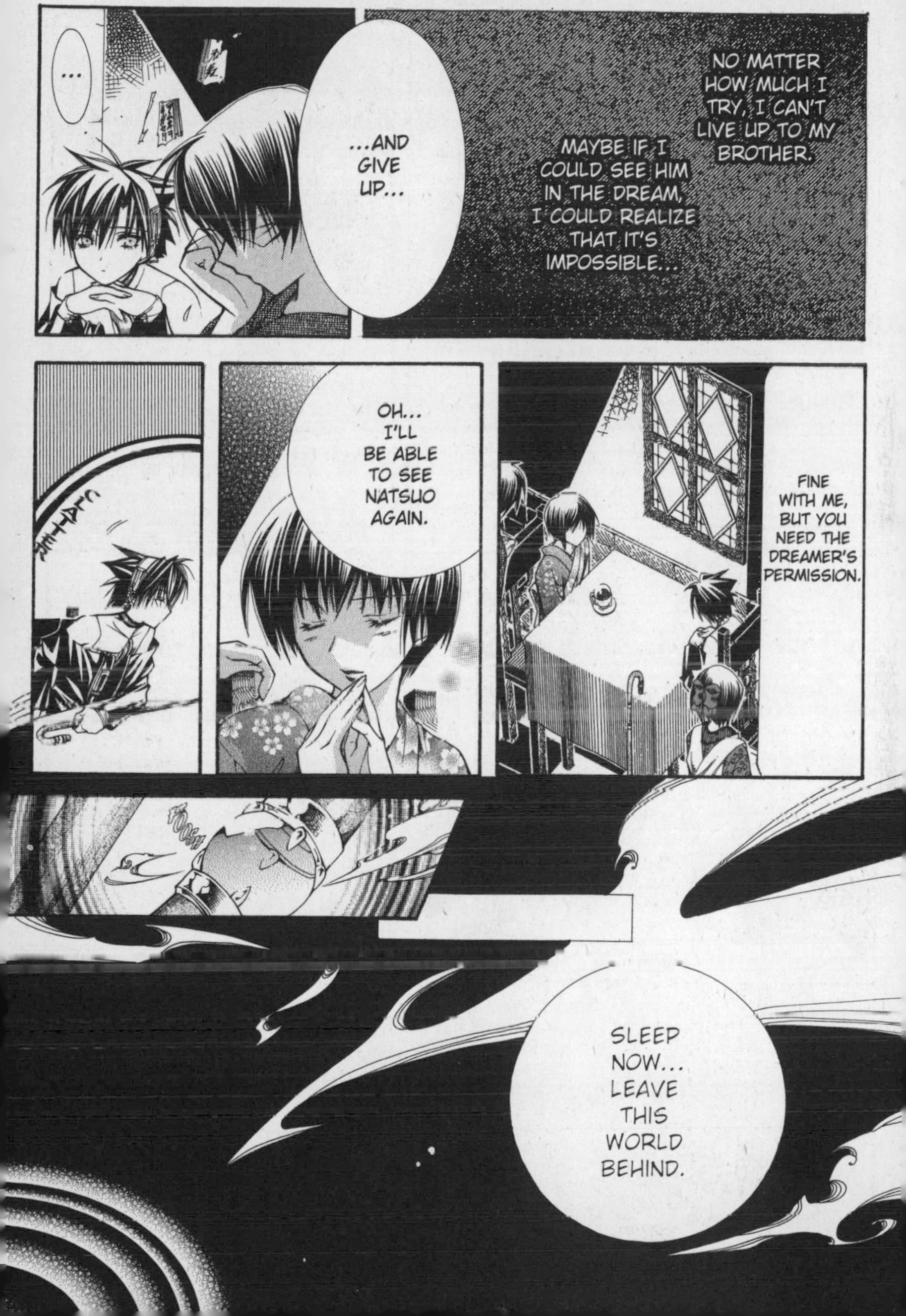
NO MATTER HOW MUCH I TRY, I CAN'T LIVE UP TO MY BROTHER.
MAYBE IF I COULD SEE HIM IN THE DREAM, I COULD REALIZE THAT IT'S IMPOSSIBLE...
...AND GIVE UP...
...
FINE WITH ME, BUT YOU NEED THE DREAMER'S PERMISSION.
OH... I'LL BE ABLE TO SEE NATSUO AGAIN.
CLATTER
FOOSH
SLEEP NOW... LEAVE THIS WORLD BEHIND.

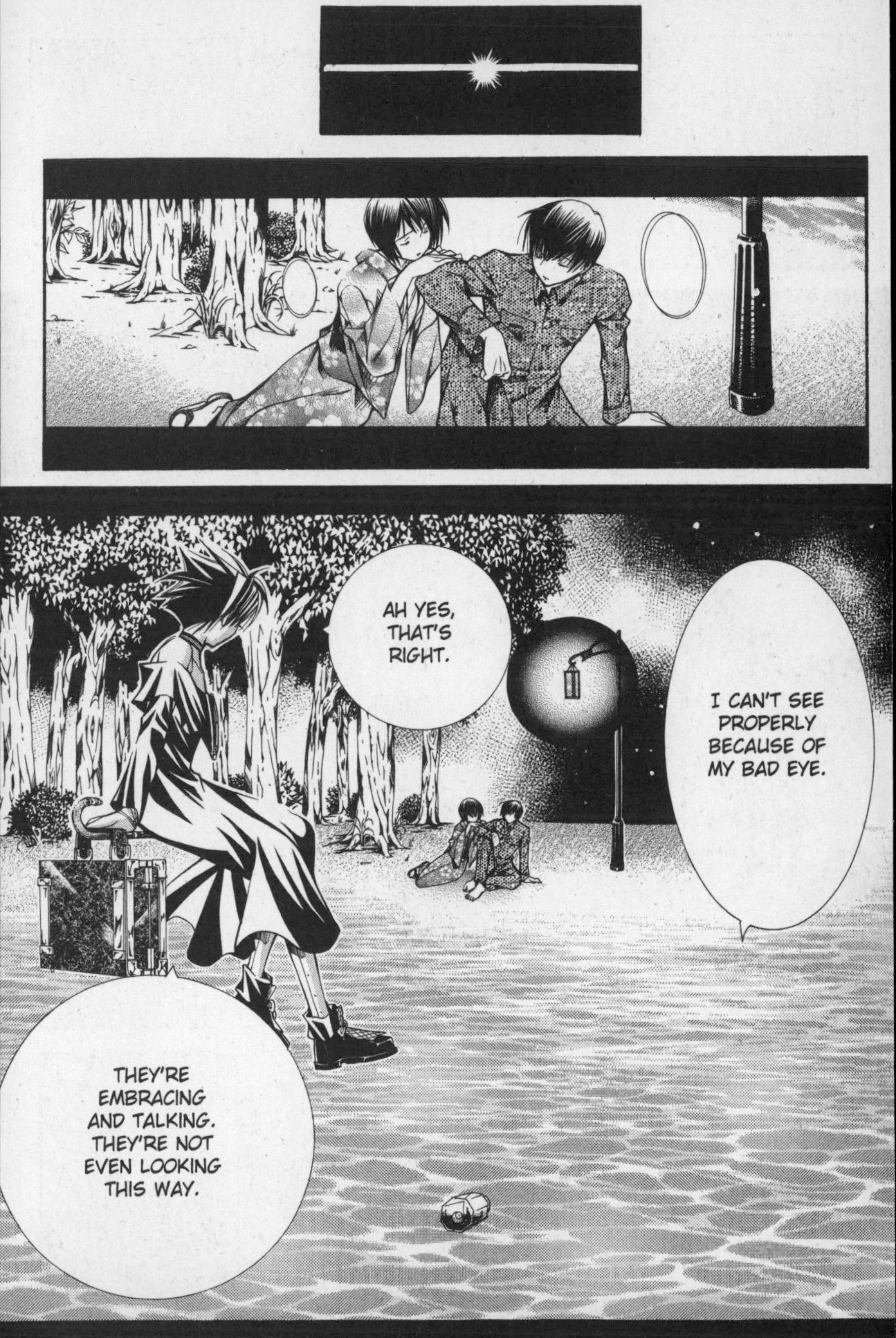
I CAN'T SEE PROPERLY BECAUSE OF MY BAD EYE.
AH YES, THAT'S RIGHT.
THEY'RE EMBRACING AND TALKING. THEY'RE NOT EVEN LOOKING THIS WAY.

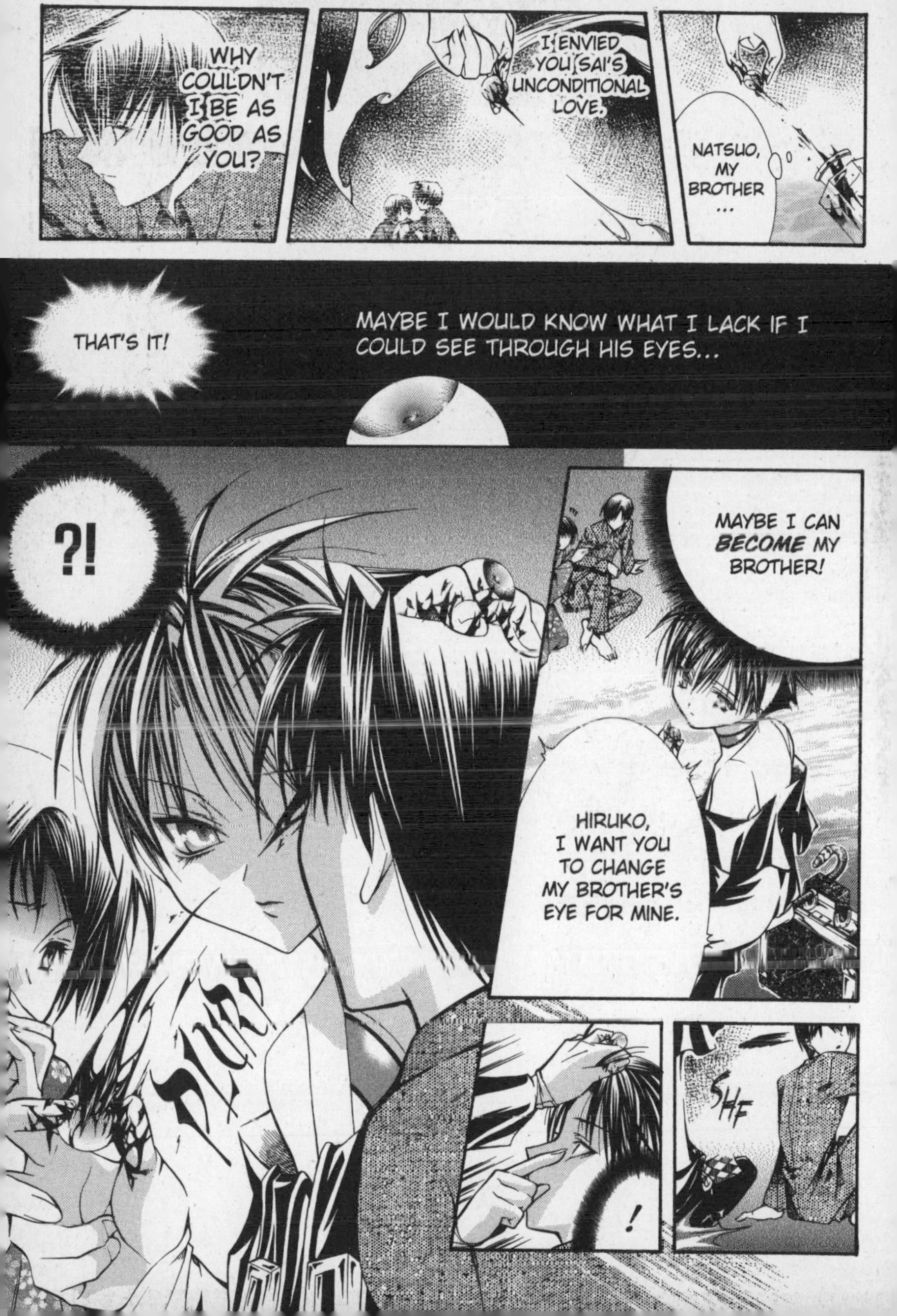
NATSUO, MY BROTHER ...
I ENVIED YOU SAI'S UNCONDITIONAL LOVE.
WHY COULDN'T I BE AS GOOD AS YOU?
MAYBE I WOULD KNOW WHAT I LACK IF I COULD SEE THROUGH HIS EYES...
THAT'S IT!
MAYBE I CAN *BECOME* MY BROTHER!
HIRUKO, I WANT YOU TO CHANGE MY BROTHER'S EYE FOR MINE.
SHF
!
?!

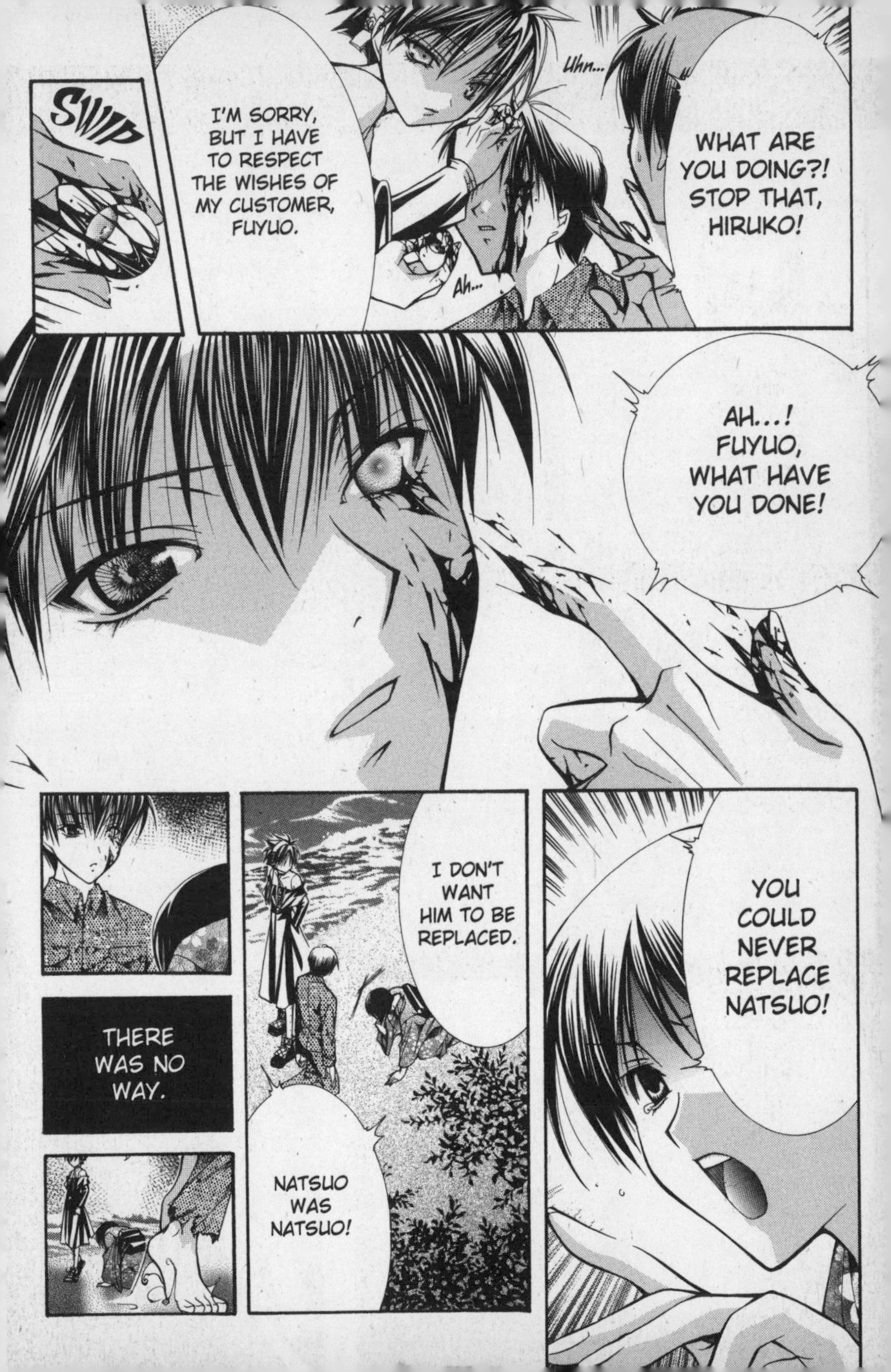
Uhn...
WHAT ARE YOU DOING?! STOP THAT, HIRUKO!
I'M SORRY, BUT I HAVE TO RESPECT THE WISHES OF MY CUSTOMER, FUYUO.
Ah...
SWIP
AH...! FUYUO, WHAT HAVE YOU DONE!
YOU COULD NEVER REPLACE NATSUO!
I DON'T WANT HIM TO BE REPLACED.
NATSUO WAS NATSUO!
THERE WAS NO WAY.

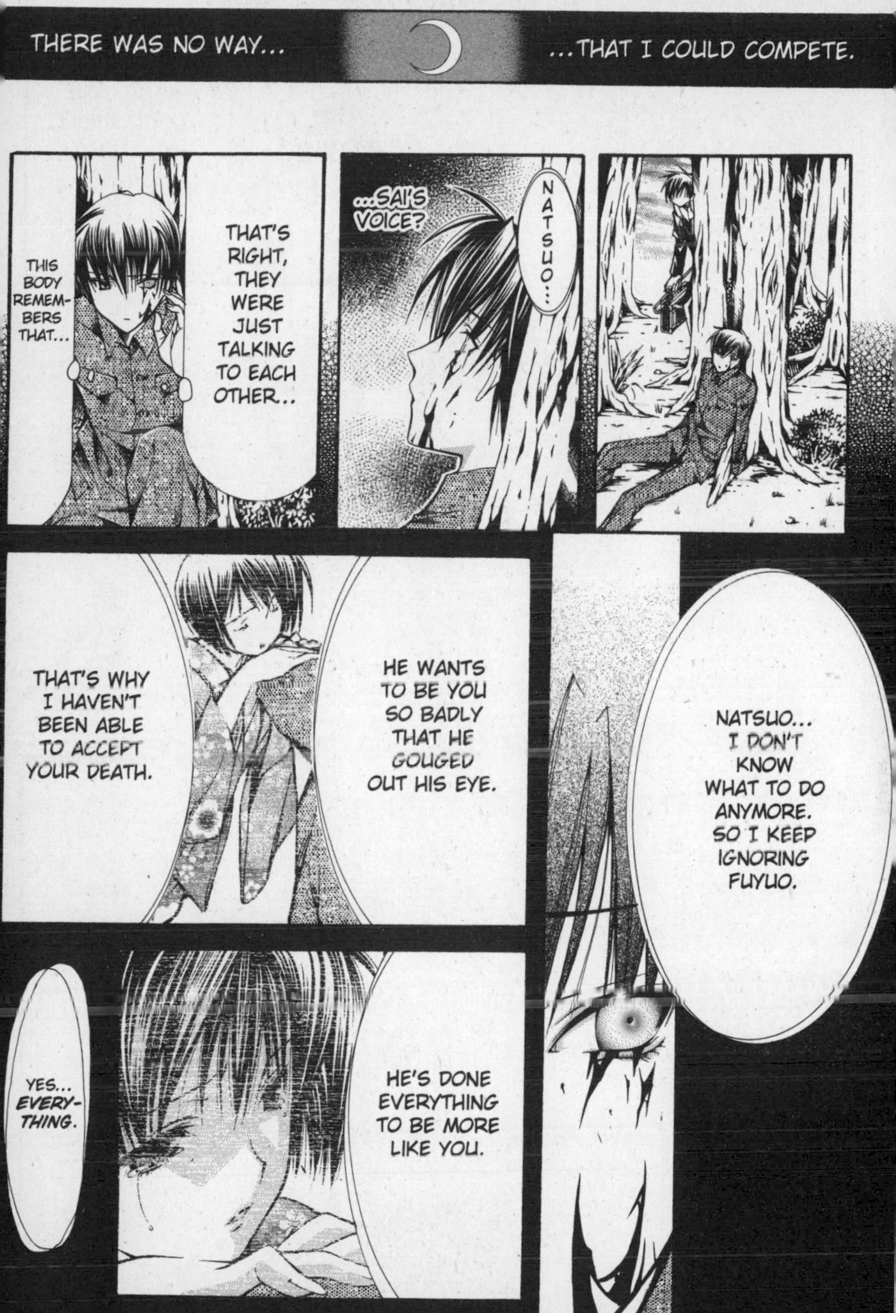
THERE WAS NO WAY... ...THAT I COULD COMPETE.
NATSUO...
...SAI'S VOICE?
THAT'S RIGHT, THEY WERE JUST TALKING TO EACH OTHER...
THIS BODY REMEMBERS THAT...
NATSUO... I DON'T KNOW WHAT TO DO ANYMORE. SO I KEEP IGNORING FUYUO.
HE WANTS TO BE YOU SO BADLY THAT HE GOUGED OUT HIS EYE.
THAT'S WHY I HAVEN'T BEEN ABLE TO ACCEPT YOUR DEATH.
HE'S DONE EVERYTHING TO BE MORE LIKE YOU.
YES... *EVERYTHING.*

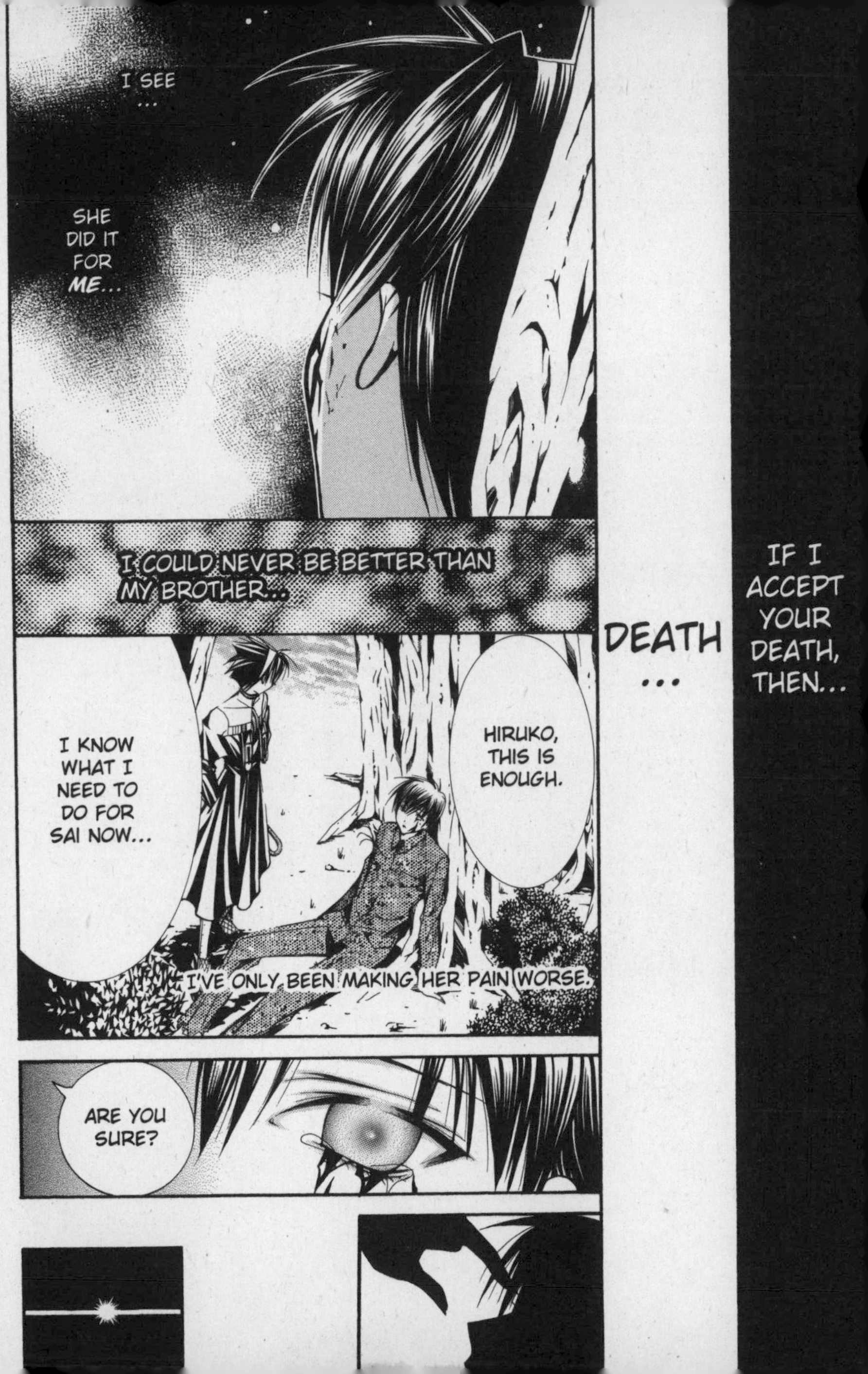
IF I ACCEPT YOUR DEATH, THEN...
DEATH...
I SEE ...
SHE DID IT FOR ME...
I COULD NEVER BE BETTER THAN MY BROTHER...
HIRUKO, THIS IS ENOUGH.
I KNOW WHAT I NEED TO DO FOR SAI NOW...
I'VE ONLY BEEN MAKING HER PAIN WORSE.
ARE YOU SURE?

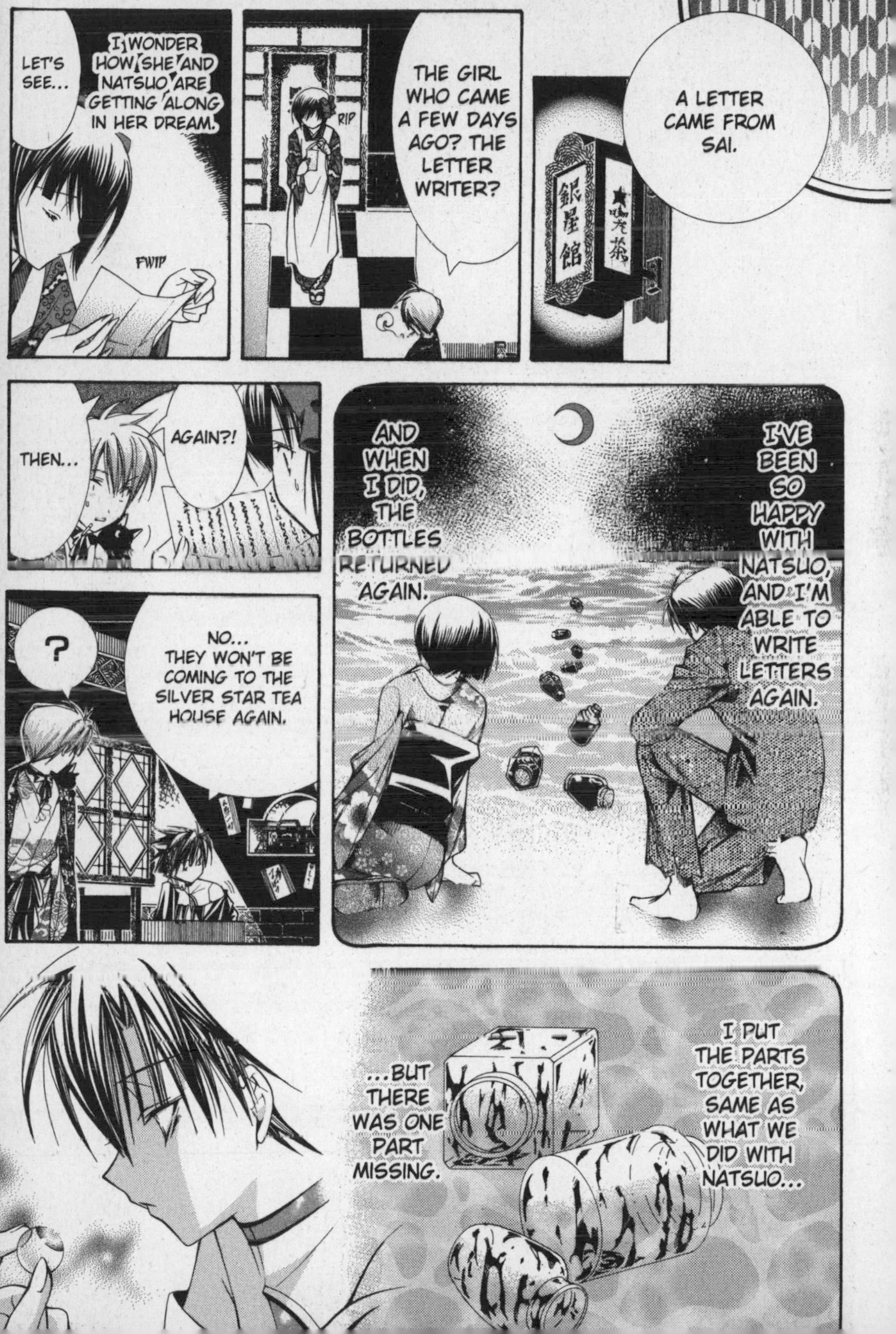
A LETTER CAME FROM SAI.
THE GIRL WHO CAME A FEW DAYS AGO? THE LETTER WRITER?
RIP
I WONDER HOW SHE AND NATSUO ARE GETTING ALONG IN HER DREAM.
LET'S SEE...
FWIP
I'VE BEEN SO HAPPY WITH NATSUO, AND I'M ABLE TO WRITE LETTERS AGAIN.
AND WHEN I DID, THE BOTTLES RETURNED AGAIN.
AGAIN?!
THEN...
NO... THEY WON'T BE COMING TO THE SILVER STAR TEA HOUSE AGAIN.
?
I PUT THE PARTS TOGETHER, SAME AS WHAT WE DID WITH NATSUO...
...BUT THERE WAS ONE PART MISSING.

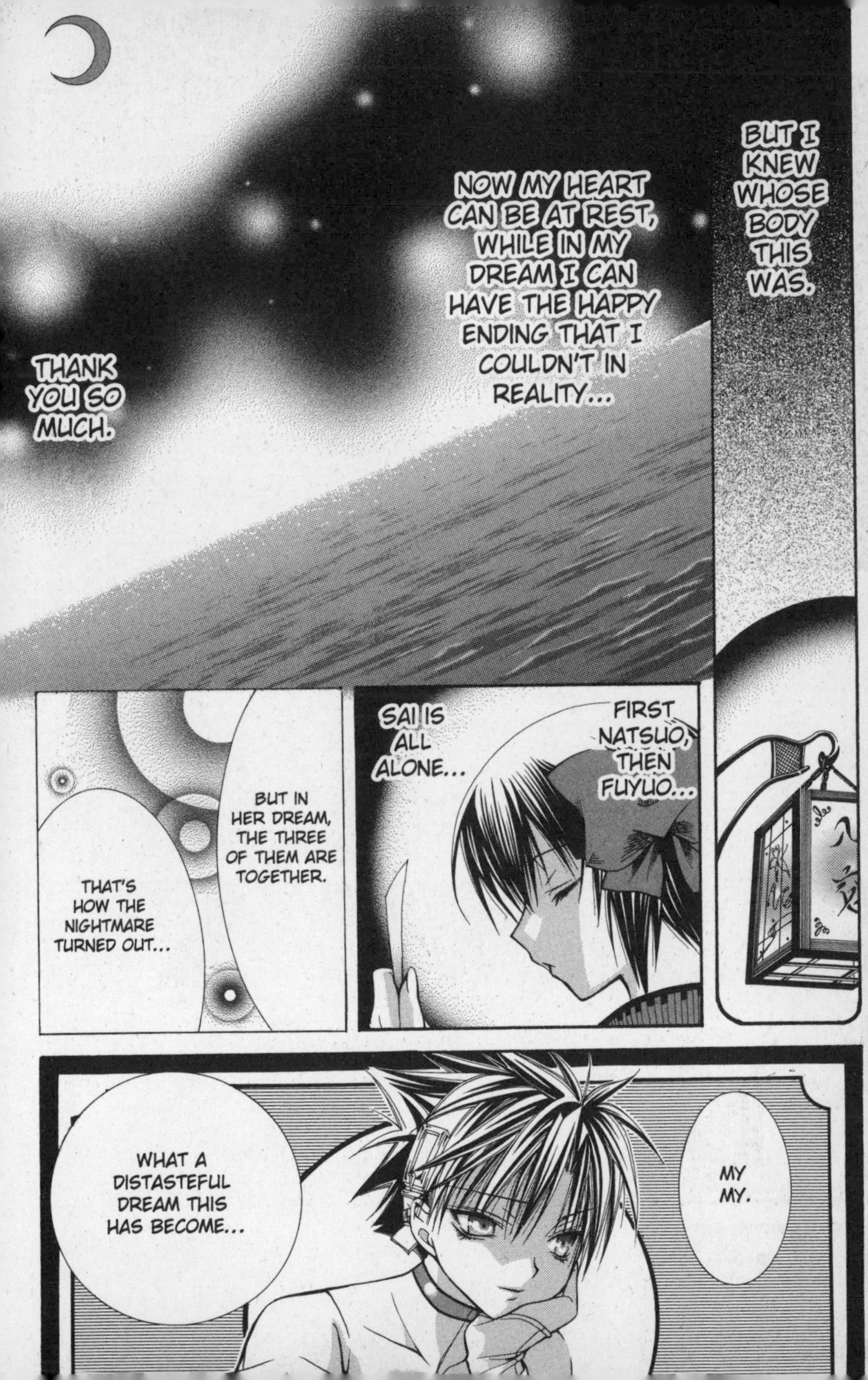
BUT I KNEW WHOSE BODY THIS WAS.
NOW MY HEART CAN BE AT REST, WHILE IN MY DREAM I CAN HAVE THE HAPPY ENDING THAT I COULDN'T IN REALITY...
THANK YOU SO MUCH.
FIRST NATSUO, THEN FUYUO...
SAI IS ALL ALONE...
BUT IN HER DREAM, THE THREE OF THEM ARE TOGETHER.
THAT'S HOW THE NIGHTMARE TURNED OUT...
MY MY.
WHAT A DISTASTEFUL DREAM THIS HAS BECOME...

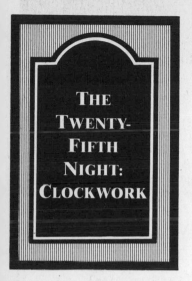

THE TWENTY-FIFTH NIGHT: CLOCKWORK
UNDER COVER OF DARKNESS...
THEY COME TO THE SILVER STAR TEA HOUSE...
...SEEKING SOLACE...
I WAS WONDERING WHY IT'S SO QUIET. HIFUMI MUST BE OUT.
HE'S GONE TO A BAR TO GOSSIP.
HOW FRIVOLOUS...
DING

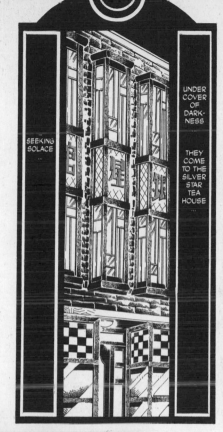

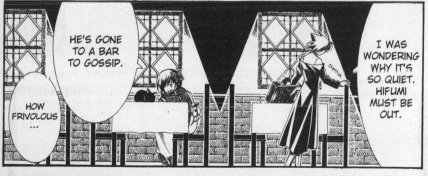

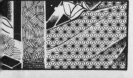

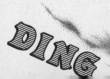

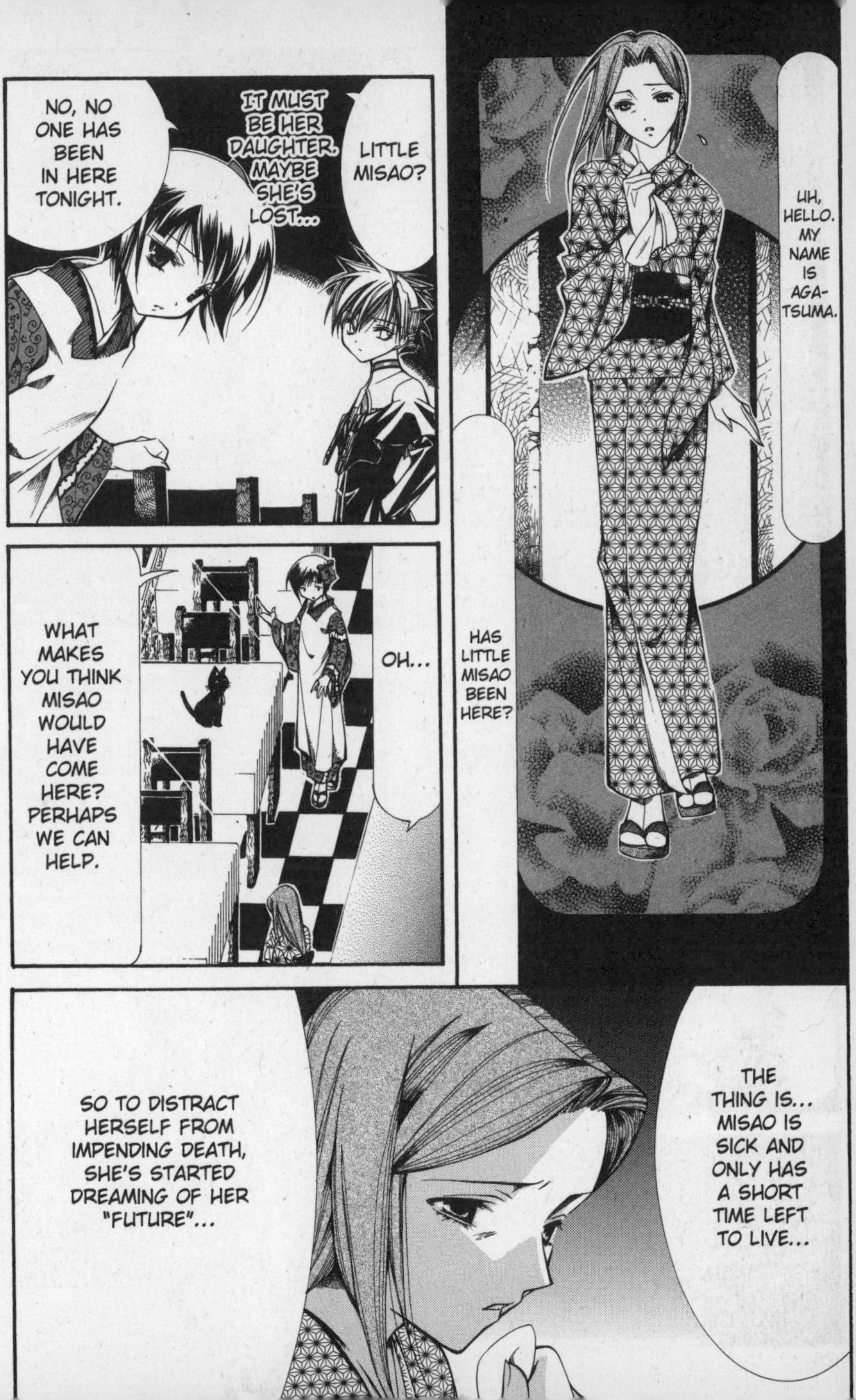
UH, HELLO. MY NAME IS AGA-TSUMA.
HAS LITTLE MISAO BEEN HERE?
LITTLE MISAO?
IT MUST BE HER DAUGHTER. MAYBE SHE'S LOST...
NO, NO ONE HAS BEEN IN HERE TONIGHT.
OH...
WHAT MAKES YOU THINK MISAO WOULD HAVE COME HERE? PERHAPS WE CAN HELP.
THE THING IS... MISAO IS SICK AND ONLY HAS A SHORT TIME LEFT TO LIVE...
SO TO DISTRACT HERSELF FROM IMPENDING DEATH, SHE'S STARTED DREAMING OF HER "FUTURE"...

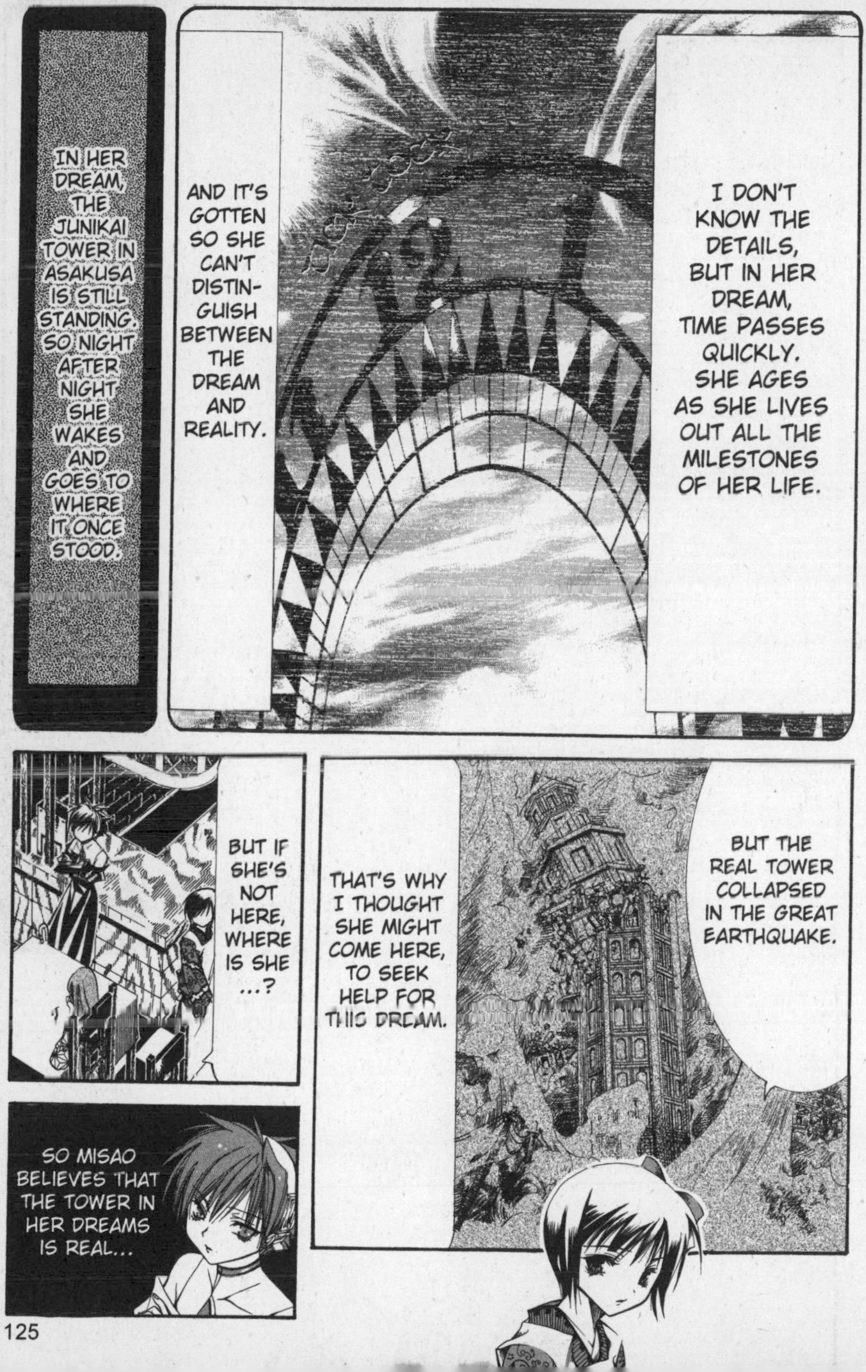
I DON'T KNOW THE DETAILS, BUT IN HER DREAM, TIME PASSES QUICKLY. SHE AGES AS SHE LIVES OUT ALL THE MILESTONES OF HER LIFE.
AND IT'S GOTTEN SO SHE CAN'T DISTIN-GUISH BETWEEN THE DREAM AND REALITY.
IN HER DREAM, THE JUNIKAI TOWER IN ASAKUSA IS STILL STANDING. SO NIGHT AFTER NIGHT SHE WAKES AND GOES TO WHERE IT ONCE STOOD.
BUT THE REAL TOWER COLLAPSED IN THE GREAT EARTHQUAKE.
THAT'S WHY I THOUGHT SHE MIGHT COME HERE, TO SEEK HELP FOR THIS DREAM.
BUT IF SHE'S NOT HERE, WHERE IS SHE ...?
SO MISAO BELIEVES THAT THE TOWER IN HER DREAMS IS REAL...

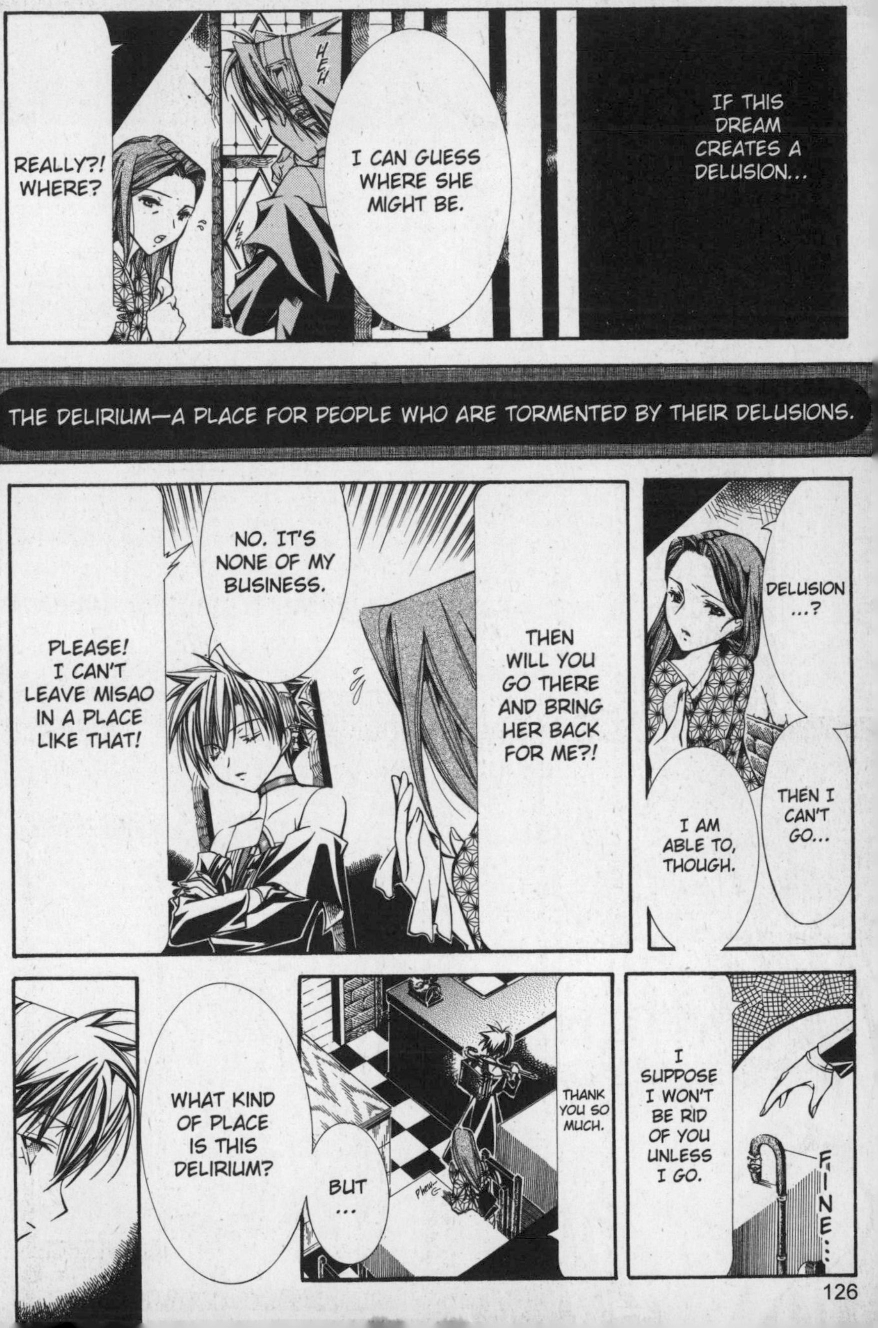
IF THIS DREAM CREATES A DELUSION...
HEH
I CAN GUESS WHERE SHE MIGHT BE.
HEH
REALLY?! WHERE?
THE DELIRIUM—A PLACE FOR PEOPLE WHO ARE TORMENTED BY THEIR DELUSIONS.
DELUSION ...?
THEN I CAN'T GO...
I AM ABLE TO, THOUGH.
THEN WILL YOU GO THERE AND BRING HER BACK FOR ME?!
NO. IT'S NONE OF MY BUSINESS.
PLEASE! I CAN'T LEAVE MISAO IN A PLACE LIKE THAT!
I SUPPOSE I WON'T BE RID OF YOU UNLESS I GO.
FINE...
THANK YOU SO MUCH.
Phew
BUT ...
WHAT KIND OF PLACE IS THIS DELIRIUM?

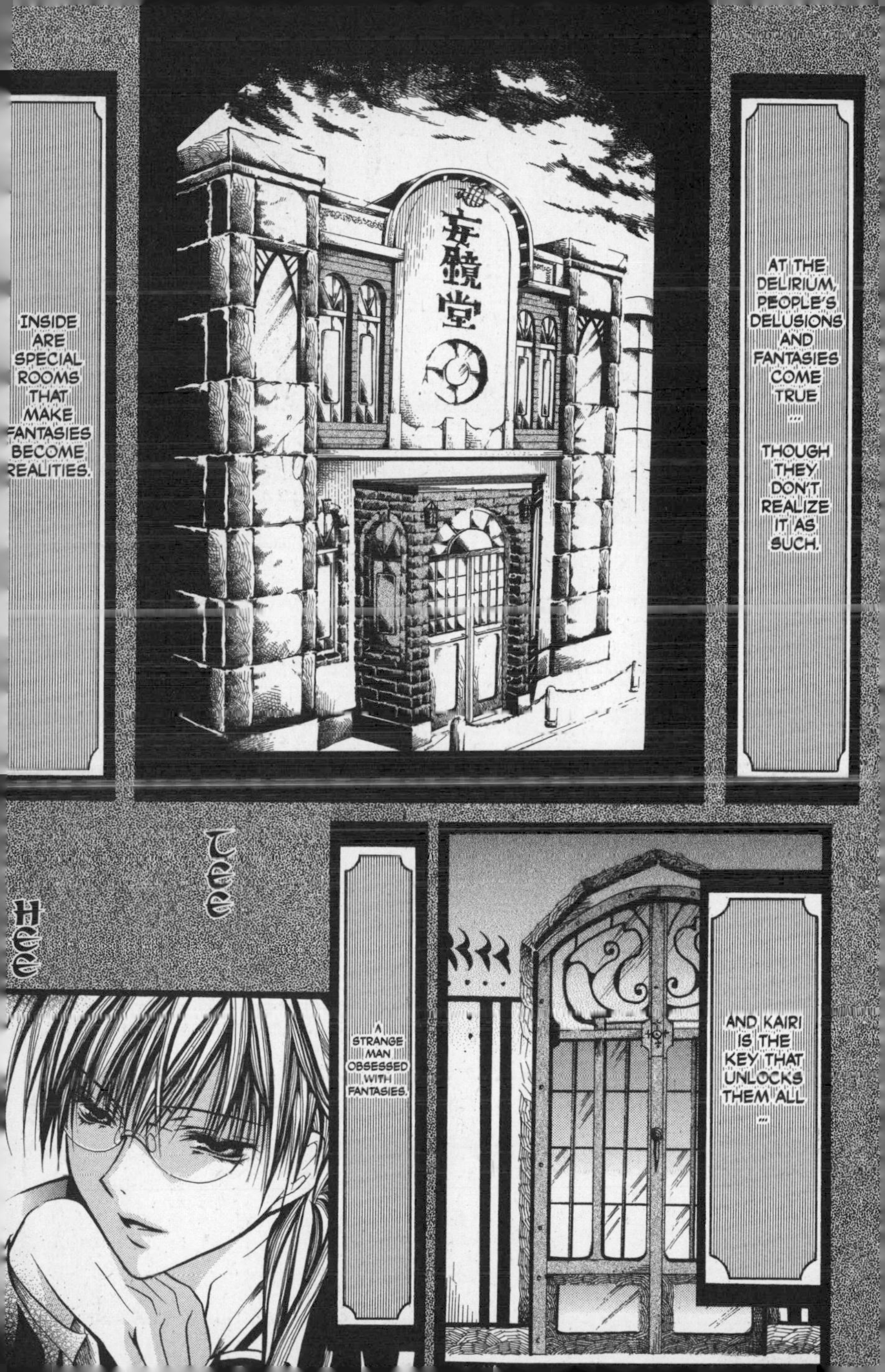
妄鏡堂
AT THE DELIRIUM, PEOPLE'S DELUSIONS AND FANTASIES COME TRUE...
THOUGH THEY DON'T REALIZE IT AS SUCH.
INSIDE ARE SPECIAL ROOMS THAT MAKE FANTASIES BECOME REALITIES.
AND KAIRI IS THE KEY THAT UNLOCKS THEM ALL...
A STRANGE MAN OBSESSED WITH FANTASIES.

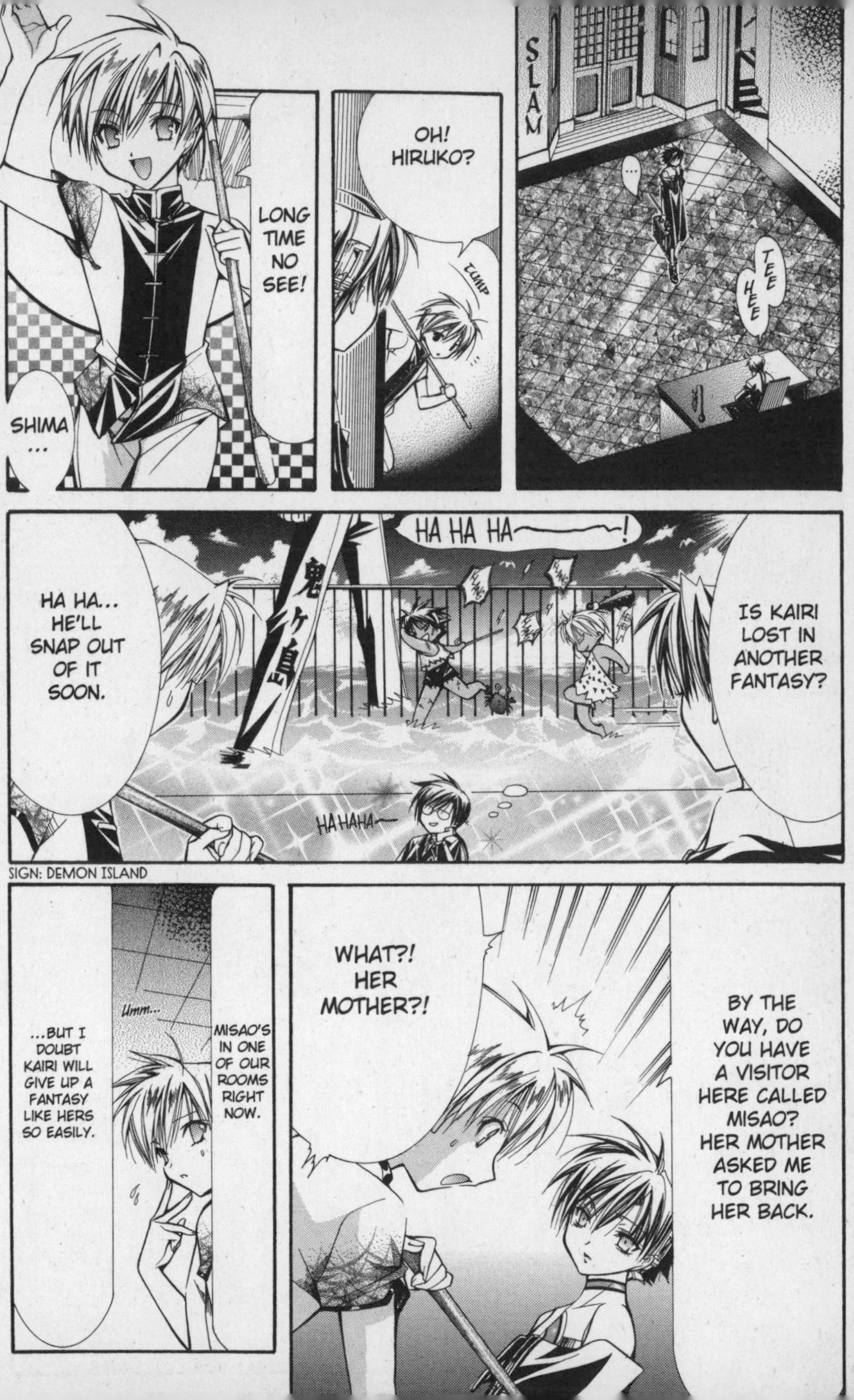
SLAM
...
TEE HEE
OH! HIRUKO?
TUMP
LONG TIME NO SEE!
SHIMA ...
HA HA HA———!
IS KAIRI LOST IN ANOTHER FANTASY?
鬼ヶ島
HA HA... HE'LL SNAP OUT OF IT SOON.
HAHAHA—
SIGN: DEMON ISLAND
BY THE WAY, DO YOU HAVE A VISITOR HERE CALLED MISAO? HER MOTHER ASKED ME TO BRING HER BACK.
WHAT?! HER MOTHER?!
MISAO'S IN ONE OF OUR ROOMS RIGHT NOW.
Umm...
...BUT I DOUBT KAIRI WILL GIVE UP A FANTASY LIKE HERS SO EASILY.

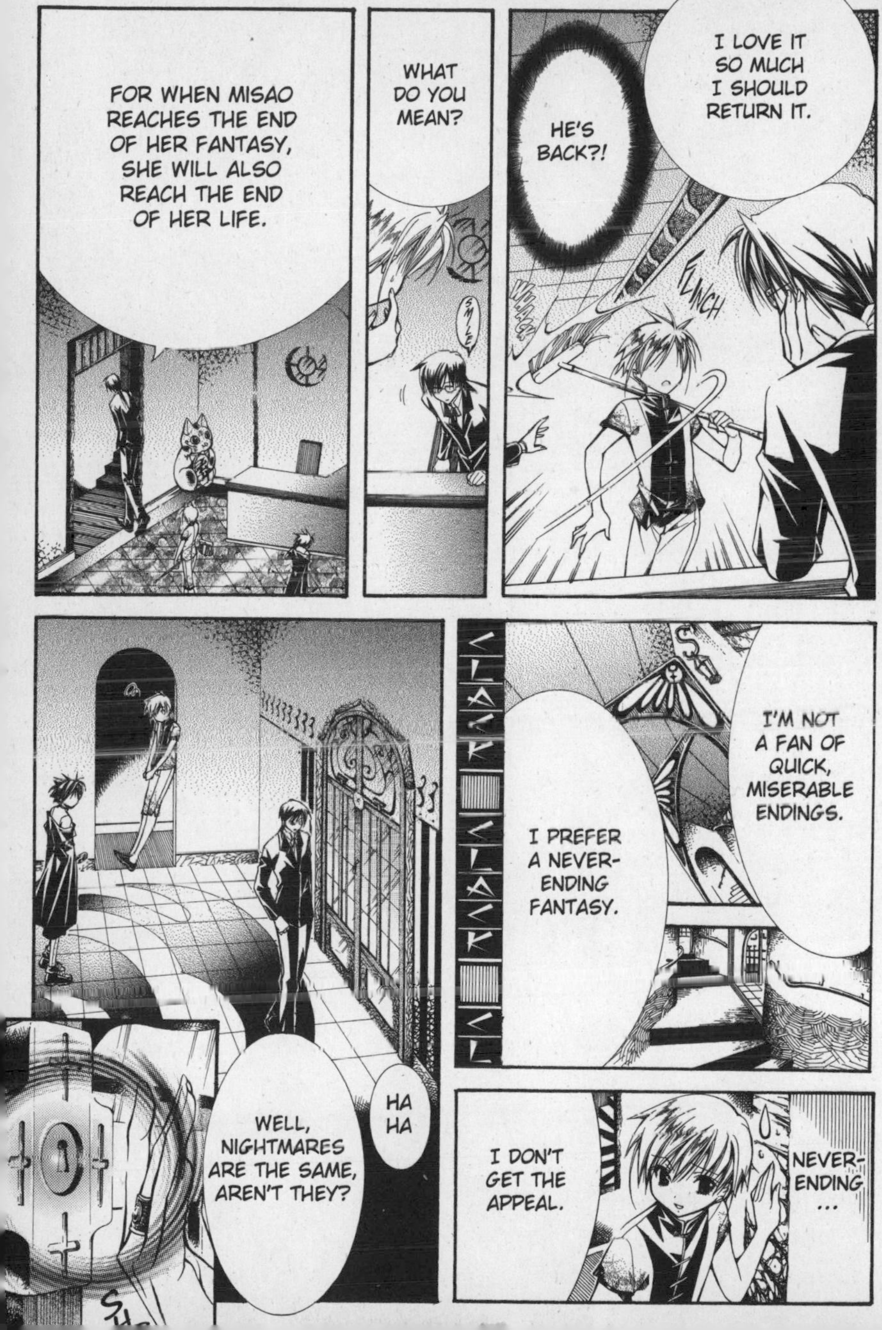
I LOVE IT SO MUCH I SHOULD RETURN IT.
HE'S BACK?!
FLINCH
WHAT DO YOU MEAN?
SMILE
FOR WHEN MISAO REACHES THE END OF HER FANTASY, SHE WILL ALSO REACH THE END OF HER LIFE.
I'M NOT A FAN OF QUICK, MISERABLE ENDINGS.
I PREFER A NEVER-ENDING FANTASY.
CLACK CLACK CL
HA HA
WELL, NIGHTMARES ARE THE SAME, AREN'T THEY?
NEVER-ENDING...
I DON'T GET THE APPEAL.

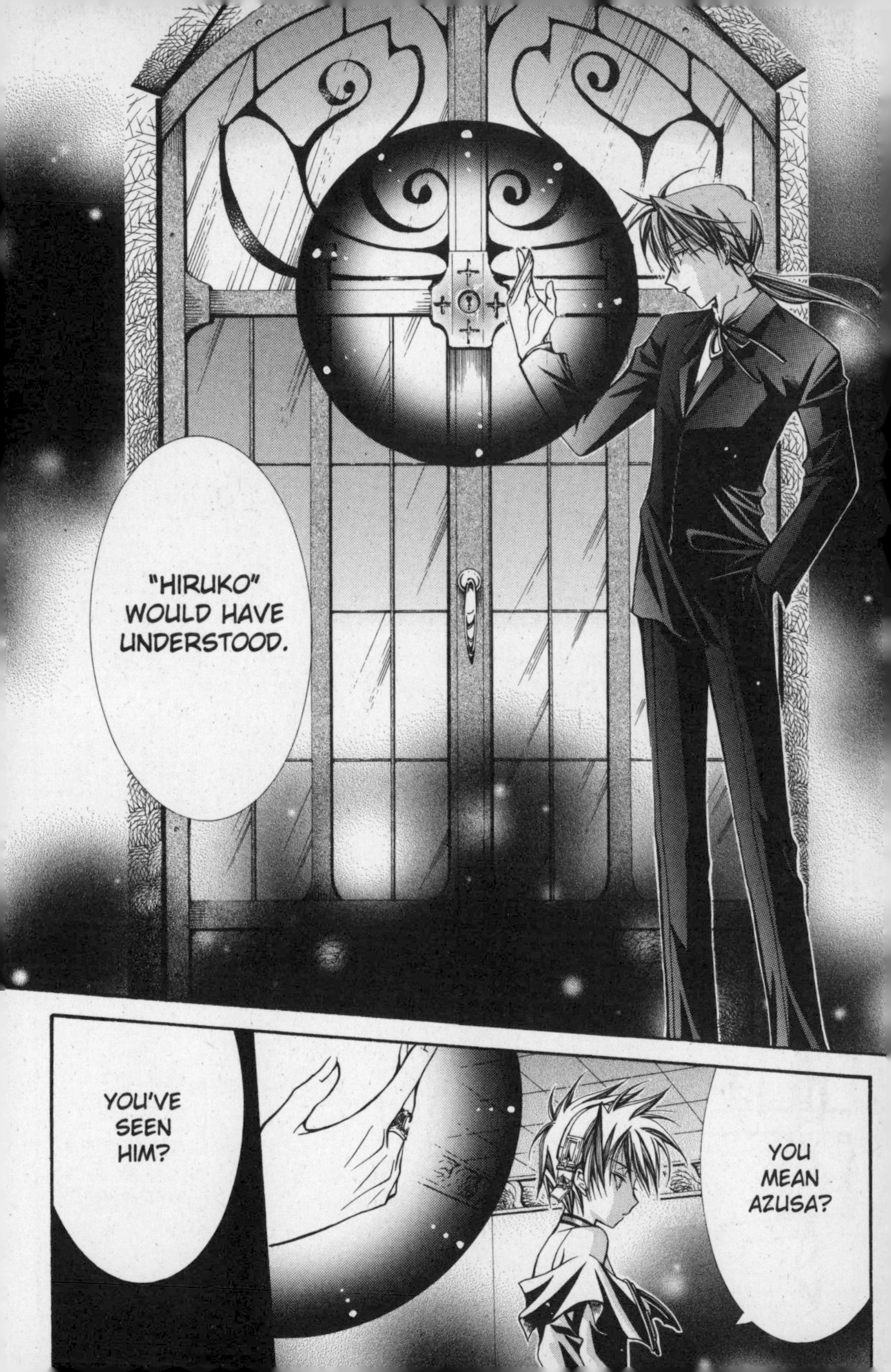
"HIRUKO" WOULD HAVE UNDERSTOOD.
YOU MEAN AZUSA?
YOU'VE SEEN HIM?

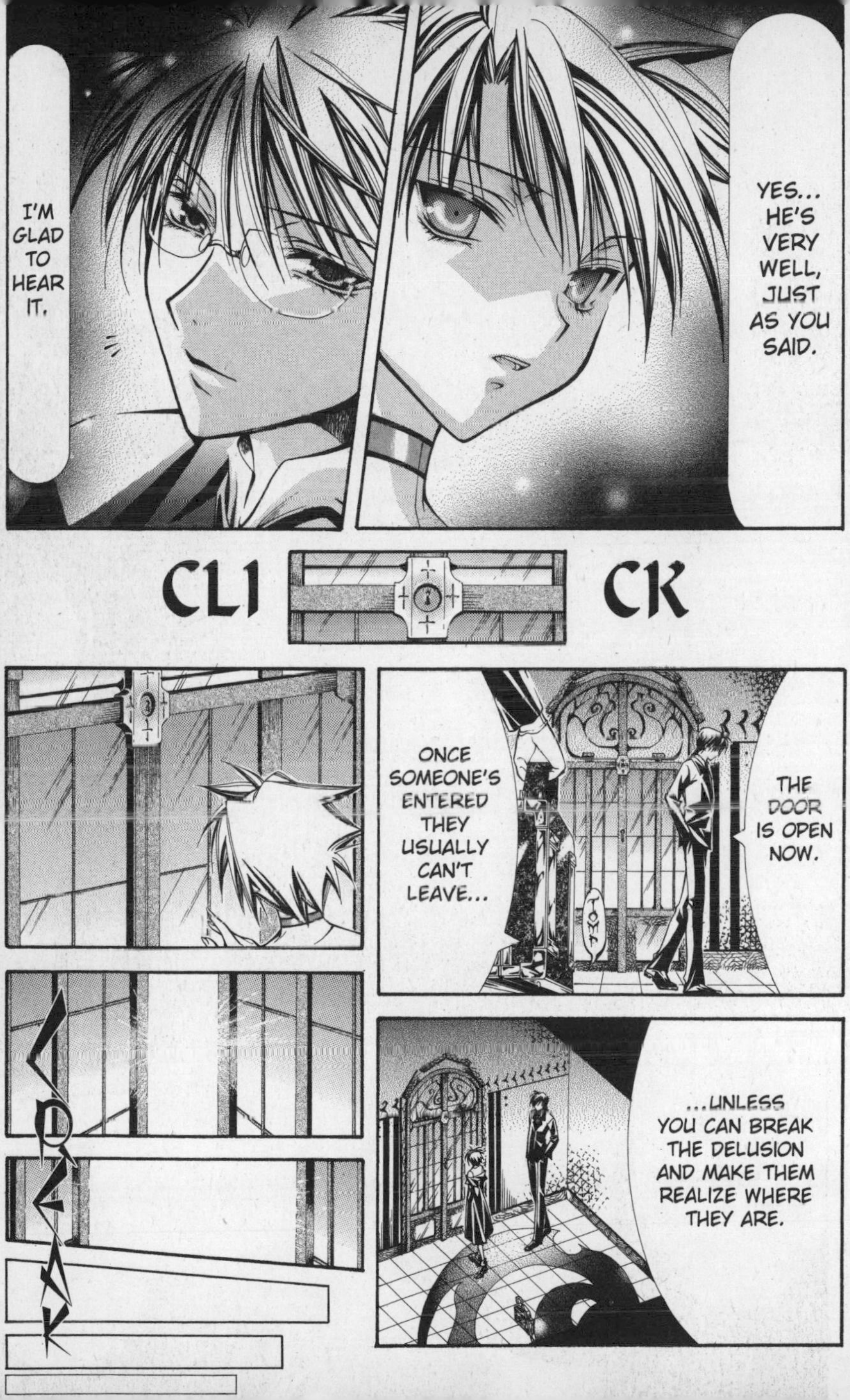
YES... HE'S VERY WELL, JUST AS YOU SAID.
I'M GLAD TO HEAR IT.
CLICK
THE DOOR IS OPEN NOW.
ONCE SOMEONE'S ENTERED THEY USUALLY CAN'T LEAVE...
...UNLESS YOU CAN BREAK THE DELUSION AND MAKE THEM REALIZE WHERE THEY ARE.

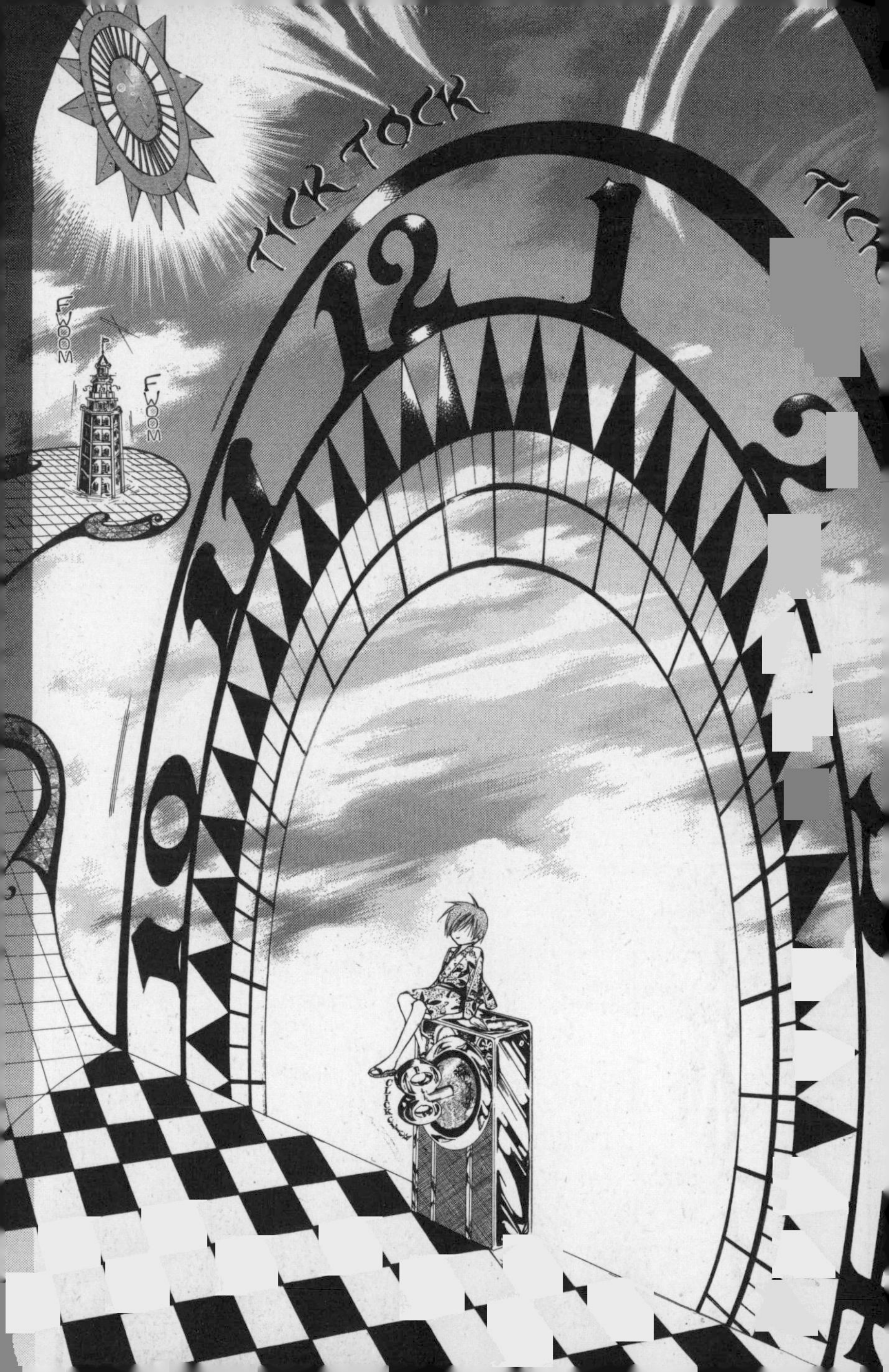
TICK
TICK TOCK
FWOOM
FWOOM
CLICK

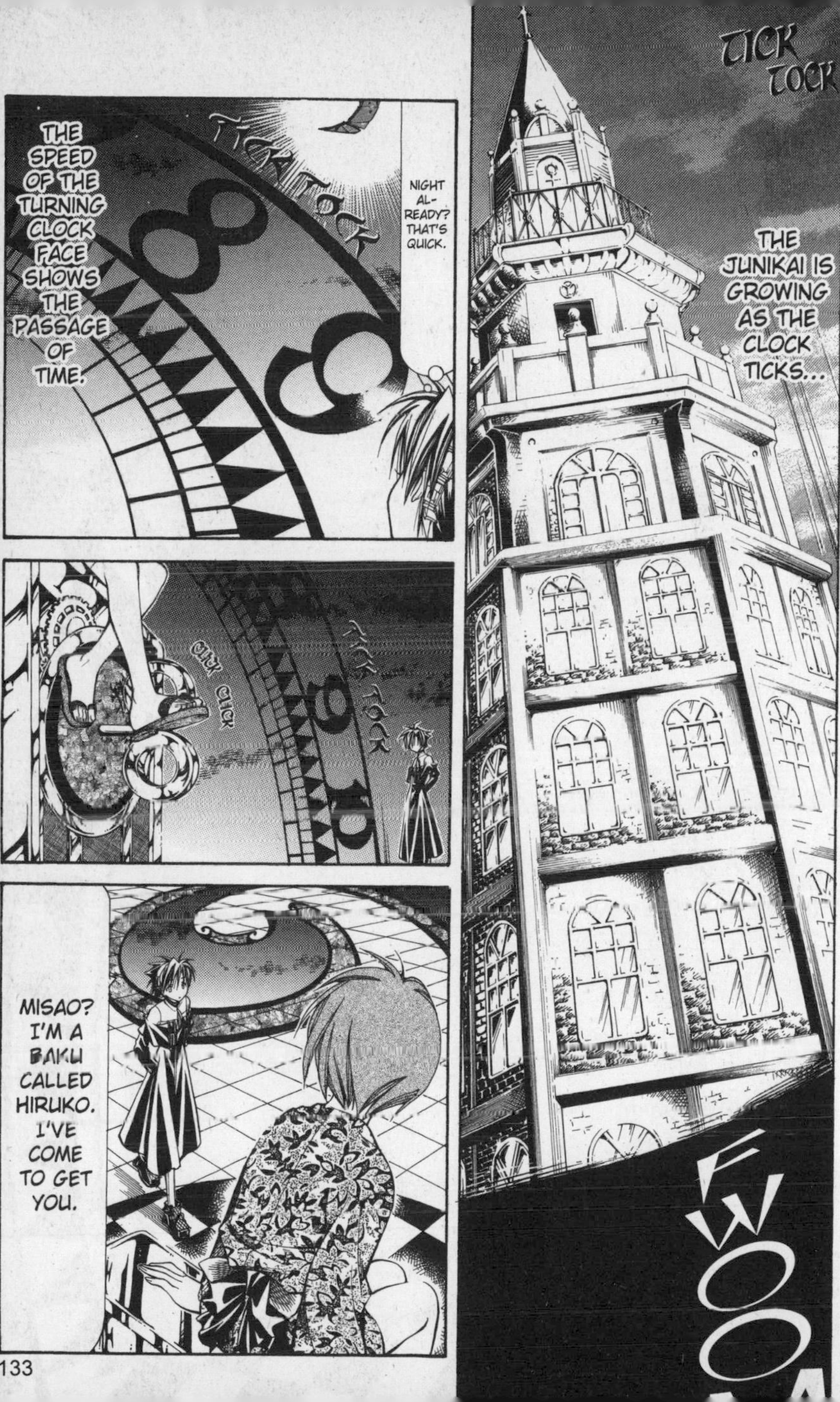
TICK TOCK
THE JUNIKAI IS GROWING AS THE CLOCK TICKS...
FWOO
NIGHT AL-READY? THAT'S QUICK.
TICK TOCK
THE SPEED OF THE TURNING CLOCK FACE SHOWS THE PASSAGE OF TIME.
TICK TOCK
CLICK CLICK
MISAO? I'M A BAKU CALLED HIRUKO. I'VE COME TO GET YOU.

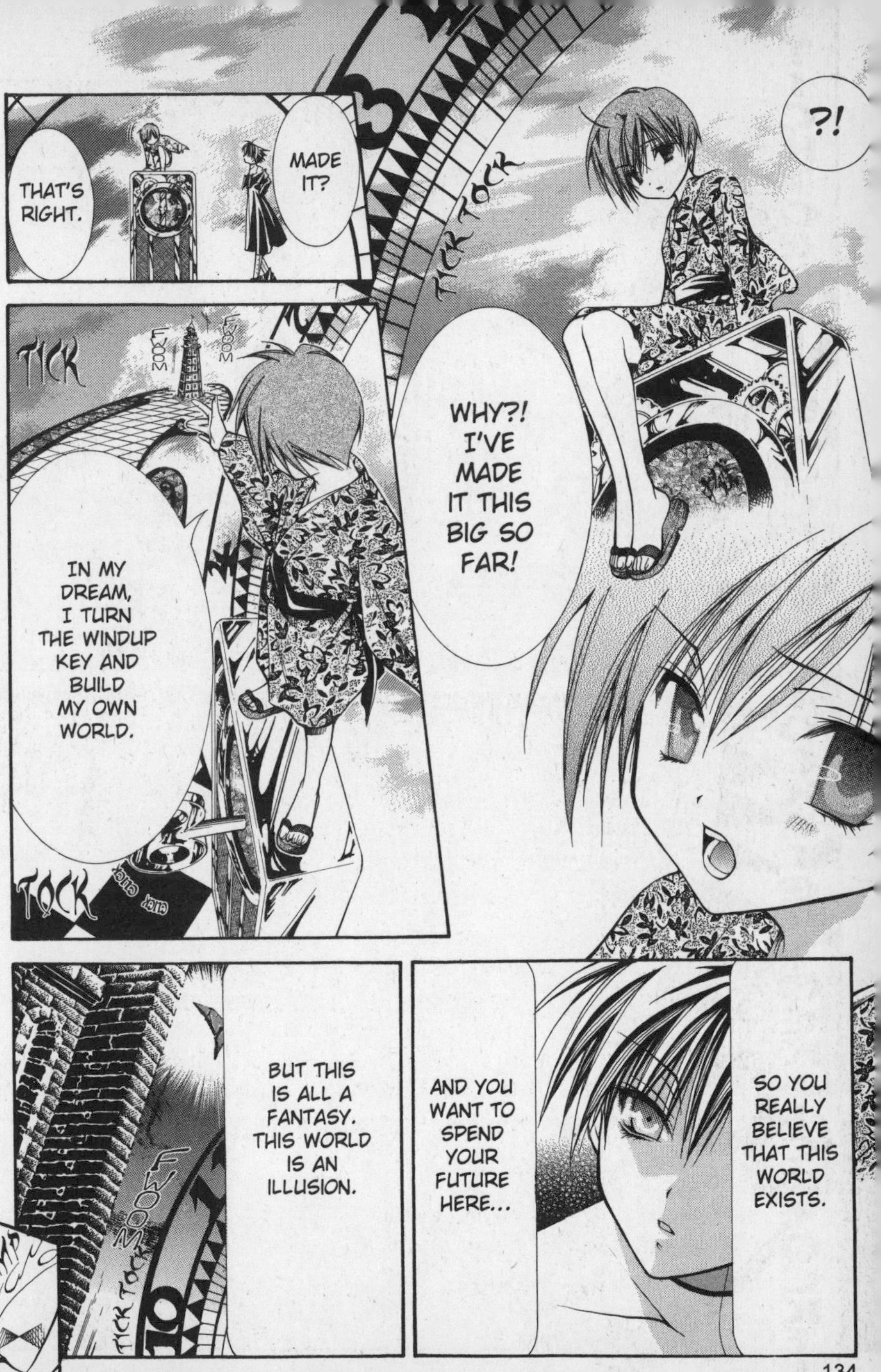
?!
TICK TOCK
WHY?! I'VE MADE IT THIS BIG SO FAR!
MADE IT?
THAT'S RIGHT.
TICK
FWOOM FWOOM
IN MY DREAM, I TURN THE WINDUP KEY AND BUILD MY OWN WORLD.
CLICK CLICK
TOCK
SO YOU REALLY BELIEVE THAT THIS WORLD EXISTS.
AND YOU WANT TO SPEND YOUR FUTURE HERE...
BUT THIS IS ALL A FANTASY. THIS WORLD IS AN ILLUSION.
FWOOM
TICK TOCK
TAP

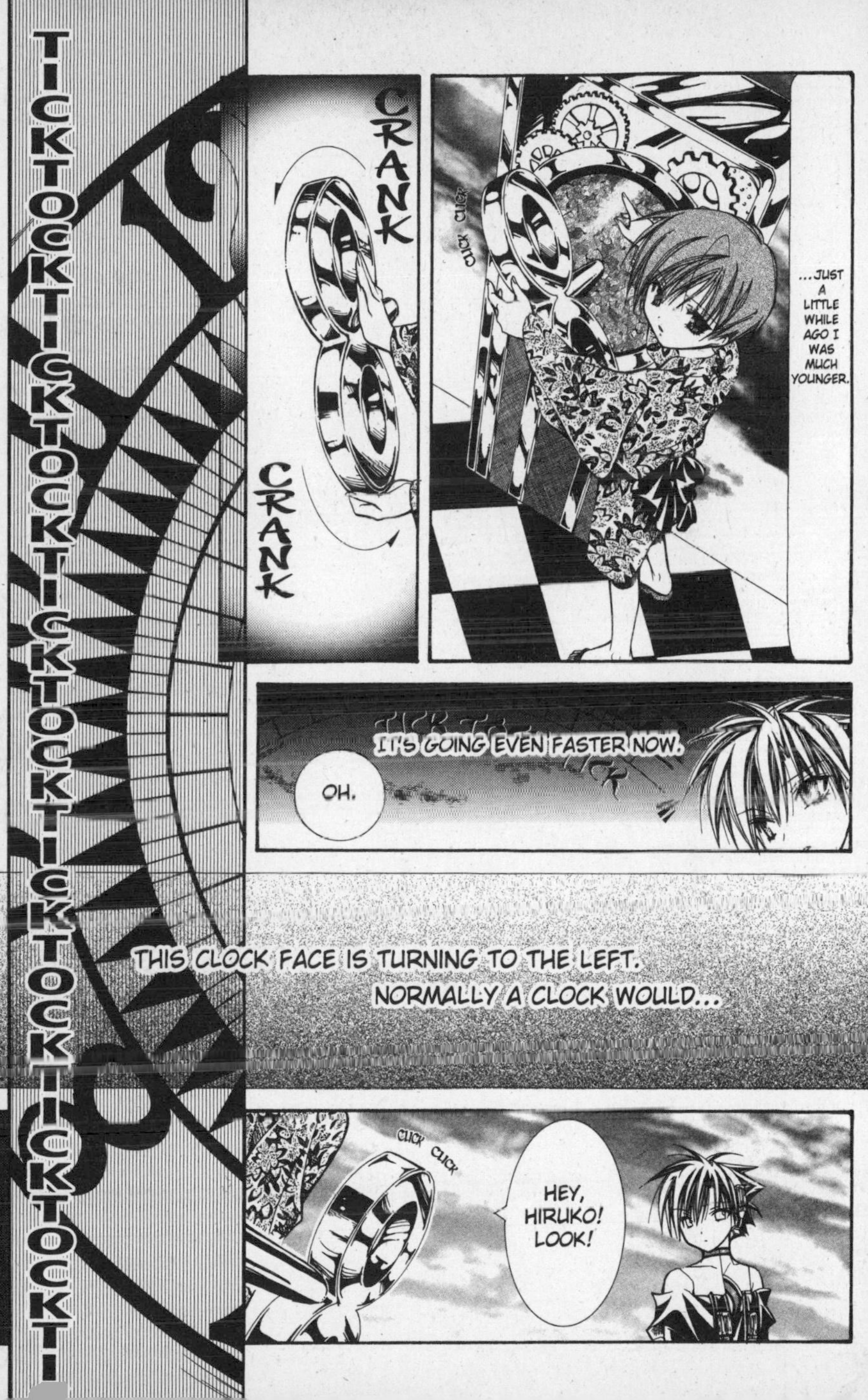

...JUST A LITTLE WHILE AGO I WAS MUCH YOUNGER.
CLICK CLICK
CRANK
CRANK
IT'S GOING EVEN FASTER NOW.
OH.
THIS CLOCK FACE IS TURNING TO THE LEFT.
NORMALLY A CLOCK WOULD...
CLICK CLICK
HEY, HIRUKO! LOOK!
TICKTOCKTICKTOCKTICKTOCKTICKTOCKTI

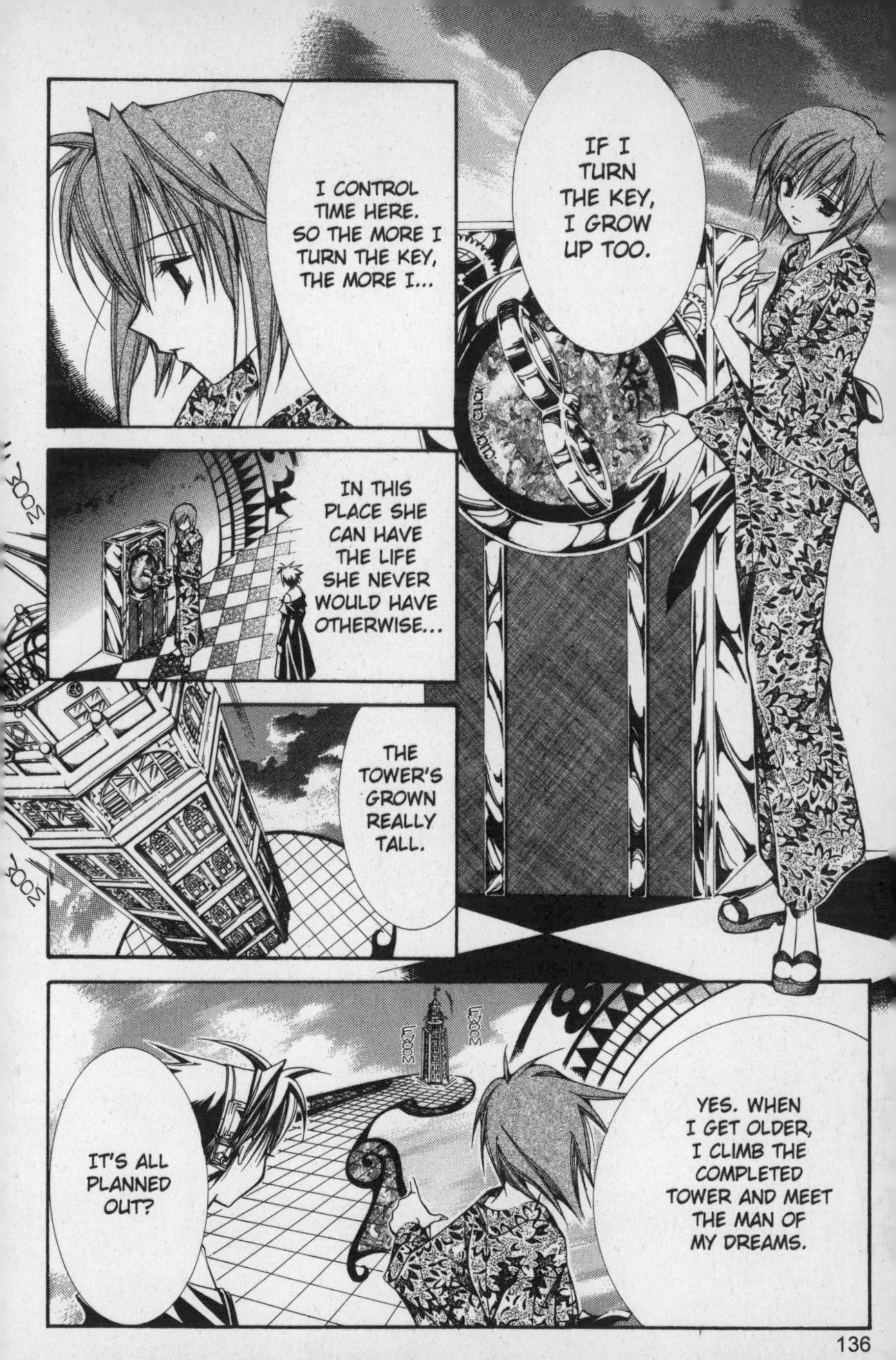
IF I TURN THE KEY, I GROW UP TOO.
CLICK CLICK
I CONTROL TIME HERE. SO THE MORE I TURN THE KEY, THE MORE I...
IN THIS PLACE SHE CAN HAVE THE LIFE SHE NEVER WOULD HAVE OTHERWISE...
THE TOWER'S GROWN REALLY TALL.
YES. WHEN I GET OLDER, I CLIMB THE COMPLETED TOWER AND MEET THE MAN OF MY DREAMS.
IT'S ALL PLANNED OUT?

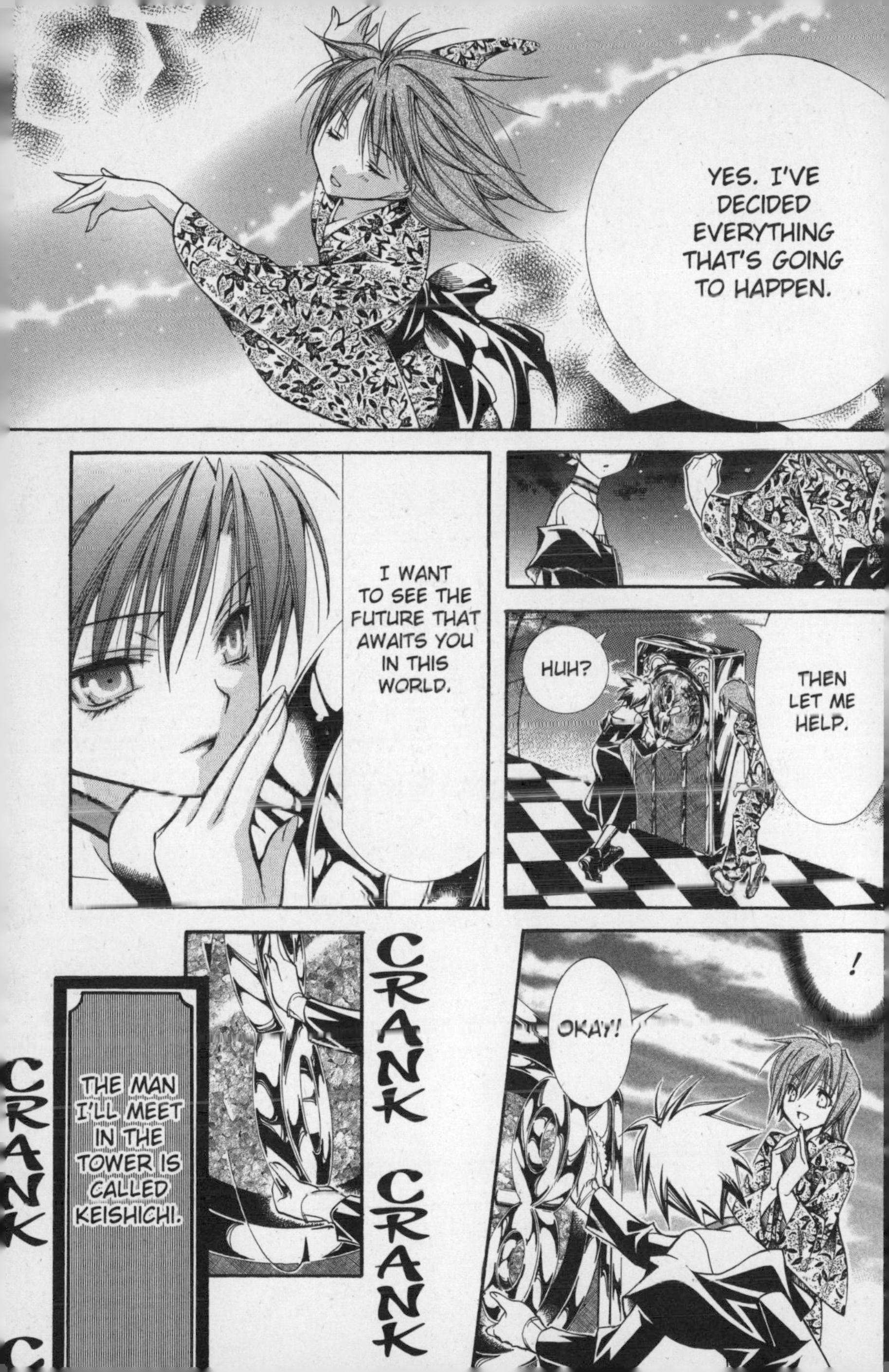
YES. I'VE DECIDED EVERYTHING THAT'S GOING TO HAPPEN.
THEN LET ME HELP.
HUH?
I WANT TO SEE THE FUTURE THAT AWAITS YOU IN THIS WORLD.
!
OKAY!
CRANK
CRANK
THE MAN I'LL MEET IN THE TOWER IS CALLED KEISHICHI.
CRANK

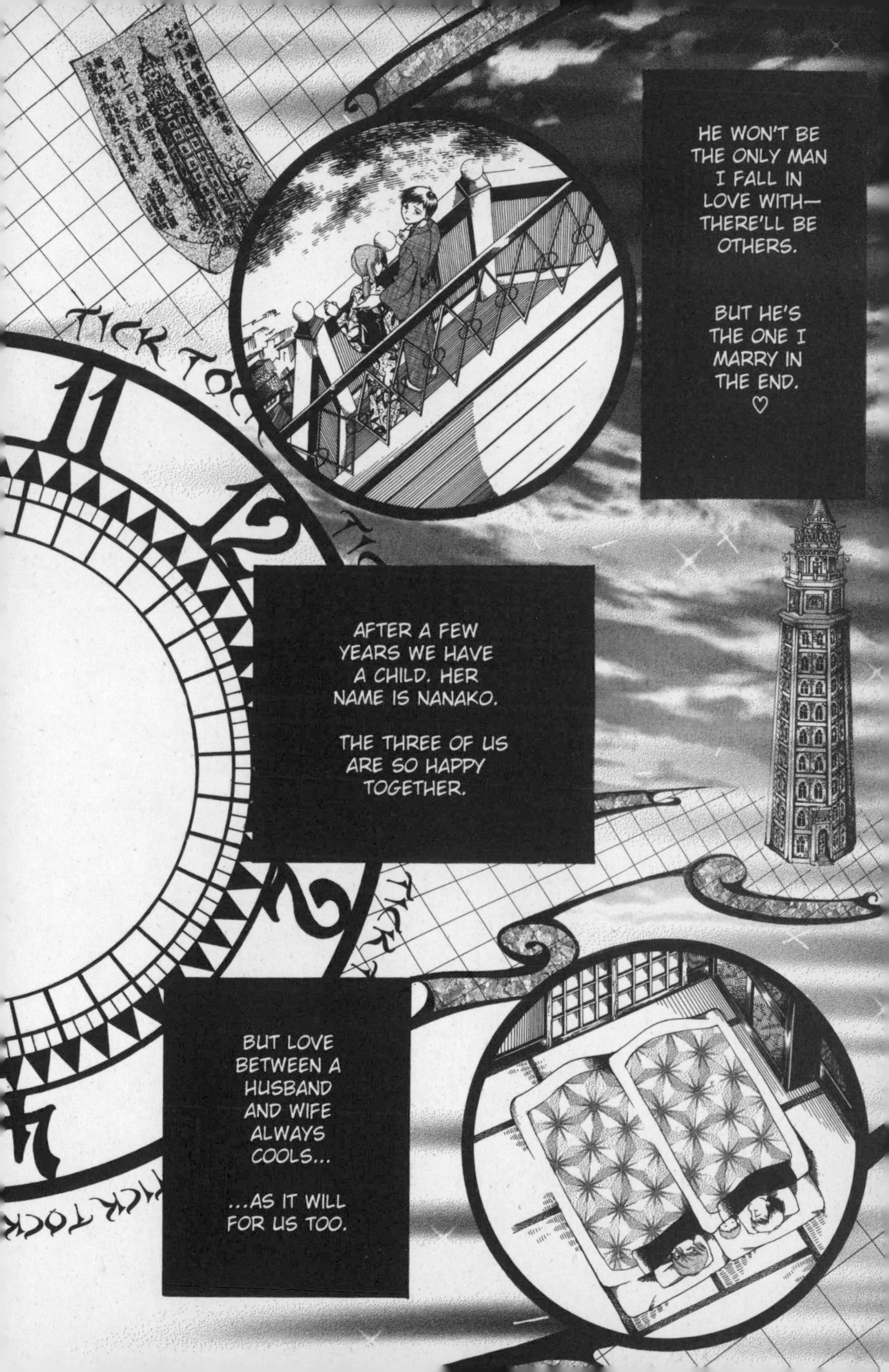
HE WON'T BE THE ONLY MAN I FALL IN LOVE WITH—THERE'LL BE OTHERS.
BUT HE'S THE ONE I MARRY IN THE END. ♡
TICK TOCK
TICK
AFTER A FEW YEARS WE HAVE A CHILD. HER NAME IS NANAKO.
THE THREE OF US ARE SO HAPPY TOGETHER.
TICK
BUT LOVE BETWEEN A HUSBAND AND WIFE ALWAYS COOLS...
...AS IT WILL FOR US TOO.
TICK TOCK

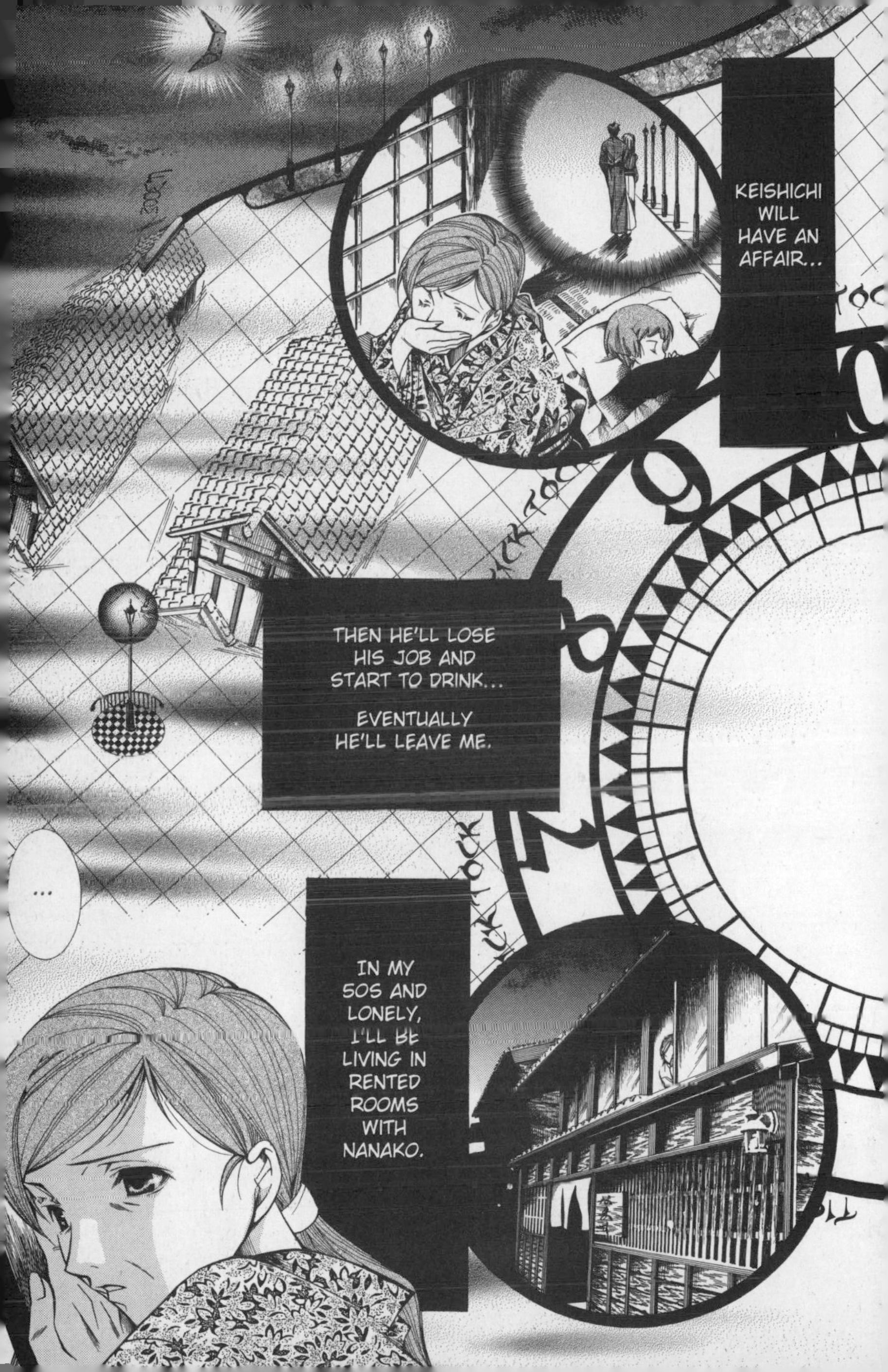
KEISHICHI WILL HAVE AN AFFAIR...
THEN HE'LL LOSE HIS JOB AND START TO DRINK...
EVENTUALLY HE'LL LEAVE ME.
...
IN MY 50S AND LONELY, I'LL BE LIVING IN RENTED ROOMS WITH NANAKO.

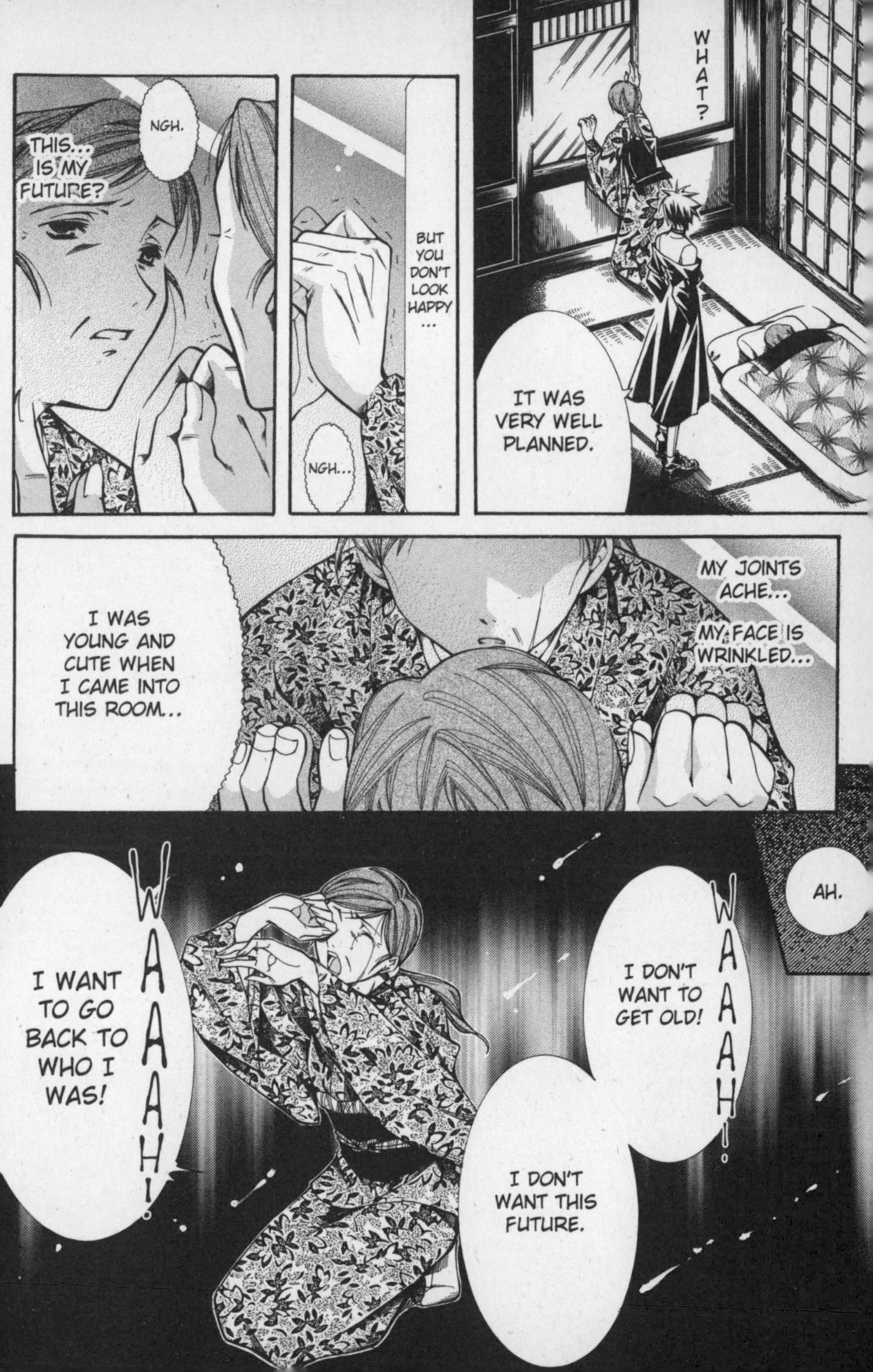

WHAT?
IT WAS VERY WELL PLANNED.
BUT YOU DON'T LOOK HAPPY...
NGH...
NGH.
THIS... IS MY FUTURE?
MY JOINTS ACHE...
MY FACE IS WRINKLED...
I WAS YOUNG AND CUTE WHEN I CAME INTO THIS ROOM...
AH.
WAAAH!
I DON'T WANT TO GET OLD!
I DON'T WANT THIS FUTURE.
WAAAH!
I WANT TO GO BACK TO WHO I WAS!

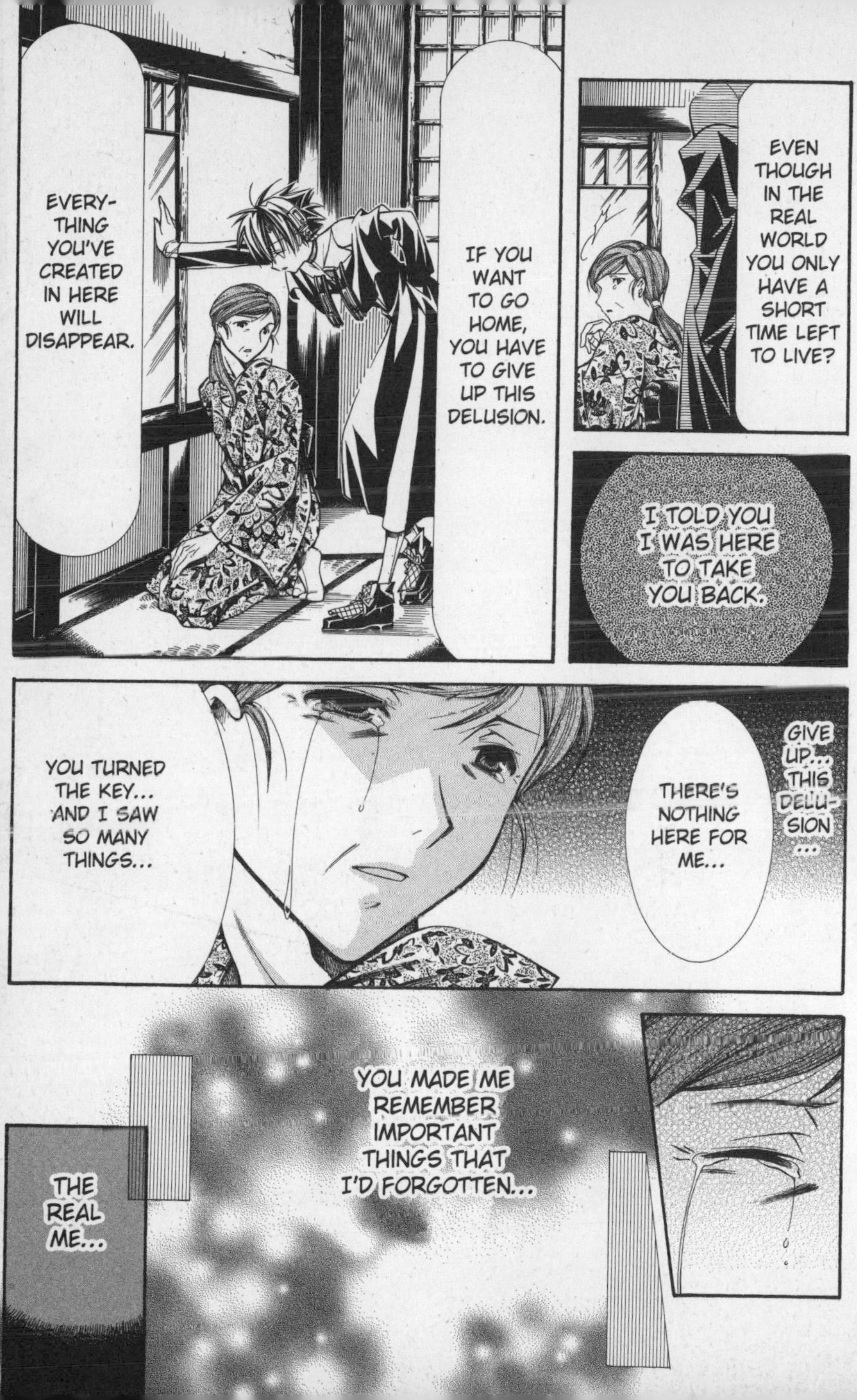
EVEN THOUGH IN THE REAL WORLD YOU ONLY HAVE A SHORT TIME LEFT TO LIVE?
I TOLD YOU I WAS HERE TO TAKE YOU BACK.
IF YOU WANT TO GO HOME, YOU HAVE TO GIVE UP THIS DELUSION.
EVERY-THING YOU'VE CREATED IN HERE WILL DISAPPEAR.
GIVE UP... THIS DELU-SION...
THERE'S NOTHING HERE FOR ME...
YOU TURNED THE KEY... AND I SAW SO MANY THINGS...
YOU MADE ME REMEMBER IMPORTANT THINGS THAT I'D FORGOTTEN...
THE REAL ME...

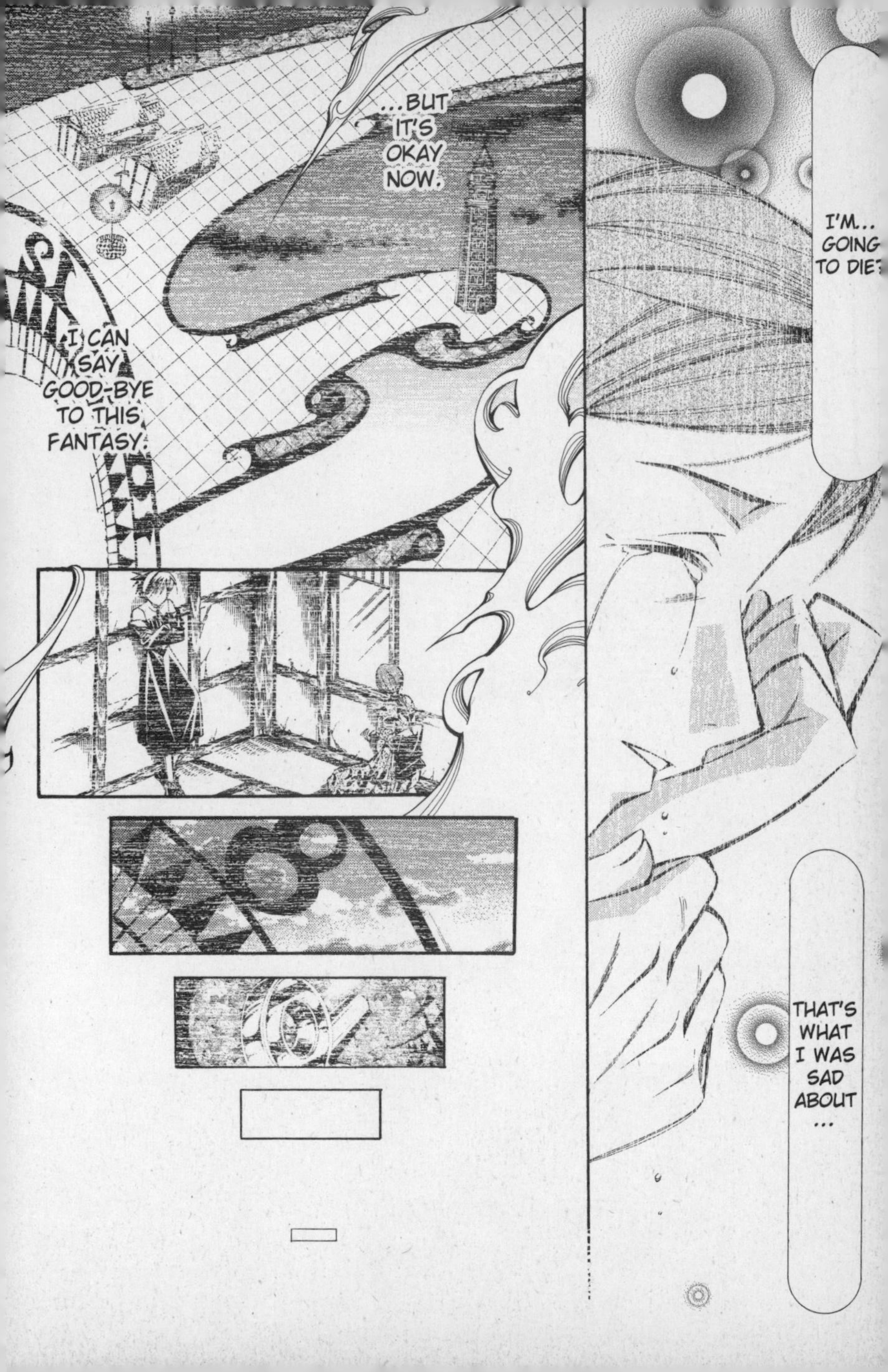
I'M... GOING TO DIE?
THAT'S WHAT I WAS SAD ABOUT...
...BUT IT'S OKAY NOW.
I CAN SAY GOOD-BYE TO THIS FANTASY.

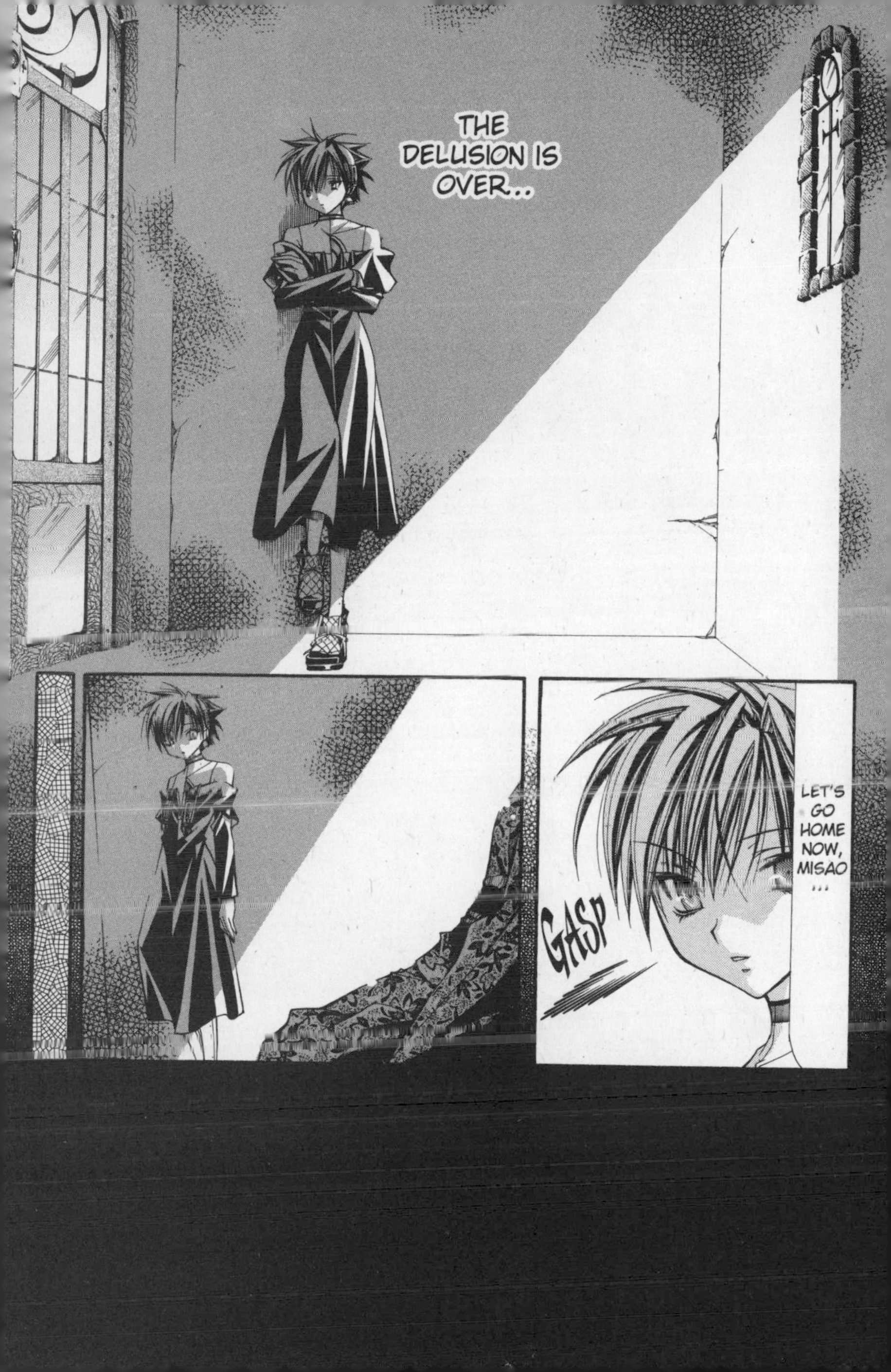
THE DELUSION IS OVER...
LET'S GO HOME NOW, MISAO...
GASP

WHAT HAPPENED?!

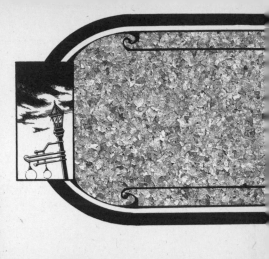

THIS ISN'T LITTLE MISAO!

SHOULDN'T SHE GO BACK TO HER ORIGINAL, YOUTHFUL FORM WHEN THE DELUSION WAS OVER?

LITTLE MISAO.

I'M SO GLAD YOU'RE BACK...

I'M NANAKO.

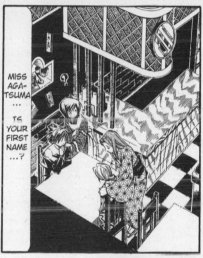

MISS AGA-TSUMA... IS YOUR FIRST NAME...?

MISAO WASN'T MISS AGATSUMA'S *DAUGHTER,* SHE WAS HER *MOTHER.*

SO YOUR FATHER'S NAME...

THEN...

AH.

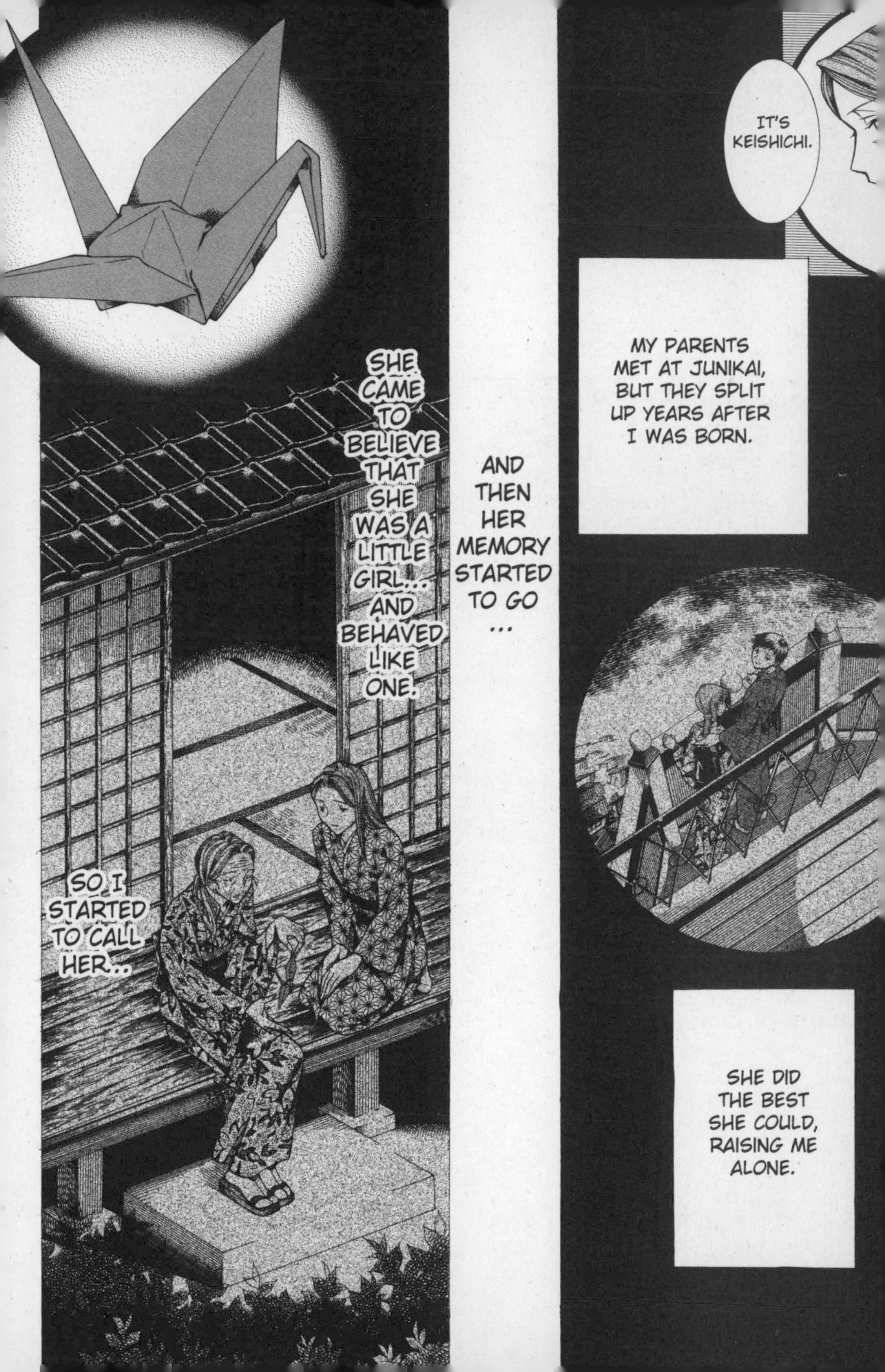
IT'S KEISHICHI.
MY PARENTS MET AT JUNIKAI, BUT THEY SPLIT UP YEARS AFTER I WAS BORN.
SHE DID THE BEST SHE COULD, RAISING ME ALONE.
AND THEN HER MEMORY STARTED TO GO...
SHE CAME TO BELIEVE THAT SHE WAS A LITTLE GIRL... AND BEHAVED LIKE ONE.
SO I STARTED TO CALL HER...

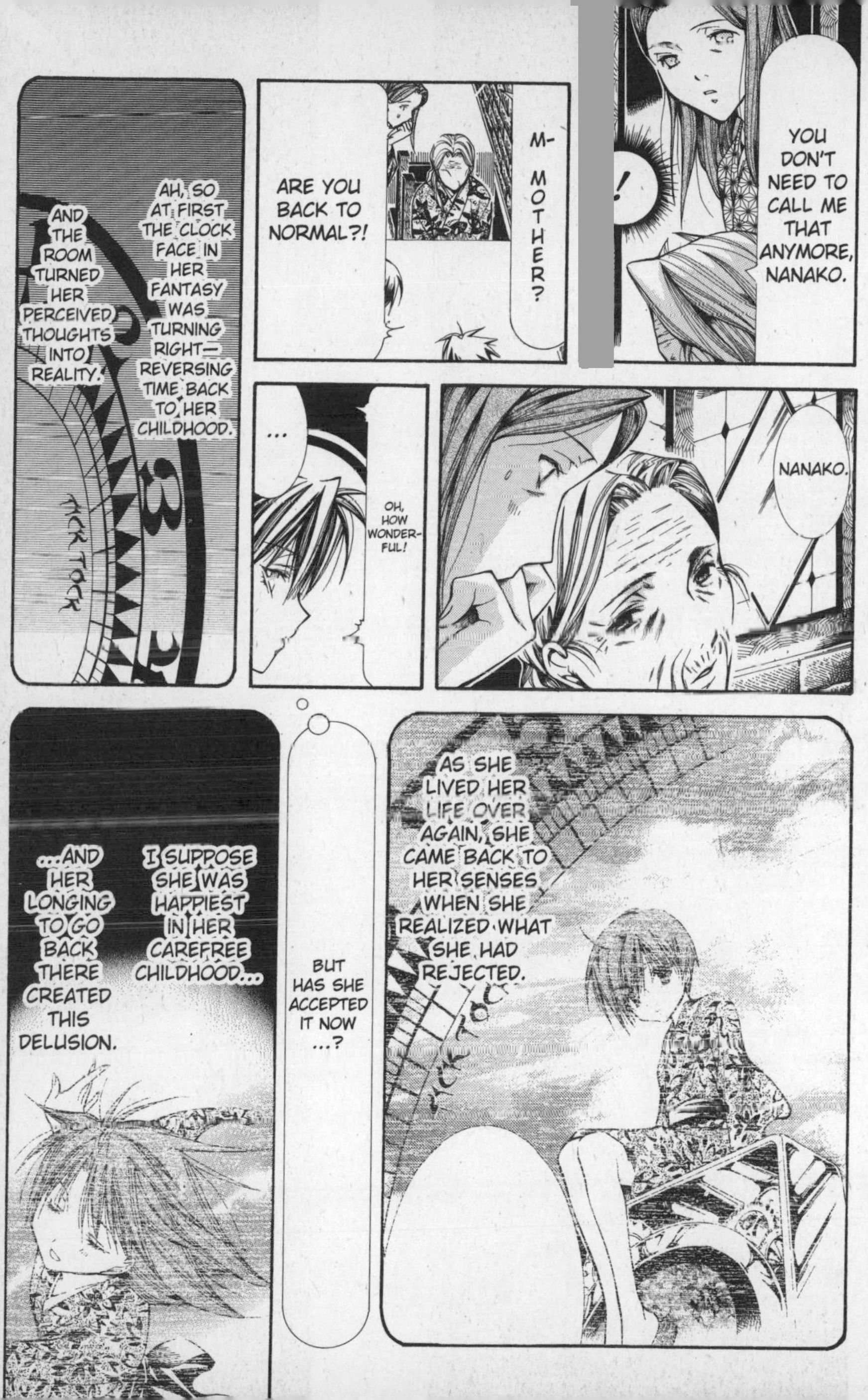
!
YOU DON'T NEED TO CALL ME THAT ANYMORE, NANAKO.
M-MOTHER?
ARE YOU BACK TO NORMAL?!
NANAKO.
...
OH, HOW WONDERFUL!
AH, SO AT FIRST THE CLOCK FACE IN HER FANTASY WAS TURNING RIGHT—REVERSING TIME BACK TO HER CHILDHOOD.
AND THE ROOM TURNED HER PERCEIVED THOUGHTS INTO REALITY.
TICK TOCK
AS SHE LIVED HER LIFE OVER AGAIN, SHE CAME BACK TO HER SENSES WHEN SHE REALIZED WHAT SHE HAD REJECTED.
BUT HAS SHE ACCEPTED IT NOW ...?
I SUPPOSE SHE WAS HAPPIEST IN HER CAREFREE CHILDHOOD...
...AND HER LONGING TO GO BACK THERE CREATED THIS DELUSION.

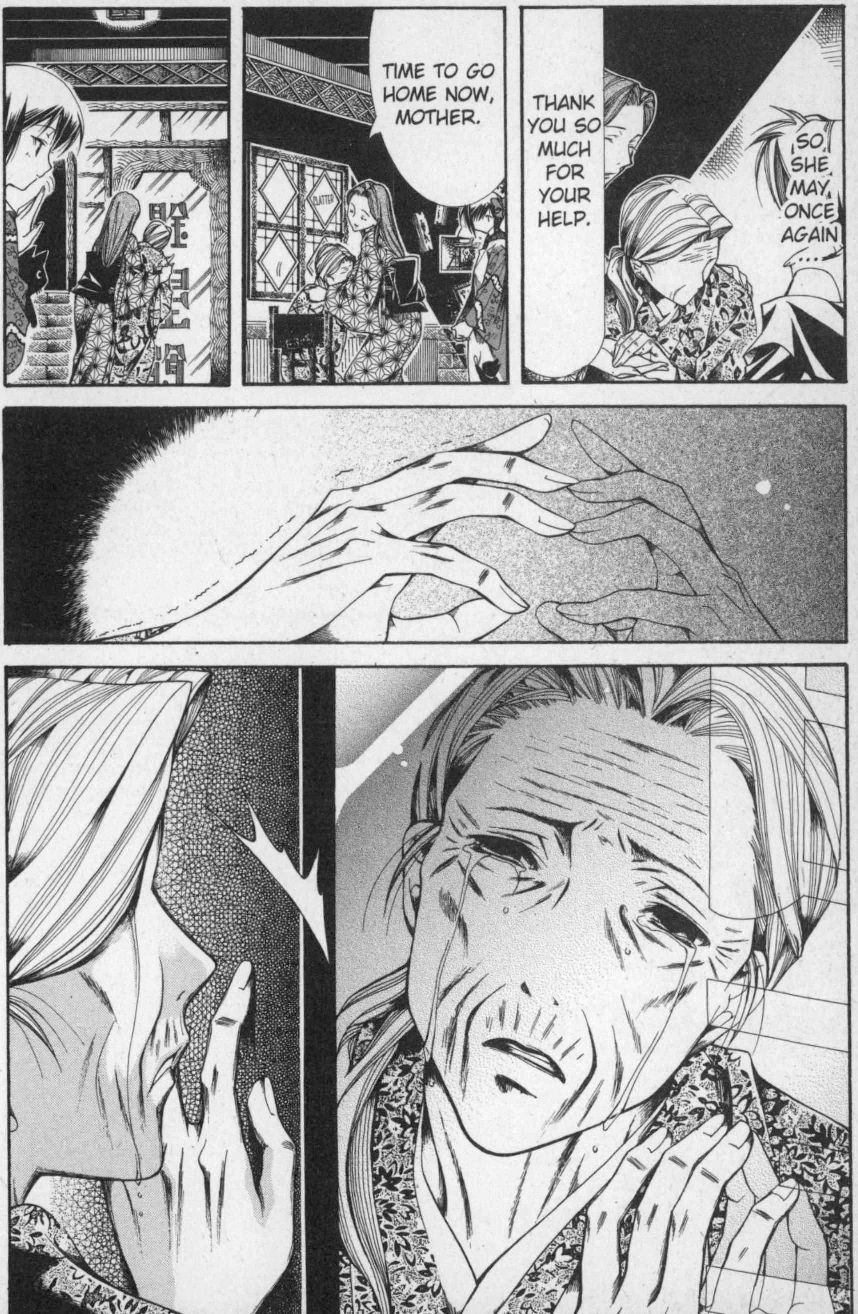
THANK YOU SO MUCH FOR YOUR HELP.
SO, SHE MAY ONCE AGAIN...
TIME TO GO HOME NOW, MOTHER.
CLATTER

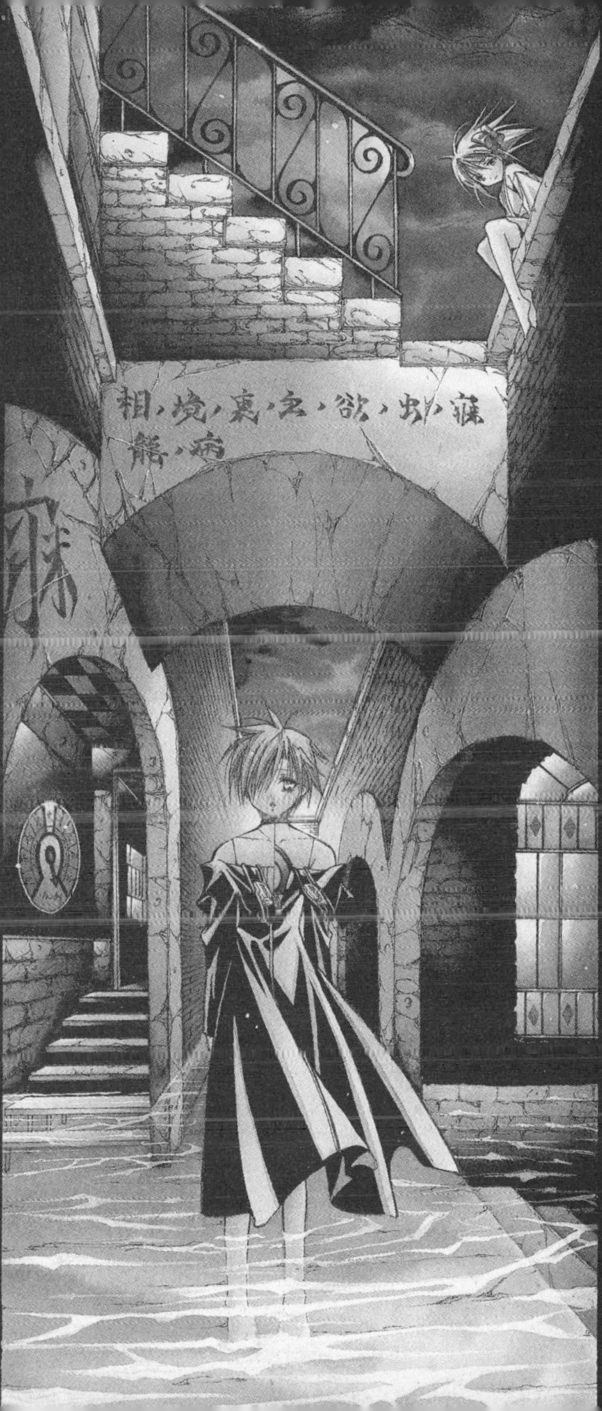

The Twenty-Sixth Night: Shadows

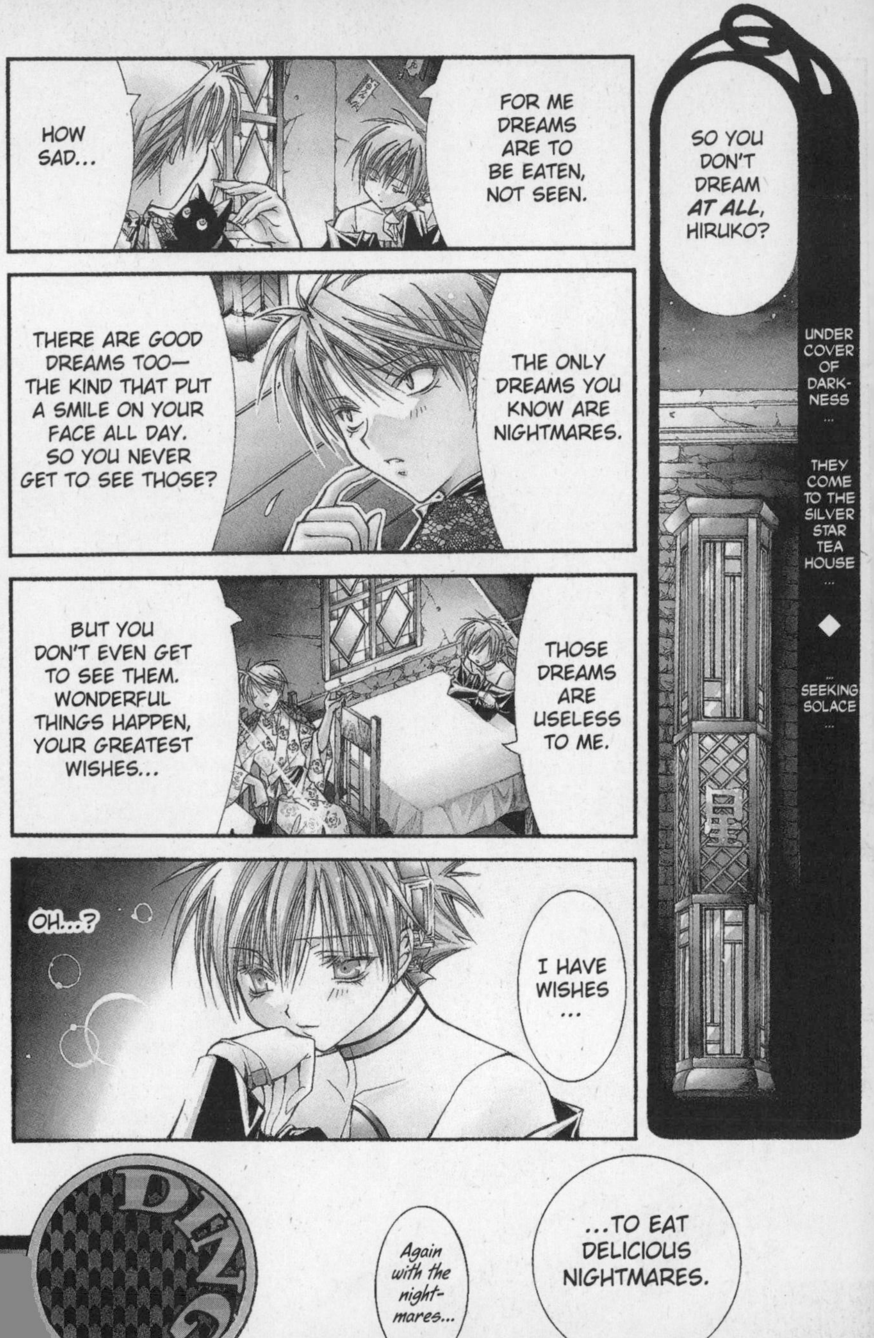
SO YOU DON'T DREAM *AT ALL*, HIRUKO?
UNDER COVER OF DARK-NESS ...
THEY COME TO THE SILVER STAR TEA HOUSE ...
◆
... SEEKING SOLACE ...
FOR ME DREAMS ARE TO BE EATEN, NOT SEEN.
HOW SAD...
THE ONLY DREAMS YOU KNOW ARE NIGHTMARES.
THERE ARE GOOD DREAMS TOO—THE KIND THAT PUT A SMILE ON YOUR FACE ALL DAY. SO YOU NEVER GET TO SEE THOSE?
THOSE DREAMS ARE USELESS TO ME.
BUT YOU DON'T EVEN GET TO SEE THEM. WONDERFUL THINGS HAPPEN, YOUR GREATEST WISHES...
I HAVE WISHES ...
OH...?
...TO EAT DELICIOUS NIGHTMARES.
Again with the night-mares...
DING

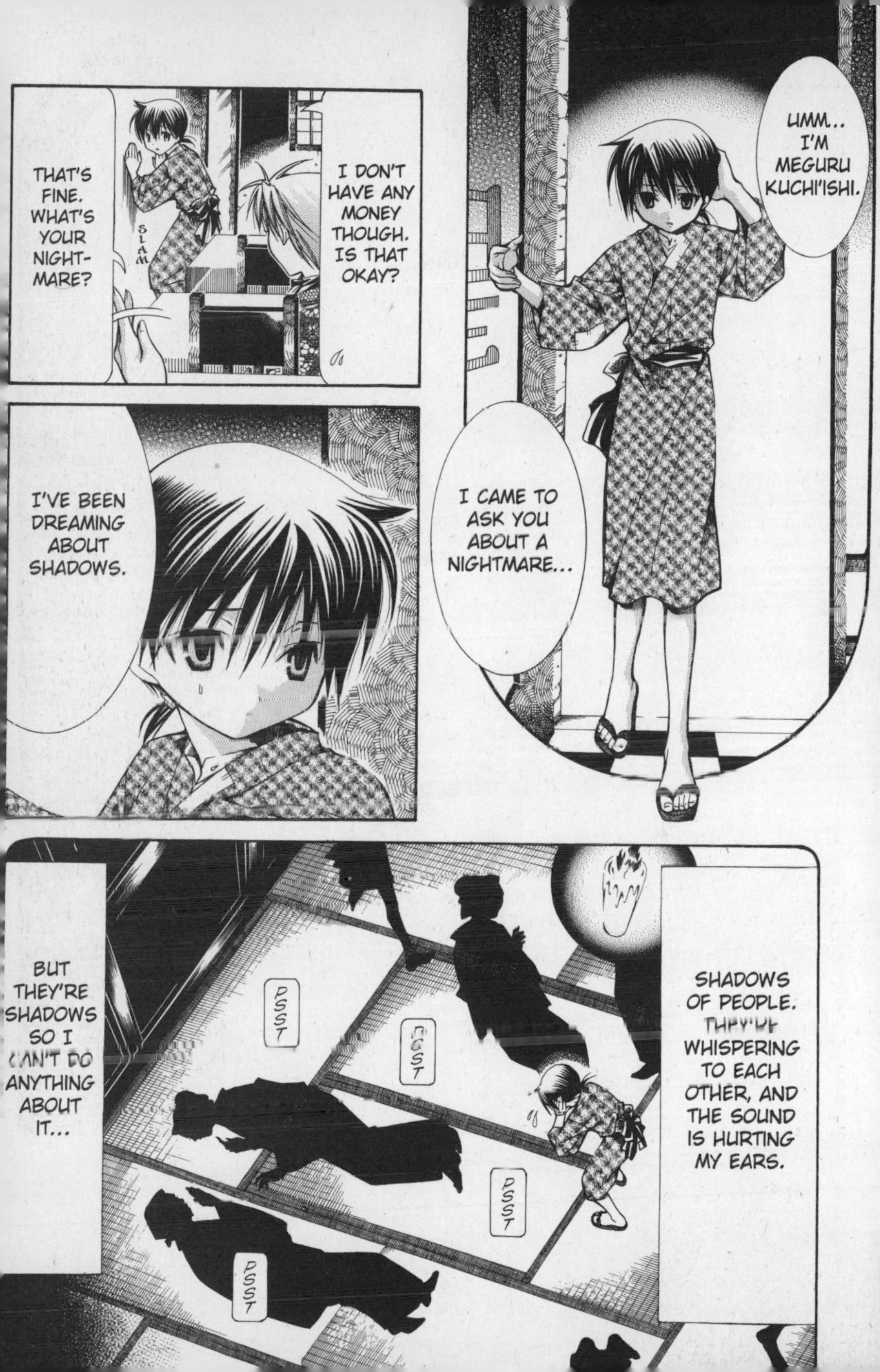
UMM... I'M MEGURU KUCHI'ISHI.
I CAME TO ASK YOU ABOUT A NIGHTMARE...
I DON'T HAVE ANY MONEY THOUGH. IS THAT OKAY?
SLAM
THAT'S FINE. WHAT'S YOUR NIGHT-MARE?
I'VE BEEN DREAMING ABOUT SHADOWS.
SHADOWS OF PEOPLE. THEY'RE WHISPERING TO EACH OTHER, AND THE SOUND IS HURTING MY EARS.
PSST
PSST
PSST
PSST
BUT THEY'RE SHADOWS SO I CAN'T DO ANYTHING ABOUT IT...

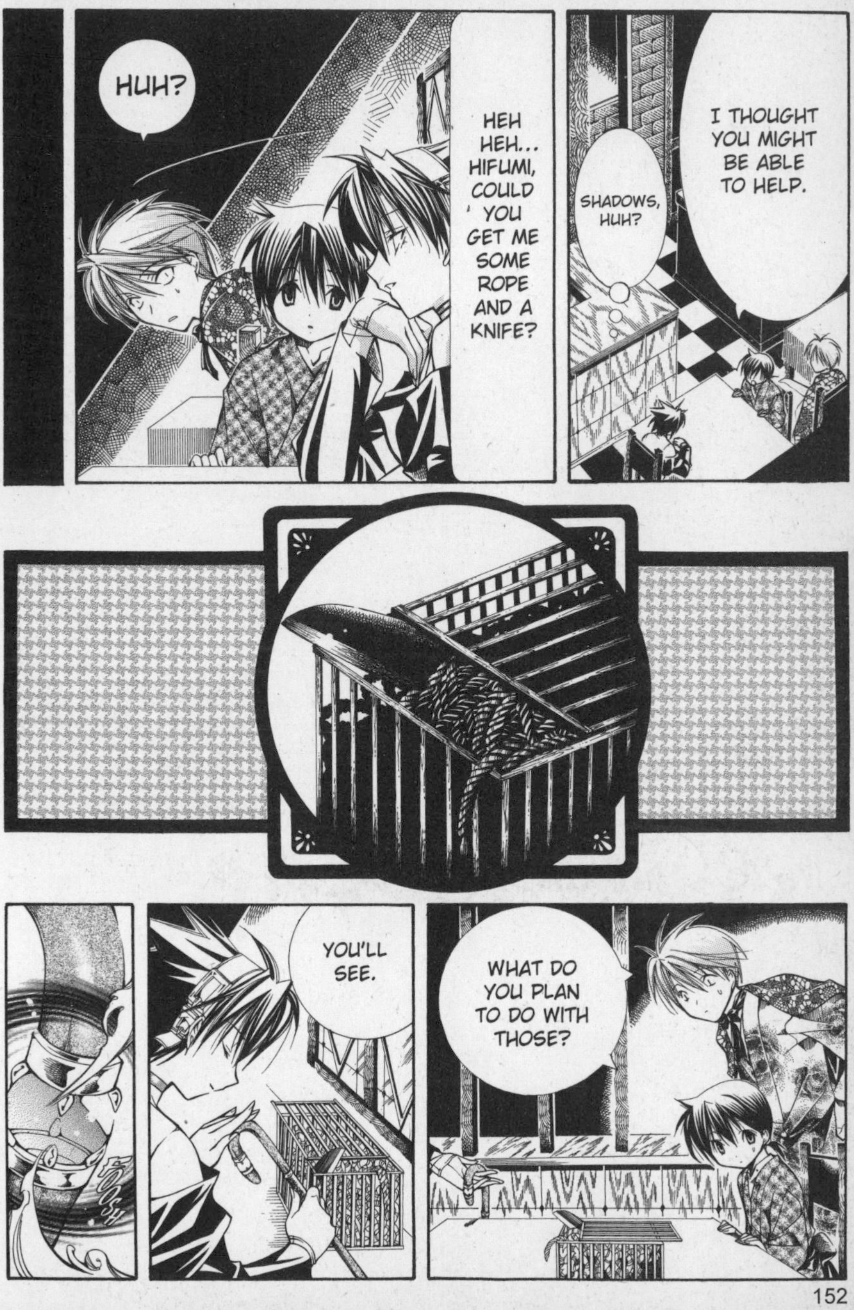
I THOUGHT YOU MIGHT BE ABLE TO HELP.
SHADOWS, HUH?
HEH HEH... HIFUMI, COULD YOU GET ME SOME ROPE AND A KNIFE?
HUH?
WHAT DO YOU PLAN TO DO WITH THOSE?
YOU'LL SEE.
FOOSH

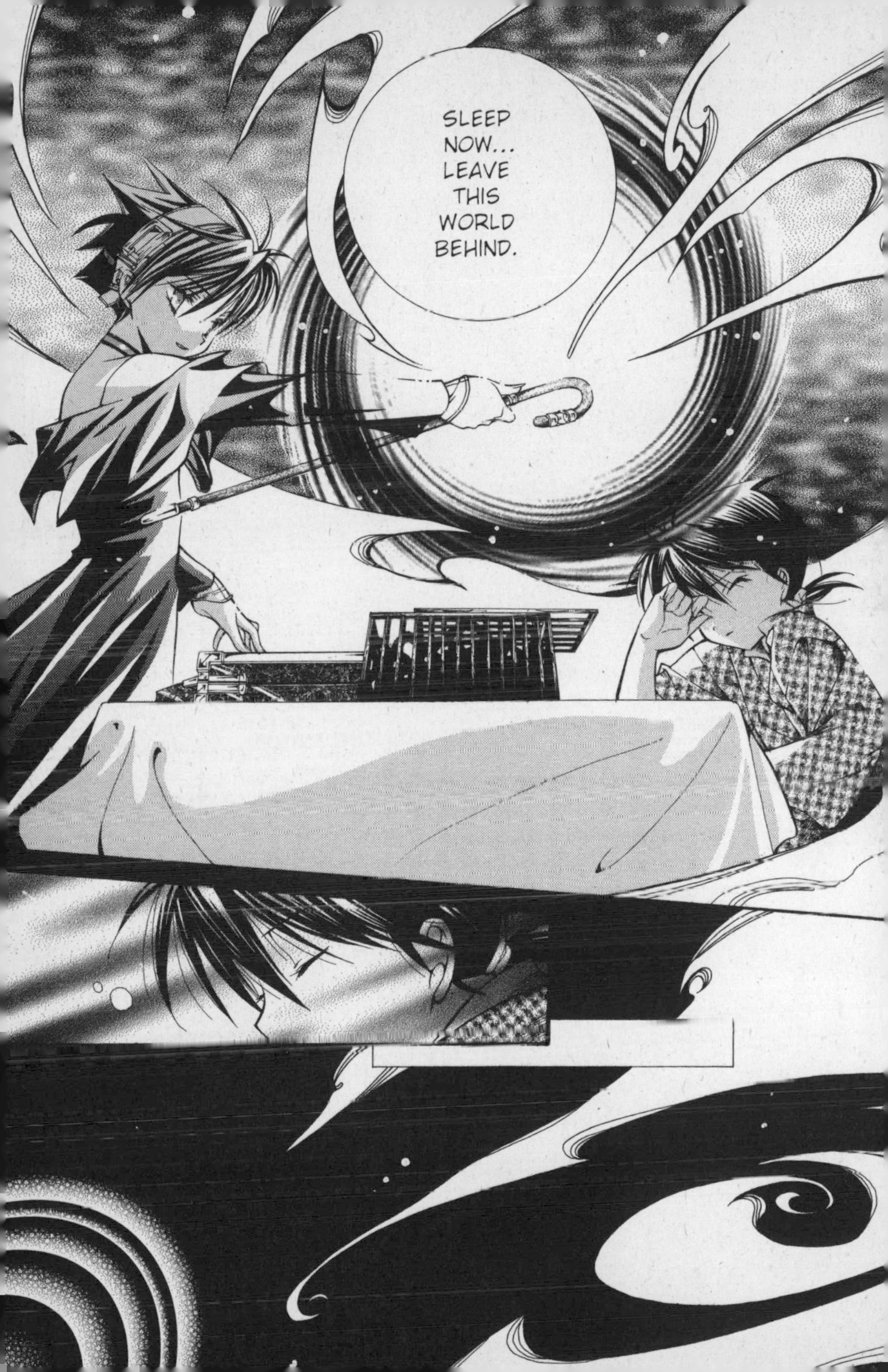
SLEEP NOW... LEAVE THIS WORLD BEHIND.

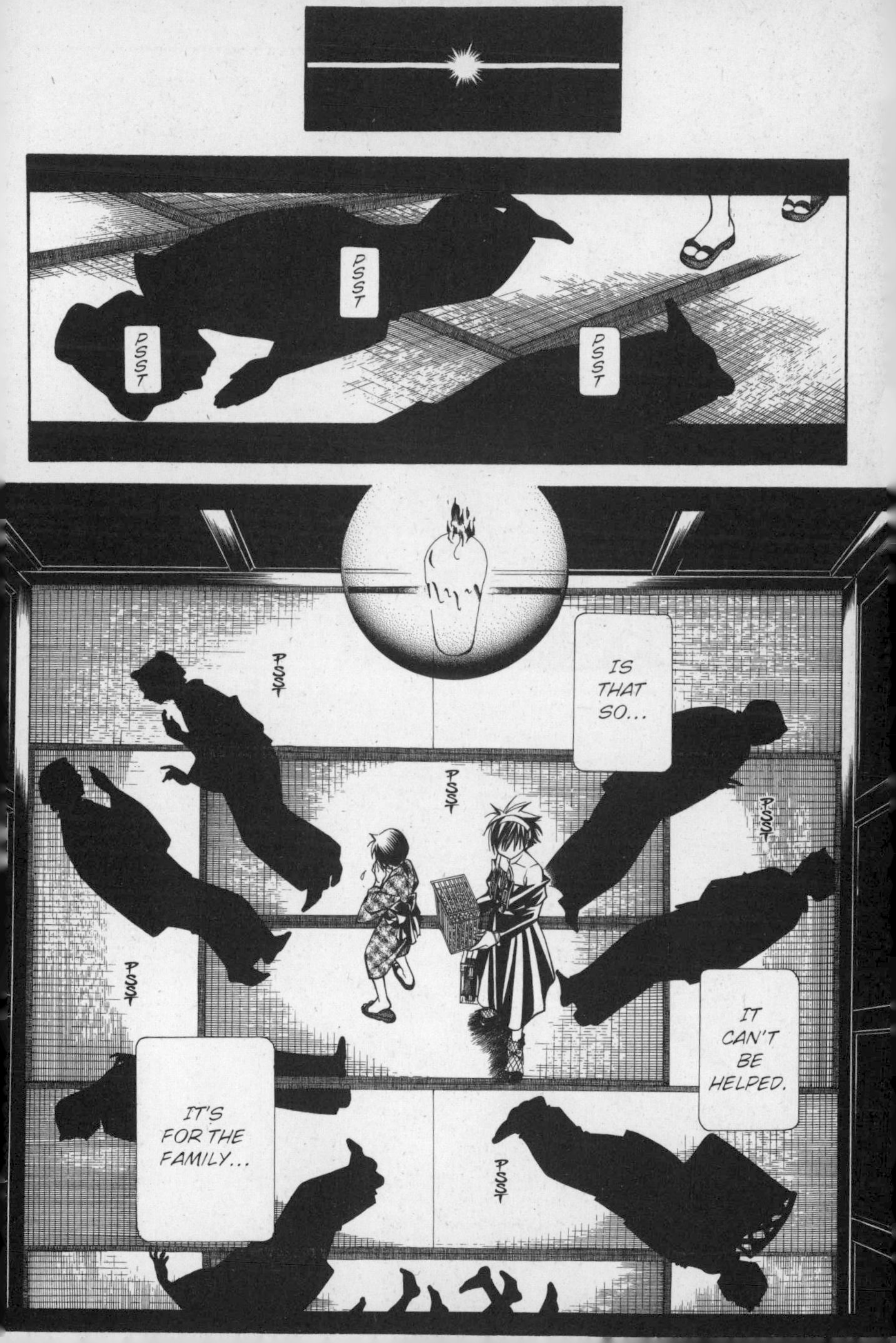
PSST
PSST
PSST
IS THAT SO...
PSST
PSST
PSST
IT CAN'T BE HELPED.
PSST
PSST
IT'S FOR THE FAMILY...

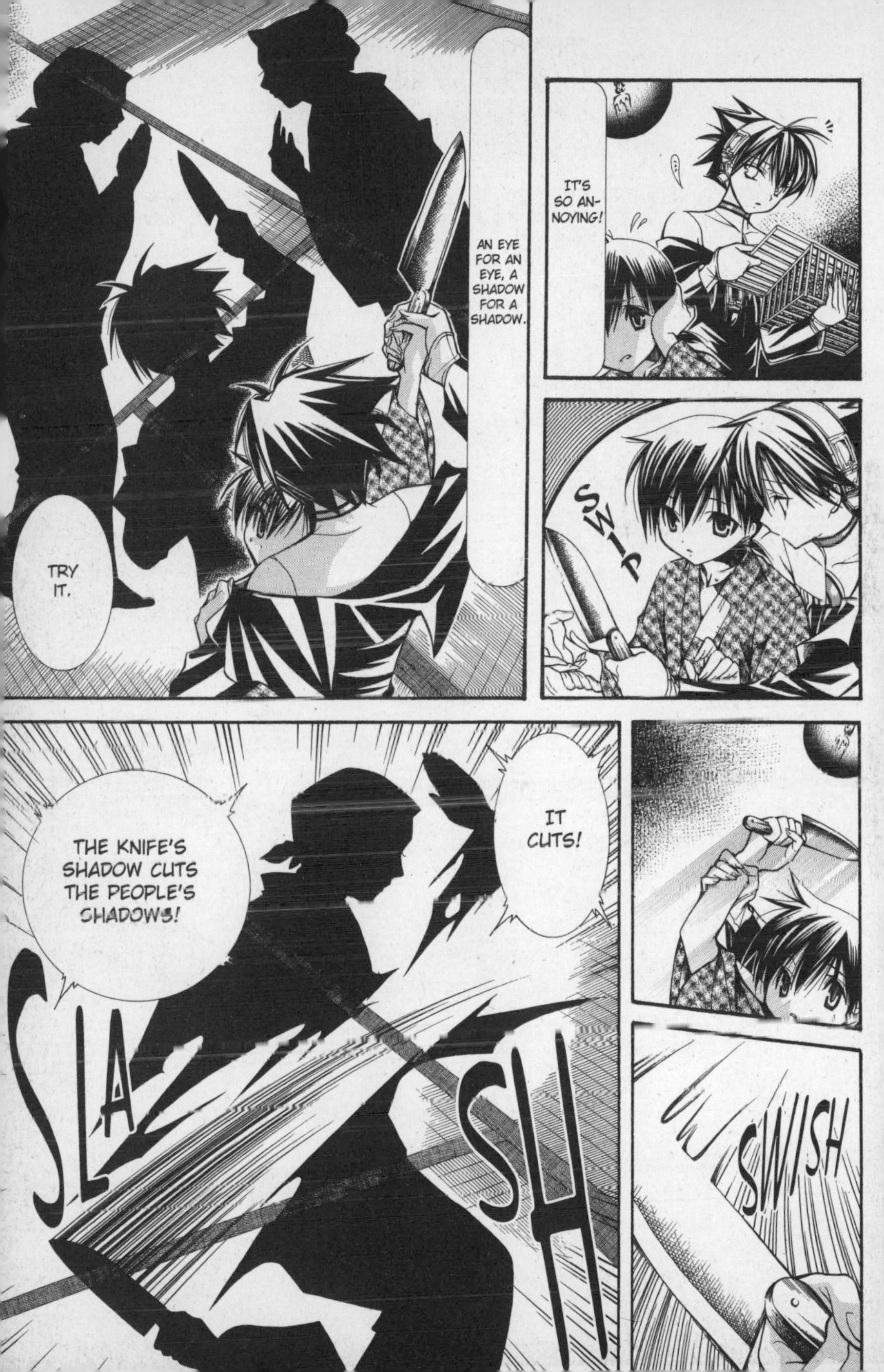
IT'S SO AN-NOYING!
SWIP
AN EYE FOR AN EYE, A SHADOW FOR A SHADOW.
TRY IT.
SWISH
IT CUTS!
THE KNIFE'S SHADOW CUTS THE PEOPLE'S SHADOWS!
SLASH

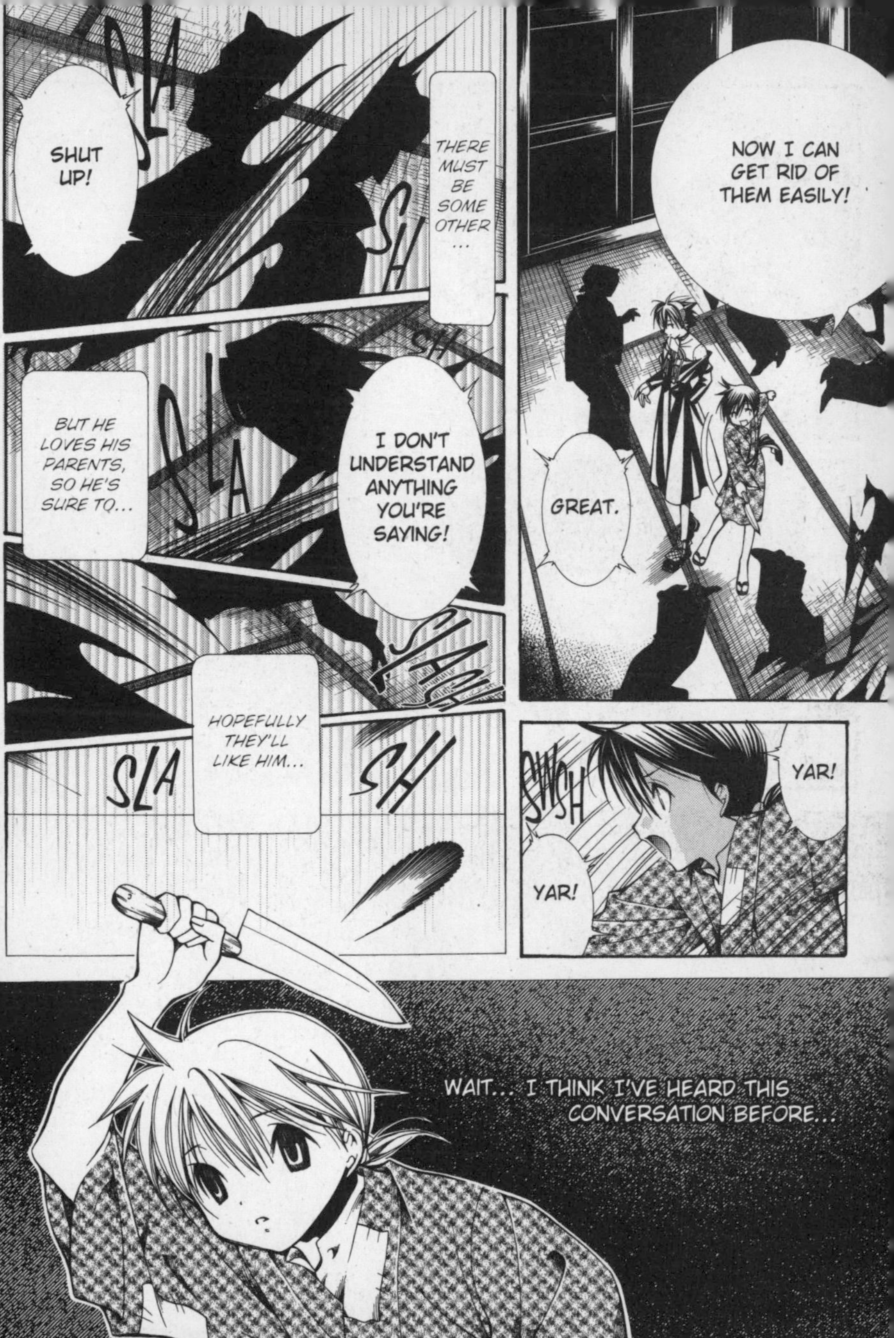
NOW I CAN GET RID OF THEM EASILY!
GREAT.
YAR!
SWSH
YAR!
THERE MUST BE SOME OTHER...
SLASH
SHUT UP!
SLASH
I DON'T UNDERSTAND ANYTHING YOU'RE SAYING!
BUT HE LOVES HIS PARENTS, SO HE'S SURE TO...
SLASH
HOPEFULLY THEY'LL LIKE HIM...
SLASH
WAIT... I THINK I'VE HEARD THIS CONVERSATION BEFORE...

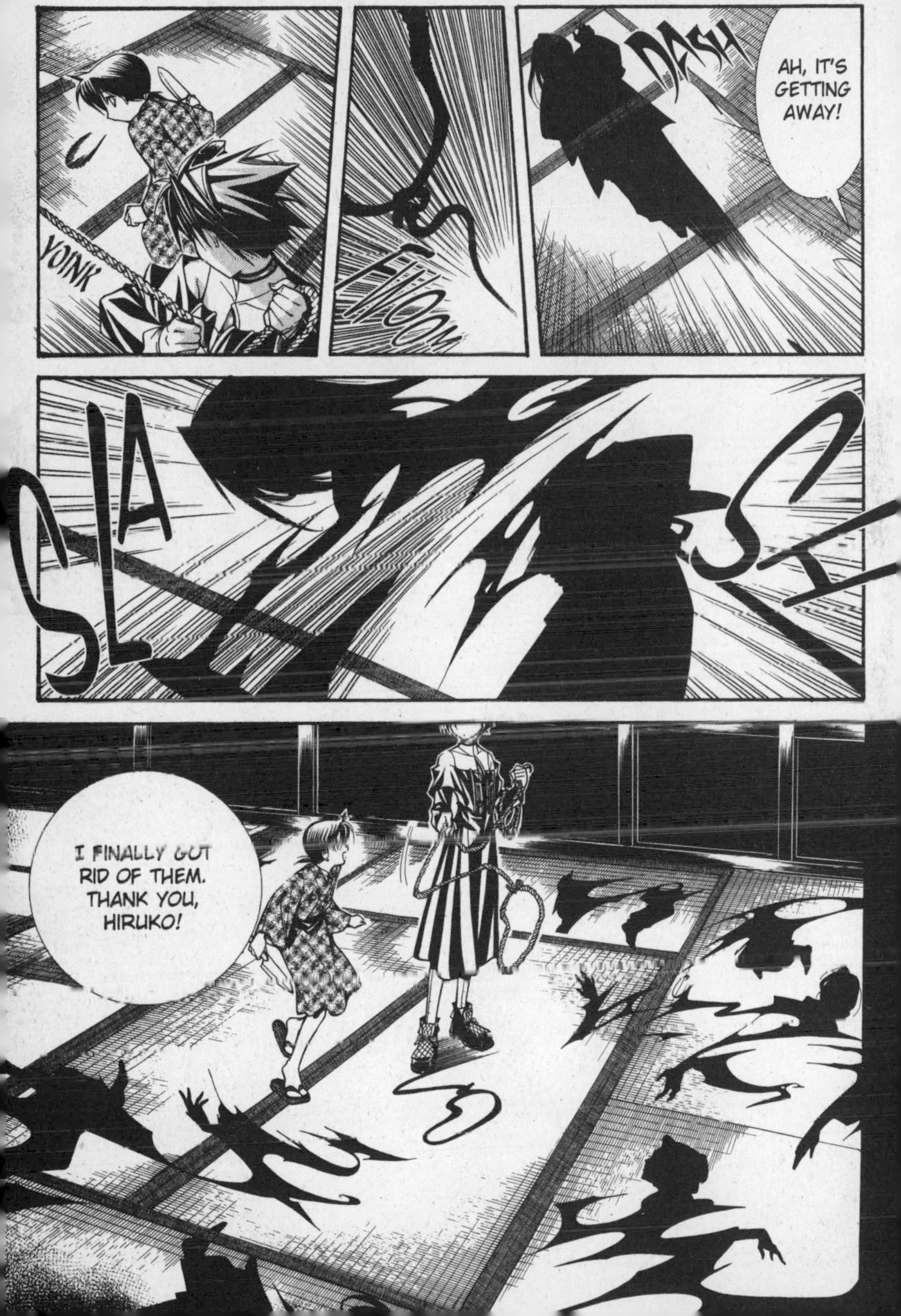
AH, IT'S GETTING AWAY!
DASH
FWOOM
YOINK
SLASH
I FINALLY GOT RID OF THEM. THANK YOU, HIRUKO!

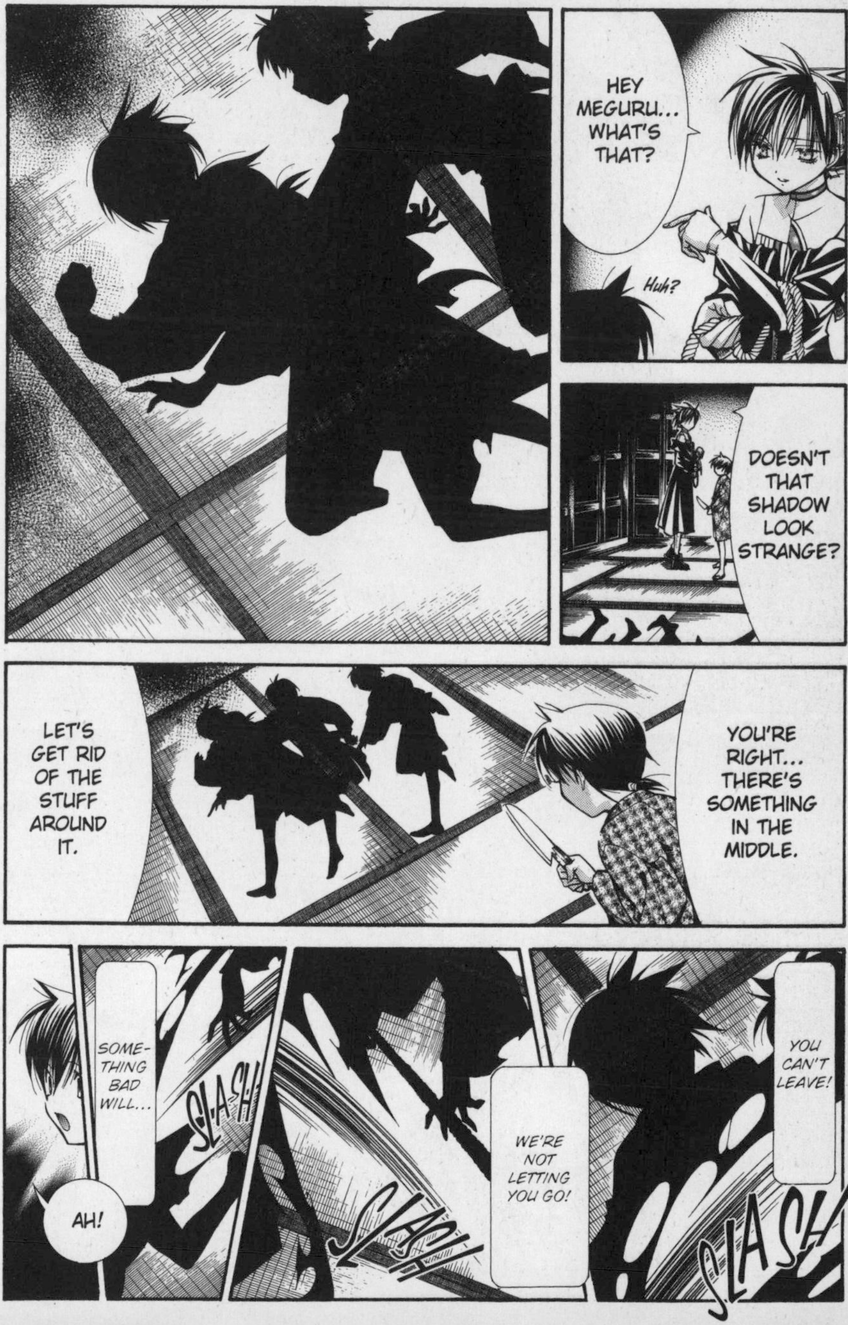
HEY MEGURU... WHAT'S THAT?
Huh?
DOESN'T THAT SHADOW LOOK STRANGE?
YOU'RE RIGHT... THERE'S SOMETHING IN THE MIDDLE.
LET'S GET RID OF THE STUFF AROUND IT.
YOU CAN'T LEAVE!
SLASH!
WE'RE NOT LETTING YOU GO!
SLASH
SOMETHING BAD WILL...
SLASH
AH!

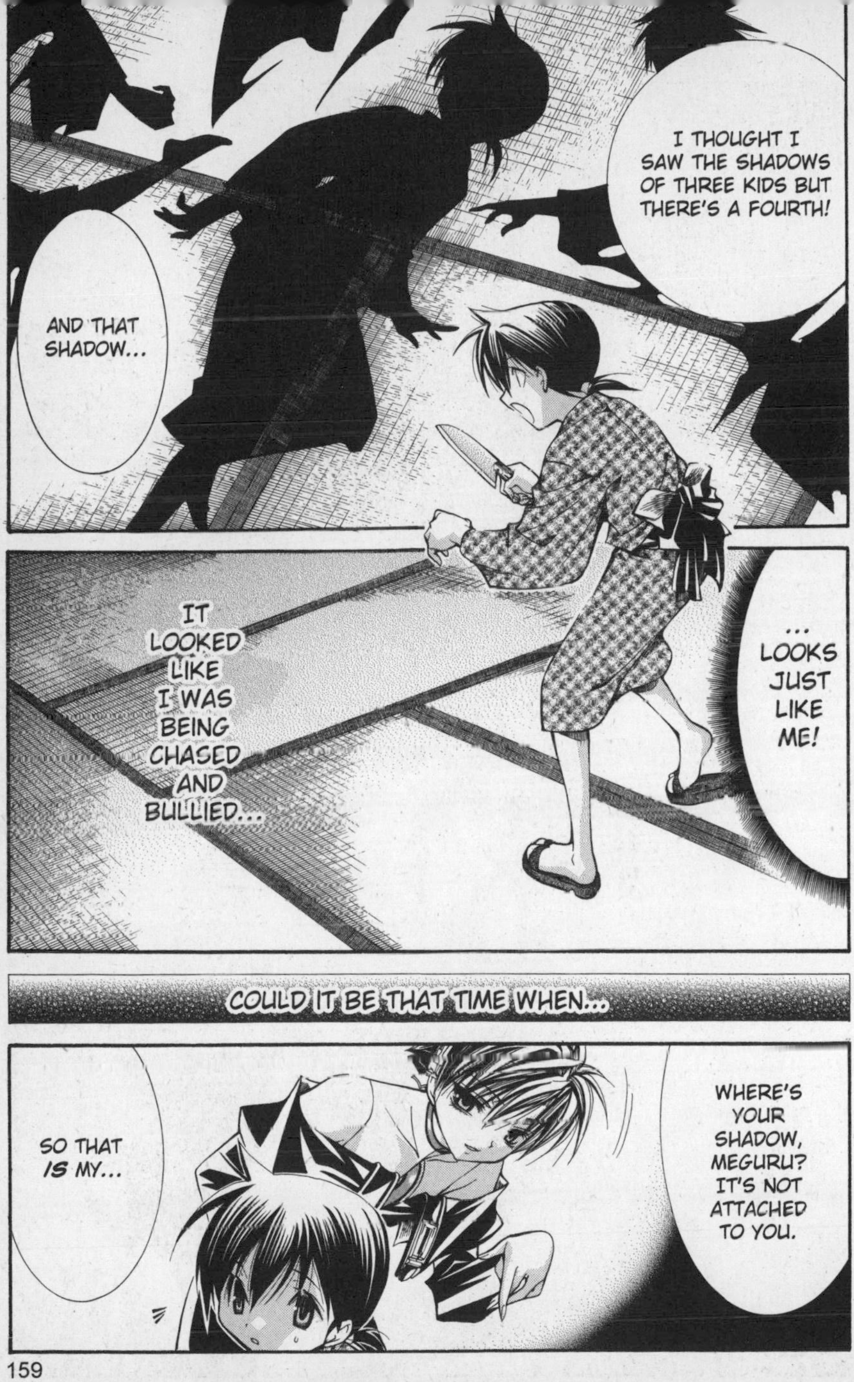
I THOUGHT I SAW THE SHADOWS OF THREE KIDS BUT THERE'S A FOURTH!
AND THAT SHADOW...
... LOOKS JUST LIKE ME!
IT LOOKED LIKE I WAS BEING CHASED AND BULLIED...
COULD IT BE THAT TIME WHEN...
WHERE'S YOUR SHADOW, MEGURU? IT'S NOT ATTACHED TO YOU.
SO THAT *IS* MY...

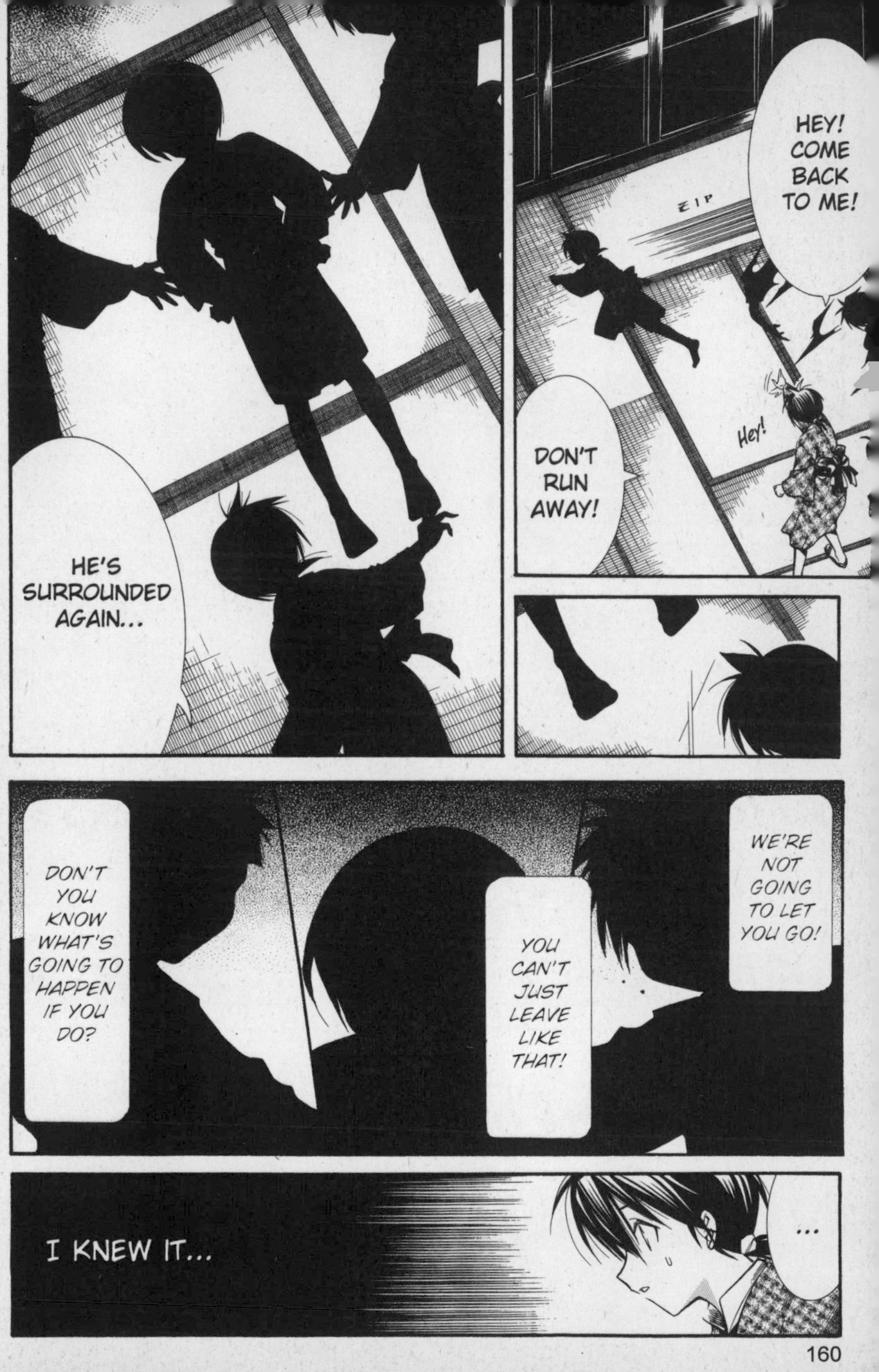
HEY! COME BACK TO ME!
ZIP
Hey!
DON'T RUN AWAY!
HE'S SURROUNDED AGAIN...
WE'RE NOT GOING TO LET YOU GO!
YOU CAN'T JUST LEAVE LIKE THAT!
DON'T YOU KNOW WHAT'S GOING TO HAPPEN IF YOU DO?
...
I KNEW IT...

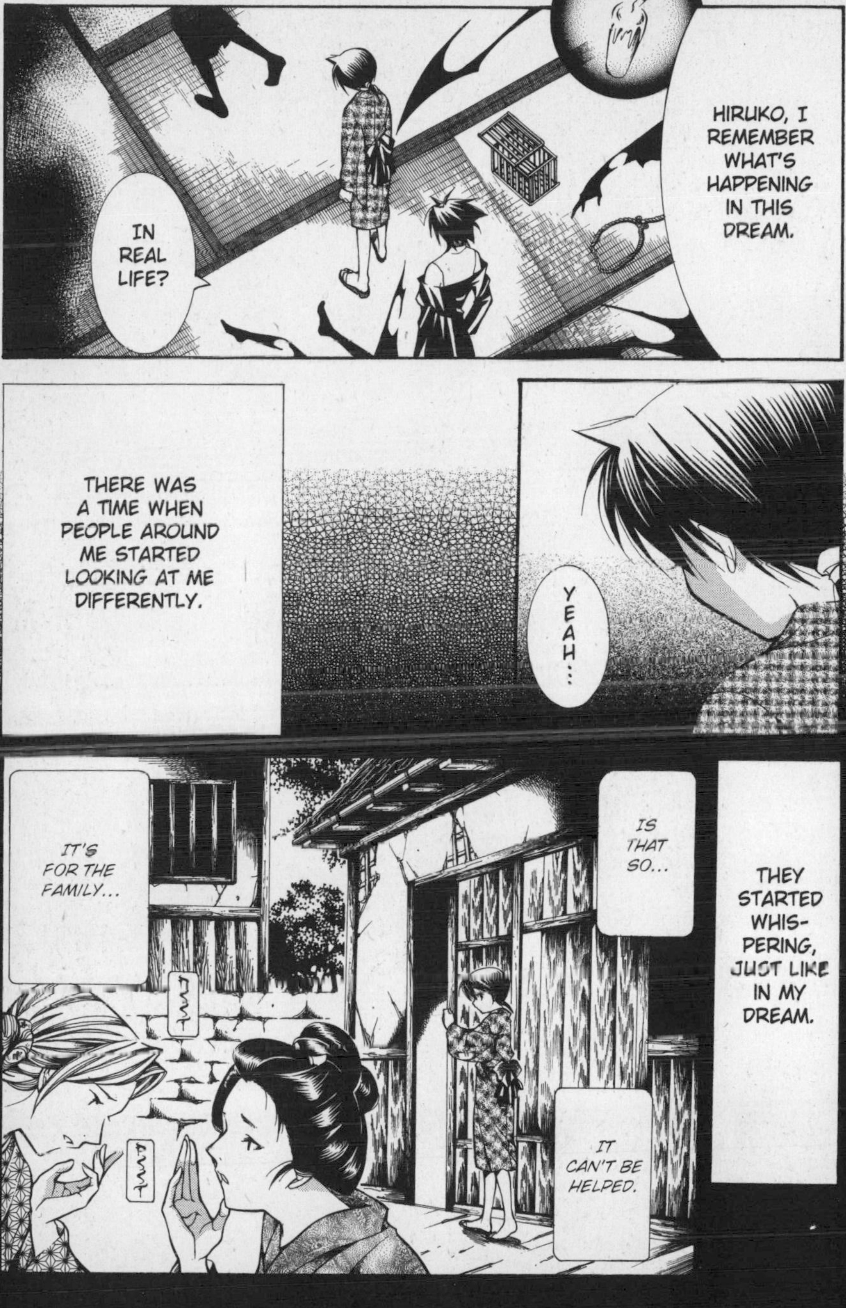
HIRUKO, I REMEMBER WHAT'S HAPPENING IN THIS DREAM.
IN REAL LIFE?
YEAH...
THERE WAS A TIME WHEN PEOPLE AROUND ME STARTED LOOKING AT ME DIFFERENTLY.
THEY STARTED WHISPERING, JUST LIKE IN MY DREAM.
IS THAT SO...
IT'S FOR THE FAMILY...
IT CAN'T BE HELPED.

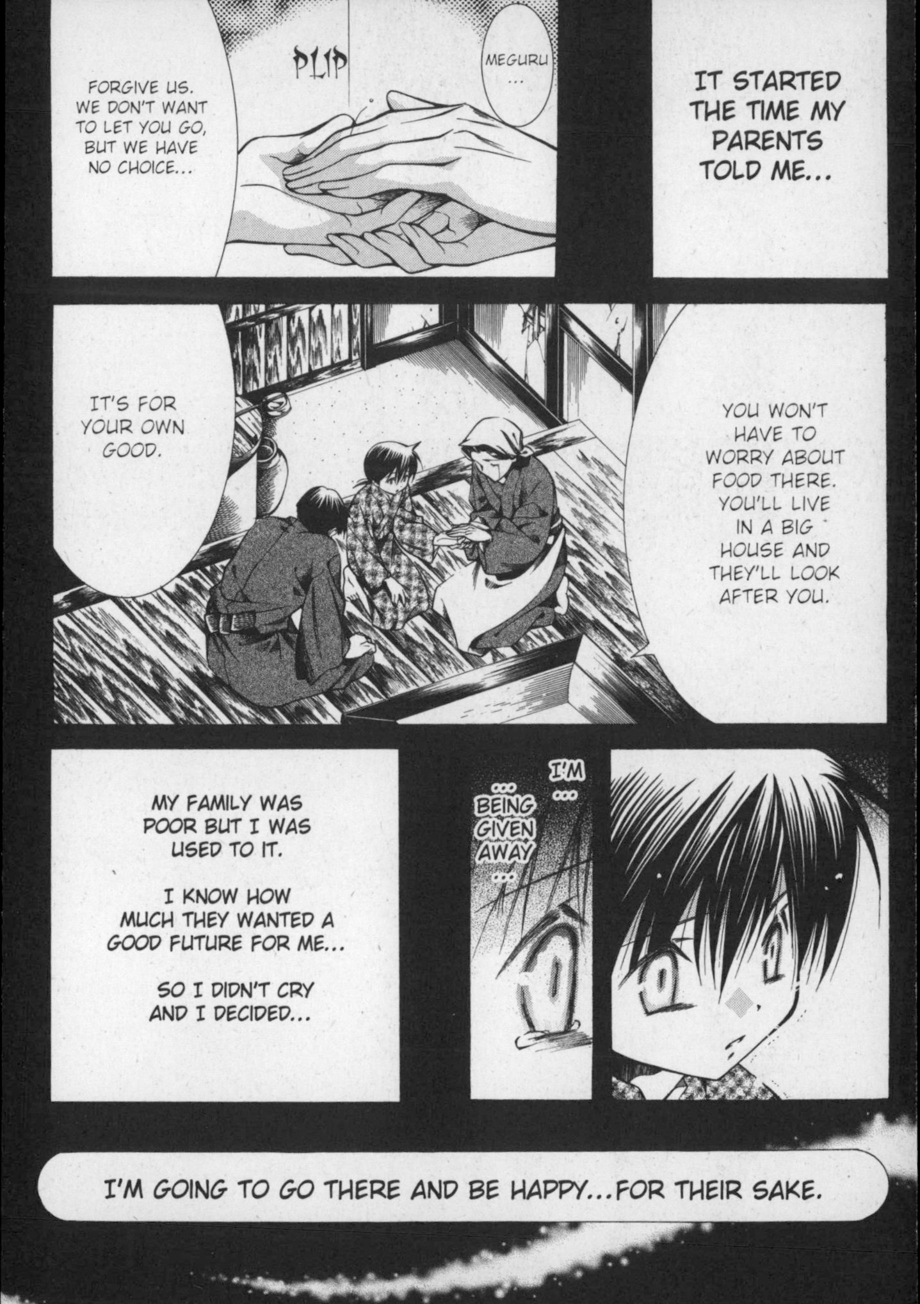
IT STARTED THE TIME MY PARENTS TOLD ME...
MEGURU ...
PLIP
FORGIVE US. WE DON'T WANT TO LET YOU GO, BUT WE HAVE NO CHOICE...
YOU WON'T HAVE TO WORRY ABOUT FOOD THERE. YOU'LL LIVE IN A BIG HOUSE AND THEY'LL LOOK AFTER YOU.
IT'S FOR YOUR OWN GOOD.
I'M ... ... BEING GIVEN AWAY ...
MY FAMILY WAS POOR BUT I WAS USED TO IT.
I KNOW HOW MUCH THEY WANTED A GOOD FUTURE FOR ME...
SO I DIDN'T CRY AND I DECIDED...
I'M GOING TO GO THERE AND BE HAPPY...FOR THEIR SAKE.

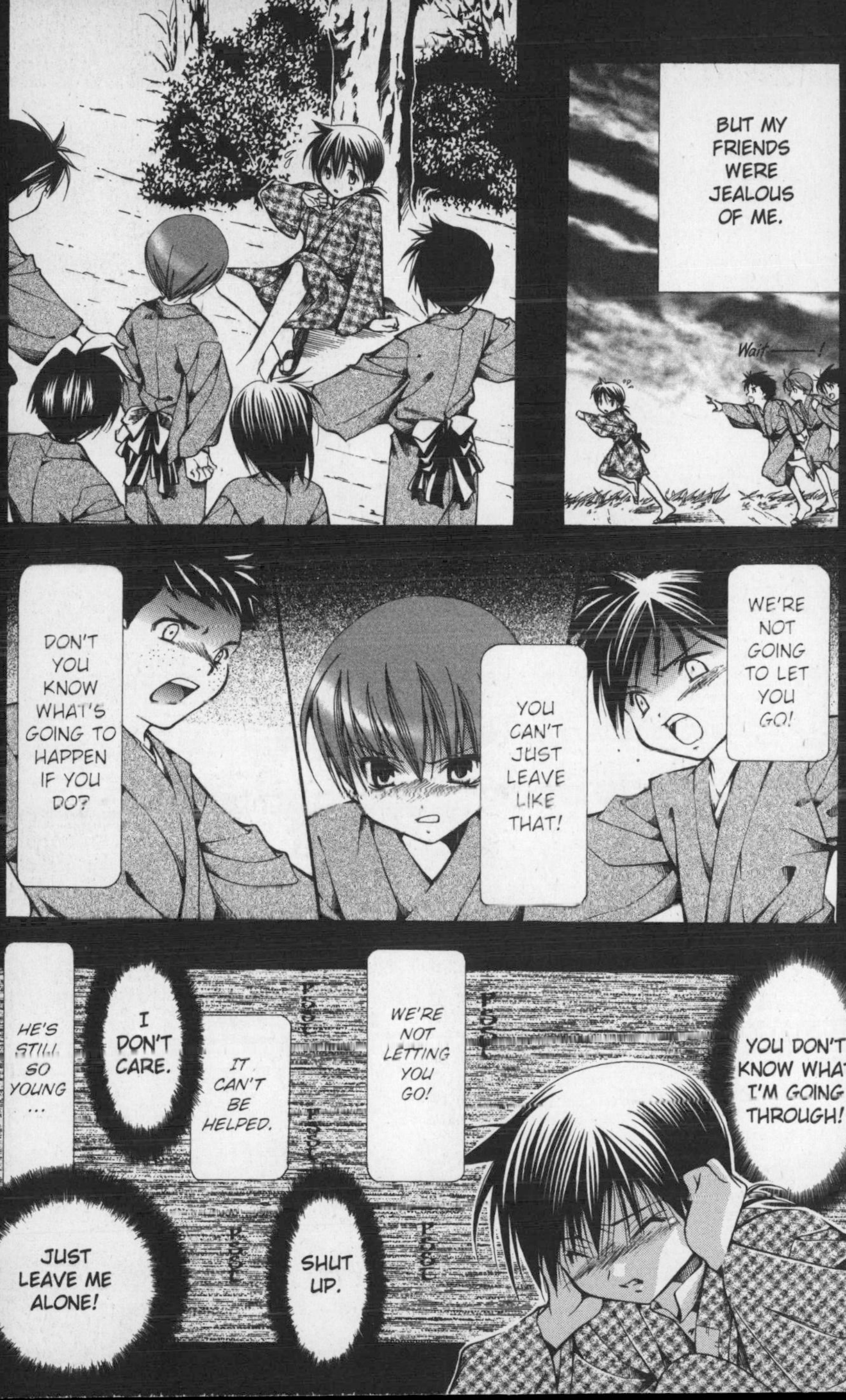
BUT MY FRIENDS WERE JEALOUS OF ME.
Wait——!
WE'RE NOT GOING TO LET YOU GO!
YOU CAN'T JUST LEAVE LIKE THAT!
DON'T YOU KNOW WHAT'S GOING TO HAPPEN IF YOU DO?
YOU DON'T KNOW WHAT I'M GOING THROUGH!
WE'RE NOT LETTING YOU GO!
IT CAN'T BE HELPED.
I DON'T CARE.
HE'S STILL SO YOUNG...
SHUT UP.
JUST LEAVE ME ALONE!

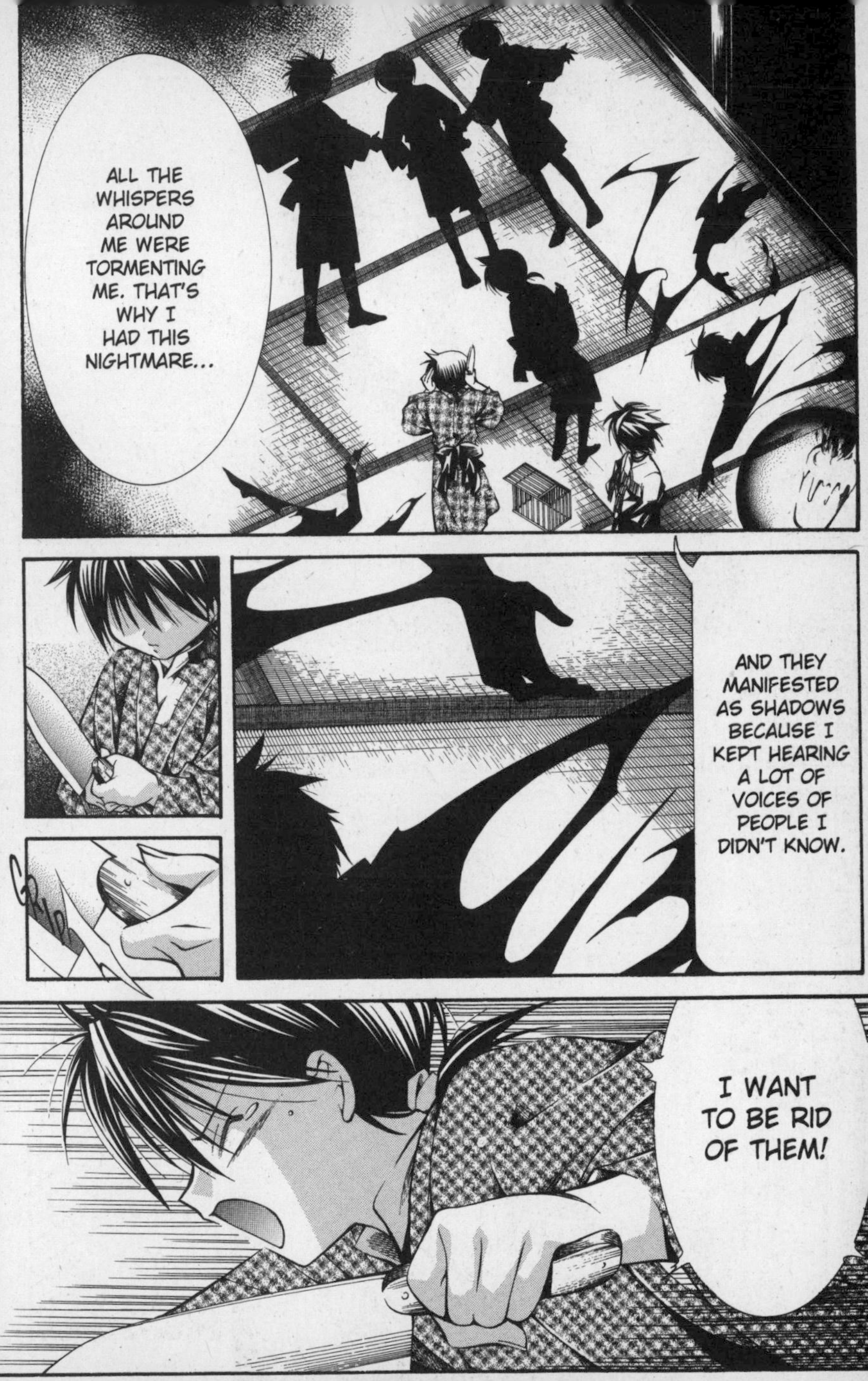
ALL THE WHISPERS AROUND ME WERE TORMENTING ME. THAT'S WHY I HAD THIS NIGHTMARE...
AND THEY MANIFESTED AS SHADOWS BECAUSE I KEPT HEARING A LOT OF VOICES OF PEOPLE I DIDN'T KNOW.
GRIP
I WANT TO BE RID OF THEM!

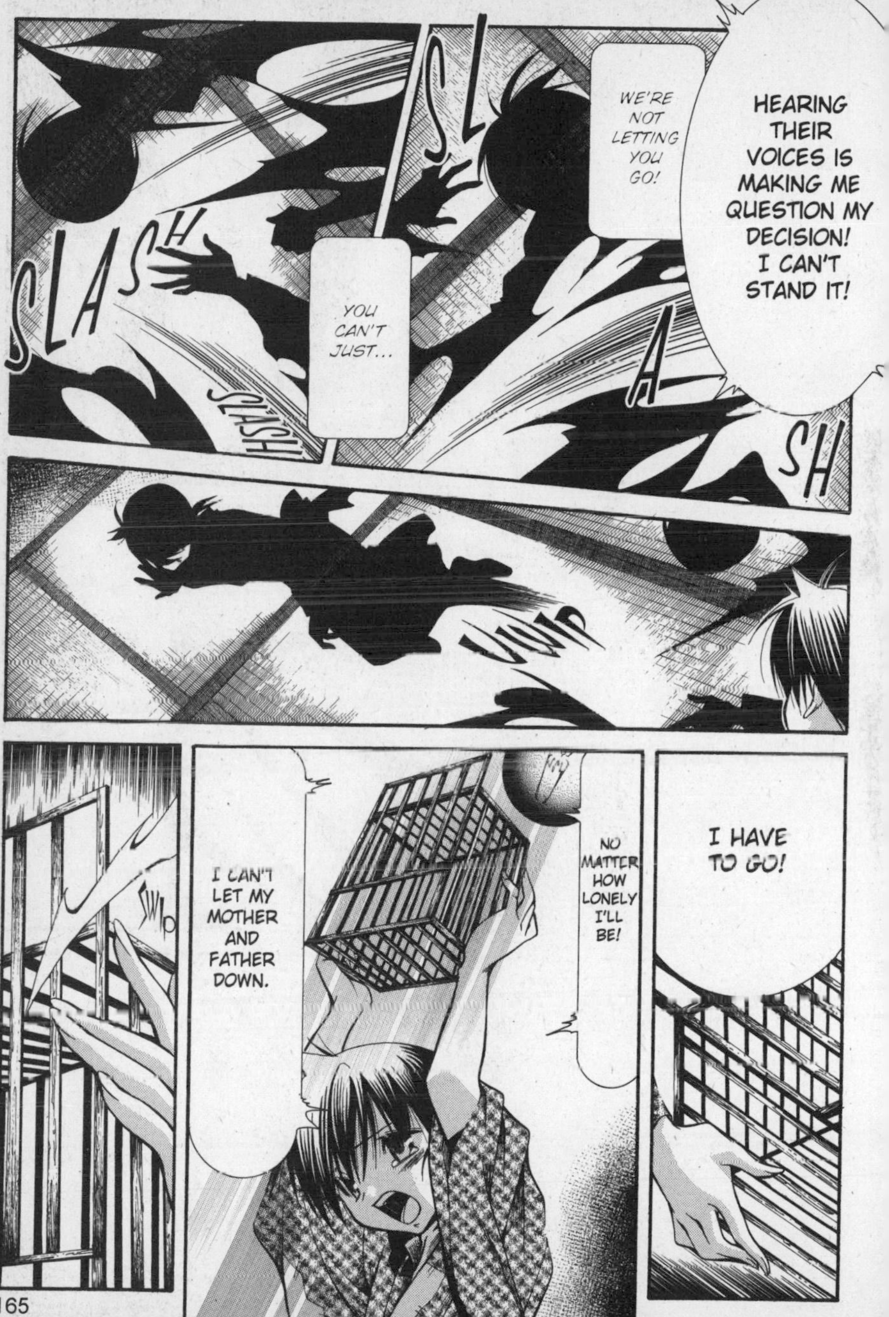
HEARING THEIR VOICES IS MAKING ME QUESTION MY DECISION! I CAN'T STAND IT!
WE'RE NOT LETTING YOU GO!
SLASH
YOU CAN'T JUST...
SLASH
SLASH!
SWIP
I HAVE TO GO!
NO MATTER HOW LONELY I'LL BE!
I CAN'T LET MY MOTHER AND FATHER DOWN.
SWIP

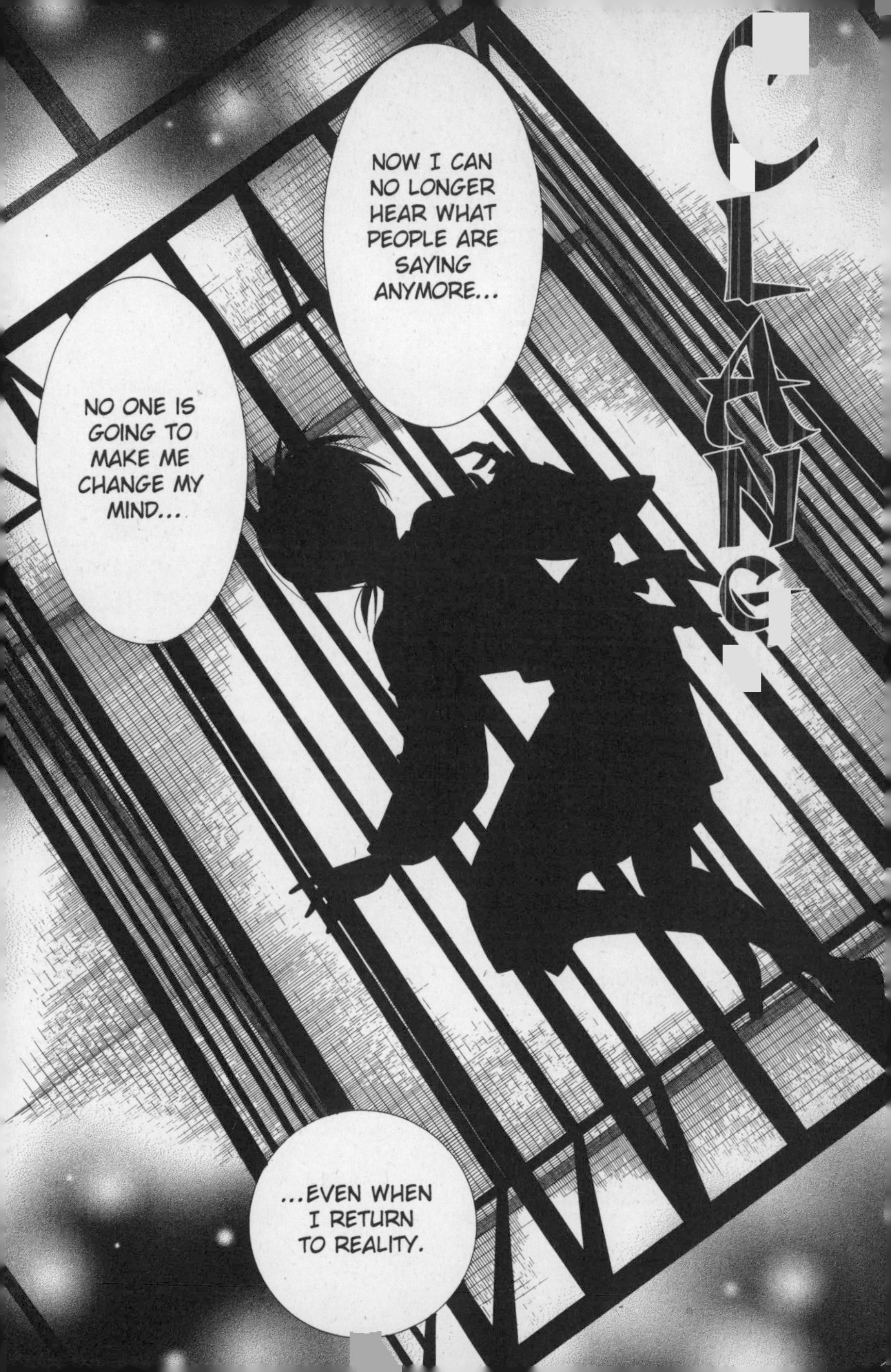
CLANG
NOW I CAN NO LONGER HEAR WHAT PEOPLE ARE SAYING ANYMORE...
NO ONE IS GOING TO MAKE ME CHANGE MY MIND...
...EVEN WHEN I RETURN TO REALITY.

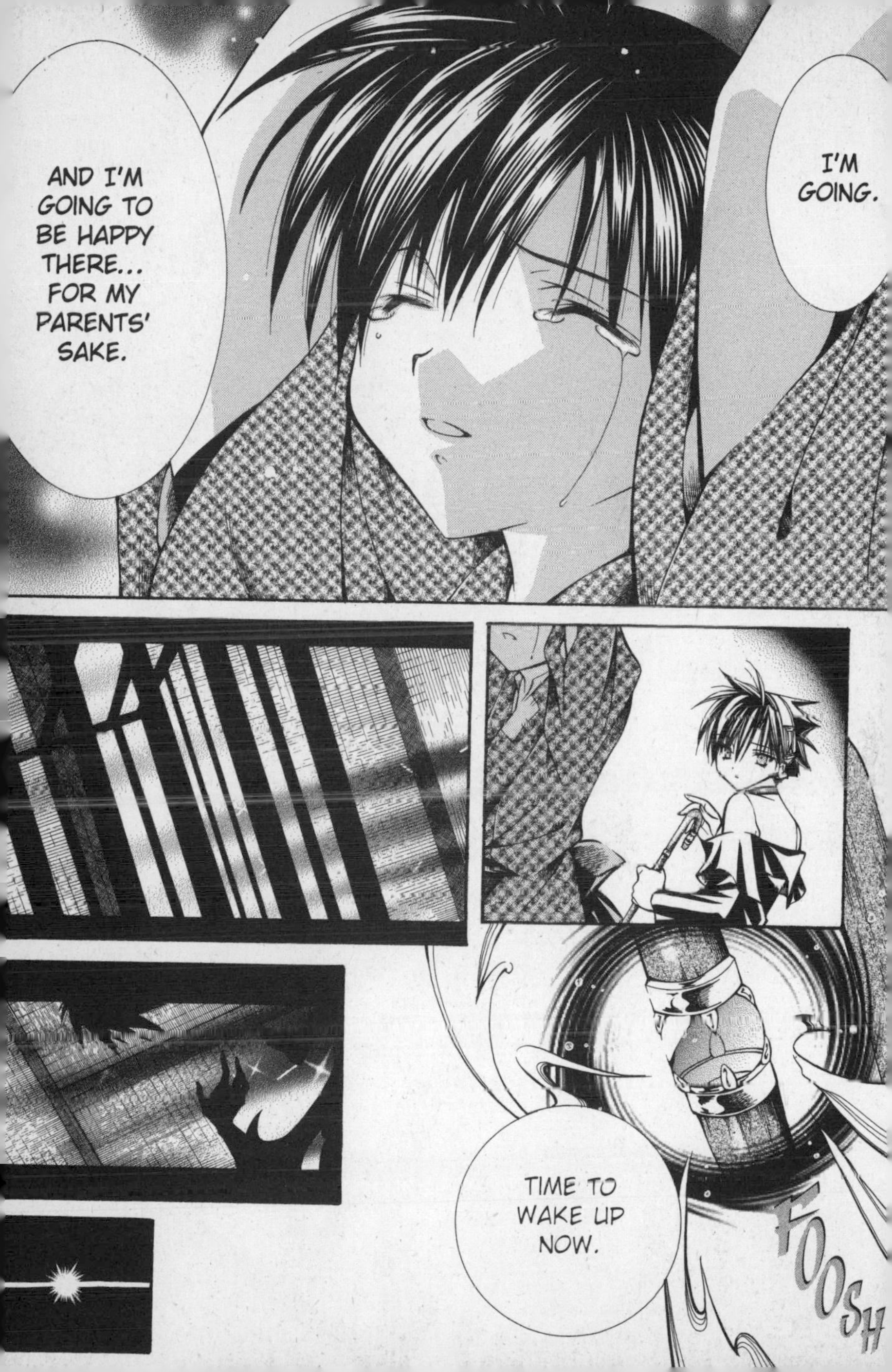
I'M GOING.
AND I'M GOING TO BE HAPPY THERE... FOR MY PARENTS' SAKE.
TIME TO WAKE UP NOW.
FOOSH

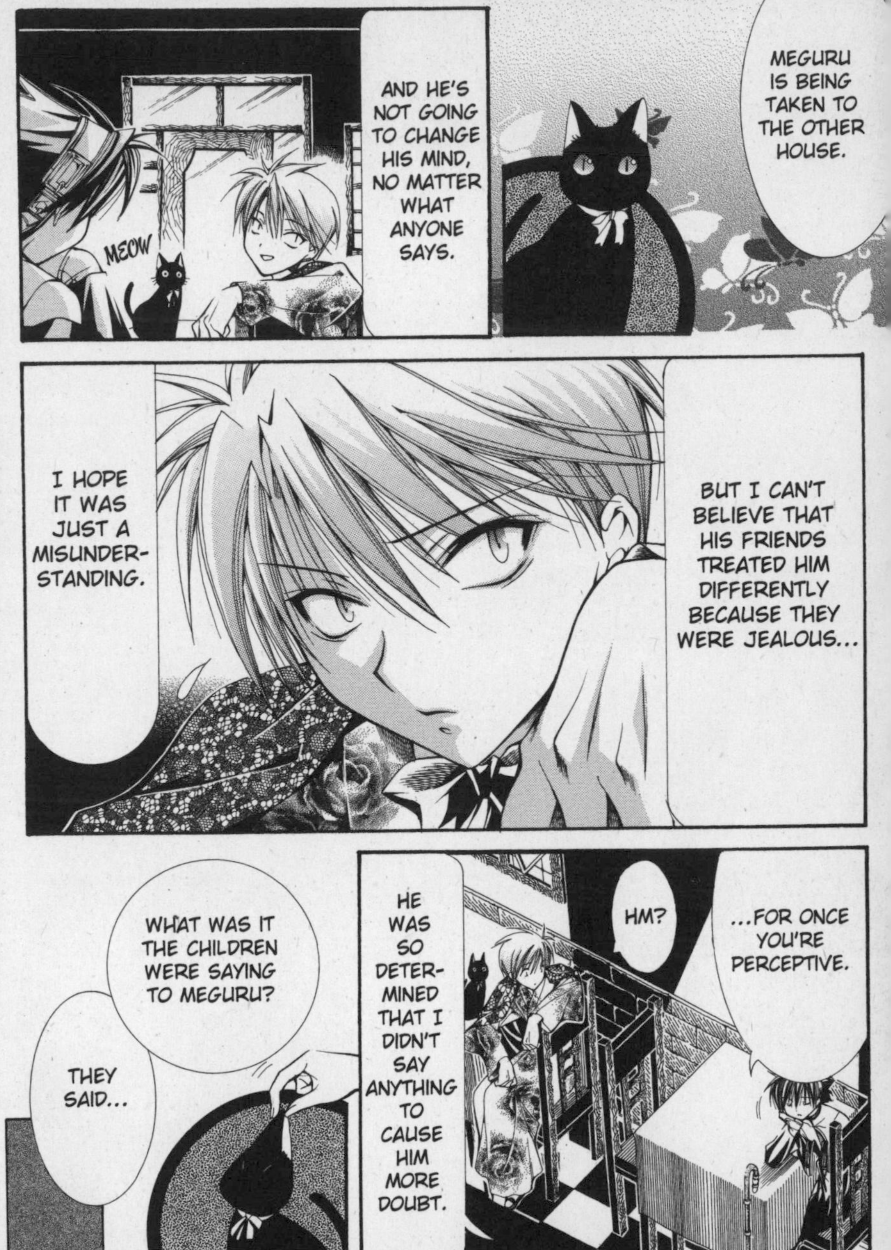
MEGURU IS BEING TAKEN TO THE OTHER HOUSE.
AND HE'S NOT GOING TO CHANGE HIS MIND, NO MATTER WHAT ANYONE SAYS.
MEOW
BUT I CAN'T BELIEVE THAT HIS FRIENDS TREATED HIM DIFFERENTLY BECAUSE THEY WERE JEALOUS...
I HOPE IT WAS JUST A MISUNDER-STANDING.
...FOR ONCE YOU'RE PERCEPTIVE.
HM?
HE WAS SO DETER-MINED THAT I DIDN'T SAY ANYTHING TO CAUSE HIM MORE DOUBT.
WHAT WAS IT THE CHILDREN WERE SAYING TO MEGURU?
THEY SAID...

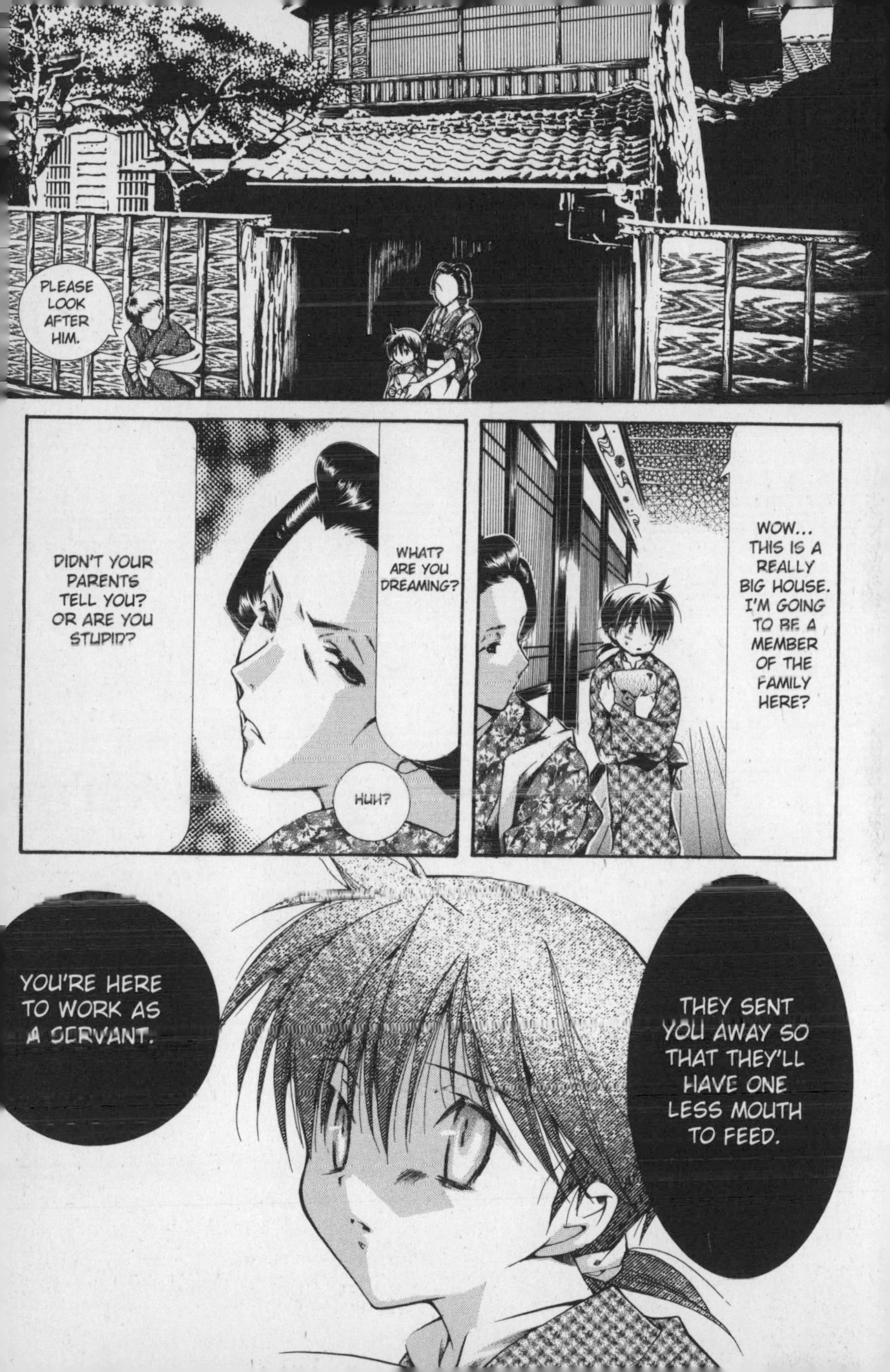
PLEASE LOOK AFTER HIM.
WOW... THIS IS A REALLY BIG HOUSE. I'M GOING TO BE A MEMBER OF THE FAMILY HERE?
WHAT? ARE YOU DREAMING?
HUH?
DIDN'T YOUR PARENTS TELL YOU? OR ARE YOU STUPID?
THEY SENT YOU AWAY SO THAT THEY'LL HAVE ONE LESS MOUTH TO FEED.
YOU'RE HERE TO WORK AS A SERVANT.

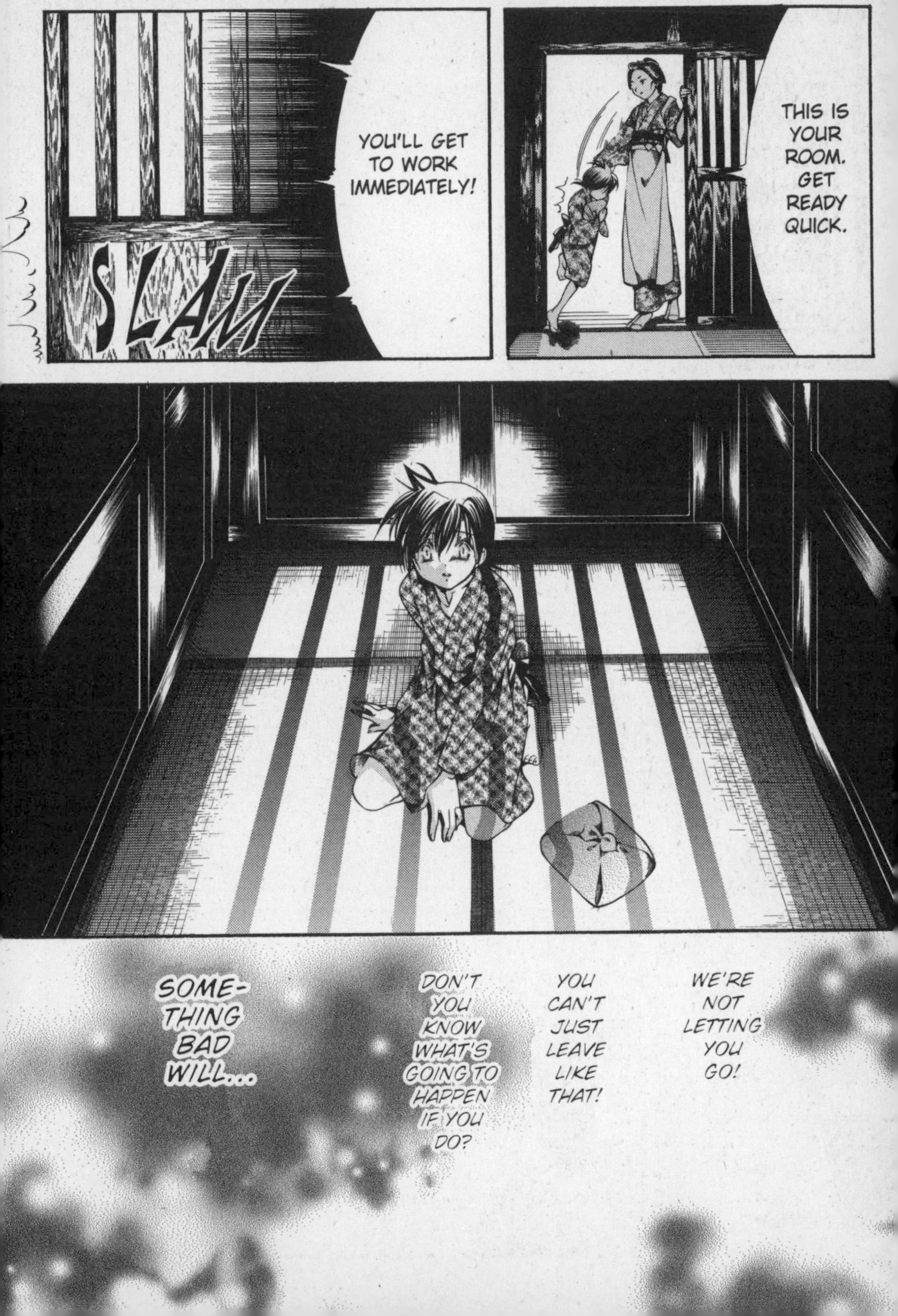
THIS IS YOUR ROOM. GET READY QUICK.
YOU'LL GET TO WORK IMMEDIATELY!
SLAM
WE'RE NOT LETTING YOU GO!
YOU CAN'T JUST LEAVE LIKE THAT!
DON'T YOU KNOW WHAT'S GOING TO HAPPEN IF YOU DO?
SOME-THING BAD WILL...

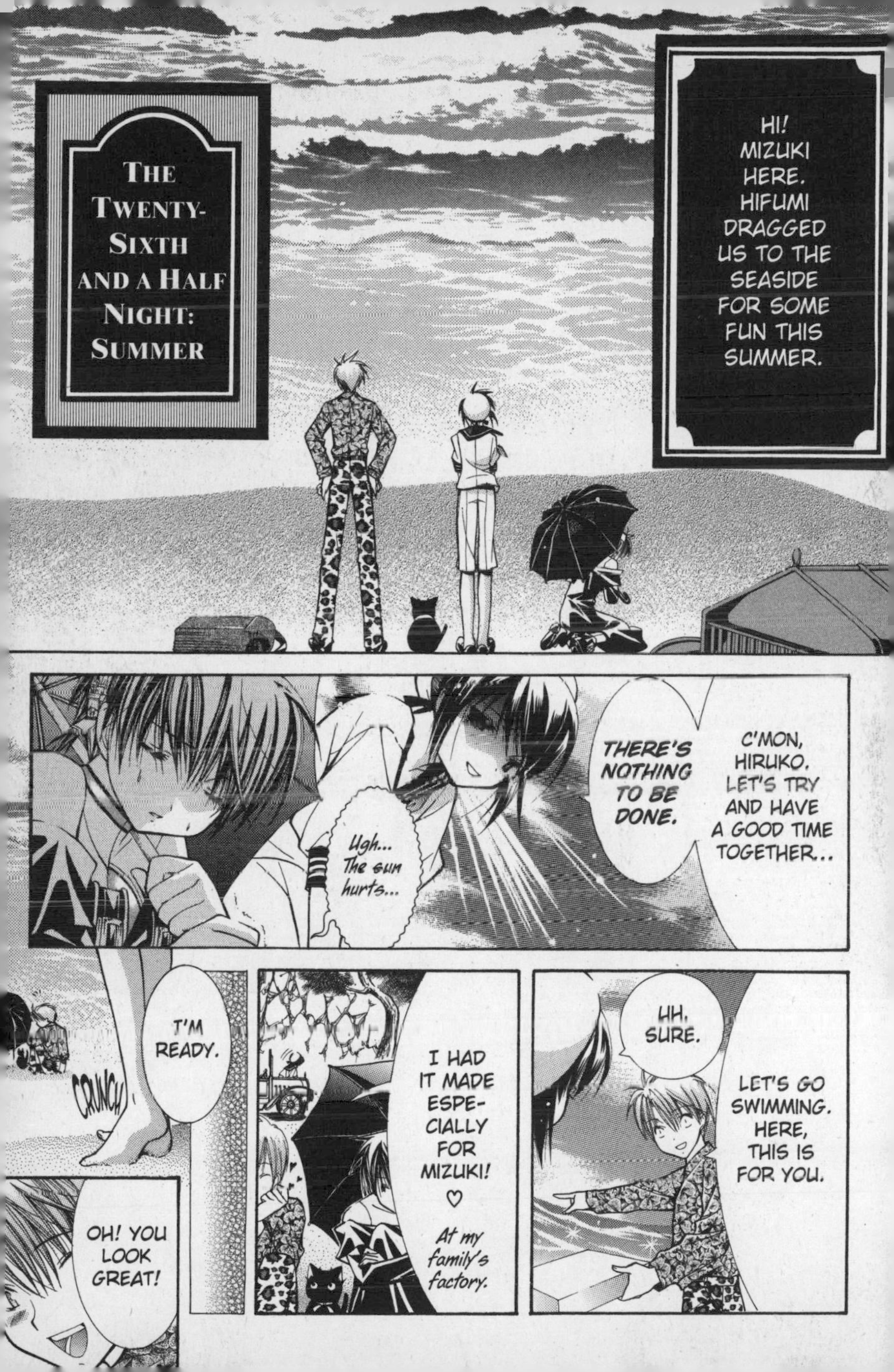
HI! MIZUKI HERE. HIFUMI DRAGGED US TO THE SEASIDE FOR SOME FUN THIS SUMMER.
THE TWENTY-SIXTH AND A HALF NIGHT: SUMMER
C'MON, HIRUKO. LET'S TRY AND HAVE A GOOD TIME TOGETHER...
THERE'S NOTHING TO BE DONE.
Ugh... The sun hurts...
UH, SURE.
LET'S GO SWIMMING. HERE, THIS IS FOR YOU.
I HAD IT MADE ESPE-CIALLY FOR MIZUKI! ♡
At my family's factory.
I'M READY.
CRUNCH
OH! YOU LOOK GREAT!

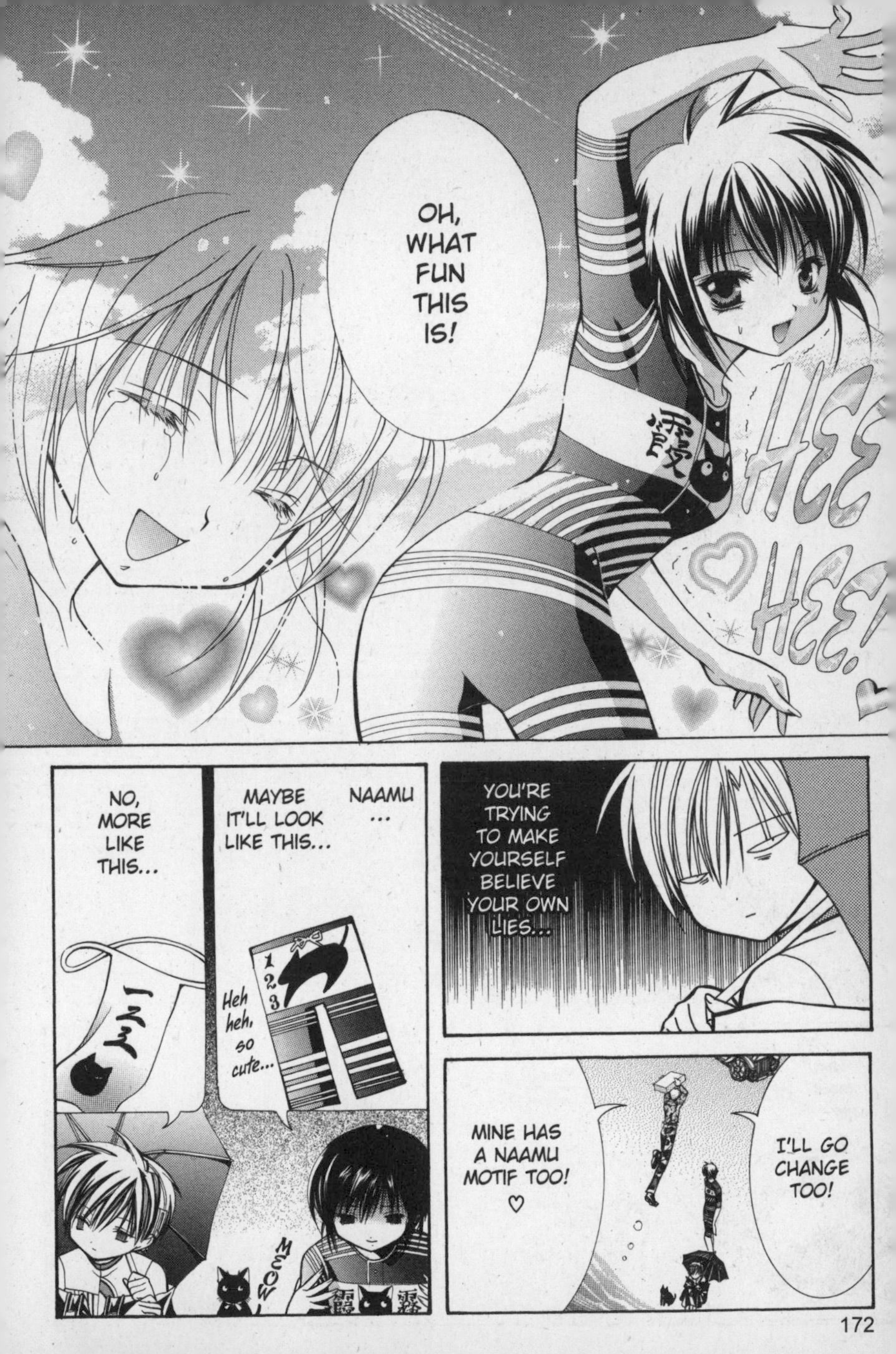
OH, WHAT FUN THIS IS!
HEE HEE HEE!
YOU'RE TRYING TO MAKE YOURSELF BELIEVE YOUR OWN LIES...
NAAMU...
MAYBE IT'LL LOOK LIKE THIS...
Heh heh, so cute...
NO, MORE LIKE THIS...
MEOW
I'LL GO CHANGE TOO!
MINE HAS A NAAMU MOTIF TOO! ♡

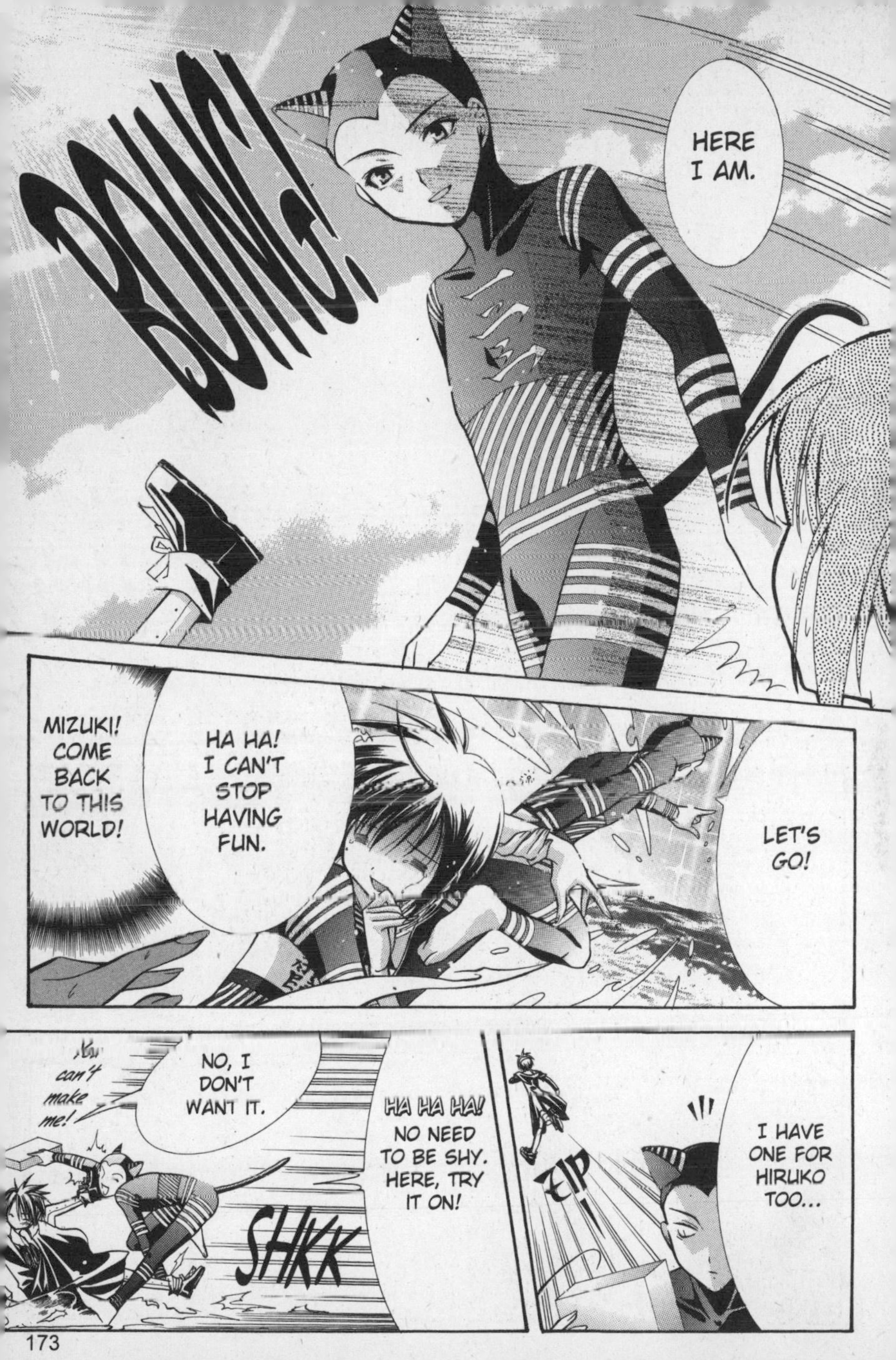
HERE I AM.
BOING!
LET'S GO!
HA HA! I CAN'T STOP HAVING FUN.
MIZUKI! COME BACK TO THIS WORLD!
I HAVE ONE FOR HIRUKO TOO...
ZIP
HA HA HA! NO NEED TO BE SHY. HERE, TRY IT ON!
NO, I DON'T WANT IT.
You can't make me!
SHKK

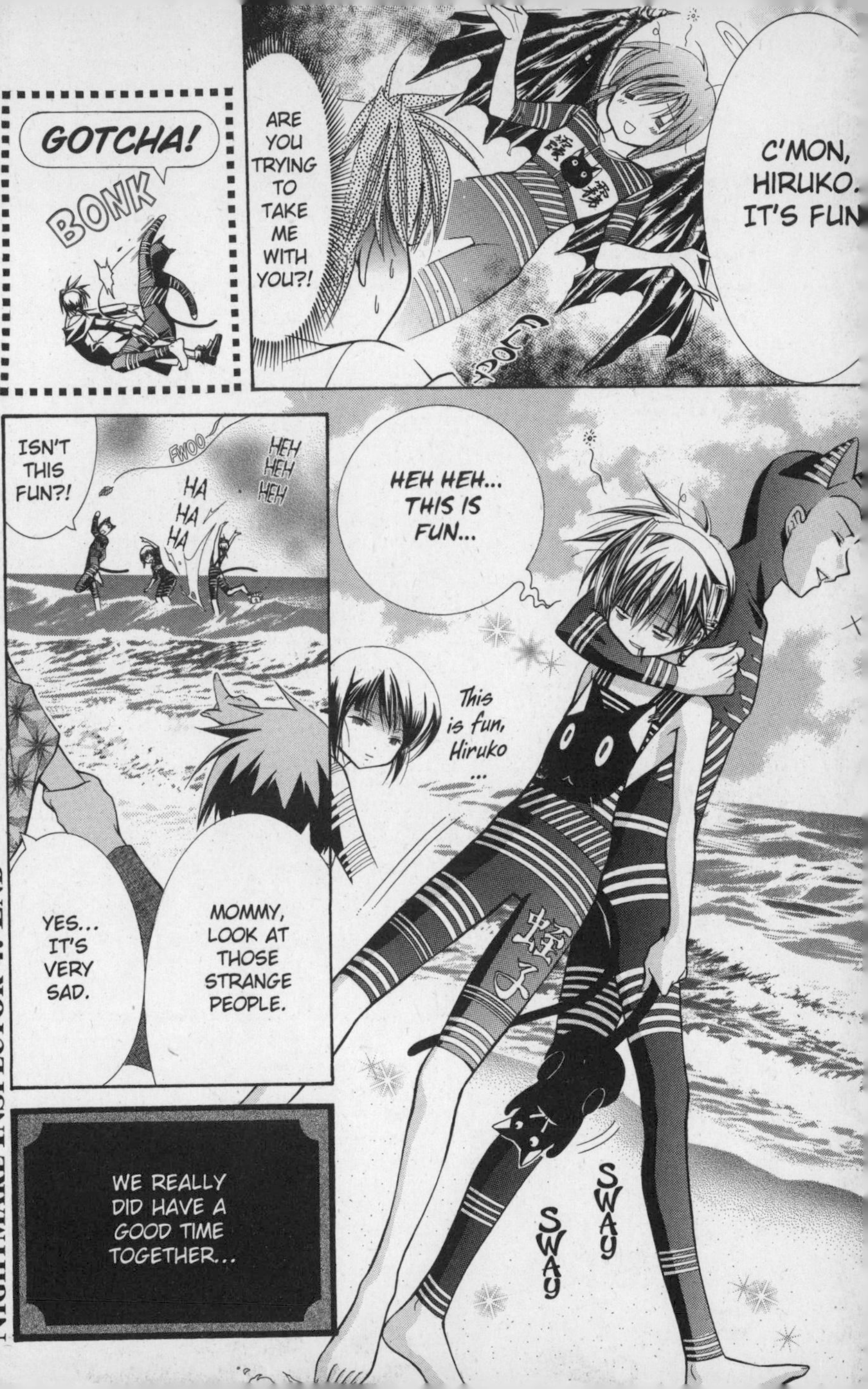

C'MON, HIRUKO. IT'S FUN
ARE YOU TRYING TO TAKE ME WITH YOU?!
FLOAT
GOTCHA!
BONK
HEH HEH... THIS IS FUN...
This is fun, Hiruko...
SWAY
SWAY
HEH HEH HEH
HA HA HA HA
FWOO
ISN'T THIS FUN?!
MOMMY, LOOK AT THOSE STRANGE PEOPLE.
YES... IT'S VERY SAD.
WE REALLY DID HAVE A GOOD TIME TOGETHER...

NIGHTMARE INSPECTOR 4: END

DREAM

Afterword

Hi! Shin Mashiba here. Thanks to you, we've reached volume four.
Thanks so much to the people at Square Enix and my wonderful
readers for all the support. Also, sincerest apologies to my editor
to whom I've caused so much trouble.

This time I tried to delve deeper into the characters' pasts. We
still haven't uncovered everything, but I hope you'll be patient.

Big Thank You

My editor Yuki Saeki and all
the people at Square Enix.
My special friends Wan Wan
Shiroi, Riru Shirayuki and
Nema.
My wonderful assistants
Katsumi Arai, Mieko Araki,
Mai Tanaka, OKASAWA and
MOAI (Info).

← Next up are Wan Wan Shiroi's guest pages, so
get ready!
(Wan Wan, thank you for drawing it all without
sketching it first! I'm so not delighted!)

← See page 178 to find out who won the contest
from volume three!

Let's Go!

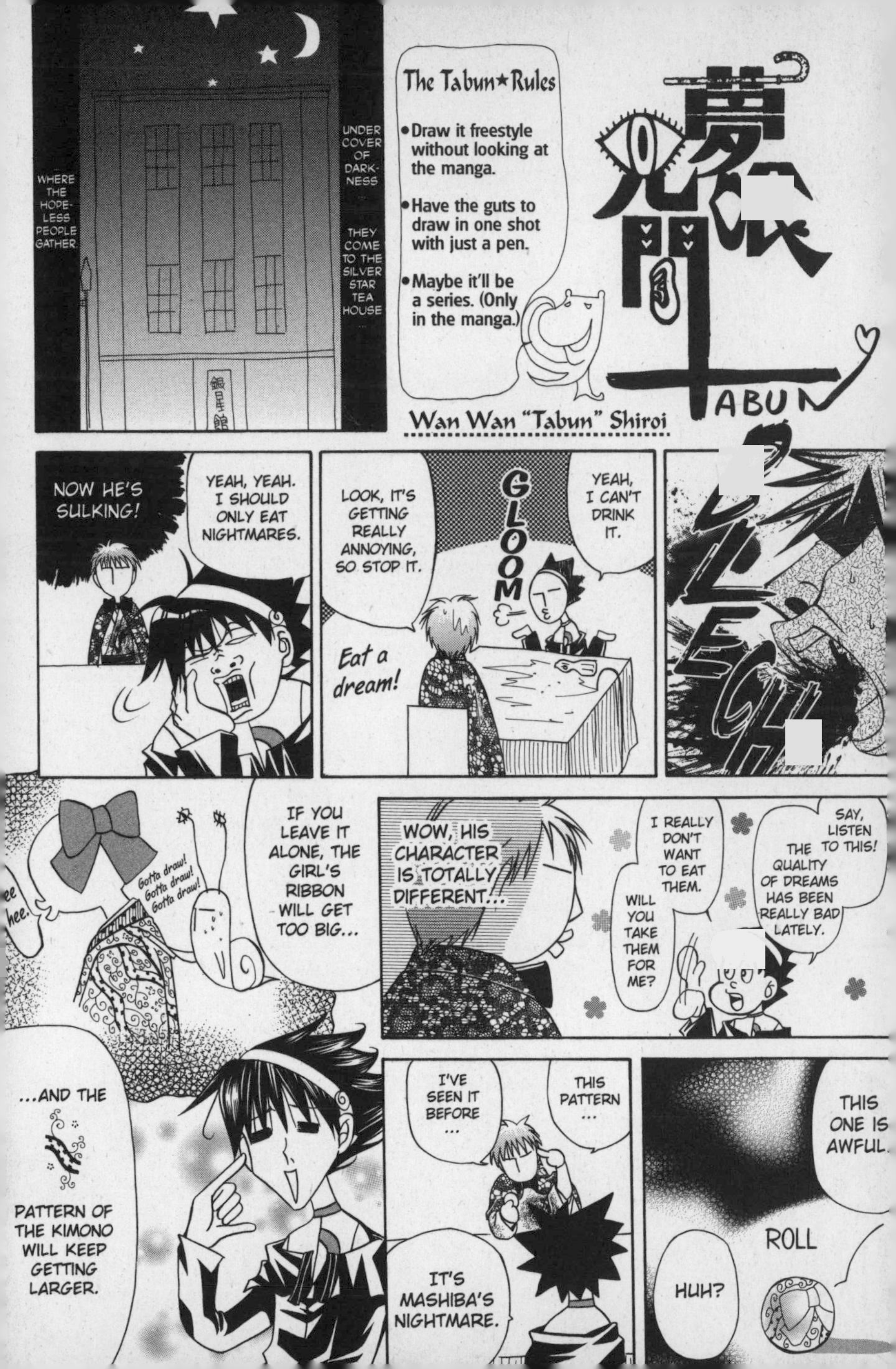
The Tabun★Rules
•Draw it freestyle without looking at the manga.
•Have the guts to draw in one shot with just a pen.
•Maybe it'll be a series. (Only in the manga.)
TABUN
Wan Wan "Tabun" Shiroi
UNDER COVER OF DARKNESS...
THEY COME TO THE SILVER STAR TEA HOUSE...
WHERE THE HOPELESS PEOPLE GATHER.
YEAH, I CAN'T DRINK IT.
GLOOOM
LOOK, IT'S GETTING REALLY ANNOYING, SO STOP IT.
Eat a dream!
YEAH, YEAH. I SHOULD ONLY EAT NIGHTMARES.
NOW HE'S SULKING!
SAY, LISTEN TO THIS!
THE QUALITY OF DREAMS HAS BEEN REALLY BAD LATELY.
I REALLY DON'T WANT TO EAT THEM.
WILL YOU TAKE THEM FOR ME?
WOW, HIS CHARACTER IS TOTALLY DIFFERENT...
THIS ONE IS AWFUL.
ROLL
HUH?
THIS PATTERN...
I'VE SEEN IT BEFORE...
IT'S MASHIBA'S NIGHTMARE.
IF YOU LEAVE IT ALONE, THE GIRL'S RIBBON WILL GET TOO BIG...
Gotta draw! Gotta draw! Gotta draw!
...AND THE PATTERN OF THE KIMONO WILL KEEP GETTING LARGER.

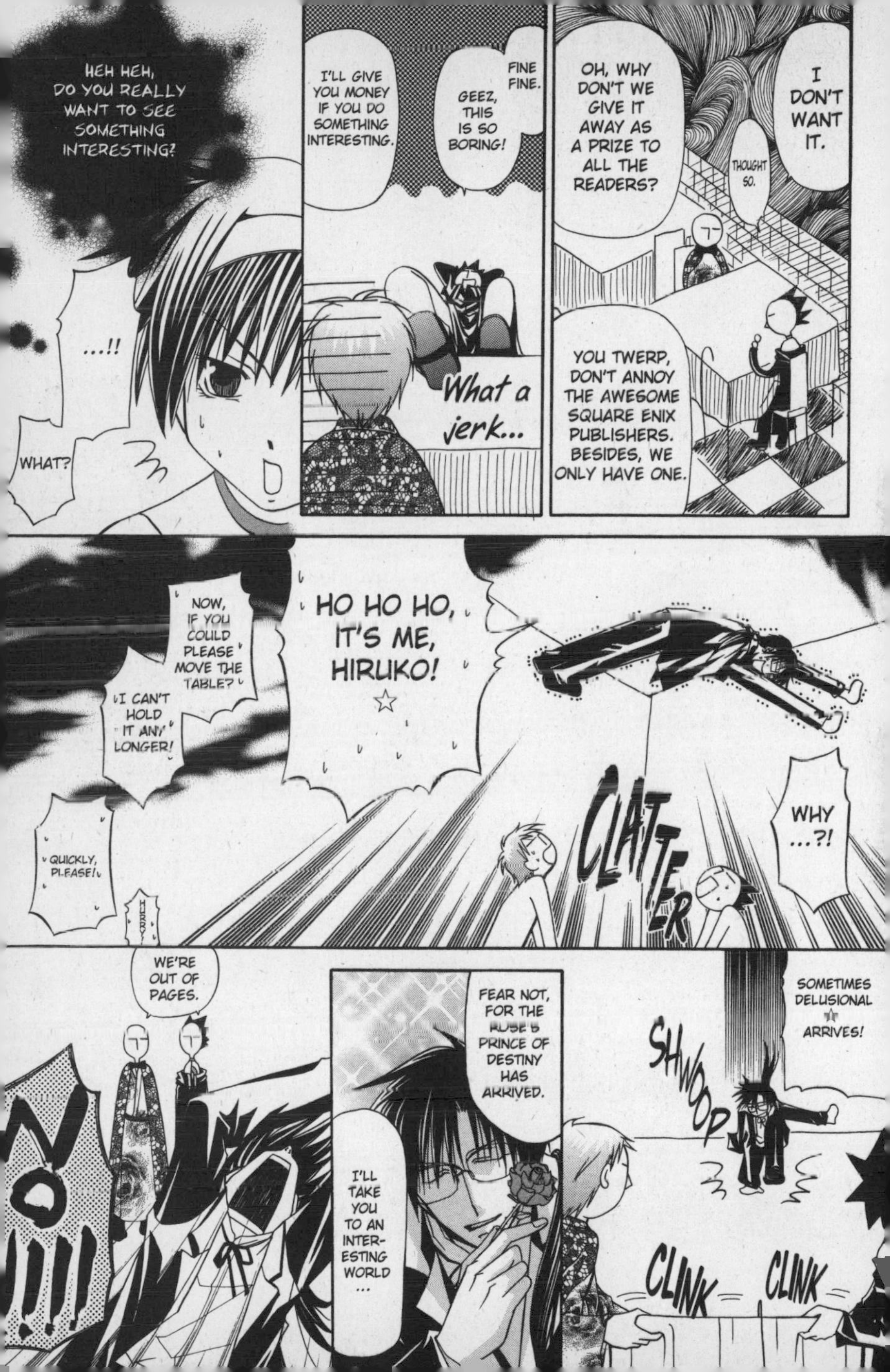
I DON'T WANT IT.
THOUGHT SO.
OH, WHY DON'T WE GIVE IT AWAY AS A PRIZE TO ALL THE READERS?
YOU TWERP, DON'T ANNOY THE AWESOME SQUARE ENIX PUBLISHERS. BESIDES, WE ONLY HAVE ONE.
FINE FINE.
GEEZ, THIS IS SO BORING!
I'LL GIVE YOU MONEY IF YOU DO SOMETHING INTERESTING.
What a jerk...
HEH HEH, DO YOU REALLY WANT TO SEE SOMETHING INTERESTING?
...!!
WHAT?
WHY ...?!
CLATTER
HO HO HO, IT'S ME, HIRUKO! ☆
NOW, IF YOU COULD PLEASE MOVE THE TABLE?
I CAN'T HOLD IT ANY LONGER!
QUICKLY, PLEASE!
HURRY
SOMETIMES DELUSIONAL ☆ ARRIVES!
SHWOOP
CLINK
CLINK
FEAR NOT, FOR THE ROSE'S PRINCE OF DESTINY HAS ARRIVED.
I'LL TAKE YOU TO AN INTER-ESTING WORLD ...
WE'RE OUT OF PAGES.
!!!

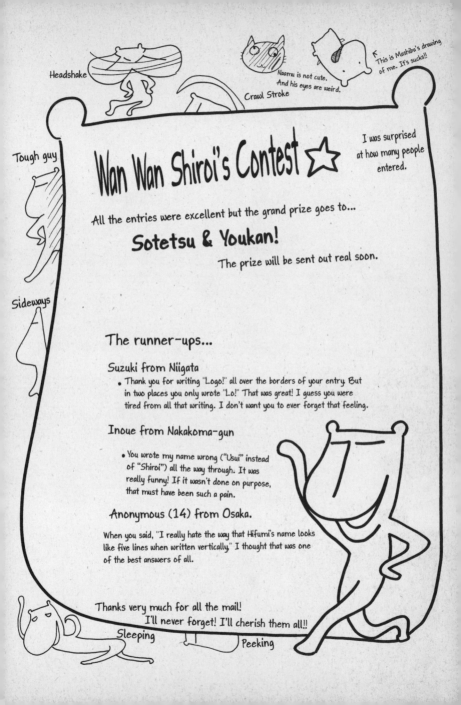

Headshake

Crawl Stroke

Naaaru is not cute.
And his eyes are weird.

This is Mashiba's drawing of me. It's sucks!!

Tough guy

Sideways

Wan Wan Shiroi's Contest ☆

I was surprised at how many people entered.

All the entries were excellent but the grand prize goes to...

Sotetsu & Youkan!

The prize will be sent out real soon.

The runner-ups...

Suzuki from Niigata

- Thank you for writing "Logo!" all over the borders of your entry. But in two places you only wrote "Lo!" That was great! I guess you were tired from all that writing. I don't want you to ever forget that feeling.

Inoue from Nakakoma-gun

- You wrote my name wrong ("Usui" instead of "Shiroi") all the way through. It was really funny! If it wasn't done on purpose, that must have been such a pain.

Anonymous (14) from Osaka.

When you said, "I really hate the way that Hifumi's name looks like five lines when written vertically," I thought that was one of the best answers of all.

Thanks very much for all the mail!
I'll never forget! I'll cherish them all!!

Sleeping

Peeking

COMING NEXT VOLUME

DARKNESS

Dreams on the menu in this volume: a woman struggling with her appearance and another trapped in darkness, a man with a sinister childhood secret, a cocoon that is more than mere silk, a delusional dream with no happy ending, a man unable to let go of past regrets, and a child's imagination that is not as innocent as it seems.

AVAILABLE DECEMBER 2008!

SHIN MASHIBA

I have recurring dreams that I'm still in school. I relive final exams, summer vacation and the last day of school. When it's finally time for graduation, I start over again at the entrance exam.

Shin Mashiba's first manga, *Yumekui Kenbun* (Nightmare Inspector), premiered in *Monthly Stencil*, a shojo magazine, in December 2001 and was then serialized in *Monthly G Fantasy* from 2003 to 2007. Mashiba-san's own nightmares include being forced to eat 50 living slugs and being chased by time.

YUMEKUI KENBUN
NIGHTMARE INSPECTOR

YUMEKUI KENBUN: NIGHTMARE INSPECTOR
VOL. 4
The VIZ Media Edition

STORY AND ART BY
SHIN MASHIBA

Translation/Gemma Collinge
English Adaptation/Kristina Blachere
Touch-up Art & Lettering/James Gaubatz
Cover Design/Aaron Cruse
Interior Design/Julie Behn
Editor/Yuki Murashige

Editor in Chief, Books/Alvin Lu
Editor in Chief, Magazines/Marc Weidenbaum
VP of Publishing Licensing/Rika Inouye
VP of Sales/Gonzalo Ferreyra
Sr. VP of Marketing/Liza Coppola
Publisher/Hyoe Narita

Published by VIZ Media, LLC
P.O. Box 77010
San Francisco, CA 94107

VIZ Media Edition
10 9 8 7 6 5 4 3 2 1
First printing, October 2008

INUYASHA

Read the action from the start with the original manga series

Full color adaptation of the popular TV series

Art book with ool art, paintings, character profiles and more

LOVE MANGA?
LET US KNOW WHAT YOU THINK!

OUR MANGA SURVEY IS NOW AVAILABLE ONLINE. PLEASE VISIT: VIZ.COM/MANGASURVEY

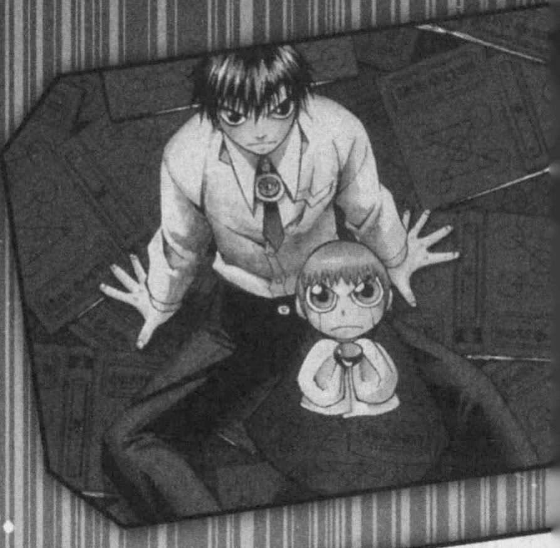
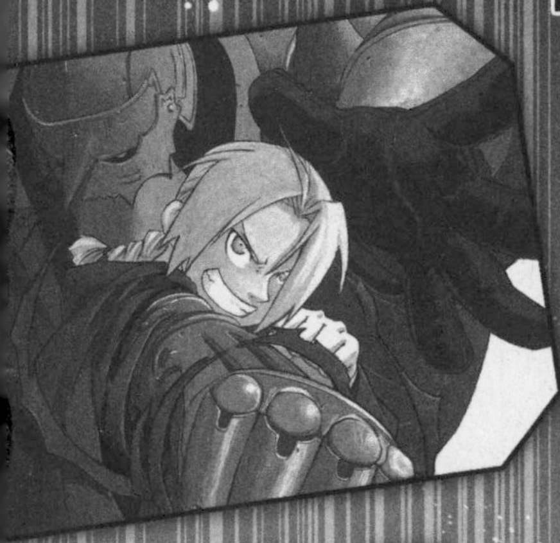
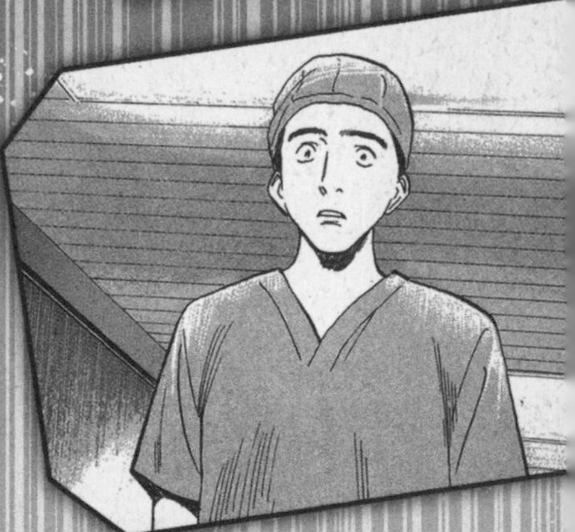
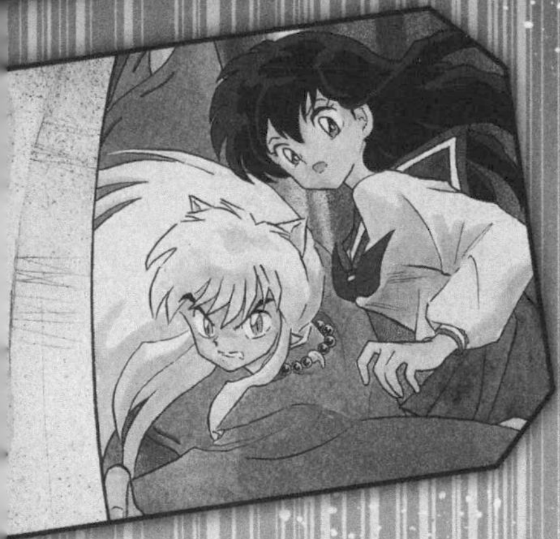

HELP US MAKE THE MANGA YOU LOVE BETTER!

viz media